This Changes Everything

This Changes Everything

The Relational Revolution in Psychology

Christina Robb

Farrar, Straus and Giroux · New York

FARRAR, STRAUS AND GIROUX
19 Union Square West, New York 10003

Grateful acknowledgment is made for permission to reprint the following previously published material: Excerpts from *The Healing Connection* by Jean Baker Miller and Irene Pierce Stiver, copyright © 1997 by Jean Baker Miller and Irene Pierce Stiver, used by permission of Beacon Press, Boston. Excerpts from *Toward a New Psychology of Women* by Jean Baker Miller, copyright © 1986 by Jean Baker Miller, used by permission of Beacon Press, Boston. Excerpts from *Trauma and Recovery* by Judith Lewis Herman, copyright © 1992 by Basic Books, used by permission of Basic Books, a member of Perseus Books, LLC. Excerpts from *Free Space* by Pamela Allen, copyright © 1970 by Pamela Allen, used by permission of Times Change Press. Excerpts from "Father-Daughter Incest" by Judith Lewis Herman and Lisa Hirschman, from *Signs 2:4*, copyright © 1977 by Judith Lewis Herman and Lisa Hirschman, used by permission of The University of Chicago Press. Excerpts from *Women's Growth in Diversity*, edited by Judith V. Jordan, copyright © 1997 by the Guilford Press, used by permission of the Guilford Press. Excerpts from *Meeting at the Crossroads: Women's Psychology and Girls' Development* by Lyn Mikel Brown and Carol Gilligan (Cambridge, Mass.: Harvard University Press), pp. 43, 50, 53, 114–117, 166, 219–222, and 225, copyright © 1992 by the President and Fellows of Harvard College.

Library of Congress Cataloging-in-Publication Data
Robb, Christina, 1946–
    This changes everything : the relational revolution in psychology /
by Christina Robb.
        p.   cm.
    Includes bibliographical references and index.
    ISBN-13: 978-0-374-27581-5 (hardcover : alk. paper)
    ISBN-10: 0-374-27581-5 (hardcover : alk. paper)
    1. Interpersonal relations.   2. Social psychology.   I. Title.
HM1106.R63 2006
305'.01—dc22

                                                                    2005016270

Designed by Gretchen Achilles

www.fsgbooks.com

1   3   5   7   9   10   8   6   4   2

Remembering

Irene Pierce Stiver,

Alexandra G. Kaplan, and

Lisa Hirschman,

pioneers of relational psychology,

and Eloise Victoria Lillemor Taylor Robb,

who gave me life,

I dedicate this book to my daughters,

Susannah Robb Kondrath

and Rachel Robb Kondrath,

who change everything

Contents

Introduction

Relational psychology is the way the women's movement and other human rights movements of the 1960s moved into psychology. It is about how our ideas about psychological development and mental health have become democratic, and it came from questioning authority—most important, questioning traditional answers about difference and relationship.

Difference—of species, habitat, coloration, size, character—gives nature depth and strength. Why should some human beings tell a story that says differences are about better and worse?

Relationships weave all creatures into the web of life. Why should some human beings tell a similar story about relationships, a story that says relationships are for weaklings and real men stand alone? And why are the human beings who tell these stories the ones who hold the most power?

These were the kinds of questions in the back of Carol Gilligan's mind when, in 1975—as a thirty-nine-year-old unpublished, part-time assistant professor of developmental psychology at Harvard, taking a year off to be with her three sons because her family had just moved from one suburb of Boston to another—she heard in the voices of women a different story about difference.

Across the Charles River in Cambridge and Somerville, Judith Lewis Herman, a young psychiatrist, and Lisa Hirschman, a young clinical psychologist, were listening to poor patients talk about incest. They weren't supposed to hear it. Their supervisors told them to ignore it when their patients talked about incest. Their textbooks said incest was rarer than rare, a case in a million. But their patients told them they had suffered incest, sexual abuse, and rape and had histories of prolonged and repeated trauma. Herman and Hirschman were women and their patients were women. They realized that what they were hearing and why they weren't supposed to hear it were political as well as medical problems, and the incidence of father-daughter incest they found was exponentially greater than medical science said it was.

They were picking up where Freud left off more than a century ago, before he retracted his discovery that childhood trauma, especially sexual trauma, can cause the most severe mental illnesses. And they were—as Freud was, and as most psychotherapists still are—listening to women and girls at a time of great and democratizing social change.

In fact, in 1975, inside a radius of about five miles, three revolutionary projects were afoot near Boston: Carol Gilligan was recording the different, not deviant, voice she was hearing in women making moral decisions. Herman and Hirschman were counting cases of incest for the first time ever. And the psychiatrist and psychoanalyst Jean Baker Miller was writing about the politics of dominance and the politics of relationship and about how being subordinate in a culture of dominance hurt her women patients and warped the dominant psychology's view of women. Working at home in Brookline, the same little suburb of Boston that Gilligan had just moved to, Miller filled her book with insights from women clients she met in a storefront clinic and in the middle-class comfort of her private office, from the explorations of two consciousness-raising groups, and from her own search for forerunners among pioneer women psychologists. *Toward a New Psychology of Women*, published in 1976, demonstrated that what male psychologists had labeled women's weaknesses—hypersensitivity, merging, dependency needs—could be seen as strengths: authenticity, empathy, a drive to connect, and the skills to stay connected. Miller saw that men and children relied on women heavily to use these strengths but mocked and devalued them because men, especially, weren't supposed to admit they needed anybody.

These early leaders in what I'm calling the relational revolution were all white women in what were still very much white men's fields. They knew they could never be department heads or make millions. But they hadn't been brought up to want those things anyway. Like Psyche, the mythical heroine Gilligan sees as a political archetype who can teach us to heal relationships, these women were all intensely curious. They were smart. Political reform was giving them access to traditionally male knowledge that women of earlier generations had had to scrape for. And the women's movement was giving them the freedom to hold this knowledge without disowning their own experience.

When I found Miller's book in a bookstore a couple of years after it was published, I did what thousands of her readers did: I read it, sent it to my mother, and gave copies to several friends. At the time, I was in the brief freelance phase of a twenty-year career on the reporting staff of *The Boston Globe*; I had time to volunteer as a music therapist at McLean Hospital, the venerable Harvard-affiliated mental hospital, and to take an adult-education course at the Boston Psychoanalytic Society and Institute. I hoped the course would help me understand the suffering I encountered as a volunteer. The course was fascinating and infuriating. The fundamental stream of proto-thought that Freud discovered and called "primary process" and the relaxed but alert, open attention he recommended paying to people in order to tune in to the way they express this primary process blew me away. Not just the idea but the experience of hearing and talking back to people in a language that I and they had been using all the time but never noticed or attended to was like adding some lush orchestration to a tune I had only known as a melodic line, to use the sort of musical metaphor Gilligan favors. But I saw that at the same time psychoanalysts opened this wide door to people's experience and motivations, they locked or kept locked a lot of other doors. I read all the Freud I could get my hands on, and I noticed a huge ignorance in the middle of psychoanalysis, Freud's system for gaining knowledge. This ignorance was most obviously about women, and I am sure it was obvious to me only because the women's movement encouraged me to see this kind of blackout of women's experience wherever it occurred. I read that Freud's first patients were women and girls who eventually traced their complaints to incest and childhood sexual abuse. But the genial, clear veteran psychoanalyst who taught our class in Boston, and who was also a physician, insisted to us that girls didn't know they had vaginas until they were about twelve. And when I say insisted, I mean that when his adult female students informed him that this wasn't true, he dismissed our response. How could anyone put stock in a theory, so centered on sexual and erotic themes, that held that half of all children had no knowledge of their own genitals while the other half were practically obsessed with theirs? And how could anyone construct ideas about girls that ignored the experience of people who had been girls in favor of the assumptions of people who hadn't been? Could it be—I thought, listening for that lush orchestration of symbolic thinking I had just learned to hear—that psychoanalysts simply didn't want to know what girls knew or how girls thought about themselves? And why not? What was so dangerous about the self-knowledge of girls?

Nearly twenty years after my epiphanies about Freud's psychology—both the epiphany of understanding what he taught about primary process and the epiphany of discovering that psychoanalysts didn't want to know what girls and women knew—I found myself sitting in Jean Baker Miller's office in the Stone Center of Wellesley College. Month after month for the past three or four years, after we had walked down to the little kitchen in the nineteenth-century brick building and waited while the water boiled and then walked back to her office with mugs of tea, I had interviewed her about her career, her ideas, her practice of psychotherapy, her collaborators, and the institutions she built. Finally we had come to the end of this exploration, and I asked her my standard end-of-interview question: "Is there anything that I haven't asked about or that we haven't talked about that you think is important?"

Jean shifted in her chair, and then was quiet for about half a minute, a long time in an interview. Finally she said, "I just hope you really understand, and can get it across, that this changes everything."

Miller is a mild-mannered, unassuming, plainspoken woman, and one of the most attractive aspects of the psychology she and her colleagues have put together is that they don't try to explain everything. They have taken their insights from listening to women and girls and applied them first to the cases that were actually before them and then slowly, as more data accumulated and as they began listening to women of color, men, and boys, to a wider group. So I was surprised to hear this rather global comment. But Miller is as brave as she is unassuming, and as bold as she is clear. She meant, she continued, that the relational-cultural theory that she created and elaborated with Judith V. Jordan, Janet L. Surrey, the late Irene P. Stiver, and other colleagues is not just about psychotherapy or even just about human relationships.

It's not that kind of theory. It doesn't just describe; it changes—*every-thing*. She believed, she said, that if she and others simply continued speaking and writing about the discoveries they were making about the power of relationships, their work would revolutionize society as well as psychology. And as the years of my preparation for this book went on, every psychologist and psychiatrist, every social worker, every patient or client I interviewed echoed her, often in the same words. And I began to notice that they were right.

In the hours after the terrorist attacks in New York on September 11, 2001, the Salvation Army arrived at Ground Zero with bottled water and grief counseling. The idea that these attacks *betrayed* as well as injured their victims and that the emergency was as much psychological as physical was new. The idea that talking about the experience with an empathic, trustworthy listener could begin to heal the betrayal right away was also new. Both ideas grew out of this relational movement in psychology.

In the days after the deadly tsunamis that killed hundreds of thousands of people in Indonesia and other coastal countries on the Indian Ocean in December 2004 and January 2005, assessing how post-traumatic stress disorder would complicate survivors' recovery was an urgent task for local and volunteer medical staffs. But when the relational movement started, there was no awareness of or respect for the effects of PTSD. Veterans of the Vietnam War and their advocates spent much of the 1970s lobbying the American Psychiatric Association to get PTSD accepted as a diagnosis, and Judith Lewis Herman and her colleagues, who had discovered that rape victims suffered exactly the same disorders as "shell-shocked" veterans, lobbied right beside them.

Nor were there victim advocates in courtrooms helping victims of crimes deal with the further victimization that results from the adversarial system that pits every victim against an offender who typically denies the offense. There were no impact statements from victims before sentencing or at parole hearings. When this movement started, there were no victims' bills of rights.

There was no psychology of trauma. There was no awareness of the epidemic prevalence of incest and child sexual abuse. There were no judges who felt that the public deserved to know how bishops and other church administrators hid evidence of sexual abuse of children by priests and ministers; there were no editors who felt that their readers and viewers deserved to know about child abuse.

There was no general understanding of how specific behaviors and attitudes in politicians, parents, teachers, toy makers, and entertainers socialized boys to be masculine and girls to be feminine. We were still in the days of women's intuition and men's manliness. The psychology of listening was a neglected and esoteric field. "Empathy" was not a common word. There were no crime shows like a 2005 episode of *Law & Order: Special Victims Unit* where a male detective who shows no feeling but anger is taken off a stressful case and a female detective who cries and admits that she worries about stress is kept on.

There was no psychology of girls; virtually no psychologists studied preadolescent or adolescent girls. Girls were supposed to operate as a sort of concave mirror image or obverse of boys. So there was no psychology of boys that compared and contrasted boys who had been studied with girls who had been studied. Women, men of color, and low-income people were excluded from psychological studies because the methodologies in use at the time were highly but invisibly politicized. The standard method required researchers to create norms by looking only at white middle-class males and to omit other genders, races, and economic backgrounds as unnecessary variables.

Relational ideas and practices were effects of the global social movements for civil rights, against the war in Vietnam and for women. This work is about how democracy overtook and transformed psychology. It's about the deepest truths we know, the ones that save our lives, the ones we go to college or turn to great authors, wise friends, and psychological experts to learn. It's about what makes love grow and what weeds love out and implants fear and contempt. It's about why expertise too often turns out to be a sort of verbal karate that experts use to prevent us from asking our deepest questions or to keep us from bringing the truths we know into the realm of expert knowledge. So it's also about the way a powerful political system cuts us off from our own deep knowledge, and about how we can build and keep up a personal and political resistance that links power to love.

The politics of how these women and men managed to develop their theories and practices is the same politics their theories describe: the politics of relationship disarming the politics of dominance, and the politics of dominance lashing back. The personal is political, and the political is psychological, in their work and in their lives.

Within the island of comparative political freedom and respect for women that was Boston in the 1970s, Gilligan started the Harvard Project on the Psychology of Women and the Development of Girls around her kitchen table. Miller got hired to direct the new Stone Center for Developmental Services and Studies at Wellesley College and turned it into a forum for the work that she and three Harvard clinical psychologists talked and laughed and cried over every Monday night in her living room. Herman joined a consciousness-raising group that dreamed up and then started their ideal mental health clinic for women. When their Women's Mental Health Collective opened in a storefront in Somerville, a working-class suburb of Boston, there were plenty of old overstuffed chairs where young clinicians could sit and talk cases and make theories.

These groups worked so well that each of them produced several waves of revolutionary work. They did not get locked into marketing or fighting to put across a single discovery. They discovered nothing less than the political and psychological power of relationship: the political use of dissociation and disconnection to widen power disparities and keep them wide, and the power of personal relationships and cultural connections to balance power and foster growth.

Why should women be the ones to discover something so important, and discover it so it stays discovered and doesn't slide back into the realm of the unsayable, like Freud's early discoveries about sexual abuse and psychological trauma? The answer is one of the first principles Miller outlines in *Toward a New Psychology of Women*: there is a whole category of knowledge that the dominant people in any society spend an enormous amount of energy trivializing, demonizing, and ignoring—knowledge about the effects of their domination on subordinates, knowledge about what subordinates know about them, knowledge about human experiences they see only in subordinates and not in themselves—because these experiences (empathy, tenderness, mutuality, and respect) make it hard to dominate people. So it makes sense that subordinates know more about dominants and about themselves than dominants know about themselves or subordinates.

However, the practice of democracy changes these rules, and we live in an era when dominant people in the United States—middle-class and wealthy white men—may choose to share power with subordinate groups, as they did in the nineteenth century when most of their representatives voted for black men's suffrage, and as they did in the twentieth century when most of their representatives voted for women's suffrage.

The payoff for this democratic generosity is that for the first time, everyone gets to own and relish all the good things that the masculine ideal hands over to the feminine because they undermine dominance—things like empathy and relational savvy. And everyone gets to enjoy equally all the good things that dominance hands over to the stereotype of the subordinate—like a rich emotional and sensual life rooted in loving relationships.

It changes everything to see and hear relationships. Not selves. Not individuals fighting or negotiating for and against separate and distinct interests and goals. But relationships, connections that join people and have their own cries for help, satisfied sighs, and whoops of triumph. It changes everything to pay attention to relationships, to hear the voice of a relationship as a dimension of your own voice and the voice of another person, or of a group of people, and to listen to that relational voice, to see what Gilligan calls "relational reality" and sense what Herman calls the "relational field."

The book in your hands is both a political history of these ideas and a how-to book. It describes a ground state of human being, a state of active connection to people that is essential for growth and creativity and even for clear and accurate perception. It is a manual for co-creating relationships that integrate perception and inspire better connections. It teaches how to recognize the best-connected times of our lives and how to use those relationships as guides to more connection. It also teaches how to catch yourself and other people in the act of disconnecting, both along the victim's range of dissociation—from micro to macro, from the simple daze of spacing out to dissociative identity disorder—and along the perpetrator's range of dominant disconnection, from teasing put-down to racism, sexism, classism, homophobia, rape, homicide, and war.

You can talk to a relationship. You can listen to a relationship, and what it tells you may transform your notion of what information is. You can learn that if people are using information for hurting, for power, to see what they can get on other people, you're in the politics of dominance. And if people are using information to care and get closer to people, you're in the politics of mutuality. Often both kinds of politics are going on at the same time, and one kind is in charge or in the open while the other is underground. You can lie to a relationship. You can break and kill a relationship. You can also join the underground and resist attempts to violate relationships. And relationships can heal.

In the course of changing many ways our society works, relational psychology has been demonized, trivialized, and mythologized. Gilligan, whom *Time* magazine called one of the twenty-five most influential people of the end of the twentieth century, has probably been misread and mythologized the most. Susan Faludi discusses Gilligan's work in *Backlash*, her 1991 study of the dominant backlash against feminism; she catalogs the way that Gilligan's work has been cited to promote conclusions, goals, and outcomes that are 180 degrees from Gilligan's conclusions, methods, and hopes. And like many of the writers who have made Gilligan's work controversial, Faludi cites only one of her books—*In a Different Voice*, the first, most preliminary, and based on the smallest studies. Not only does Gilligan not say that girls and women are essentially or biologically more relational or "caring" than boys and men; she actually suggests that everyone starts out being relational but that boys are pressured to stop thinking and acting relationally as early as preschool. These days Gilligan cites decades of research on infants, as well as her own work with girls, boys, and adult couples, that supports the hypothesis that empathy and other relational skills are innate—that all human beings are literally born to connect, and the interesting question is not about why some of us are more relational than others but why some of us are less so.

More recent critics, such as Rosalind Barnett, a clinical psychologist, and Caryl Rivers, a journalist, in their 2004 book, *Same Difference: How Gender Myths Are Hurting Our Relationships, Our Children, and Our Jobs*, continue to cite only Gilligan's earliest work, and misread that. They create a myth about Gilligan's findings, and then debunk their own misreading. So they only cite work that Gilligan did in the 1980s and before, and they cite criticisms of her from the early twenty-first century, ignoring everything that she and her many colleagues have written and done for decades to respond to criticism and refine their theories. A culture of dominance constantly generates pressure to co-opt, distort, demonize, trivialize, or ignore insights into the unfair and undemocratic ways people are made more or less powerful in human societies. It also ignores the democratic basis of mental health and the fundamental idea of relational psychology, which is that people who are psychologically healthy have honest relationships with political equals. In their willingness to spar with the distortions and myths that have been made of relational psychology rather than the actual content of the new field, critics like Barnett and Rivers seem to be making a political compromise; it's almost as though they're saying that if relational theory is going to be distorted and abused to keep women down, let's scrap the theory.

In their chapter "The Caring Trap," Barnett and Rivers tell a story that perfectly exemplifies how the culture of dominance has quickly learned to put on a mask of relational thinking and feeling that nonetheless fails to conceal what big teeth it has. I am deeply chagrined to say that the villain in their story backs up her villainy with an article I wrote for *The Boston Globe Magazine* about Miller, Jordan, Surrey, and Stiver and their work at the Stone Center in 1988. Barnett and Rivers write that when a girl asked to do an independent, advanced math project in school, her teacher told her she had to do it with math novices because girls learn cooperatively, and when this student protested, her teacher read to her from my article about how "for women, 'the apex of development is to weave themselves zestfully into a web of strong relationships that they experience as empowering, activating, honest and close.' "[1] Of course, this teacher was abusing my words the same way a politician abuses words when he says an intercontinental ballistic missile is an instrument of peace or a tyrannical regime is a republic. She was using words about freedom and mutuality to mask the fact that she was forcing this girl to teach or at least babysit some of her less gifted students. This girl wasn't zestfully weaving herself into anything; she was being ordered to work with students she did not want to work with because they could not have an equal or mutual relationship about math. But ideally, and surprisingly often in practice, the world of mathematical research is generously collaborative. And in real scientific research, still a largely masculine preserve, women are less likely to find themselves ordered to collaborate with colleagues not up to the task than to find themselves excluded from collaboration with able male colleagues. Thirty years ago, in a chapter of *Toward a New Psychology of Women* called "Doing Good and Feeling Bad," Miller took on the way the dominant culture forces women to be good cooperators and then condemns them for it.

The conservative polemicist Christina Hoff Sommers has written a couple of books that oppose the political look at gender that relational psychology insists on. She has given her books titles that accuse her opponents of crimes: *Who Stole Feminism?* and *The War Against Boys.*[2] Yet I doubt she really believes Carol Gilligan is a thief or warmonger. She criticizes Gilligan and David Sadker, who has studied gender bias in school classrooms, for not publishing in peer-reviewed journals; in fact, peer review has been part of the structure and progress of their research many times over, as it is in all university, foundation-approved work, from the time their studies were designed through publication in academic books and journals and every time they have been vetted for faculty posts and promotions. Sommers quotes a lot of newspaper stories about psychology, too, but she is neither a psychologist nor a journalist. She doesn't know the rules of the fields she writes about. She doesn't understand that a psychological study is different from published reports about the study. She doesn't understand that clinical observation is as legitimate a source of scientific information as controlled experiments or longitudinal studies but that it produces different, if equally valid, kinds of information. I believe her work is a protective mask for masculinity and its privileges. The backbone of her work seems to be her refusal to see that masculinity is cultural, that the behavior and attitudes we think of as masculine could change. To Sommers, women are gendered but men just are. Men are mostly strong and right and very patient and long-suffering compared with outrageously demanding "gender feminists." And a social commitment to learn about or help girls jeopardizes boys.

Gender stereotypes are deeply rooted in the dominant culture. Relational psychology focuses on the politics of gender—and eventually race, class, and sexual orientation, the politics of difference, really—in the way we see and treat violent crime, the idea of self, psychopathologies like depression and anxiety, and child development. Because they see and hear stereotypes at work, relational psychologists are repeatedly accused of creating or supporting the stereotypes whose damage they study. Human development is a political process. Relational psychologists have begun to trace the lineaments of power in the way our children are raised or the way we adults organize and regulate our communities; they collect accusations of "essentialism" every time they insist that the gender differences they notice are political. The only essential thing about white boys' early disconnection from growth-fostering relationships and about their training as privileged, dominant members of their societies is that it is essential for a large group to be trained this way if the politics of dominance is to persist. The only essential thing about girls' much longer and wider experience of free and mutual relationships is that it is essential for someone to raise infants and young children in growth-fostering relationships or they will die. Relational psychologists are saying not that women are essentially nurturant but that nurturant human connection is essential. Somebody has to stay close to babies if they are to live. Somebody has to stay close to children if they are to develop. Somebody has to stay close to adults if they are to know happiness. Somebody has to get close to traumatized adults if they are to regain happiness. Yet many men have been pressured since toddlerhood to walk away, to disconnect, just as women have been pressured to stay connected, to listen, to empathize. Janet Surrey quotes a client describing how alone white middle-class America leaves her as a mother: "It takes a village—but *I'm* doing it."

Worse than criticism, Judith Herman says, is the risk of being forgotten or ignored. And that happens to this relational work, too. Just as Freud started out talking to girls and Freudians ended up ignoring them, many would-be experts on relationship never mention relational psychology. Just to pull an example out of the current media: a special issue of *Time* devoted to "the science of happiness" reports that both male and female respondents most commonly attribute their happiness to relationships with children, friends, family, and spouses. But then the magazine more or less "disappears" relationships, as Gilligan or the organizational psychologist Joyce Fletcher might say, in the remainder of its coverage. Instead, it explores spectator sports, laughter, money, and other more stereotypically "guy things" as causes of happiness, even though both male and female respondents say these factors are less important to their happiness than close relationships.[3] While supposedly focusing on happiness, the magazine ignores what it reports are the most common sources of happiness—or "zest," as Miller has it.

And despite the tremendous impetus their work got from movements for human rights in the 1970s, the first relational psychologists also had to endure the shift of focus in the 1980s. In the 1970s, Massachusetts integrated schools and passed its own Equal Rights Amendment; it was cool to strike for peace and boycott lettuce for Cesar Chavez and the United Farm Workers. In the 1980s, white flight fueled real-estate speculation that made home ownership practically a white privilege; HUD money turned Columbia Point, a public housing project on Boston Harbor, into luxury waterfront condominiums; Donald Trump became cool. The War on Poverty, as so many observed, became a war on the poor as year after year Congress took billions of dollars of entitlements to food, child care, education, job training, and housing from hungry, uneducated, jobless, homeless people and gave them to the defense budget or to wealthy people in tax breaks. Managed care, the idea that people's health can be profitably manufactured like cars or cotton cloth, created major disconnections in the clinical world as insurance companies and health maintenance organizations cut average mental hospital stays from ninety days to four or five and began refusing to pay for more than half a dozen psychotherapy sessions a year.

But even as the gulf between rich and poor widened stupendously, the movement for victims' rights that had come out of the women's movement moved into the conservative political ambit and led to the victims' rights acts of the 1980s. This legislation underwrote the rapid progress Herman and her colleagues were making in treating the psychological trauma of incest, rape, political torture, and war. Revolutionary advances in neurochemistry and pharmacology supported discoveries that Herman and her colleagues at the Victims of Violence program in the Cambridge Health Alliance were making about the experience of healing from psychological trauma—and about the importance of education and group support in treating trauma victims. Today they know how to educate and empower trauma survivors to choose the drug and talk therapy that will work best for them.

I was moved to write this book because whenever I wrote magazine articles and reviews about relational psychologists, psychiatrists, and social workers in the 1970s, '80s, and '90s, I found myself swamped with calls and letters. The people who called and wrote didn't say this work was interesting. They said it changed their lives. Mothers, daughters, wives, sisters, friends, husbands, and lovers said they were talking now, meeting again, finding the courage and desire to connect in ways they hadn't for years, or ever.

I spent more than a decade interviewing and following dozens of these psychologists around to offices, clinics, conferences, workshops, seminars, institutes, Girl Scout gatherings, and kitchen-table conversations. Several of them had become friends by the time we started and are closer friends now. Eventually, because their methods are so open and inclusive, I found myself teaching or leading a few workshops and sessions of the Working Connections programs at the Stone Center, and I lectured at the Harvard Medical School conference these psychologists teach together every other year. I had to immerse myself in their thinking and practice to write about them, and they were endlessly generous teachers. All the women and men whose interview material ended up in this book went over their contributions with me to clarify their ideas and amplify my interpretations—though of course any mistakes that remain are mine alone. Above all, for me personally, my immersion in the life and growth of relational psychology had the invaluable benefit of keeping me honest as a mother through every phase of my daughters' growth. By that I mean I never left them, never got into a place where I had to say, "Well, if you're going to be like *that*, you're on your own." When they grew and changed, our relationship grew and changed, and so did I. It was never time to separate; it was often time to change, always time to grow, eventually time to become equals. We had wonderful times of laughter and invention and stories and play. And when I made mistakes, or life imposed disconnections because our family had to move to another town, we had difficult but vibrant times when I listened to their pain. I gave one daughter a rose every day she went to a new middle school where she was shunned as a newcomer. I gave another daughter an album to put photos of our old house in, and every day I listened to her talk about how much she loved our old house and how sad she was to lose it. After days, or weeks, or sometimes months, they no longer needed to talk about pain, because they had made new connections and weren't in so much distress. Now they live far away, and we designate five minutes a day to send each other love. Holding that pain of disconnection with them, feeling the hope in that pain as we continued to listen to each other, trusting our relationship to hold us while they and I changed, "waging good conflict" (as Jean Miller teaches) during adolescence—these are priceless lessons for parents, and I can attest that they work.

At the turn of the twenty-first century, these psychological revolutionaries no longer design their work to discover how the social system of dominance distorts psychology. They know a lot about that by now. Now they set out to help heal the culture and the people dominance hurts or holds back: a dozen or more of Gilligan's former students are working and writing about how girls and boys develop in relationship. Gilligan herself—"the mystic of the movement," as her friend the actor, director, and founder of Shakespeare & Company, Tina Packer, calls her—has moved from psychological research at Harvard to teaching at New York University and has opted for art as the cultural healer, writing fiction and adapting plays. Judith Lewis Herman, Mary Harvey, and many others have made the Victims of Violence program an award-winning training and healing center. They consult to the archdiocese of Boston in the wake of clergy sexual-abuse scandals and to trauma clinicians on every continent, carrying to Bosnia, Croatia, and Northern Ireland protocols about war wounds and healing they learned from Boston streets. Miller and her colleagues direct the Jean Baker Miller Training Institute at the Stone Center, where they teach psychotherapists how to make relationships that heal. The women who sit on the panels at their conferences reflect the rainbow. The white women who started these groups were already working with lesbian psychologists and psychologists of color when I began following them more than two decades ago. By now their groups have become multicultural, and they have undertaken to learn about their own whiteness, their own un-earned privilege, and use that knowledge in their work.

Finally, it must be said that these three groups of relational psy-chologists who did their primary work in Boston are part of a nation-wide and to some extent worldwide movement of relational thinking, oriented to human rights, that is revolutionizing psychology, psychiatry, criminal justice, politics, and art. Another version of this story could be told about psychologists in New York and California, where many of these women and men grew up and were educated—or Paris, London, Berlin, or Tokyo, for that matter. Just as they have been allies and wit-nesses for each other, they have colleagues, allies, and supporters all over the world, and that global support has been indispensable to them. Nonetheless, their story, their work, does change everything. And it starts in Boston, in 1975.

This Changes Everything

1.
Difference I

One day, late in the fall of 1975, Carol Gilligan sat down at her dining room table with a pad of paper and wrote "In a Different Voice" at the top of the first page. She was a thirty-nine-year-old part-time assistant professor at the Harvard Graduate School of Education, taking a year off to help settle her three sons in a new neighborhood. Later she said she started writing that day "for no reason." She was speaking in exactly the same way that girls do when you ask them what they've been doing on the edge of the playground during recess while the boys have been playing pickup ball and chase and steal-the-hat and the girls say, "Nothing."

"The men whose theories have largely informed this understanding of development have all been plagued by the same problem, the problem of women, whose sexuality remains more diffuse, whose perception of self is so much more tenaciously embedded in relationships with others and whose moral dilemmas hold them in a mode of judgment that is insistently contextual," Carol wrote. "The solution has been to consider women as either deviant or deficient in their development."[1]

But what—Carol asked, as she wrote on long yellow sheets in a room looking out over a wide lawn filled with moss-footed beeches planted a century before, a dining room walled with elegant paintings of merchant ships and schooners, of men and boys fishing in an eighteenth-century Dutch sea—what if the problem is not women? What if the problem is the theories that say women are a problem?

In 1972, the year Nixon beat McGovern in a landslide, Gilligan began asking men and women students at Harvard how they faced moral conflicts. She had also decided to study young men forced to choose whether or not to fight in Vietnam, a moral dilemma that was ripping American families and the United States apart.

The war was so unpopular, and yet so many U.S. troops were there—half a million at the peak—that you had to be involved. Either you were fighting in Vietnam or you were fighting about Vietnam somewhere else. In Cambridge, Massachusetts, the songs on the radio—"Universal Soldier," John Lennon's "Imagine"—were about putting an end to war. The atmosphere was charged with antiwar feeling and rang with the protesters' chant "Hell, no! We won't go!" Marches, protests, rallies, sit-ins, and strikes pitted a civilian army of student war resisters against an army of police in riot gear virtually every time you turned on the TV news or picked up a newspaper.

Then, in 1973, the U.S. Supreme Court conceded to women the power to make a moral decision as wrenching as the choice of whether or not to go to war: whether or not to have an abortion. The Court's decision came after an intense nationwide struggle by women activists that had already led to liberalization of abortion laws in California, Colorado, and North Carolina in 1967 and to the repeal of New York's antiabortion law in 1970.

Gilligan, meanwhile, was planning her draft study and lining up draft-age men to interview. But the draft ended before she could start interviewing. So in 1974 she decided to study women who were in the throes of deciding whether to have first-term abortions.

"I'm talking with pregnant women at a time when the Supreme Court of this country has said that women can speak their thoughts aloud, that women's voices can guide women's decisions, can be the decisive voice. The women are battling the accusation of selfishness, the threat that if they speak they will disrupt, they will lose relationships. Is it selfish to listen to oneself rather than to others saying that to be a good woman means to be without a self, to be selfless? What does that mean? To be self-less? What is love? What is truth? What does it take to sustain a life? What is the responsive—that is, the present, the responsible—way to act at a time and place when there's no way of acting that will not cause hurt? What does it mean to act rightly or well in a world that is intrinsically relational, where there's no way of taking even one step," Carol tells a class of graduate students in 1995, "without having the relational fabric shift under one's weight?"

What is love?

What is truth?

You could say that all of Gilligan's work—from "In a Different Voice" to *The Birth of Pleasure*—has simply allowed into psychology all the big questions she entered psychology to try to answer, because the first thing they taught her when she started studying psychology at Harvard was that those big questions were inappropriate. In fact, at the beginning of her studies, not only were her questions inappropriate, but, according to the head of the department, she herself was inappropriate. In 1958, when Gilligan arrived at Harvard from Swarthmore for graduate study, she recalls, "the head of my department announced, 'We only take women students to keep our junior faculty happy. They're going to have children and put their diplomas over the washing machine.' I thought, Well, I take your program about as seriously as you take me."

His kind of bias was so common, so expected, that she was nowhere near seeing it as a distortion that falsified all the psychology she read and heard. She was working in a university that paid white men to do research based on the assumption that they were at the top of the economic and social pile because of hereditary mental superiority. And these researchers were merely the latest to be rewarded for shoring up a system that rewarded intelligence in people of one skin color by making a theory that only found intelligence in people of one skin color. Richard J. Herrnstein, who had a Ph.D. in psychology from Harvard and finished a term as chairman of the Harvard psychology department in 1971, ignored the continuing legacy of slavery, Jim Crow, school segregation, redlining, and other forms of racism and focused on I.Q. test results. "We do not know why blacks bunch towards the lower end of the social scale, or, for that matter, why Jews bunch towards the top," he wrote, and went on to conclude, based mostly on data about white men, that intelligence is 85 percent inherited and that the political and social system rewards intelligence.[2]

He and his colleagues were renowned as experts in manipulating statistics and followed all the proper protocols for psychological research. They had no training in political or social analysis, and their work rested on the untested assumption that inherited intelligence—

rather than education, cronyism, luck, appearance, or the ability to conform to a white male ideal—is the engine of social mobility. The game is fair, and the winners have to be smarter than the losers. That was their theory about intelligence, and there was a whole intellectual tradition, with its own jargon and buzzwords like "eugenics" and "progress," that supported their theory.

But the civil rights movement had changed the rules—not yet of playing the game, but of seeing and hearing the game. And the women's movement was giving women courage to speak. Herrnstein's book found a lot of white critics who just couldn't swallow its psychometric social Darwinism. In 1973, the year Herrnstein's book *I.Q. in the Meritocracy* came out, you couldn't go to a dinner party in Cambridge 02138, the zip code that includes Harvard, among the academic stars Herrnstein dubbed the best and the brightest, without seeing somebody walk out screaming and slam the door, furious that a host or a fellow guest could stomach Herrnstein's ideas. Many of the door slammers, it must be said, were white women—the people who raised white men of superior rank, class, and intelligence that Herrnstein said were simply smart by nature. Couples divorced over his book. For some women, the discovery that their husbands actually believed that their power and wealth came from merit based on natural endowment was more than they could take. The argument was almost always about African-Americans—few of whom, it also has to be said, were at those tables. Banks and mortgage agencies had redlined black middle-class people out of Boston's white neighborhoods, suburbs, schools, and colleges, and at the moment the city was inflamed by a bitter fight about school busing to achieve integration. The fight showed an intensity of race hatred that embarrassed dinner-table integrationists in a region with a long history of opposing slavery and legal segregation. But at least in the courts and in the first round, integration won in the Boston public schools. Affirmative action had only just begun to put talented white people to work beside talented black colleagues whom the white people might then invite to dinner. So, trendily dressed white people—in jacket, tie, and jeans, or silk blouses and jeans, or cheap Indian silk caftans—would eat their coq au vin and sip their *grand cru* wines, almost all still under ten dollars, and rant: How could Herrnstein add insult to injury and call it science? Didn't he read the newspaper? Dismantling Jim Crow in the South and school desegregation in the North were exposing generations of racist chicanery that amounted to a national policy of preventing African-Americans from acquiring wealth. How could Herrnstein imply that black people, so long oppressed and so many of them still at the bottom of the economic and social heap, were on the bottom because they were mentally inferior?

Few white women argued against Herrnstein from their own experience, even though they had a very damning argument: If humans were smart by inheritance, and intelligence was rewarded by merit in the system, why did a white upper-middle-class woman's brothers get top corporate jobs while she ended up doing laundry and pouring all her intelligence and ability into raising a white upper-middle-class man's sons and daughters? Herrnstein mentioned the huge difference in status and earnings between white men and white women but made nothing of it, noting only that one woman with an I.Q. of 192 had been happy to be a housewife raising eight children in the 1950s.[3]

One of the things that must have infuriated women about Herrnstein's thesis is that it made their work invisible. Many suburban Boston schools still sent children home for lunch in 1973. Home was where Mom was supposed to be waiting with soup—and with time to nurture intelligence. Before kids started school, and after school, it was up to white middle-class mothers to teach their kids, while Dad might not get home from the office until after they were in bed. In school, most teachers were women. Not only did Herrnstein's book fail to account for the very different way the "meritocracy" treated men and women born of the same white middle-class parents; it failed to notice the incredible amount of work—women's work—that went into educating white middle-class men. And if this is how psychologists were researching class and race differences, who noticed what they were doing about gender? Though psychologists talked about their field as a body of knowledge based on clinical and experimental observations of human beings, they didn't talk about their political program, their mission, which was to use their observations to create a set of beliefs about who was human and who was not quite human, who should rule and who should be ruled. Fortunately, Carol Gilligan's knowledge of two worlds, and her sense of belonging more in the world that was not welcome at Harvard University, protected her from caring too much about getting ahead in a tacitly politicized field of psychology.

Most people who shift paradigms in science aren't looking for what they find, and Gilligan fits that description. But she wasn't looking for what she was supposed to be looking for, either. Again and again, when I talk to her years and then decades later about what she was thinking and feeling when she made her first discoveries, she uses metaphors of water. It was as though the world she was about to bring psychology into were a different element, a different medium for life, and she had to be amphibious to survive in both worlds. Air was Sigmund Freud and Erik Erikson and Jean Piaget and Lawrence Kohlberg, the dead and the living theory makers in her field who had set the terms of the current debates in her brand of psychology, the psychology of human development. And water was where she went when she listened to the women and men she was studying. She found the lost treasure of women's voices underwater. Then she hid her knowledge about women and girls there to keep it safe. "It was like I'd been holding the work on women, which was the center of my work that touched me personally most centrally, absolutely underwater," she would say. Air was the thin stuff she maintained herself on as she waited for the dry, nitpicky process of tenure review to finish with her. And then, more than a decade after she sat down and wrote "In a Different Voice," she got tenure and a dolphin existence, air breathing and yet joyously, stylishly waterborne.

Certainly by 1975, her senior Harvard colleagues who knew what she was doing regarded Gilligan's work not as important or dangerous but as trivial and irrelevant, at best a fad.

The fad was women.

Gilligan was a research psychologist working with women on women's development at maybe the best time for women's rights in the history of the United States. By 1975, the 1970s had already become famous as a decade that was listening to women. Women's activism— starting with the Women's Strike for Equality in 1970—had prodded Congress into passing more laws to expand and protect women's rights than ever before. Even the Equal Rights Amendment had risen from the dead. Though the amendment was drafted in 1923 and introduced every year after that, Congress failed to report the ERA out of committee for forty-seven years. But by 1972, both houses of Congress had passed this ultimate protection of women's rights with huge majorities. By 1974, thirty-three of the thirty-eight states needed for ratification had passed the ERA.

And that was it. The crest of the second wave of the women's movement rose and broke. Tennessee, whose legislature had made women's suffrage law by one vote in 1920, took back its ratification of the ERA in 1974. In 1975, one more state ratified, but seven Southern and Western states rejected the ERA, and Nebraska rescinded. In 1975, the second wave started to crash into backlash.

A liberal political oasis, Massachusetts tried to compensate. I remember walking up to see what was going on at a table in Harvard Square on a beautiful New England Indian summer day in 1975. A tall, grinning, sandy-haired man in shirtsleeves began to lecture me about why I should vote against the state ERA on the Massachusetts ballot. "You already have equal rights. You don't need an ERA," he told me. But most men did realize that women needed equal rights, and many of them realized faster than women. A national Gallup poll taken in 1975 suggested that 63 percent of men and 54 percent of women favored an equal rights amendment for women; in the East, 67 percent of all respondents said they favored the ERA. The Massachusetts state ERA passed in the legislature and by referendum and became law in 1976. The next day the place felt a little different. A friend of mine walked down a narrow Boston sidewalk and saw a man making straight toward her. "What do we do now?" she asked herself. "Bump?"

The 1970s were a bumpy ride for women and men. But since the late 1960s, a political movement had cushioned women. Tens of thousands of women met in places where they felt safe, usually their houses, to talk about the politics of being women: too often these were the politics of getting coffee, of getting jumped, of getting raped, of getting confided in by bosses who would never promote them, or of getting left out of the Western canon, the history of civilization, and the study of psychology. Some of these meetings were consciousness-raising groups where all kinds of women, not just professional thinkers, got together to explore for themselves the political truths of their personal lives that most social scientists ignored. But a few of them were groups of women social scientists who were starting to go about their business in the same way—by looking at good data they knew didn't fit conventional science and by asking questions they really wanted answered.

It began to dawn on women that they were paying a high economic price for equal, or no longer quite so unequal, rights. Few women would have traded their new rights—to education, jobs, credit—for their old security. But by 1978, the sociologist Diana Pearce would notice that women now made up two-thirds of poor adults in the United States. In 1959, just before the women's movement began its resurgence, women had been half the nation's poor, equal at least in poverty.[4]

The first wave of the women's movement had started in 1848 at a convention in Seneca Falls, New York, and ended with the passage of women's suffrage in 1920. It had forced public U.S. colleges and universities to include women despite a bias against educated women that was a very effective barrier to their advancement. Though psychology was really born after the women's movement, and women persisted in entering the field from the beginning, the first women psychologists were prohibited from taking courses, then refused degrees, and then never hired by schools that taught men. In 1904, the respected psychologist G. Stanley Hall declared that intellectual women were "functionally castrated."[5] In that same year, the president of the Experimentalists, a new learned society of the most distinguished experimental psychologists in the United States, refused to accept women members; this man remained president, and his policy remained in place, until 1929. By 1950, women made up the majority of the U.S. population but were only 10 percent of U.S. college graduates. By 1946, fully one-third of all U.S. psychologists were women, but almost all of them worked in applied fields—not in research or on university faculties, which remained almost exclusively male. During nearly two generations of setbacks for the women's movement— roughly coinciding with the years the ERA couldn't get out of committee on Capitol Hill—the world of official, academic knowledge did its best to ignore women. In psychology, hardly anybody taught anything that psychologists had learned from women. The psychoanalyst Karen Horney, first working in Berlin and then teaching in New York, was something of an exception. But from the 1920s right up to the 1970s, research psychologists were taught that the most scientific way to treat women—and black people and Asians and basically anybody who wasn't white and male—was to leave them out of their studies. That is what Gilligan had been taught. But, almost by accident, that is not what she was doing in 1975.

Carol had gotten her Ph.D. in psychology from Harvard in 1964, only the second year it gave doctorates to women. In 1975, the school agreed with Radcliffe College, the female annex where Harvard had begun to practice a genteel gender apartheid in 1879, that it would abolish gender quotas. But Harvard still made sure most of its students were men. It was one of four Ivy League colleges that lobbied hard for exclusion from Title IX of the Education Act of 1972 because it wanted the right to exclude women.[6] And although women could finally get Harvard graduate degrees by the 1970s, the odds that any woman would end up teaching at Harvard were atrocious. In 1971, the year Carol became an assistant professor at the Harvard Graduate School of Education, 3 percent of Harvard's faculty were women. And it wasn't as though a woman teaching at Harvard, or any other university, had nothing more to worry about. A national survey by the Educational Testing Service, released early in 1975, found that salary discrimination against women with Ph.D.'s teaching in universities actually increased the longer they taught.

Gilligan retreated from the psychology program of Harvard's Department of Social Relations to the Graduate School of Education—the Ed School, as it was called. The psychology department was considered tougher and more hardball, and therefore more prestigious. But Carol felt the prestige came at too high a price. She had gotten her Ph.D. in psychology next door to B. F. Skinner and his cadre of trained pigeons and pigeon trainers, and the place almost drove her out of the field. Her graduate courses were supposed to prepare her for clinical work. In one clinical course, she recalls, "The supervisor said, 'What you say to a child is, "This is not the happy way to be." ' And coming from reading Virginia Woolf—and the Holocaust . . ." Carol can't finish her sentence. She felt almost desperate to escape the stultifying psychological boosterism that passed for theory and practice in Harvard's clinical psychology program. When she finished, she couldn't imagine responding to a child's pain with the heartless pap she'd been taught, so she decided not to be a clinician.

More than a decade later, in the late 1960s and early 1970s, when she was teaching with Erikson, it became fashionable to do research on morality, which psychologists labeled "pro-social behavior." The notorious Kitty Genovese murder in New York prompted an experiment at Harvard that was a watershed for Carol. Although thirty-eight neighbors witnessed Genovese's murder outside a Queens apartment building, no one had helped the victim or called the police until after she was dead, even though the young woman screamed for the better part of an hour and her attacker left and returned three times; for weeks afterward every news show served up at least one sound bite about whether America had become hopelessly unneighborly. The Harvard psychology department reacted by sponsoring an experiment: researchers were to run into a drugstore, cry for help, and see how many people responded. Apparently none of the experimenters felt it mattered that the main reason bystanders give for not responding to someone who is calling for help is that they think the person is faking. The researchers would be faking, but they believed their deception would not affect the kind of responses they would get. "That was research on ethical and pro-social behavior, and empathy and altruism: 'Okay, let's lie to them and make it harder to do something that's hard anyway,' " Carol remembers. "I was really appalled," she says. "They were confusing people's ability to trust when cries for help are genuine." She didn't keep her outrage to herself. "I said it in the department. I said it to the person who was doing it. You can imagine how warmly it was received. I said it. I said it all." And it made no difference—except to Carol. From then on she knew, she says. "I couldn't be a member of that faculty if *that* was the way they did research."

At the Ed School, Carol taught under the man who had made moral psychology an acceptable research topic. Lawrence Kohlberg had been trained at the University of Chicago in a psychological scientific method that left morality out. He had been taught that motives and drives, not reasons and principles, propelled people. But Kohlberg's own experience smuggling Jewish refugees into British Palestine after World War II had convinced him that psychology had to pay attention to moral development or else add to the kind of moral apathy that had brought Hitler to power. As it stood, he felt psychology was too corruptible. Germany, a great world culture and a center of psychological discovery and innovation, had defined millions of people as proper subjects for extermination. And then Britain, the last of the great empires and an adoptive home for German psychologists, and the rest of the allies that defeated Germany had kept the survivors in camps for what they called "displaced persons."

Kohlberg started his research on Jewish Sunday school boys. In his psychology, Jews would define the norm, so they could never be treated as deviants. But even after he broadened his base to include other ethnic and religious groups, Kohlberg did his basic research on moral development by putting hypothetical moral puzzles to white men and boys. "Whom would you throw out of the lifeboat?" That kind of question. Only he preferred questions about drugs. Should Heinz steal the impossibly expensive drug that could cure his wife, who would die without it? That was one of his favorites. Kohlberg graded the answers he got to his questions and plotted them on a rising scale he divided into six stages of moral development. From lowest to highest, his stages ranged from self-interest to interest in abstract justice. The person who was out for himself was at the bottom, and the person who acted out of a commitment to a principle of justice, without regard to how it affected himself or others, was at the top. The quality of mercy—shown by a person who attempted to act in a way that would not hurt others— was at stage three. After Kohlberg created his scale from tests of boys and men, he got around to charting women's development. And because they acted more out of care than principle, the women he tested ended up as stage-three moral mediocrities.

Carol respected Kohlberg's passion for putting moral development at the heart of psychology. She herself was the granddaughter of Jewish emigrants from Germany and Eastern Europe, raised in New York in a tradition that saw morality as part of scholarship, music, art, and every other part of life. But she felt very uneasy about Kohlberg's method of moral grading. Since she knew caring didn't make women morally inferior to men, she felt there had to be something wrong with Kohlberg's approach. The flaw she focused on first was his certainty that the way people said they would respond to a moral as-if puzzle was a fair measure of their true morality. Why not ask people how they actually dealt with real-life moral dilemmas?

Underneath this question—underwater, let's say—Carol had another question, a big question about the possibility of asking questions in psychology. She lived in two worlds. One was the world of conventional achievement, the world of the good grades she'd always gotten, starting in elementary school. This was the world of ideas about being human based on the idea of standing alone—preferably on some pinnacle of success, though it was understood that only a handful of people ever actually attained such eminence.

But Carol also lived in another world, a world of art, music, beauty, her mother singing to her in four languages, her own mastery of the piano. And while she was playing, or dancing in an interracial modern dance group, or singing in an interracial chorus, the graded, academic world seemed to be a dream or a crude sketch, while this creative world was real.

The creative world could hold sadness, and terror, and the Holocaust she grew up knowing about because she was born two years before Kristallnacht. Her parents found jobs for Jewish refugees in New York, and sometimes put them up. Her grandfather, who lived in the Manhattan apartment where she grew up, had emigrated from Hungary and lost friends and relatives—Carol's relatives, too. But that sadness was in the same world that Carol and her grandfather and their pets created when her parents went out and left them the whole apartment to play in.

Carol says she felt this world of feeling and relationship was stringently excluded from the world of abstract thought and autonomous academic achievement. Yet it was essential to her, and it was the source of her deepest and most urgent questions. It held her friends—school friends, camp friends, college friends, graduate-school friends—and it was the world of her marriage and her child rearing. It was the world she explored with her three sons when they were babies and as they grew up. It was the world where she gardened and spent summers on Martha's Vineyard. It was also the emotional world of being shamed and put down simply for being female by the head of the department where she was supposedly being taught about human psychology. And everything in that world of feeling and relationship, good and bad, was supposed to stay outside the psychology department.

In the elegant Gestalt school experiments on human perception that she learned about as an undergraduate at Swarthmore, and in the riveting case studies of Sigmund Freud, who wrote like a novelist, Carol had felt a possibility of bringing these two worlds together in psychology. But at Harvard, all that counted as psychology seemed to be logic and gamesmanship, the -ology, you might say. Where was psyche, the soul? Without ever completely distinguishing the two worlds, Carol kept wondering. At the Harvard Ed School, the psychology department's poorer but freer relation, she worked briefly as Kohlberg's teaching assistant, and she wondered: Why did most of the women and almost none of the men drop his course? Why did women show up as morally inferior on his principled, abstract scale of morality?

Despite the progress women were making in the law books, Carol started her research at a time when university women were more used to being treated as objects than they are now—whether they were studying object-relations theory (in which women were always cast as the Other, the mother, the object men needed so they could develop separate selves) or whether they were the direct objects of harassment by men who were still powerful enough to toy with them and get away with it.

"It used to be said in faculty meetings that I had good legs," Carol remembers. "People propositioned me all the time. It wasn't called sexual harassment. It was called propositioning." And at the time, propositioning was a normal job hazard for all women who worked with men. For a woman like Carol, who had some powerful connections to men —a husband who was a psychiatrist in Boston, a father who was a founding partner of a Wall Street law firm—the harassment was never terribly intense, because the harassers knew she had protection available. "I would just say no," and that would end it, Carol says.

Her male colleagues liked having her around, even when she chaffed them about women's issues and they had to cast her as the rebellious adolescent daughter. They let her be a mother, too. She insisted on taking every third year off as long as her children were at home, and 1975 was a third year.

And already, even as a junior faculty member, she had played the role of the professors who had shut her down when she was a graduate student. She would face "students with burning questions," she says—questions about civil war in Nigeria and Vietnam, or about the nature of love and power. "And I remember saying to them, 'That's a very good question, but it's not what we're talking about here.' " The power put-down: Your question doesn't belong here. Your question has to drink from a separate spigot at the well of truth, and you have to find it on your own. Later, having decided that they had to undermine Gilligan's reputation if their work was to continue to have currency, some traditional psychologists would tell her she was a poet and her work was beautiful, but not psychology. And Carol would do the same double take—first flattered, then enraged because her work was being disqualified. But as a beginning professor, she had to feed that line to her students, and she remembers feeling awful about it. "I mean," she remembers, "really feeling that they were asking my question, but I had learned not to ask my question."

In the previous fifty years, psychology had not entertained many questions from or about women. Without really noticing, the field had defined women not as part of normal humanity but as an abnormal subset. According to Freud, Piaget, Erikson, Kohlberg, and other psychologists who theorized about human development, most women did not develop in the "normal" human way. They meant most women did not build a strong ego to defend themselves from other egos and did not strive to stand alone, to win, to be "independent" individuals who prized above all their power to reason abstractly. Of course, Carol knew, in the part of her mind that came up with all those inappropriate questions, that no one is independent, that everyone depends on many people every day, no matter how independent they believe themselves to be. But she also knew that the major theories of human psychology upheld a separate self as the be-all and end-all of growth. And as she lived the split between what she knew about being human and what she knew she was supposed to think, she began to realize that the great theorists of human development were really in the business of disconnecting ideas from experience.

For Erikson, whose psychosocial stage theory of development gave Freud's ideas a new lease on life in the 1960s and '70s, the crux of development was forming a sense of individual identity, a sense of how you were unique and not like other people. Kohlberg thought people only arrived at a mature morality when they married an ideology, a set of principles that replaced a sense of lived connection to relationships. But these developmental steps could also be described as a movement into permanent dissociation. ("Dissociation" is a psychiatric term that had been out of favor almost from the moment in the 1890s when the French physician and psychologist Pierre Janet, followed by Freud and his collaborator Josef Breuer, began to use it.) Carol was beginning to understand that developments like identity and principled morality fractured the self and divided the two worlds she lived in. Many women, who never managed to develop the firm identities and clear principles Erikson and Kohlberg thought were crucial, never lost touch with these two worlds. And why was that?

Working with Erikson and Kohlberg as a teaching assistant, Carol had seen that both of these eminent psychologists did their best work on questions that came straight out of their lives and their hearts. Both Erikson and Kohlberg had been political resisters as young men. A decade before, Kohlberg had smuggled Jews into Palestine. Erikson had left Freud's Vienna in the 1930s, when it was starting to become Hitler's Vienna, and he had given up a professorship at the University of California because he would not sign a loyalty oath in McCarthy's 1950s. As a teenager, Erik learned that the loving pediatrician he thought was his father was actually his stepfather. He never learned the identity of his biological father, and he named himself Erikson as a way of agreeing to become his own father and of creating an identity that defined himself. Not surprisingly, the question that lit up his psychological work was this question of identity. But Carol also saw both of these men founder on the world of feeling and relationship that their discipline discouraged them from exploring. This was her first inkling that dominant men knew they were losing out on something essential for happiness when they split mind from body, head from heart, thought from feeling, and tried to live as though they didn't really need anybody.

Kohlberg was a poor little rich boy. He had been a very young child of divorce at a time when divorce and especially divorced mothers were rare and stigmatized. His wealthy father more or less bought custody of him from his mother in a way that could be very neatly expressed in a one-line moral dilemma: Should the poor divorced mother give her son up to a rich father who can provide him with the best, or should she keep him with her where he will share her love and her poverty? Kohlberg virtually *had* to say connection was worth less than principle if he was to approve of his own mother's decision to give him up. And he almost had to avoid looking at women's moral decision making if he was to avoid the most broken places in his heart. Gilligan also saw Kohlberg slip in and out of paranoia so severe he had to be hospitalized.

The story of Carol's discoveries is something like the story of the princess and the pea. Only in her case, the prince's family (a.k.a. developmental psychologists) didn't know the pea was there and had become numb to feeling it. When Carol woke up feeling bruised, most of the local royalty acted as though she was deluded. But Carol, losing sleep on that pile of traditional psychological mattresses, kept getting up with an ache that grew into an insight: in all developmental theories, the stages billed as the climaxes of individual growth—building a strong ego, finding an identity, embracing a principle—marked a stupendous dissociation from the experience of life as we live it with the people we love or hate, the people who care for us or hurt us. I am I; I know who I am; I know right from wrong; I would never compromise my high principles: that was the voice of moral maturity in the theories of human development that Carol was supposed to pay attention to. Yes, it was supposed to be good if the principles were about justice and bad if they were about, say, greed, but the way the beliefs were supposed to be held, and the kind of self that was supposed to hold them, fit a tyrant or a bully as well as a prophet or a reformer. And where does absolute commitment to principle leave love, solidarity, or the need to heal and be at home with people? Nowhere. Yet that dissociation, that inner divorce of thought from feeling, of belief from experience, of self from community, was always masked as maturity. Echoing the culture, psychologists were saying you have to stop knowing what you know about relationships, cut yourself off from them and build yourself into a bunker of identity or ideology or principle, or you'll never grow up.

The end of the Vietnam War and *Roe v. Wade* had moved Carol's research from a moral problem that faced only men (whether or not to resist the draft in a war many felt was wrong) to a moral problem that faced only women (whether or not to have an abortion). Working with three clinics, Gilligan and a tiny research team got in touch with twenty-nine women of different races and classes who were considering first-trimester abortions. "We start listening to people talk about their experience of conflict. We're kind of creating a psychology of daily life. And we're just doing this," Carol remembers, typically evoking her past in the present tense.

She wasn't teaching and doing research because she had ambitions to become a Great Man. She wanted to do something interesting and make a little money now that her kids were all in school, and she was smart, educated, talented, and lucky enough to get part-time work at Harvard. She and her student researchers were a small-time operation—one dissertation study and a couple of seat-of-the-pants investigations. They had moved from asking hypothetical questions to exploring real moral choices, and from a population of men to a population of women—huge moves in the staid and mostly white male world of academic psychology. When Kohlberg noticed that they were looking at the morality of women deciding whether to have abortions, he asked the students in his class, also mostly white and male, to vote whether abortion was a moral dilemma. The majority voted that it wasn't. Carol had already had some experience with voting in the early 1960s: while her husband was in medical school and she was finishing her doctoral thesis, she had spent warm summer nights in Cleveland wheeling her infant son Jon in a stroller up and down the streets of Hough and sitting around kitchen tables in the ghetto, registering black voters. She knew what disenfranchisement was, and she knew what re-enfranchisement was. Because she didn't need anything from Kohlberg, didn't depend on him for academic advancement, and didn't even really think of herself as a candidate for academic advancement—yet—Carol could learn without fear or discouragement that he had led a class to vote that abortion wasn't a moral issue. She says she thought Kohlberg's vote was funny. And Kohlberg didn't push it any further at that point. Later, intimidation and campaigns to define her work as trivial, muddleheaded, and demonic were not so funny. But in the beginning, she and her band of students were just too marginal to matter to the big professors in the Ed School. Carol's abortion study was truly defiant. But nobody thought it was defiant, because almost no one had heard of her and her students. Carol was one very junior, part-time assistant professor. She was working with a few, mostly female, graduate students.

At first, Carol and the students she was working with didn't realize that the shift from the Vietnam draft to the abortion clinic had shifted their sample from the norm to the untouchables of psychology research. But in fact the only people they could put in an abortion study were supposed to be "controlled for" by being left out of every study. All their subjects were women: white women, black women, poor women, middle-class women, single women, married women.

"She dreamed it up," Mary Field Belenky says of Carol, who was then her thesis adviser. "She had a small group meeting that talked about real-life moral decisions and was an ongoing group." That first group of graduate students "had a lot of men in it," Belenky remembers. When history took away the draft and gave them abortion as a moral dilemma, Carol invited them all to an open brown-bag lunch every Tuesday to discuss the new project. The men dropped out. "Once the topic was abortion decisions, I think all the participants that came to the lunch were women," Belenky says. But still, nobody talked about gender.

Mary reaches back to her days as a master's student at the University of Chicago to remember a required course on research methods in psychology. The professor "had been a teacher of Kohlberg's," she says. "He told his class, 'You should leave women and blacks out of your research sample. They mess up the data,'" Belenky remembers. "It took me a decade to think what it meant to 'mess up the data,'" she confesses.

Gilligan, on the other hand, had a genius for relating to people as friends and companions rather than as categories or roles, whether they were students, professors, or research subjects, Mary says. "I was her student. I'm ten years older than she. And I was her colleague. And we were friends," Mary says. They were friends who'd been neighbors and mothers together in a suburb where their kids came home from school for lunch every day. Now they sat around Carol's kitchen table and brainstormed a way of really listening that could also pass as psychological research. "We talked in a laughing kind of way about kitchen-table research," Belenky says.

Carol "apprenticed herself" to her subjects, learning from them even what questions to ask them by holding practice interviews with students and with women who answered an ad in *The Real Paper*, an alternative Boston tabloid. The women researchers spent hours refining an interview designed "to give voice to these people who have been unheard," Mary says, "and Carol of course is just brilliant at that."

The research meetings worked like a consciousness-raising group, Mary explains. At last they asked all those questions Carol had been put down for asking and had found herself having to put students down for asking in class. No one competed. No one sucked up. "We created together, a bunch of us, a very supportive, very affirming community. We had a good time," she says. "Her social science was so remarkable, because she brought to it the sensibility of the artist," Belenky says of Carol. Most of the students had been taught to stop asking the questions they had gone into psychology to answer. "I think those meetings really gave them courage to begin that kind of work in their own lives," Mary says.

So Belenky learned from Gilligan how to do "messy" research, including studies of women and people of color from all social classes wrestling with real-world decisions that had been seen as too complex for academic psychology, and she also learned something about how messy writing could be. "I thought people wrote papers by just sitting down and writing them," she says. But that is not what Carol did. Mary saw draft after draft of "In a Different Voice," first in Carol's "small and light" handwriting on lined yellow sheets, and then on typed drafts that got written all over, too. "That went on I thought for months and months and months. It dawned on me that this is how people write," she says. "I think watching that paper unfold was for me a major learning experience." A decade later Belenky was to share authorship of *Women's Ways of Knowing*, a collaborative book in which she invented "pajama-party research" with Blythe McVicker Clinchy, Nancy Rule Goldberger, and Jill Mattuck Tarule. The four psychologists did for women's minds and experience of coming to know things what Gilligan's work did for women's voices and experience of making relationships.

I have heard Carol tell the story half a dozen times of how she wrote her essay "In a Different Voice." She always tells it in the present tense. Sometimes she is at her kitchen table. Sometimes she is in the dining room. Sometimes she types the title right at the top of the first page, and sometimes she starts in on the text in longhand: "The arc of developmental theory leads from infantile dependence to adult autonomy." In that version of the story, she doesn't come up with the title till 1977, when she and her friend and student Michael Murphy are riding around in her Volvo trying to think of a name for the essay that was finally going to be published in the *Harvard Educational Review*. And sometimes the idea for the title is Murphy's and sometimes it is hers. She knows she doesn't remember exactly. Sometimes she tells both these stories and says she is pretty sure one or the other is true. There were, after all, more than ninety titles on her résumé under the heading of publications by 1996, when *Time* called her one of the twenty-five most influential people in the United States. She has written a lot of things, some in the kitchen and some in the dining room. She has come up with a lot of titles, some on the top of the page and some while riding around and brainstorming.

Why should she remember that one moment indelibly? There was nothing traumatic about it to singe all its particulars into her memory, nothing triumphant about it to prepare her for the students and biographers who would be asking her decades later just where she was and what she did that day.

She remembers being at home in Brookline with her kids and with her study results and living and mulling and finally getting it. Finally she knew for sure what she wanted to say about her real-life studies. But she was also sure that nobody who counted in psychology would bother to listen. She had seen the men drop out when she started to research abortion decisions. She had laughed at Kohlberg's vote, but she hadn't forgotten it.

Then Dora Ullian dropped in one afternoon.

"I was looking at those interviews that Mary and I were doing with those women. And I do remember that sense of suddenly seeing it. I remember Dora Ullian coming over, and I remember saying to Dora, 'You know, Dora, I understand why. I understand that these women have a completely different sense of self,' " Carol tells me in the light-filled living room of the Cambridge house where she lived through the 1990s. " 'And that leads to a different understanding of morality.' The sense of self in relation was so clear. And it was very focused for me," because the interviews with women who were deciding whether to have abortions so clearly didn't fit the terms of the public debate about abortion, she says. "You know, the public abortion discourse was right-to-life and right-to-choice, and mother and fetus were posed as two ad-versaries in a moral contest. It was like the whole construction was wrong, and I could see how it was impossible for a woman to bring her understanding into the public realm without having shouted back at her, 'You're selfish!' or 'You're a murderer!' or 'You're this!' or 'You're that!' No way she could be heard because the whole framework com-pletely missed the connection and distorted it." Traditional politicians and developmental psychologists simply dismissed a woman's commit-ment to finding the best way to act as a moving part of a living network of relationships, Carol says. " 'She's not autonomous. She had no sense of self. She was indecisive. She couldn't make a moral decision. She had no principles.' And I could see she just had a completely different sense of self.

"And Dora said to me—this is just absolutely crucial, I can remem-ber the day, I can remember the light—Dora said to me, 'Why don't you write about it?' "

So somebody did want to hear about it.

"She thought it was interesting. Otherwise it could have just gone up like skywriting. But *right* there was that kind of resonance: 'Why don't you write about it?' " There was no assignment. Carol had not been asked to present a paper at some prestigious conference or sub-mit an essay to a refereed professional journal. Dora was interested. That was her motive.

"I write 'In a Different Voice' for no reason, for nothing. I write it for myself," Carol tells me on a different day. But there was also Dora, a graduate student in Kohlberg's program on moral psychology at Har-vard. There was Mary Belenky. There were the women psychologists and psychiatrists who went to postgraduate seminars on women's psychology at Brandeis University and at the Boston Psychoanalytic Society and Institute, and there was her own Tuesday brown-bag lunch. So I hear Carol's "for myself" as just the sort of self she was about to describe in her famous essay—a self that is intimately bound up in a network of close relationships in which people feel free to speak their hearts and minds.

Gilligan knew now that she had to look at gender. So before she quoted any of the women she had interviewed, she cited some studies of sex stereotyping. They showed that most men and women thought the qualities essential for adulthood—thinking for oneself, making clear decisions, acting responsibly—were masculine. Autonomous and independent men were admired; autonomous and independent women were seen as unfeminine, callous, and self-absorbed. And when women acted the way they were supposed to—loving and caring instead of autonomous and independent—most men and women considered them immature. Gilligan had uncovered her first paradox: "The very traits that have traditionally defined the 'goodness' of women, their care for and sensitivity to the needs of others, are those that mark them as deficient in moral judgment."[7] But what if women really weren't children? What if men weren't the only adults? What if the habits of paying attention to relationships and of feeling and thinking at the same time were not, as Carol wrote, a "developmental deficiency" but simply the result of "a different social and moral understanding"?

Then Carol let a young woman in her study of Harvard students speak. The woman described her personal morality, a way of thinking and feeling all at once that was not like anything the male theorists who were seen as authorities had observed. "I personally don't want to hurt other people. That's a real criterion, a main criterion for me. It underlies my sense of justice. It isn't nice to inflict pain. I empathize with anyone in pain. Not hurting others is important in my own private morals," the student said. "My main moral principle is not hurting other people as long as you aren't going against your own conscience and as long as you remain true to yourself." And she added, "There are no moral absolutes."[8]

Because she says there are no absolutes, the student disqualifies herself from top ranking on Kohlberg's scale. This woman is saying she doesn't act out of obedience to an abstract principle that she uses as a standard. She says she relies on a live sense of empathy that works with her thoughts about justice. Moral thinking and moral feeling together guide her. She doesn't call this inner moral guidance system a principle, because it doesn't do the work of a principle. It doesn't force her to dissociate, to split off and ignore her experience of love and relationship. Male theorists of the time saw this refusal to segregate thought and feeling as a failure to rise to the pinnacles of abstract thought. Carol saw it as a way to integrate thought and feeling, a way that even so renowned a moralist as Gandhi, who made "not hurting" a universal principle, had missed.

Quoting Erikson on Gandhi's inconsistency, Gilligan implied that Erikson and Kohlberg were inconsistent, too. Gandhi had taken the ancient Hindu idea of ahimsa, not killing, as a basis for nonviolent political action that brought India its freedom from Britain in 1947. But he hadn't taken it to heart. Instead, he had made the move that people like Erikson and Kohlberg regarded as a crucial developmental step: he had elevated his principle of nonviolence to a level of abstraction that tore it loose from personal experience. Ahimsa for him became an excuse for private dissociation as well as an inspiration for public action.

Gandhi could inspire his whole country to achieve independence without war. Yet he shamed and beat his wife and justified his own personal violence by saying he was trying to teach her to do right. "I was a cruelly kind husband. I regarded myself as her teacher and so harassed her out of my blind love for her," he confessed. He also scorned, ridiculed, and preached celibacy to his son before his son committed suicide.[9]

The American psychologist Kohlberg, the European-born psychoanalyst Erikson, and the Indian political activist Gandhi had all made what Gilligan saw as the same mistake. And, she realized, these three innovators from three continents had other things in common. They all had formative experiences of being outcasts—Erikson the young artist with no father; Kohlberg the Jewish boy whose mother gave him away, and who cast his lot with Jewish refugees from Hitler; Gandhi the Indian who learned about color lines by being on the wrong side of them in Britain before he fought colonialism in South Africa and India. They were all classed as great men. (Kohlberg, the least known of them, ranked himself as one of five men in history who had arrived at stage six of his scale of moral development—along with Socrates, Jesus, Gandhi, and Martin Luther King, Jr.) They all spent a tremendous amount of energy devising ways to hold people accountable for fair treatment of others and to define morality as an intrinsic part of everybody's growth and everybody's politics. And yet they all cast women as another breed. And when they followed their principles—to justice for Kohlberg, to autonomy and identity for Erikson, to chastity for Gandhi—at some point each of them believed he had to let go of care, that care could neither be a principle nor cooperate with principle. Gilligan began to sense that a pattern or system was screening and editing experience in these men, and to some extent in herself. Here it was editing moral experience; and she glimpsed a pattern, a way of seeing that made it almost impossible to take in how seamlessly principle and care can go together. Instead, the system seemed to cleave justice from love, and right from comfort, and to force a choice. And the system linked that choice to gender.

Women care. Men are fair. Women feel responsible. Men manage rights. Women want to know who might get hurt and how to avoid hurting as much as possible, because caring for people and leaving people in a condition to grow and thrive is so important to them. Men want to know what is the just thing to do whether or not somebody gets hurt, because universal principles are so important to them. Gilligan didn't call either one of these ways better, or at a higher stage, or more complete than the other. Instead, she described them as complements that integrate mercy and justice when women and men work together. But in fact only one of these ways of being moral had any current standing in the field of psychology and in the political world.

Women's "reluctance to speak publicly in their own voice, given the constraints imposed on them by the politics of differential power between the sexes," was also an enormous problem in women's moral development—and one that really had nothing to do with women, Gilligan wrote.[10] Many women in the early 1970s didn't feel they had a right to use their "different" way of making moral decisions, or any way at all. Gilligan quoted a woman, a mother of adolescent daughters, who had only begun after her divorce to notice the subordination she had felt all her life: "As a woman, I feel I never understood that I was a person, that I can make decisions and I have a right to make decisions. I always felt that that belonged to my father or my husband in some way, or church, which was always represented by a male clergyman."[11]

This difference was not really allowed for in the prevailing theories. Some people, including many women in 1975, say they do not have the political power to make decisions about the moral problems that confront them. Working with the testimony she gathered in her studies, Gilligan painted a complicated picture of how the women she had listened to were different from the "human" norm that current theorists who looked only at men had created.

A stage of realizing that you exist did not appear in the developmental stage theories derived from research on white middle-class men and boys. White middle-class men and boys seemed to know that they counted from the start. The challenge for them was coming to see that somebody else counted, too. And Gilligan found that some women in her abortion study also began with an attitude that the problem of abortion was simply their own personal problem. She called this take on decision making "selfishness," deliberately and provocatively using the old shame word for women who think of themselves.

She found that a lot of women got stuck at what she saw as the next stage, "responsibility." They realized so profoundly how much their decision would affect other people that they could only think of the other people and they left themselves out.

But many women arrived at a third stage that she called "the morality of nonviolence." These women guided their decisions by the commitment not to hurt—and applied it to others and to themselves. Some women went through all three stages in the course of making a single decision.

Gilligan was still using the old methods to understand the new, different voice she was hearing. She was still caught in psychology as rating system. Her "morality of nonviolence" was better—more developed, more mature—than what she called selfishness. It was not just different. I think she wanted to stay in this ballpark because she wanted to show that women were in the game, not just spectators. Her stages of moral development meant that she could reposition (as it were) women—and that advertising word is just right for what she was doing.

She could position "not hurting" as a universal moral principle. And if "not hurting" was a moral principle, it qualified the people who went by it for consideration as fully moral humans. Women did not come out as fully human in the theories of Freud, Erikson, Kohlberg, and Piaget. Carol laid out a theory that said that some women, rated on their own morality by norms established in research on women, were as moral as the men Kohlberg's system rated as the most moral in human history. So Carol did some conceptual magic. She waved the wand of principle over care, and poof! women were moral.

"In a Different Voice" did in academic prose what George Eliot, Margaret Drabble, and Joan Didion—all cited in Gilligan's essay—did in fiction. Gilligan drew her conclusions about women's morality from research, and she drew them in a standard way that made the research seem to spill her conclusions spontaneously into facthood. Other psychologists could not immediately dismiss her essay as poetry or fiction, though some tried, and as time went on, some tried harder and harder. She only used the active voice when she was writing about her subjects: only her subjects ever did anything. For the researchers and the research, she used a pervasive passive voice in which no one ever does anything, though much is accomplished and revealed. That passive voice had become the voice of science, the prose key to creating the illusion of objectivity that science depends on.

It would be a long time before Carol would achieve the courage, skill, and knowledge to pay researchers, including herself, the same active, honest attention she had paid to research subjects in her first studies. But by itself, this caliber of listening, described in a scientific style, was enough to start a revolution in psychology, or at least to get Gilligan labeled a leader in a revolution that had been building for more than a century.

Gilligan quoted and described anonymous young women, not just men. These nameless young women had a kind of morality that made it impossible for them not to know, or care, that they were hurting someone, because they never shut out empathy. And this is the contrast that rang such a loud and liberating bell for Dora and the women who made Carol's essay a much-photocopied underground classic long before it was in a book.

Before it was published anywhere, "In a Different Voice" started a public life as samizdat. It was xeroxed and handed and mailed from friend to friend. I first saw it in a xeroxed copy a friend of mine gave me, saying it had saved her marriage and I had to write about it. The psychologist Janet L. Surrey first heard about it from Jean Baker Miller. "I remember Jean talking about it very early in the group, before it came out," Surrey says. "I remember a lightbulb going off—something you know but that had never been said." Surrey got her copy from a social worker in her discussion group in the same form I did, as a third-hand Xerox. "I remember actually Sarah Greaves giving me a copy of the *Harvard Ed Review* article. I also remember that was very exciting," Surrey says.

"In a Different Voice" said what many women knew and had often almost thought but never expressed: we cannot feel that we have acted morally, without hurting, unless we can actually see and hear the people around us being unhurt from day to day. Simply knowing that we haven't used a weapon or broken a law, or knowing that we have advocated nonviolence from a pulpit, doesn't constitute nonviolence for us. We have to use an empirical test: we have to experience, by feeling with the people around us, that we have not violated our relationships.

In time, some women, and men, would criticize Gilligan and other feminist psychologists for focusing on women's differences from men. These critics said that pointing out differences gave men ammunition for blasting women as worse than men and gave powerful men an excuse for continuing to exclude women.[12] Very quickly, Gilligan's research would show significant overlap among men and women—so that even where these "care" and "justice" voices were distinct, about 20 percent of men and boys used the "care" voice and about 20 percent of women and girls used the "justice" voice. Eventually, she and her colleagues would work out a new research method that revealed a four-part fugue of moral voices in both men and women. But many of her early and later critics forgot that Gilligan's first work was a response to major theorists who had used the methods of psychology to prove that women's differences from men made them inferior because they didn't fit male norms.

The problem with this kind of criticism is that it pretends there is no political system of dominance that skews and co-opts *any* insight into how the system works. People in the system of dominance use certain differences—gender, race, income, age, size, health, religion, place of birth, sexual orientation—as sluices or barriers for power. In the system—and psychology and psychological proofs, results, and conclusions are in the system—there is no way to talk about these differences that dominant people will not use to put down the people whose differences mark them as less powerful. If you say or prove that women have a culture that is different from but equal to that of men, the men and women whose voices are amplified in the current system of dominance will call women's culture silly or inferior. If you say or prove that women have no distinctive culture and are exactly like men, and are therefore completely equal—if you demonstrate that women don't need affirmative action or any other special help, thank you—the men and women on the search committee and in the boardroom and the executive suite will somehow just happen to hire white men for the highest-paying and most powerful jobs. The insights of that early research on gender stereotyping that Gilligan quoted in her classic paper still hold: men and women with the same qualities are still seen by men and women as decisive or pushy, commanding or bossy, articulate or garrulous, principled or out of touch—and wimpy or caring, ineffective or modest, indecisive or good listeners—depending on gender alone.

Some psychologists—Jungians are the best known—do claim that gender differences are archetypal forms that have a Platonic reality, pooled in a collective unconscious or accessible to human minds in other ways. But Gilligan and other relational psychologists are not talking about gender differences they think are essential. They are talking about gender differences they think are systemic, inculcated by socialization for political ends. And they are talking about human work they think is essential—caring, listening, healing. They are saying that for the most part, in the system of dominance that makes Western culture tick, a small number of men have the power to structure work for everyone else, and they leave women to do the essential work of helping people grow by making good, equal relationships.

When she wrote "In a Different Voice," Gilligan was saying that most women were different from most men. Different. Not worse. She didn't talk a lot about why women were different. To do useful scientific work, you don't have to explain the genesis and cause of everything you discover. But she hinted that the differences her work turned up might be cultural and political—that because women were taught to rate themselves as less valuable and because they had less power to make decisions, they made different kinds of decisions, decisions that were much more alert to the risk of inflicting pain.

Still, almost until the last sentence in her essay, Gilligan never spotlighted the problem of drawing conclusions about all people from studies of white men and boys. She never thought and still doesn't think that the problem with the old psychology was studying only men and boys. Not every study needs to be comparative. There are a lot of interesting conclusions about men and boys to be drawn from studying men and boys. The problem was that white middle-class men who were psychologists had studied white middle-class men and boys and drawn conclusions about all humanity.

Almost as an afterthought, she did name this problem in the essay she started that fall afternoon.[13] But only when the essay found an audience did she realize she had pulled the pea out from under all those mattresses.

Of course, the image of a princess doesn't really fit a researcher talking to women and girls about the hardest times in their lives. All her water metaphors suggest that Gilligan thought of herself as a marine explorer who had come upon a magnificent undersea city. When she leaned over the side of her ship, she thought she saw underwater terraces and towers, but when she blinked, she saw only surface weeds and a reflection of sun and sky. Then she dove in.

When Gilligan came to the end of the months of revision, of finding words to admit what she was learning from women, she scarcely realized how revolutionary were the implications of the "different voice" she had described. She had played back ordinary women's voices beside the developmental psychology of Freud, Erikson, and Kohlberg, and the activism of Gandhi, and she had shown these giants all to be blind and deaf in the same way: despite their commitment to combating "otherism," all of these men had treated women as abnormal Others, in a way that exposed a rift in their thinking. Could separation and autonomy play the same role in psychology that separation and segregation play in politics? Could these ideas be used as covers for domination, for prejudice, for tilting the game board?

More than a decade would pass before Gilligan would entirely grasp again what she had hold of as she wrote "In a Different Voice." By then, she and her students had created a body of research and a way of going about it that transformed psychology. When she wrote this first essay, she was simply following an inner voice, writing right up to the edge of what she knew and beyond. "It felt like fishing something up from the bottom of a well. It was something that was so deep inside of me," she says.

After reading over the typescript, she realized she had said everything she wanted to say, then thought about how her colleagues at Harvard would take it. "I thought, I've said it. I'll bury it in my garden, and it'll help things grow. I didn't want to bring it out into the glare of day, because I didn't think it could be heard," she says. "It was written out of my soul, out of the part of me that was raising my children, out of the part of me that had a garden." Carol knew too well how Harvard psychologists felt about that particular *s* word. And as for children, gardens, and intelligence that is in touch with children and gardens, she had only to remember the head of the psychology department who had welcomed her as a first-year graduate student with the comment that teaching women was a waste of time. "Everything in my experience knew that you couldn't bring that voice into the outer world because it would always be met with disbelief or criticism, contempt, dismissal."

She never lived out her fantasy of composting her essay. But she knew enough to put it aside. "The whole of 'In a Different Voice' came in response to a question: 'If you'd like to know what I think about this . . .' But nobody had wanted to know. Instead of saying it, and, you know, being shut down or told it was wrong or stupid, I had decided that nobody wanted to know and therefore I was—out of there," she says. "Once I wrote it, I just kept it. I didn't do anything with it except start to show it to a few—you know, the kind of people I was in conversation with," she says, "all students."

Students loved it. They xeroxed it and sent it to their friends. Eventually, one student, Roger Landau, convinced Carol to let him take it to the *Harvard Educational Review* to try to get it published.

Then, in the spring of 1976, Carol read "In a Different Voice" to the seminar on women at the Boston Psychoanalytic Society and Institute. The seminar was a discussion group where she could always find the handful of Boston-area researchers and clinicians, mostly women, who were interested in learning from and about women. "There was a sense of special closeness" among them, she remembers. "We didn't get into . . . who-said-it-first," she says two decades later. "We really didn't want to get into that sort of world of competitive theories." After Carol read her paper, a small, slender woman with pale hair and eyes came up to her. "I think you'll be interested in a little book I wrote," Jean Baker Miller said. "It'll be out in the fall."

2.

Difference II

From the time Jean Baker Miller started practicing as a psychiatrist, the theory she had been trained to go by told her the problem with distressed women was that they hadn't come to grips with their feminine role. The line was, "She's upset because she hasn't developed beyond a certain psychosocial stage," Miller remembers. But listening to women taught her something else. "Almost all along in my clinical work, you know, I always felt something's not right here," Miller says. "Look what strengths women really have—look what they really do to hold the world together, and they think they're doing nothing," she would tell herself. "Isn't it terrible that women can't take strength from what they're doing?"

Miller says she got the sense that when women she treated despaired over relationships with more or less absentee husbands and fathers, "they were like the sick ones sent to the psychiatrist while the husband pushed on." Women were left alone to supply the nurturing relationships it takes to raise a child. And even though many of them felt that they were doing nothing or next to nothing of value, many of them were actually very effective at holding their families together.

Throughout her training, when she worked in state hospitals, and then afterward, when she taught in medical schools, most of Miller's clinic patients were low-income single mothers, many of them on welfare. "But then in my private practice I saw middle-class women," or women who aspired to be middle-class—"sometimes they didn't have that much money; they were students or something." But whatever class they came from, they were left with all the responsibility for relationships. "I would say that in both groups I saw these strengths—very much. The working-class and the middle-class women were providing all of the what we would call now growth-fostering relationships, all the connecting, trying to help the kids develop, and trying to help the family work," Miller says.

Even among her middle-class colleagues in psychiatry and psychoanalysis, Jean noticed that women did the relational heavy lifting. "I even remember once coming in after some meeting from my psychoanalytic school at night—we all went, you know, maybe ten, twelve people to a restaurant, to continue talking. And it would be the women who would pull the tables and chairs together," she says with a belly laugh, "somebody's wife often, a woman whom one of these psychoanalysts would bring." And while the women were moving furniture, "the men were, you know, continuing their talk," she says.

Miller saw all kinds of unrecognized strengths in all kinds of women. "But the working-class women had to have even more of these strengths, I think, just to survive and try to do well for their kids," she says. Listening to them "helped me to stick more with women's experience and drop some of the old formulations," Miller acknowledges. "Maybe that helped me to move over and see that what women were doing with relationships was very valuable."

In her small private practice, Miller had no trouble telling housewives what she knew they needed to hear rather than what she was supposed to say. "From way back, I would say, 'Look, it's not nothing,' " Miller recalls. "I'd always be pointing out to these women what they really did and what they really *cared* about." So much of what they did was caring. White middle-class women took care of the men society said were taking care of them. They took care of their children, and they taught their children what they were supposed to teach them: to value what their fathers did at the office more than what their mothers did at home with them. Then, when their children finally got old enough to become their friends, true mothers were supposed to separate from their children. So they did that, too. They sent their adult sons out into the world of work that was closed to women, and they sent their adult daughters into separate but identical versions of what Betty Friedan was to call "a kind of suicide."[1]

Miller encountered these women in private practice in the mid- and late 1950s as they were starting to fail. The white middle-class mothers she treated raised a generation that rejected what their mothers tried to hand them. Many of their daughters did not grow up to be unpaid domestic workers but broke down the gates that had barred their mothers from well-paying jobs and piled through. The middle-class women Miller treated were the last of a very short line, and one probable cause of their depression was that younger women, including their own daughters, were about to join men in devaluing what they did.

Miller also had the strange but common experience of being able to uphold the value of women's skill and commitment in relationships when she was with them and not being able to mention it when she was in case conferences with her supervisors. "I sort of said it. I knew it but I didn't" is how she describes her fluctuating state of knowing what women needed when she was in her office with them, knowing that this working knowledge flew in the face of the prevailing theory, but having no alternative theory to put in place of the old one when it came time for diagnosis or clinical discussion. "I was always trying to construct this alternative theory" that would include the strengths she saw in women, she says.

Then, in 1964, the head of her psychiatry department asked her to give a talk on Betty Friedan's current bestseller, *The Feminine Mystique*. Miller read the book, and a light dawned: she finally recognized that the discrimination against women she had witnessed and encountered all her life, without noticing or naming it, was really and truly discrimination against all women, including her.

Jean was both brilliant and lucky. Her talent and her good fortune made it hard for her to see the forces that kept women down. In 1964, she was in her mid-thirties, a mother of two sons under the age of ten, and a psychiatrist. She was the daughter of a municipal clerk who was poor but kept his job in the Bronx during the Depression. She had gotten into Hunter College High School, a New York City public school for top female students. Her teachers urged her to apply to a women's college for a scholarship, and she got that, too, at Sarah Lawrence. She went to medical school on a full scholarship. Luckiest of all probably—certainly rarer than all her scholastic honors—at Upstate Medical Center in Syracuse, New York, she found a department head who let her finish her psychiatry training part-time while she raised her kids.

But it was not an easy time for noticing oppressions. The price almost every social critic had to pay to find fault with the United States in public was very high. Miller couldn't even get many interns and medical students to join an organization advocating better health care. "People were afraid of anything," she says. In fact, a medical-school classmate threatened to report her to the FBI for belonging to this organization, and Columbia cut off her scholarship in her last year when she refused to leave the group. The country was recovering from an episode of paranoia, the media feeding frenzy of anti-Communism, set off by the junior United States senator from Wisconsin, Joseph McCarthy. In 1950, McCarthy first spoke out on the theme he was to espouse and eventually die for, at least politically: the U.S. State Department, he insisted, was harboring Communist infiltrators. His obsession with adulteration by foreign ideas in a country populated almost entirely by immigrants and their descendants, his incendiary way of responding to calls for evidence with accusations of treason, and the investigations of thousands of Americans by his Senate subcommittee made headlines for years and created a monstrous and long-lived political red herring. Not only was it hard to work against homegrown dangers like racism, sexism, and classism during the McCarthy years; it might be "un-American," too, since Communists also thought that at least racism and classism were bad.

The same year McCarthy's anti-Communist fanaticism in the U.S. Senate began to inflame the country, Miller heard a very different kind of speech by a brave man, and she heard the shaming response it met. At a psychiatric conference in New York, Bernard S. Robbins, a psychoanalyst, suggested that women's "deviant" psychological traits might actually be strengths—strengths many men didn't have. It was an idea whose time had not come. Robbins's mostly male listeners ridiculed it, and Robbins never tried to publish it. But one third-year medical student in his audience never forgot what he dared to say.

The 1950s were "a bleak time for women," Miller wrote later. Postwar popular culture—movies, magazines, the new medium of television—told women to stay home. Psychoanalytic theory said women should have children and devote their lives to raising them, and then it blamed children's problems on their mothers.

During college in the late 1940s, Jean had seen enough high-profile women to know the culture could and should cast women in more flexible roles. She heard and saw that white women had been freer until recently. Her tutor at Sarah Lawrence was Helen Merrell Lynd, co-author of *Middletown*, the famous Depression-era study of small-town America that taught the nation what sociology was, and "she made all the difference for me," Miller says. In Lynd's social philosophy course, which Jean took as a freshman, she read books by Frieda Fromm-Reichmann, the empathic and imaginative psychoanalyst whom Joanne Greenberg later portrayed in *I Never Promised You a Rose Garden*. She read Harry Stack Sullivan, a psychiatrist who worked with Fromm-Reichmann and stressed the importance of preadolescent friendships for boys' development. She also read Karen Horney, the Berlin-trained psychoanalyst who dared to claim that women's development was their own, not just the opposite or mirror image of men's. "I never had a psychology course in college," Miller says, but the psychology that she learned as an undergraduate at Sarah Lawrence, a women's college, in the 1940s, was more complex, sophisticated, and careful about difference than Gilligan's clinical course work in graduate school at Harvard University a decade later.

Miller majored in history. She loved the history of ideas. "But," she says now, "there were no women"—in the field or in the ideas. So she went in for medicine, entering medical school at Columbia University in 1948. Her choice was practical: she had grown up in the Depression, and she knew that even in the toughest times, doctors always had work. For Jean, medicine was also a chance to join the sodality of doctors and nurses who had seen her through several childhood surgeries and long hospitalizations after polio left her with a bad leg as an infant. That experience of illness and the lameness it left had taught her how much—and how little—of a difference difference can make. Ten of the hundred students in her medical-school class were women, and two were black—a high proportion of Others for a traditionally white male medical school at the time.

Years later, she realized how invisible the women at Columbia had been when she remembered the great scandal of her time there. All of a sudden a critical mass of people at the medical school found out that faculty members held special cram sessions for WASP men only, so WASP men would do better than Jewish men on exams. This revelation spotlighted the school's admissions quota for Jews and made it look ugly and unfair. And it led to protests about the way Columbia denied advancement to the few Jews it did admit, since no matter how high their class rank Jewish medical graduates could rarely get jobs and training as residents at non-Jewish hospitals. Meanwhile, the school also had a 10 percent quota for women, and almost all hospitals, including Jewish hospitals, made it difficult for women to become residents. As one of the ten women in her class, Jean had gone through medical school thinking she had to be a good sport about what she calls "jokes in bad taste." The only comment she remembers any woman student making about gender came in her last year, when a woman classmate asked her if she'd noticed that only men students fainted at the sight of blood. She hadn't. All through what became an intense debate at Columbia about anti-Semitism, no one—including the women students, and Miller among them—said a word about discrimination against women, or against men of color. "It's amazing how you can know and not know," she says now. "I knew it was very hard for women and other marginalized people to get into medical school, but I didn't know. We just didn't put it together with anything."

For her training as a psychoanalyst, Jean chose the "other" psychoanalytic center in New York, the one founded by dissenters from both the orthodox Freudian center and Karen Horney's center. The Comprehensive Course in Psychoanalysis at the New York Medical College was full of men who were—she smiles—"Freudians and not Freudians," the way psychiatrists today might be called biologists and not biologists. "It was all the dissenters," she says. Jean was ready for an alternative to Freud, because all through her residency in psychiatry Freud alone was the name of the game and Freud had said women were creatures who never recovered from the early trauma of realizing they weren't men.

It isn't that Freud ignored relationships, the way today's biopsychiatrists often seem to. He saw them as essential, as Miller's friend Carol

Gilligan likes to point out in her talks on the history of psychological thinking.

In 1994, Gilligan took time out from a year as a visiting professor at Cambridge University, England, to fly back to Cambridge, Massachusetts, and teach two weeks of a seminar at Harvard. One afternoon she traced the twists of Freud's theories about women that Jean Miller had been taught to work by two and three decades before: Freud saw "the capacity to love as essential: if we can't love, we are going to fall ill, and if we fall ill, we are going to lose the capacity to love," Carol paraphrased. But Freud came to think that loving and being loved were separate processes, instead of being part of one relationship. Men loved; women were the objects of this love. Freud invented a complementary opposite to the healthy, loving man he thought himself to be that reduced his theory to a "zero-sum game," Carol said: "If men can love, women can't love; if women can love, men can't love." And Freud had to say men could love, because he was a man and knew he could love.

"Suddenly Freud has a problem," Carol said. "Either women can't love or his theory is wrong." Freud corners himself. Instead of letting reality break through and remind him that people can love and be loved, too, "he holds his theory, and in an extraordinary passage—you read these things and you're astounded," Carol said—Freud writes that women can only love themselves, and then when they have children, they can love their children because they mistake them for parts of their own body. Then he says he knows he's right about this because of "the fact that tendentiousness is alien to me" and because he knows the biological basis of these differences in men and women match his psychological explanations of how men and women love. Carol marked the prestidigitation in this argument: "We talk about women's capacity to love, and suddenly we're talking about the development of women's sexual organs." And then she read from Freud's essay "On Narcissism: An Introduction," written in 1914, when he elaborated this odd bit of theory:

A different course is followed in the type most frequently met with in women, which is probably the purest and truest feminine type. With the development of puberty the maturing of the female sexual organs, which up till then have been in a condition of latency, seems to bring about an intensification of the original narcissism, and this is unfavorable to the development of a true object-love with its accompanying sexual overestimation; there arises in the woman a certain self-sufficiency (especially when there is a ripening into beauty) which compensates her for the social restrictions upon her object-choice. Strictly speaking, such women love only themselves with an intensity comparable to that of the man's love for them. Nor does their need lie in the direction of loving, but of being loved; and that man finds favour with them who fulfills this condition. The importance of this type of woman for the erotic life of mankind must be recognized as very great. Such women have the greatest fascination for men, not only for aesthetic reasons, since as a rule they are the most beautiful, but also because of certain interesting psychological constellations. It seems very evident that one person's narcissism has a very great attraction for those others who have renounced a part of their own narcissism and are seeking after object-love; the charm of a child lies to a great extent in his narcissism, his self-sufficiency and inaccessibility, just as does the charm of certain animals which seem not to concern themselves about us, such as cats and the large beasts of prey. In literature, indeed, even the great criminal and humorist compel our interest by narcissistic self-importance with which they manage to keep at arm's length everything that would diminish the importance of their ego.[2]

"If you start with a man and make him the model, women are deficient," Carol summed up. "You have to say, where were women reading these passages? What would it mean to take in these passages, particularly if you were a woman reading it?" Carol asked her graduate students in 1994.

Thirty-five years earlier, Jean Baker Miller had been that woman. "From the beginning I felt it was wrong. I also knew that women had strengths that weren't recognized. What I didn't have was a way to put it all together in what would sound like convincing theory," she says. Though she couldn't come up with a theory that worked when his failed, Miller had seen that Freud's descriptions of women were trance readings given at a sort of cultural séance he thought of as psychiatric investigation. And she began to notice the crack that gender makes in the Cartesian wall between body and mind.

But Freudians of the 1950s, who taught the seminars Miller had to take, left this little rift alone. They taught that women could be calmed down or cheered up by being brought around to accepting their femininity, which usually meant becoming unpaid, full-time housekeepers and governesses for their husbands and children, and liking it. "I had other seminars," Miller says, where she searched for but couldn't find other ideas about women. "There weren't any other people talking about women," she says. Karen Horney had once offered a courageous critique of Freud's ideas about women, but by the time Miller was becoming a psychiatrist, Horney had produced a general theory of human psychology that applied equally to men and women. "Horney thought that she had moved beyond talking about women and had developed a universal theory, so then she didn't talk about women anymore," Miller says.

Of course, the Freudian definition of womanhood meant that women who worked at paying jobs were seen as failures or simply weren't seen, like men who didn't work at paying jobs. But most of Miller's patients were working women. What's more, this strange division—not just of labor but of the parts of their humanity that women and men were allowed to express—meant that women, who were defined as hopeless narcissists in Freud's theory, often carried responsibility for all the relationships in a family. And Miller saw that responsibility in all of her women patients.

Betty Friedan couldn't stand what this arrangement made her give up, and she wrote *The Feminine Mystique* as a very personal yet thoroughly researched scratch for her itch to have a professional life. Friedan was a journalist and housewife who'd dropped graduate training in psychology to marry and have children, because, like millions of other white middle-class American women, she felt pressured to choose between a profession and a family. Her book exposed the culture that kept highly educated white women at home with the kids while highly educated white men worked long hours somewhere else, but she missed the race and class bias that went with it. Millions of black, Latina, Asian, and white working-class women were—and still are—forced to work in a women's vocational ghetto where jobs were underpaid and never led to better jobs, and Friedan didn't think of them. She wrote about battered children, marking only mothers as abusers, and she ignored wife beating. She missed the brute force that kept the whole social arrangement in place. And she missed the way sexism straitened men's as well as women's roles—pushing men away from doing anything that smacked of tenderness or active caretaking, requiring them only to provide money and stand by as protectors and punishers.

Friedan did see that the restriction of white middle-class women put them into "comfortable concentration camps" and not—as the prevailing psychological theory had it—at the peak of female development. Freud's theory was wrong: the problem was not that women who hated being housewives hadn't grown into being women. Friedan turned the theory on its head. "*Women have outgrown the housewife role,*" she wrote.[3] The occupation of housewife—at one time a manager, doctor, tailor, farmer, brewer, baker, weaver, florist, artist, and entertainer—had become depressingly less than full-grown women were capable of. More powerful men had split the job into trades and professions for men only, and left women with just the bits about care. Political and economic change, not psychotherapy, was the only way out of this "housewife trap," Friedan said. She suggested something like a GI Bill to fund professional education for middle-class housewives who had been kept out of paid, professional work. She pointed to the Commission on the Status of Women that President John F. Kennedy had appointed in 1960, with Eleanor Roosevelt at its head, as a possible source of political and legislative solutions. And she opened Miller's eyes.

When Friedan described the "mutations" who might initiate social change for women, she described Jean's life: women with professions and children, made practical by later births and part-time training and work. Somehow, through a kind of canniness she was completely unconscious of, Jean had slipped past all the barriers into the fullest life that was possible for women in the mid-1960s, at least according to Betty Friedan. So if it was that easy to put it all together—work, marriage, kids—what was all the fuss about? Why shouldn't every woman be able to have it this good? Jean never asked these questions, because she was too close to women who didn't have it good at all.

By 1967, Jean was teaching at Albert Einstein College of Medicine, treating mostly working-class single mothers, and reading every book about women she could find. She had seen expectations and opportunities for women shut down from the 1940s to the 1950s, and now she saw they were opening up again, but she also saw that in the first years of this second wave many women seemed to think they were inventing possibilities for themselves instead of reclaiming them. The reading Miller had done at Sarah Lawrence had stayed with her. "I felt when the women's movement started, like, Gee, am I the only one who remembers?" she says. She had never forgotten her reading about the greater professional opportunities women had had decades before, and yet during the decade of her medical and psychiatric training she had never noticed the gender prejudice that was barring women from doing what they had been able to do even ten years earlier. The books and articles she read one by one as they came out in the 1960s showed her that middle-class women hadn't just jumped out of the professions, including her own, into full-time housekeeping and motherhood between the 1930s and the 1950s. They had been pushed—by the kinds of forces that kept the number of women in her medical-school class "high" at 10 percent. Betty Friedan, Gloria Steinem, Phyllis Chesler, and *Our Bodies, Ourselves*, the self-help guide to women's health in the original newsprint edition—"These books really did influence me," Miller says. "But nothing is really as good for whanging you as the reactions of people."

Miller joined a consciousness-raising group in 1968, one year after the first women's consciousness-raising groups met in New York. A young psychiatric resident Jean was training pushed her into it. At first Jean, at forty-one, said she was "too old," but the resident said, "I'll find you a group with old people." And so Jean began to meet with two secretaries, two teachers, and a nurse; with them, she heard the same voice she had heard from her patients, the voice of the supposedly maladapted female. Only now the context of the discussion was frankly, intimately political. And Jean found that she, too, had a lot to say.

Nineteen sixty-eight was a brutal year in the annals of social change: Protesting students in Paris barricaded the city, and protesting students in Palo Alto burned the office of the president of Stanford. Protesting students at Columbia struck and took over the campus until police drove them out, injuring more than one hundred and arresting more than seven hundred. Martin Luther King, Jr., and Bobby Kennedy were assassinated. Lyndon Johnson decided not to run again, and Hubert Humphrey tried to inaugurate a "politics of joy" at a Democratic Convention in Chicago where Mayor Richard Daley's machine police clubbed and teargassed demonstrators and arrested journalists. In August, Soviet tanks rolled into the streets of Prague to end a heady, liberalizing spring that would not bud again in Eastern Europe for more than two decades.

The noise women were making didn't seem particularly loud in this context. And at this stage, women made much of their noise in private spaces—living rooms, kitchens—where they met and talked to each other for the first time about what they went through just because they were women.

Women had always helped each other, Miller says—even neighbors who didn't particularly like each other helped each other when children were sick or cars broke down. "I was in many ways *very* moved by those women who helped me," when they were all raising toddlers in a city neighborhood. "But you didn't begin to talk about what was really going on in your life, and certainly not between you and your husband," Jean says. "That was all hidden," she remembers. "Women didn't tell these stories—at least in my life it had been hidden." To Miller, this sound, of women supporting each other emotionally as they began to talk through the politics of gender that molded their lives, helped her hear false notes. When the leaders of this new women's movement started playing politics as they began to imagine female liberation, she could say, "You're calling men the oppressors, *and* you're wanting to take on their way of being and their values."

In *The Feminine Mystique*, Friedan tried to leave to at least some psychology the appearance of apolitical objectivity. She wanted to use a few psychologists as allies in her cause of unshackling white middle-class women from a crushing domestic ideal. But Miller could not be as hopeful, kind, or blind. In 1971, she presented a paper called "Psychological Consequences of Sexual Inequality" at the annual meeting of the American Orthopsychiatric Association. She was about to try to do again what Bernard Robbins had tried to do in an era when it had been shameful for a psychoanalyst to admit he was learning something from women rather than simply subjecting them to his expertise. This time the response was warmer. Ira Mothner, an editor at *Look* magazine and a summer neighbor of Jean's on Shelter Island, heard her give the paper and rewrote it with her in a form he hoped he could persuade *Look* to print. *Look* didn't buy it, but the lecture was published the next year in the book *The Women's Movement*.

"Open conflict, if understood, offers far more productive possibilities for both men and women than the covert conflict it can replace," Miller announced in a lecture that was designed to bring covert conflict between the sexes into the open. And then she read out loud the rules of the game of dominance that had been—and often still are—kept so secret that the people who use them most proficiently may never actually spell them out to themselves. She numbered the ways that dominant and subordinate groups work and don't work together, and the first item on the list was "They need each other." That was as close as she got, on this first try, to the fundamental, omnipresent human need for relationship. In time, she would get much closer.

Her paper was a kind of manifesto, describing all political relationships between unequal groups. Miller put everything in the gender-race-class-neutral language of "the dominant group" and "the subordinate group." She was really looking for ways the political system of dominance chews up all differences and spits them out as generic Other, to be put down, marked and measured as inferior, and kept from power. Her list covered characteristics she said "all relationships that are irrationally unequal (e.g., blacks and whites, women and men) share."

She traced political twists and turns in relationships that had never been described by a psychiatrist as having any political dimension. She talked about the way a dominant group makes conflict inevitable "and yet it insists there is no cause for conflict." She caught dominant groups calling subordinates names and then denying them power because they had a bad name. Yet despite these dirty tricks, "the dominants actually come to believe that both groups share the same interests," they wrote.[4]

The dominant group uses power to force the subordinate group to do its will. The subordinate group tries to survive. The dominant group has the power to kill subordinates who tell truths it doesn't want to hear. So "direct, honest reactions to destructive treatment are avoided" when subordinates deal with dominants. For women, Miller said, "economic hardship, social ostracism, psychological isolation and even the diagnosis of personality disorder by some psychiatrists" can come of "open action in their own self-interest." But while a dominant group is putting down a subordinate group, the subordinate group may put on the dominant group, often with a smile meant to please, she said, and she cited black, Jewish, and women's folk traditions about getting around white, gentile, male masters.[5]

"The dominant group obscures . . . the very fact of the existence of the inequality itself. It rationalizes the situation by other, always false, explanations, such as racial or sexual inferiority," she wrote. And then she brought her analysis home to her audience of psychoanalysts: "This point has particular application to psychoanalytic theory, which, despite overwhelming evidence to the contrary, is still rooted in the notion that women are meant to be passive, submissive and docile—in short, secondary." However, she continued, "in the short period since the women's movement began, many women in therapy are beginning to raise the issue of their own needs and interests. Previously, they would have felt no right to define an issue this way, rushing on instead to question what is wrong with them that makes them unable to fit their husband's needs and plans." Miller believed this change was not just born of a temporary shift in the openness of the culture. She thought it came from a constant tendency among subordinates at any time "to move towards free expression and action." History is full of slave revolts, outspoken women, labor movements, race riots—and their suppression.

She described subordinates who absorb the attitude of the dominant group and obediently begin to feel inferior. She saw that people who get put down as subordinates may turn around and put down other people in relationships where they are dominant. "Blacks put down women; working men put down blacks and women," she wrote. She didn't get to white women putting down black women or to straight women putting down gay women and men. But she did make the crucial observation that this political system of dominance biased virtually all relationships. Relationships between unequals that were supposed to be equalizing—between parents and children, teachers and students, perhaps even doctors and patients—tended to remain dominating and to stifle conflict. "We have no idea of how to treat unequals constructively and respectfully. We have no full concept of the process of change from unequal to equal, having experience only of enforcing inequality. We want children to grow. But when their growth challenges us, we shift rapidly to the tactics of closure and intimidation that characterize our irrationally unequal relationships."[6]

Miller still worried that many of the women in this new movement seemed not to know how many of their insights about women's place had been gained and lost before—even in her own field, some of them less than a generation before. So she put together *Psychoanalysis and Women* to bring back the insights of Horney, Clara Thompson, Alfred Adler, and others, from the second decade of the twentieth century to the 1960s, and to introduce her own insights.[7] "Alfred Adler," she wrote, "was the first psychoanalyst to condemn society's conception of women and to see this conception, in itself, as a root contributing cause of the psychological problems not only of women but also of men and children."[8]

She recycled the American psychoanalyst Clara Thompson's insight that "warfare between the sexes" had nothing to do with Freud's brainchild "penis envy" and was "not different in kind from any other struggle between combatants, one of whom has definite advantage in prestige and position."[9] In the early 1970s, Miller reminded women that back in the early 1940s, Thompson caught Freud disguising cultural beliefs about women as biology. Freud called girls' depression and distress at puberty a reaction to a shift from clitoral to vaginal sexuality. Thompson wrote that puberty was the time when "it became necessary for the girl to accept the restrictions placed on women, and that this was usually unwelcome." In other words, "the difficulties of adjustment found in the girl at puberty are the results of social pressure and do not arise from the difficulty of giving up the clitoris in favor of the vagina."[10] Freud hadn't learned a thing about women, Thompson said. The "characteristics and inferiority feeling which Freud considered to be specifically female and biologically determined can be explained as developments arising in and growing out of Western woman's historic situation of underprivilege, restriction of development, insincere attitude toward the sexual nature and social and economic dependency," she wrote.[11]

Freud had imagined that one of his greatest contributions would be freeing men and women for sexual enjoyment. But forty years after the old man died, his sexual revolution had become a trap for women—and their expected response had become a role as restrictive as the housewife's routine. In the Victorian era before Freud, women were damned if they did. Now they were damned if they did and damned if they didn't. At first, many women tried to share Freud's vision of sexual pleasure as the motive force of life. They thought it could make them freer. But they hadn't reckoned with Freud's impossible ideas about their sexuality.

Freud's model of girls' development into vaginally orgasmic women incapable of love was, if not pure fantasy, then a code for the moment when freedom to look for real pleasure meets name-calling and pressure to start faking; girls were politically pressured to make this shift from real to fake at adolescence in every aspect of their lives, not just sexually, and psychoanalysis became part of the pressure. When women failed to fake vaginal orgasms, or the joy of housework, psychoanalytic theory said they were immature and hadn't developed into real women. In other words, Freudian analysts—whose outlook became the basis of what educated people took to be normal or okay—pushed women to fake pleasure, sexual and otherwise. The analysts didn't exactly know or think they were doing this, but they didn't do the research that would have shown them what they were doing. Alfred C. Kinsey cast doubt on the physiology of vaginal orgasms in 1953, and William Masters and Virginia Johnson would correct Freud's mistaken idea of sexual physiology only in the 1960s.[12] But even after Masters and Johnson showed that what Freud expected of women in bed didn't happen, Freudians' theory didn't really change. Psychoanalysis never actually moved into the empirical mode Freud claimed for it at the start. Freud's stress on autonomy, and his masculine point of view, meant that sex to Freudians came to mean a man's pleasure in a woman, or a woman's ability to create that pleasure—not the mutual pleasuring of two people in an affectionate relationship.

In her own contribution to *Psychoanalysis and Women*, Miller remembered Bernard Robbins, the psychoanalyst who had galvanized her as a medical student by standing up in public and saying that women might have certain strengths that men didn't. Robbins had also been the first to see that in Western culture, men have the job of keeping sex and love separate, she wrote.[13] "It makes sense that civilizations which developed inequalities enforced by power, and which forced the vast majority of people to spend most of their lives doing work without pleasure, should also have evolved all manner of ways to separate and isolate people from pleasurable interaction with each other. It follows that sex, one force that impels people toward each other and provides so much pleasure, should suffer the most extreme distortions and limitations. It does not follow that sex, per se, is the road back to greater equality, mutuality and satisfaction," she wrote.[14] In fact, "sex, per se"—sex that isn't all tied up in affection and relationship—is an artifact of the sort of divide-and-rule dominance Miller was describing.

Psychologists who took on the deep questions after Freud—men like Abraham Maslow and Erik Erikson, working in the 1950s and '60s—dealt with human development in a more social and complex way than Freud and traced development beyond adolescence. Maslow emphasized the importance of inner fulfillment, which he called self-actualization. Erikson, as Gilligan was to learn from working with him, made forming an identity the gateway to adulthood in his interwoven stages of psychosocial growth. Betty Friedan cited Maslow and Erikson when she said that the current culture of white middle-class America put women in a role that stunted their growth and deprived them of the self-respect required to form an adult identity.[15] Women thinkers like Friedan and Miller took up this post-Freudian stress on growth because it promised women more freedom than Freudian sex, but immediately they had to deal with the way post-Freudian psychologists had defined psychological growth: real growth, it turned out, was for men only.

"We have all grown up in a world within which one half of the people have been portrayed as a lesser breed. Thus growth for men has tended to be conceptualized as movement away from those attributes identified with women," Miller wrote.[16] Passivity, for instance, "which women, in fact, do not exhibit or they could not take care of an infant," is identified as a female trait, she wrote, and men are encouraged to give it up and to give up any identification with anything else women do, like take care of infants. "The father's current abandonment of the mother and the child in the process of child-rearing is a characteristic of our society so accepted that we hardly recognize its destructiveness," she wrote. America had bought into a system in which "the child is led to believe that he or she has a father, and in essence, he or she does not."[17] But the skills needed to raise children "would probably be salutary for everybody to identify with rather than renounce. The negative ideas are not good for anybody, and are ideas falsely linked to both women and babies. Underneath it all runs the interdiction of another, even more basic process, which, as demonstrated here, seems the most frightening prospect of all: close and direct emotional engagement with another human being who is different—and female."

In 1971, Miller had written about power, and how power distorts relationships. Now she wrote about growth and said, "Only from direct and emotional involvement does growth proceed. It is when such engagement is thwarted or distorted that problems occur and that people are forced into devious routes in their attempts to grow."[18]

She turned stereotypes inside out and showed they held snips and snails and puppy dogs' tails. Women's growth isn't thwarted if they get paying jobs, Miller wrote; men's growth is thwarted when they allow dominant stereotypes to keep them from loving actively and creatively. "What is rare is a man who has incorporated an image of himself as a person who takes care of his equals—both men and women—who feels this identification as a critical part of his inner sense of self, equal to or more important than other inner images, like that of being superior to his 'equals,' for example," Miller wrote.[19]

By the time she got to Boston in 1973—when her husband, the sociologist S. M. Miller, began teaching at Boston University—Jean Miller had been writing about relationships for years without quite "getting it." She had written that power distorts relationships without quite seeing that power depends on relationships. She had written that growth requires "involvement" and "engagement" without yet seeing that people always and only grow together, in relationship. Like a cartoon character who runs off a cliff and treads air unawares, she had escaped the theoretical foundations of psychoanalysis, but her ideas still rested on the empty notion that when people developed, what grew was a self; equality made this self grow better, but equality wasn't fundamental. A lot of her friends in the field thought the same way, she says, so it was hard to find colleagues who could follow her thinking as it started to shift.

"I remember talking to a friend. I can remember driving with her and saying, 'You know, women need relationships.' And she said, 'But men need relationships, too.' She didn't see that there was a distinction to be made here."

Miller had been trained to think she had to help her patients find a hidden problem, one they didn't know about, one they were keeping from themselves because they were ashamed of it or couldn't handle it. Once that problem was dug up and named, the treatment was basically over, she'd been taught. "Coming out of the traditional training, I had crammed in my head the basic notion that the person is doing something wrong and they're perpetuating the trouble for themselves, and that's your responsibility to figure out, so you can help them," she says. But, she adds, "I think somewhere, without ever saying it, I really knew you had to relate to the person you're working with or nothing else matters."

By the early 1970s, she had realized that the problem was often not in the patient at all; patients were often responding to a difficulty the society dumped on everyone in their position. Women had too little power. But most of the women she saw in therapy didn't want to hold power the way the men around them did. What women valued and knew they needed was something that men were supposed to grow out of: relationships. She saw this now. Everyone needs relationships, but most women want them in a way men usually don't and often make women feel bad about. "It is extremely important to recognize that the pull toward connection that women feel in themselves is not wrong or backward; women need not add to the condemnation of themselves. On the contrary, we can recognize this pull as the basic strength it is. We can also begin to choose relationships that foster growth," Miller wrote in her still-epochal book, *Toward a New Psychology of Women*, nearly a quarter century ago.[20]

Jean says she wrote the book because two women pushed her: "Mary Ann Lash and Anne Bernays. Without them I never would have written the book. They were the ones who clearly were saying this is something important—more than anybody else."

Bernays, at home in Cambridge in the early 1970s, was between book projects when Mary Ann Lash called her from Beacon Press and asked her to work on a book about her great-uncle Sigmund Freud and women. "The more I read, the more I realized it was going to be absolutely hopeless, because I was a complete novice," Bernays remembers. When she described her plight to a friend who taught high-school English in Brookline, the friend told her to look up a woman whose son she was teaching. So Bernays called Jean Baker Miller and went to see her. "She didn't talk about psychoanalysis," Bernays remembers. "She talked about women."

Almost immediately Bernays realized Miller had the knowledge she lacked. "I have this project, and I'm just totally at sea, and I think you're the person to do this book," Bernays told her. Bernays called Lash, who let Bernays out of her contract and signed one with Miller. And then "the two of them got on me and pushed," Miller says. Through 1975, when Gilligan was writing "In a Different Voice" about a mile away, Lash was telling Miller, "We've got to hurry up and get this out, because they're saying the fad is over," Miller remembers. Lash cut about two-thirds of the first draft—"which was very right to do, I recognize," Miller says. But Lash was wrong about the fad.

"That book changed my life," says Bernays, who later dedicated a novel to Miller. "It was Jean who said, 'No change without conflict,' " and for Bernays, who had been taught to avoid conflict in marriage at all costs, Miller's words were a godsend. "I initiated some conflict and, luckily, my husband saw the justice of it," she says. "I changed some of the rules."

By now Miller had come to see that human growth didn't just happen to take place in relationships; human psychological growth depended on relationships to move it. "We all grow via conflict," she wrote. Difference was a source of conflict, and growth stalled without it. "The infant would never grow if it interacted with a mirror image of itself. Growth requires engagement with difference and with people embodying that difference," she wrote. But of course she knew that people in power also used some differences to mark other people for inclusion or exclusion, privilege or poverty. So "open conflict around real differences, around which they could grow," was often completely distorted or suppressed, for children and adults. "Instead, inequality generates hidden conflict around elements that the inequality itself has set in motion."[21] Women had taken to the streets not about the difference between men and women but about the inequality.

Miller took the psychic reality of human growth as she found it in late-twentieth-century North America—totally gendered. Boys were supposed to grow one way, girls another, and the men and women they grew into were supposed to raise the next generation of boys and girls so that men would continue to have more political power than women, generation after generation. But Jean's generation had a chance to change all that, and the mechanism was simple: listening to people who had not been heard before.

She began her book with the analysis of power relationships between dominants and subordinates that she had already worked out with men and women in mind. But now she fleshed out the agonies and anxieties of masculine and feminine—not with what she called the "ahistorical," symbolizing eye of Freud's younger Swiss contemporary C. G. Jung, but with the eye and voice of a woman who noticed social change and its effect on psychological change, both in herself and in her patients.[22] The problem was not what men are or what women are. The problem was power, and power turned out to be a stunting, painful psychological problem for everyone.

One of the hardest knots in the snaggle of cultural ideas Miller was sorting out was the way these ideas made inequality "normal." The rules of dominance and subordination were so rooted in social norms that it had become hard *not* to define the person with less power as inferior, hard *not* "to treat others destructively and to derogate them, to obscure the truth of what you are doing, by creating false explanations, and to oppose actions toward equality." To dominate was normal. The subordinates were the ones the dominants defined as abnormal, inferior, dependent, incapable of knowing what was good for them, only fit for the mindless drudgery or—idealized—for the sacred calling of unpaid or low-paid work. Anyone who tried to tamper with these labeling practices, which made up the day-to-day maintenance work of domination, got labeled a troublemaker or a reformer or, more usually, both. Troublemakers and reformers were abnormal, too, of course. "But to keep doing these things"—to keep shaming, bullying, ignoring, to keep trivializing as too unimportant, demonizing as too evil, or idealizing as too saintly to need equality—"one need only behave 'normally,' " Miller wrote.[23]

It made sense that subordinates would be the people who would want to change this system. Subordinates were certainly the most uncomfortable. In fact, "since women have had to live by trying to please men, they have been conditioned to prevent men from feeling even uncomfortable."[24] Women also knew the most—but only about dominant men. How could they learn about themselves? And why would they want to? To change the system? It was certainly far from obvious that their trivialized and denigrated point of view was a key to world peace and justice. "Indeed," for a subordinate, "there is little purpose in knowing yourself. Why should you when knowledge of the dominants determines your life?" Miller asked.[25] As long as the system of dominance kept operating, Miller's question could never have a positive answer. But real political challenge—consciousness-raising, marches, protests, boycotts, petitions and lobbying, and, finally, changes in the laws that kept the system in place—made it possible for Miller and other pioneers of what might be called "post-dominant psychology" to learn about themselves.

The women's movement gave women a chance to know themselves, and to be known, not only for what they could be if they acted just like men but also for the culture that they carried as women—"that is, the intense, emotionally connected cooperation and creativity necessary for human life and growth," Miller wrote.[26] The culture of taking care, of comfort, of weaving networks of relationships, is instilled in women over a lifetime. "Women stay with, build on, and develop in a context of connections with others. Indeed, women's sense of self becomes very much organized around being able to make and then to maintain affiliations and relationships. Eventually, for many women the threat of disruption of connections is perceived not as just a loss of a relationship but as something closer to a total loss of self," she wrote.[27] "Women are geared all their lives to be the 'carriers' of the basic necessity for human communion."[28] These relational needs and skills are not in any way "essentially" female but "common and inevitable to all," men and women, she wrote. However, "our cultural tradition unrealistically expects men to discard rather than to acknowledge them" and leaves women to care for everybody.[29]

Women are supposed to be weak and at the same time have limitless love and care. They are called selfish when they say no, something men are called focused and commanding for doing. Women's work of fostering development is seen as doing nothing. Their learning is not seen as learning, because it's learning to make new applications to a constantly changing, growing relationship or person. The "real world" is defined as the place where the things women are supposed to do— put others first, work for free—never happen. The tasks assigned to women are all called essential—raising children, caring for the old and the sick, serving sexual needs—but they are also defined as marginal and inessential to the "real work" of the dominant culture, which is what men are supposed to do. Because most women live with children, women live change. They do many of the things the culture holds up as being good—helping others, giving care, giving service, going with the flow—and yet they often don't feel good about it.

Miller titled one chapter "Doing Good and Feeling Bad." One reason women find themselves in that position, she explained, is that they are taught not to judge for themselves but always to see themselves from the point of view of a dominant other, whose judgment they have to learn to predict because it is the one that counts. Many men treat women as things to possess or barter, and many men teach women to look at themselves as things, even though "to be treated as an object is to be threatened with psychic annihilation."[30] Women feel bad because it's a bad system, Miller wrote. The system of dominance is so bad that just about everyone in it would feel bad if women were not the only ones the system allowed to feel much of anything after infancy. "Our dominant society is a very imperfect one. It is a low-level, primitive organization built on an exceedingly restricted conception of the total human potential. It holds up narrow and ultimately destructive goals for the dominant group and attempts to deny vast areas of life," but because that view is dominant, its inadequacy is obscured by all the political forces that make it hard to tell a boss to his face that he's totally out of touch and even harder for a boss to pay attention to such a comment.

"Some of the areas of life denied by the dominant group are relegated and projected onto all subordinate groups, not solely women," Miller wrote. Women, black, and low-income people are stereotyped as being less intelligent and as living more in their bodies than dominant men, for instance. "This partakes of the familiar scapegoat process," she wrote. "But other parts of human experience are so necessary that they cannot be projected very far away. One must have them nearby, even if one can still deny *owning* them. These are the special areas delegated to women. Based on their intimate experiences with them, women feel the problems in these areas most acutely, but they are even further diminished if they mention the unmentionable, expose certain key problems."[31] So men disown tenderness and active care in themselves and instead treat women who care tenderly as their possessions.

And even women, marked as subordinates and therefore emotional, have trouble knowing what they feel at times, Miller wrote. When women offer their special skills for taking care of people emotionally, for being with people, and their service is accepted without acknowledgment or return, it is hard for them to notice the resentment they feel at being used. When women try to change their roles, the system still holds them responsible for doing everything the dominant group wants of them. Like Cinderella, women can only go to the ball after they have cleaned the house and done the laundry. When white middle-class women began working for pay, they were held responsible for making sure their children were well cared for while they were working. As women began to take an equal share of paid work, it was abnormal, the act of a troublemaker, to ask how society could rearrange itself so that men and women would have an equal responsibility for child care.

In the dominant system, women are supposed to suppress conflict, and if they refuse to do so, they are accused of causing it. But at such times "women are not creating conflict; they are exposing the fact that conflict exists," Miller wrote.[32] Women are taught that it's wrong to assert themselves and that even the threat of conflict is evil, but since the system gives them responsibility for relationships and also gives them permission to feel, in a sense they are experts in relationships and in feelings. "We would assert that when women feel in conflict, there is often a good reason to believe they should *be* in conflict," she wrote.[33]

Here were *ideas*—about women, about cultural history, about politics. They were the kinds of ideas Miller hadn't found in intellectual history when she'd fallen in love with the field and then realized that she and other women had no place in it. And as soon as these ideas about the politics of gender, race, and class got loose in Miller's book, they began setting people free.

The poet Linda McCarriston, for instance, then a young housewife and mother married to a man she was putting through medical school, found Jean's book and began to base an inner resistance on the "conceptual thunderbolt" she heard in it.

"Women's 'job' is to protect men from the knowledge of the impact of their actions on the lives of others. This is how women are permitted to survive as 'subordinates,' to keep a roof over their—and their children's—heads," McCarriston, now a professor at the University of Alaska, remembers learning from Miller. "In other words, women's 'ascribed' moral superiority, which they supposedly exercise to improve and rescue males, is in fact arm-wrestled (usually through women's necessity to provide for kids) down to an immense lie. This has been my story," McCarriston says. "Seeing it in simple language *still* has a stunning impact on me, still informs all I see of pain between men and women."

"Put simply," Miller wrote, "subordinates won't tell."[34] The good girl won't tell anyone her father's binges and tantrums shatter her; the good wife won't tell her husband or anyone else that his intimate disrespect is destroying her.

"That book saved my life," McCarriston says.

3.
Difference III

In 1975, the *Comprehensive Textbook of Psychiatry*—the big book that defined the field of psychiatry for American doctors—said incest was a rare aberration with an incidence of one in a million.[1] At the same time, substantiated incest cases made up about 10 percent of the caseload for social workers in Boston child protective agencies. In other words, in the early 1970s psychiatrists didn't talk to social workers, or, more precisely, psychiatrists didn't listen to social workers. And once again, gender marked this gulf, since most psychiatrists were men and most social workers were women. With a very different pedigree from psychiatry, social work had grown out of nineteenth-century middle-class responses to what were considered the lower-class sins and crimes of alcoholism, wife beating, and child abuse, and social workers had been coping with incest for a century.[2]

What this divide meant for Judith Lewis Herman, a psychiatrist in training straight out of Radcliffe College and Harvard Medical School, was that when her patients complained of incest, her supervisors told her to ignore it. The classic Freudian line—which was still the main line for psychiatric treatment, as it had been during Jean Miller's training two decades before—was that children are very sexy beings and that when a patient thinks she remembers incest, she is really just remembering that as an infant or child she wanted it. The assumption made since Freud's maturity was that children long for sex with their parents, but their parents know it is bad for them and resist. With her colleague Lisa Hirschman, a psychologist in training at Boston University, Herman was about to discover that when it came to incest, the textbook was off by a factor of about ten thousand, even for father-daughter incest. And they were to find that for a very large portion of the population of people who sought psychiatric help, the truth about incest and other sexual abuse was exactly the reverse of the psychiatric assumption: all too often fathers longed for sex with their children, who knew it was bad for them and didn't want it.

Herman had chosen to do her psychiatric residency at Boston University Medical Center, where she could treat some of the hardest cases. Her problem was that when she went by the book and ignored her patients' reports of incest, the treatment didn't work. Besides, she couldn't swallow the notion that her poor patients were making up stories of incest or that they had wanted it. "They'd been so severely mistreated in so many ways"—repeatedly beaten, given up into foster care, beaten there, taken back and beaten again—that the idea that a father might have raped them didn't seem far-fetched at all. She didn't have to contend with what she calls "that 'oh, this doesn't happen in middle-class families,'" the line of denial by which psychiatrists had come to absolve their own class. Herman's patients came from very low-income, disorganized families. "It just didn't compute that it was a fantasy," she remembers. "Why would it be?"

Then her patients started complaining of ailments that weren't supposed to exist. For instance, while Herman was a fellow in community psychiatry at Boston University, a patient who'd been in treatment with her for a year and a half took an overdose, called Herman, and told her what she'd done.

"I said, 'Get thee to an emergency room, get your stomach pumped, and call me. If I don't get a call in fifteen minutes, the police will be at your door,'" Herman condenses.

The woman called from the emergency room and later called to debrief.

"I said, 'What happened?'

"The patient said, 'I didn't do it. *She* did it.'

"At that point," Herman comments, "the hair on the back of your neck starts to stand up."

"Split personality," the shattering of traumatized personality and identity now familiarly named multiple personality disorder or, more accurately and recently, dissociative identity disorder, was supposed to be a myth. Psychiatrists were supposed to dismiss patients' claims of being inhabited by vivid alter egos, the same way they were supposed to dismiss memories of incest, as fantasy or fakery. Doubt was the recommended treatment for people who, despite medical insistence that they didn't exist, sought help for the pain and confusion of starkly fragmented psyches. So when "the first multiple I ever treated came out to me after a year and a half of treatment," Herman remembers, "I didn't have a clue."

This same cultivated blind spot in psychiatry also meant that two decades of experience as a therapist had not prepared Jean Miller for what she started hearing when she got to Boston. In 1974, Jean had just arrived from New York, after a year in London at the Tavistock Clinic. She was looking for feminist therapists to go on thinking with. She felt she needed women allies to keep her focused on the way gender politics had skewed both human development and theory about it. Meanwhile, she heard about a new storefront clinic for women in Somerville, a white working-class town just north of Cambridge. Herman had persuaded Boston University to pay her a fellow's salary to do community psychiatry there, and the new clinic needed supervisors. Jean volunteered. She had already taught in a community psychiatry storefront in New York, through Albert Einstein College of Medicine. But her patients had not said much about violence or incest then. "I remember some of the cases we presented just appalled her, and she didn't know what to do any more than we did," Herman says.

But Jean helped with one problem they all shared: being daughters of their mothers. Standard psychiatric supervision would certainly not have included sessions on helping young practitioners think about their mothers, and most supervisors would have regarded it as unprofessional gossip. But for these young women clinicians, talking about their mothers was essential consciousness-raising. It was not hard for them to see the political nature of the model clinicians they were supposed to become, because they so obviously didn't fit the picture: they weren't men, and they weren't interested in making sure their patients adjusted to a world where, one by one, patients or their mothers were held personally responsible for all their problems.

"We did a lot of consciousness-raising about our own mothers and sort of trying to understand our own mothers differently, because part of the male tradition in training was harshly mother-blaming and emphasized the horrible competition between mothers and daughters," Herman says of her supervision with Miller in the new Somerville Women's Mental Health Collective. "Most of the women in the collective really didn't have in their mother a model of what they possibly could be. They had more of a model of compromise and being concerned about what the limits of being a woman could be. So Jean filled a hunger."

Herman's own mother, the psychologist Helen Block Lewis, taught her her most important lesson about the limits professional politics could set. "My mother certainly encouraged me academically," Herman says. "When I told her I wanted to be a psychologist like her, she said, 'Go to medical school. You'll have more power.' So I did."

Her mother was a first-generation American daughter of Eastern European Jews. Helen Block walked the three miles from home in New York to Barnard College starting when she was sixteen, ran the student newspaper, embraced radical social ideals, and became a Communist; but on cold or rainy days, her beloved nanny, Sally, still met her after class with a sweater or an umbrella. And though Block abandoned Communism after Stalin made his pact with Hitler, it was not early enough. She became an experimental psychologist, married Naphtali Lewis, a classicist, and taught at Brooklyn College till the late 1940s, when she realized she would not get tenure because she had once belonged to the Communist Party. When she found she couldn't get a job anywhere else, either, she took her inheritance from her father and trained as a psychoanalyst. "My mother's intellectual career did not end when she was blacklisted. She went on to publish several influential books and many articles, founded a journal called *Psychoanalytic Psychology*, and in the last decade of her life was a professor in the psychology department at Yale," Herman says.

Herman was born in New York in 1942, and her early childhood was filled with stories about relatives of her grandparents and their friends who had survived the Holocaust and were displaced persons trying to get out of Europe. "There was always this talk about visas," she remembers.

As she grew older, "the discussion around the table was of who was an informer and who would stand up for what they believed, what the college administration did, and who would take a loyalty oath and who wouldn't, and all the rationalizations that people had for their various degrees of complicity and cooperation with the anti-Communist purges. My mother was merciless about them. But she had a fine ear," Herman says. "I'm afraid I've inherited some of my mother's judgmental attitude—a lot of it. And also she didn't mince words about people, in private or in public." Her mother taught her about living a politicized life and what that could do to relationships. "The lesson was sort of 'Keep your wits about you; know who your friends are; keep your passport active.'"

So Herman cut her teeth on politics. "I was a red-diaper baby," she says. The first major influence on her life, she says, was "the world of my parents, both of whom were active members of the New York Jewish intelligentsia."

Herman remembers playing with some of the patients she found in her mother's waiting room at home. As a child, she says, she had no idea what the people in her mother's waiting room were there for and never connected her mother's work with her own future. She dreamed of growing up and being in the circus, and perhaps there are days when she believes that's pretty much what happened. None of her friends' mothers worked, so her own mother taught her the lesson that was such a major discovery for white middle-class girls in her generation: a woman could have a job.

"I don't think it's a coincidence that Carol and I are second-generation Jewish Americans" from New York, Herman says, "and Jean is steeped in that environment. There was already both a tradition of scholarship and a tradition of radicalism that infused our culture, that was part of the air we breathed, and it was also an assimilation of that into a very American ideology of equality and democracy that came together in the civil rights movement and the antiwar movement and the women's movement." In high school at Fieldston, a progressive New York private school with a required ethics course, in the days of the first sit-ins and Freedom Rides, Herman's heroes were Quakers who stood in silent vigils outside of weapons installations and activists who swam in front of the first nuclear submarines. "Those were always my people," she says.

She accelerated out of her freshman year at Radcliffe and in 1963 married Peter Herman, a high-school classmate. She took a seminar and volunteered at a state mental hospital. But the community she found for herself during college was in France—in Chanzeaux, a conservative farming village in Anjou where she studied as part of a Harvard seminar that the anthropologist Laurence Wylie taught. The Chanzeaux group "was sort of where I found a home in college," Herman says.

Wylie began to teach her feminist methods almost before there was a women's movement. He was a gregarious, democratizing sort, "very good at fostering cooperation" and at inspiring students to use their own talents rather than parrot his, Herman says. Also inspired by Quakers, Wylie "emphasized direct participant observation and cooperative learning rather than obeisance to abstract theory, and he encouraged us to look at the connection between very domestic and private matters (such as child rearing) and political attitudes and behavior," she says. Herman was one of four students Wylie listed as co-editors of *Chanzeaux, a Village in Anjou*, which Harvard University Press published in 1966, when Herman was halfway through medical school. "I sort of even briefly entertained the idea of doing graduate work in anthropology," she remembers, "and Wylie said, 'Now, don't be ridiculous. You want to be a psychiatrist, you should be a psychiatrist.' "

After graduation she went to Mississippi for the Freedom Summer of 1964, with the Student Nonviolent Coordinating Committee, at a time and place where the Ku Klux Klan and its white allies could and did treat black voter registration as a capital crime. Herman taught French ("which was sort of a joke") and the anthropology of the rural South to black students at Tougaloo College. "Talk about anthropology—both ways: we were bringing Northern, Harvard culture to these students who were raised on the Bible," Herman remembers. When it came to the anthropology, their students, young black undergraduates, "of course knew it better than we did, but they never had a name for it," Herman says.

Freedom Summer led her to the heart of "the phenomenon known as the Sixties, what we called the Movement," and she calls it the second major influence in her life. "To me, the core of the Movement was its radical vision of freedom, justice, and beloved community."

The Movement's approach to social change—"nonviolent but direct action"—had appealed to her since high school: "Let's not just take ads out in *The New York Times*. Let's confront the oppressor on his turf. Let's go into that restaurant. Let's go down to the voting booth. Let's swim in front of the nuclear submarine. Let's put our bodies on the line. Now, that's what I aspired to do, that's what I admired, that's what I thought was the most effective way to make change," she says. "But I was also scared to death to do things like that—still am."

Scholarship felt essential to her, too, as a kind of comfort and balance to her commitment. "The Tougaloo project was perfect for me, because it allowed me to be part of Freedom Summer but sort of in the rearguard" and to do it in a way that had her teaching French. Student civil rights workers "wanted to have a kind of a cultural wing of the movement," Herman says, "an educational exchange that went from basic literacy up to a college education." Marian Wright, a black SNCC organizer, met and later married Peter Edelman, a white Harvard student, during Freedom Summer. Bob Moses and Wright organized the Tougaloo program as an exchange of Tougaloo faculty, who went to summer school at Harvard, and Harvard graduate students and a few professors, who taught summer school in Tougaloo. "I wasn't as brave as Kathie Sarachild, who went out into the small towns and did voter registration or taught freedom in the freedom schools, and the workers who were followed and whose places were firebombed. At Tougaloo, it was like the base camp. It was relatively safe. It was a college campus," Herman explains. Vigilantes fired a few potshots into the campus, and black students had to hide when they rode into town with white students. But Herman says none of them was surprised when a week after they got there, three students who had been registering voters were killed. The three deaths only strengthened the students' commitment, Herman says. "The night they disappeared we all got together" in church and sang 'Ain't Gonna Let Nobody Turn Me 'Round' and 'This Little Light of Mine.' "Mississippi was a fascist state," Herman says. "They were so used to getting their way by intimidation because it had gone on so long," but she knew, she says, that they weren't going to get their way this time.

"We know how much courage it takes, but this is how we're going to get our freedom," Moses would tell the black and white students he recruited, or the families he asked to put workers up and feed them. "And people *did* it," Herman recalls. "The purpose of it was to confront oppressive power at its source and, by bearing personal witness, to expose its secret crimes. That is why the 'new abolitionists' of SNCC went to the totalitarian heart of the Deep South and put their bodies on the line in defiance of the Klan, knowing that the response would be murder. Mississippi Freedom Summer was organized to put an end to the state-sanctioned terror that maintained the system of white supremacy, and in this aim we succeeded. Though I was not on the front lines, I was a conscious participant in this project, which I certainly count as one of the formative experiences of my life."

And then, at the end of the summer, she went back to Cambridge and into a very different kind of frontline experience. "I came back and I went right to medical school, and at least I knew how artificial my world was. I had elected to withdraw from active participation in the Movement because I was chosen to do this other path, but the Movement was my home. Medical school was where I was studying to have something to contribute. In some ways I saw it as lesser. It was what I was better suited for, but I think I knew that eventually I would use my skills to be part of the Movement." That meant "when I went to antiwar demos, I'd be on the medical van. That way I didn't get as much tear gas, and you know I didn't get beaten up as much, but I also helped out, so it was a good compromise," she says with characteristic tense vivacity and ironic idealism.

At the end of Freedom Summer, the students who'd been part of it carried their education in radical change in half a dozen directions, she says. "People from Berkeley went back and started the free speech movement. The women who came north gave birth again to the women's liberation movement, but I think those of us who were there in Mississippi saw and understood and lived what it was to commit yourself to radical change and that a small group of people who made that commitment and made that decision could change the world," Herman says.

Medical school was a shock after this kind of close and generous community of idealists. Herman was one of 14 women in her medical-school class of 140: women in the 1960s made up the same 10 percent at Harvard Medical School that Jean Miller had been part of at Columbia in the 1940s. By 1964, that 10 percent was "typical" for medical schools, Herman says, while in 1948 it had been high. This rate of change was not exactly liberating.

But women's attitudes were changing much faster than medical schools. A new movement that seemed almost instantly to become worldwide, or at least West-wide, was hurtling out of civil rights and antiwar activism. By the time Herman was applying for medical internships in 1968, some of her old friends from the Freedom Summer, like Kathie Sarachild, had come north again and begun a women's movement cell in New York. "The radical feminists (like Kathie Sarachild) who matured in the civil rights movement applied the same political analysis to male supremacy. We knew that ultimately this elaborately ritualized system of domination could not simply be a matter of custom or psychology or 'sex-role socialization'; it had to be maintained by force," Herman explains. "This is the reason that we were able to see what others could not. We focused our inquiry on the hidden crimes of rape, wife beating, and incest, because we came to understand that these crimes were a culturally sanctioned system of terror that served the same function in the politics of sex as did lynch law in the politics of 'race.' "

Not afraid to bait red-baiters back or boast of their bluestocking seriousness with tongue in cheek, these radical feminists called themselves Redstockings. In the second Redstockings anthology—which was also the second to acknowledge the help of Judith Herman—Sarachild described the beginnings of second-wave feminism in New York: Like many other tactics and methods of the women's movement, consciousness-raising was borrowed from the early civil rights movement, Sarachild wrote. Anne Forer, at a planning meeting for a protest by New York Radical Women in 1967, suggested that they prepare by "raising consciousness" in small groups, as they had in Mississippi, to look at their own experience of oppression with an emphasis on asking, Cui bono? Who had an interest in keeping them oppressed? "We were in effect repeating the 17th century challenge of science to scholasticism: 'study nature, not books,' and put all theories to the test of living practice and action."[3] However, Sarachild continued: "There turned out to be tremendous resistance to women's simply studying their situation, especially without men in the room. In the beginning we had set out to do our studying in order to take better action. We hadn't realized that just studying this subject would be a radical action in itself, action so radical as to engender tremendous and persistent opposition from directions that still manage to flabbergast me."[4]

No combination of goals, methods, and enemies could have suited Herman better. Her respect for observed and interpreted data and her appetite for community politics had already been sharpened in Chanzeaux and Tougaloo. The women's movement was organized in the same anarchic but intimate and radically egalitarian manner as friendship. It had none of the tighter, more controlled, hierarchical approach that eventually dominated the civil rights movement and then the student left and antiwar movements. Herman threw herself into the Boston branch of women's movement politics just as she found the prejudice against women in medicine shutting her out of the internships she wanted.

"In those days, the discrimination was overt. It wasn't against the law or anything," Herman remembers. The department she applied to at Boston City Hospital "basically said we don't take women on this service." Their rationale was "something about 'That time of the month' and 'You would be useless to the other interns because of your moodiness'—and physical strength: 'You couldn't deal with rowdy drunks.' " So she ended up interning at Mount Auburn Hospital, which she says "got bargain-basement women" in this kind of gender-bar climate. She interned with "three crackerjack women" and "six all-right men."

Her marriage didn't survive this internship year. And the following year she joined a Bread and Roses consciousness-raising group in Cambridge—where she met Mary Belenky. Then, with a nominal research fellowship at Beth Israel Hospital, Herman took a year off to recover from medical training and to divorce and do women's politics—always the Movement kind, never the party kind.

It was "radical feminism—as opposed to liberal feminism or NOW feminism or cultural feminism for that matter—separatist feminism," that drew her and that she quickly "felt completely part of and identified with," she says. "It's the difference between thinking of equal rights and the ERA as the central demands and thinking about reproductive freedom, sexual liberation, the reconstruction of family as your central demands," she explains. "When we thought about sexual politics, we thought that sex was the main thing to talk about in sexual politics." Because she and the women she was talking with believed women were oppressed in their bodies, "it meant not just talking about political participation and citizenship and rights or economic participation and discrimination, but it meant talking about our bodies, talking about sex, talking about reproduction and child care." Talking about their experience as women was a revolutionary political method, and they used it for political reasons.

"Consciousness-raising, the method of inquiry that we used, was adapted basically from speak-bitterness sessions in the Chinese revolution," she says, taking it a step back from the U.S. civil rights movement, where radical feminists like Kathie Sarachild learned it. "The purpose was to understand our situation so that we could make a revolution," and the revolution was intended "to radically democratize an oppressive society." So though they spoke about the most deeply personal things, "the purpose was not personal liberation or self-actualization—although many of those things happened. The purpose was to understand our oppression as women, and that meant talking about things like sex and our bodies and beauty and relationships with the opposite sex and relationships with women. And the secrets that were revealed in that context had to do with those aspects of sex and relationships and our bodies that we had felt so ashamed of and so intimidated about that we didn't dare to name them.

"So people talked about orgasms—or the lack thereof. One of the sessions we had I remember—one of the stunning revelations to me was that every single woman in that room had faked an orgasm, without exception. Now, why would you fake an orgasm?" Herman asks. "We felt that was our job, to protect the male ego and cater to it, and who was sex for, anyway? And then from that it went to all the elements of coercion in sex, psychological and then physical. That was another thing that came out in the consciousness-raising groups—about rape. In most of them, it was three or four women in ten had been raped, or molested. We didn't know that was the national statistic then; I mean, the formal studies came after. Abortion—how many women had had illegal abortions, and what the circumstances were. People came out with their secrets, and there was an enormous rush of excitement and relief and the feeling of laying down a tremendous burden of secrecy and shame, and enormous feelings of connection and solidarity. But it was in the service of understanding that we had had our bodies taken away from us; our bodies did not belong to us; our sexuality did not belong to us. Our capacity to bear children did not belong to us. Contraception, the struggles to get contraception, the struggles to get men to use condoms."

A married Radcliffe classmate invited her to join. Thirty years later, Herman can rattle off the names of all twelve members of the group, including Mary Belenky, who thus met Herman before she worked with Carol Gilligan. The group met in people's houses once a week from 7:00 or 8:00 p.m. until "well into the night, because nobody wanted to leave," Herman says. Many members were graduate students, and they fell into two groups: women in their late twenties, like Herman, and older women who had had children, like Belenky. It was very hard for one young mother, who was "on call and on duty at every moment" for her husband and children, just to get to their meetings, Herman remembers. "One of the most moving sessions was when she talked about how she felt that she had just gone under, that she didn't have a self anymore, that her body and her energy and her existence were at the disposal of her children, whom she adored, and her husband, whom I think she felt incredibly afraid of and subservient to. But for her to voice those feelings that she wasn't happy in her marriage and that she was oppressed in her marriage, that she had not a second of spare time for herself—you know, she was being a 'bad' woman to voice such sentiments, and it was very moving for all of us to give a witness to that, to support her."

Then there was "our Marxist," who used to say, "Men are alienated in their penises, but women are alienated in our whole bodies." Herman laughs and adds, "Which is true," then laughs again.

"We talked about the actual conditions of our lives. Those who were in school talked about the trivialization of our work—not only the overt discrimination, sort of 'Why should we give you a place when you're never going to have a profession?' Sexual harassment, which wasn't considered inappropriate—in fact, heck, you were supposed to be flattered, because the alternative was that as an intellectual woman you were obviously a dog."

On "another incredibly moving night," Herman remembers, they heard from the belle in the group. "Here was this tall, exquisitely beautiful blond woman—beautiful according to the white WASP standard. And she talked about how her beauty had made her life a living hell— how from the time her face appeared in the freshman register, she would get constant calls from people she didn't know asking her out. It was clear that guys would sort of compete to see who could get her, if they could score with her. People would come by her window, throw stones at her window, try to get her underwear, you know. She was constantly harassed and grabbed. And that was, I think, a breakthrough for me in terms of seeing how our ranking in the hierarchy of beauty divided us from one another and how there was no ranking in the hierarchy of beauty that felt good."

Herman told her own story. "I talked about separation and divorce, because at that point Peter and I had separated, and I think I talked about the fact that becoming a doctor had cost me my marriage, which it did, and that even this man who I thought was not threatened by my intelligence or my ambition in fact was. And you know we saw that as an example of the ways that women are punished for trying to be free."

And as they talked even about the worst, most shameful things, she says, they felt the shame shift into liberation: "It was a liberation to me to feel that whatever I had lost in my marriage, I had more than gained in recompense this tremendous sense of connection and solidarity with other women, which I had not had before." In the past, even as students at Radcliffe, and "like many high-achieving intellectual women," Herman and her women friends had male mentors, she says. "Our fellow students were men. We didn't look to women for intellectual support—the big exception in my case of course being my mother," Herman says. They had been chosen to go where smart men went, so they were supposed to be different. "We started off as exceptional women, and I think the great gift of the consciousness-raising group was to make me feel that I was not exceptional, that I didn't have to think of myself as different from other women. We really understood from hearing how each of us had struggled—we understood that there were no personal solutions, because being a beauty was not a solution; withdrawing from the whole arena of sexual politics was not a solution; marriage was not a solution; divorce was not a solution; being single was not a solution. We made the best choices we could in a situation where none of us was free."

When she began her residency in psychiatry at Boston University in 1970, her raised consciousness met teachers who were, for the most part, masters of the high art of sexism, often in a completely unexamined way. "I was quite confrontational," Herman says. In fact, her problem was how to avoid spending all her time fighting classroom sexism, to leave herself time to learn psychiatry. "I actually made a decision that I would only comment on every tenth sexist remark—and I was constantly running my mouth," she says, laughing. For instance, she recalls, "The guy who taught the psychopharm[acology] course started off with a joke about two lions, and one of them ate a barmaid and had indigestion, and the other one said, 'It must have been the bar bitch you ate.' I said that using demeaning, derogatory stereotypes of women was not a good way to teach psychopharm or anything else and that I felt personally insulted and I would appreciate it if he wouldn't use that kind of language. He was extremely shocked."

She also organized the nurses and eventually ran consciousness-raising group meetings in hospital conference rooms. "I must have been a real pain in the butt," she admits.

She was least sure of herself in dealing with patients. Some feminists almost seemed to feel that because patriarchy had invented ineffective treatments for mental illness, mental illness shouldn't be treated at all. Herman remembers a feminist mental health conference in the spring of 1971. With typical Movement accommodations ("in those days you had to apologize for not sleeping with people"—both male and female), the conferees had to sleep on the floor. "I remember sleeping on the floor and eating this god-awful granola and thinking, I don't like these people. I think they're childish, on an ego trip, and I think I will stay out of this as much as I can," Herman says.

Later that year, when she was on call at the hospital, she took an emergency phone call in the middle of the night from a women's group. They described a woman in what Herman recognized as a florid manic episode. They told Herman they didn't want to send the manic woman to an oppressive Establishment institution like a mental hospital. They wanted to take care of her themselves, sort of round-the-clock consciousness-raising with an exhausted, sleepless, raving comrade. "I said, 'Hospitalize her.' I said, 'Maybe someday we'll have alternative things, but mental hospitals are there now, and she's psychotic, and mental illness is not just a myth," and not simply caused by injustice.

But then what was it? And where did politics fit in? And who and what would be of use in figuring that out?

Though the swirl of movements for civil rights and women's rights that she calls the Movement was Herman's social environment in this period, it did not direct her unerringly toward the truths she was about to uncover or toward a practice of psychotherapy, based on her discoveries, that would be truly effective for women. Precisely because of its open, participatory, inventive style, the Movement was a very mixed bag that included such major political successes as the right to abortion; equal rights to housing, education, credit, and the franchise; the end of the Vietnam War; and much acute observation and theoretical insight; but it also included an ample number of woeful political boners and excursions into left field. Not infrequently it was all these things at once. For example, along with the granola-on-the-floor mental health conference, Herman remembers an all-night student meeting at MIT sometime during this period. Leftist students had gathered in the student center to give sanctuary to a soldier who had gone AWOL and wanted to make a public protest against the war in Vietnam, then widely seen as no longer worth losing lives to try to win. Eric Mann, later a leader of the student left Weathermen "action faction," gave the main harangue. (Mann was "later busted for stealing long underwear in Vermont," Herman footnotes drily.)

"As the night wore on and it was two in the morning, he gave this incredible speech about imperialism and the war machine and links to the local and the global," she remembers. "Or maybe it was just two in the morning," she adds with the wry self-mockery that is such a constant and disarming accompaniment to her unyielding idealism. In any case, she found the speech "a fascinating and mind-expanding experience once you saw the whole dialectic in operation. And his conclusion was, so tomorrow we should go out and throw rocks. And I thought,

What? Am I missing a crucial step here? It really was from the sublime to the ridiculous."

The Movement gave them a place to stand outside of traditional psychiatry. Standing there, Herman and her friends had to invent their own way to use the practice and the insights about power they had learned from consciousness-raising to help women suffering from mental afflictions. Failure helped. Seeing that the things she did by the book didn't work freed Herman to try something else.

One senior psychoanalyst and psychiatrist on the Boston University faculty, Davide Limentani, a refugee of war in Europe and "a little bit of a maverick," she says, also helped. He became a mentor while she trained at Boston State Hospital. "He was a good clinician and a good teacher—and there were plenty of them around. They weren't all pompous blockheads," Herman says with a smile, mocking her own critique. Limentani "was very committed to doing analytic work with very sick patients, including psychotic patients, schizophrenic patients." And, to trainees, "his attitude was that if you were willing to see very tough cases, then he was willing to back you up."

Herman arrived for supervision with Limentani as the brand-new psychiatric resident trying to learn by working with the most chronic cases in the state hospital. She admitted right off that she felt she'd gotten nowhere with a profoundly depressed patient. The senior clinician riffled through some pages, and handed her an open book:

Mine eyes are blind and darke; I cannot see;
To whom, or whither should my darkness flee,
But to the Light? *And who's that* Light *but Thee?*

My path is lost; my wandring steps do stray;
I cannot safely go, nor safely stay;
Whom should I see but Thee, my Path, *my* Way?

O, I am dead: to whom shall I, poore I,
Repaire? To whom shall my sad Ashes fly
But Life? *And where is* Life *but in thine eye?*

And yet thou turn'st away thy face, and fly'st me;
And yet I sue for Grace, and thou deny'st me;
Speake, art thou angry, Lord, or onely try'st me?[5]

Limentani gave her a seventeenth-century metaphysical poem of desperation and abject surrender to God. Not Freud. Not the textbook. He invited her to imagine the poem as the outpouring of an abused and neglected child who was feeling utterly rejected by a parent who seemed all-powerful. The supervisor's lesson: use anything you can any way that helps you vividly and viscerally know the feeling state of your patient.

"He identified the core relational issues of a neglected child," Herman says. "He helped me empathically enter the patient's world," and he taught her to assume that was a good thing to do, essential for successful treatment. "He was very good about that. He asked me, how did I feel about my sessions with a patient? I said I often dreaded seeing her. He said, 'Well, now you know about her state.' " Her own feelings about her patients were not a mirror of their feelings but "a clue, information to be used," Herman learned.

And then, with incest, came a breakthrough case—"a so-called borderline patient who was malignantly suicidal," Herman says. "It was one of those cases where the incest was indisputable.

"We dealt with the issues."

The issues in incest hadn't been dealt with for almost a hundred years. But now here came a young psychiatrist who was so politically bonded with other women that she didn't have a blind and deaf spot about incest; she had a supervisor who told her it was always her job to listen; she had been to Tougaloo; and she had done consciousness-raising. "After that experience, I had some distance from the extraordinary elitism and condescension which was ingrained in us—particularly in medical school, but certainly at Harvard, throughout. The idea that you should listen to the patient and the patient will tell you what's wrong. I took that to heart—I mean, it's the kind of thing that the emeritus professors would say when they were thought to have gotten soft. But they said it because they knew it, and God knows how long it had taken them to learn it. But I took that seriously."

What Herman's patient told her was wrong dawned on her with a shock of recognition. Incest, she realized, fit all the many shapes of political oppression that she had set herself to learn about.

"It seemed to me that incest was a way to look into the heart of oppression, of the psychology of oppression. Just that the dynamics of it were so complex, that love was mixed up in it, that it was such an airtight system, that it was a way to turn everything that was a strength—the victim's ability to love, her endurance, her determination, everything—it was a way to turn all those strengths against the victim and use them to perpetuate her enslavement. How much of ordinary relations between the sexes and the generations was reflected," she says, noting that the normal and familiar power imbalances between male and female, and father and daughter, made incest possible, so that "the extreme form of oppression illuminated the ordinary. And how condoned it was, how integrated into the culture," she says twenty-five years later, remembering "just seeing how well it worked, how ingenious it was."

And she found its politics. "If you want to create someone whose sense of pride and dignity comes from how much oppression she can voluntarily submit to, that's how you do it," she realized: father-daughter incest. The problem of what to do about incest began to seem especially pressing to Herman as she encountered more patients who suffered from it and as she met more therapists who said their patients complained of it.

By 1970, Herman's Bread and Roses group had "sort of fizzled out," because they had more or less finished with their political review of their personal experience. "At a certain point, we'd done it, and then we were staying together because we cared about each other and for the camaraderie," Herman says. But they also felt an obligation to do something with the political knowledge they'd created together. "A lot of the energy in radical feminism came from the fact that we were radicals first, and our radical brothers were screwing us, literally and figuratively, and we were getting not a whole lot out of it except VD and pregnancy and broken hearts, and not even a whole lot of orgasms," Herman says. "So our entry into psychology was, you know, based on our experience of sex, which was: Would somebody please explain to me what a vaginal orgasm is? We started with our bodies, we started with our feelings, we started with our own experience of relationships, and we noticed how cockeyed, how just ludicrous, the theories were. Here was an anatomical impossibility, right? The vaginal orgasm. It was like so many of the other anatomical impossibilities, like the pediatrics text that said when *children* had gonorrhea, they probably got it from toilet seats, even though it was clear that biologically the gonococcus, like the AIDS virus, doesn't live outside of human tissues for any appreciable length of time."

That fall all the Bread and Roses groups organized a meeting in Boston where women could begin to sort themselves by interest into action projects that were to affect the lives and health of millions of women in the next decades. "The pressure was then to take our understanding into action, and the way to take it into action was as varied as" the women who had been doing the consciousness-raising, Herman says. "There was so much to be done. You could start anywhere. You could start with trying to make a list of good health-care providers, which is how *Our Bodies, Ourselves* started. Good gynecologists. Well, there weren't any." So a group of women started the Boston Women's Health Book Collective and put out another of those cheap New England Free Press newsprint pamphlets about how to live in their own bodies. "Or you could start with a group that tried to shelter women who were fleeing violence, fleeing a vengeful spouse, and start out by hiding women in your home and end up with Transition House," which is now the oldest shelter for women victims of domestic violence in the Boston area. "Or you could come together as a group that was interested in psychological care, mental health care, for women, which is what our group was," Herman says. So Herman began meeting with a group of women who had all been in consciousness-raising groups that had run their course, and these women took it upon themselves "to understand and critique the existing ideology as it applied to mental health," just as they had spent a couple of years understanding and critiquing the current political system as it affected their individual lives in their particular bodies. "There wasn't a split between understanding our bodies and understanding our minds; there wasn't a split between fighting for the things we needed to control our own bodies and what we needed to know to control our own minds."

It was still Movement politics. And as they critiqued and analyzed the training for all the professions that did psychotherapy—psychiatry, psychology, and social work—the group of women who were or wanted to be psychotherapists in Herman's clinical consciousness-raising group began dreaming up their ideal clinic together. They found many of the same writings that Jean Miller pulled together for *Psychoanalysis and Women*. They began to get a good idea of what not to do for mentally ill women—but what to do? They realized that psychotherapists could easily get drafted into the cultural police that enforced the status quo. They wanted to do something different. The rationale of the women's movement and the student left was that old institutions had failed and the only way forward was to abandon them and create alternatives. That rationale had gotten Herman through the rote grind of medical school, where gender put-downs had been part of the program. Now, in the new collective clinic in Somerville that came out of their consciousness-raising, Herman and her clinical comrade Emily Schatzow "shared families," Herman says: Schatzow treated the teenage girls and Herman saw the parents, to help them stop and recover from incest. In one family with daughters aged thirteen, twelve, and eleven, Schatzow started seeing the girls as a support group for each other, and Herman saw the battered mother. "We learned an awful lot from that family," Herman says.

At about the same time, in 1973 or 1974, Herman began doing peer supervision—that is, talking about cases as equals—with a doctoral student in counseling psychology at Boston University. Both Herman and the doctoral student, Lisa Hirschman, had gone to the Fieldston School in New York City, and both came from the same New York Jewish intellectual world, with its traditional vocations of science, scholarship, and justice. Hirschman had spent five years of her childhood in Colombia. While her father, the economist Albert O. Hirschman, was studying Third World development, Lisa at the age of seven started a school in her backyard, "because I discovered the beggar children in the mountains didn't know how to read," she recalled. Her parents shut down her backyard school but encouraged her sense that governments and authorities could make gross and cruel mistakes that even a child could see and fix. "I was very conscious in my whole life that there were things people didn't think about or address," Hirschman said. "I often got restrained" for trying to right wrongs, she remembered. And she, too, found in the women's movement and the student left an ethos of hope for justice with a do-it-yourself style that suited her.

"We were part of the women's community," Herman says. "It

seemed like a natural connection. We began just talking about some cases, and she had a lot of incest cases. So did I."

"We were sitting in her kitchen," Hirschman remembered more than twenty years later, at home in San Diego. "I said, 'I have quite a few cases of father-daughter incest or what seems to be, and when I talk to my supervisor, the first question from him is whether it's fantasy, and I don't think it is.' "

Herman and Hirschman were making their observations in a time of immense distrust. When they were in their teens and twenties, a motto of their generation had been "Don't trust anyone over thirty." Now, as they turned thirty or thereabouts, they knew themselves as part of a huge postwar generation with a common experience of being lied to—about race, about women, about men, about war. As some members of every subordinate group realized how completely their political experience—of pressure, harassment, control, rape—was whited out of the official picture of them in virtually all fields, they became the only experts they could trust. Herman and Hirschman couldn't help seeing that women were far more likely to feel helped by what they heard about women's psychology from peers in a consciousness-raising group than by what they heard from trained therapists—at least if the therapists were using their Freudian or pharmacological training, which was so dismissive of women. Some of this distrust of the Establishment led to granola on the floor, and some of it led to political, social, and medical reform. This was the era of empiricist activism—find it in your life, feel and think about it, talk it over, change it. The Cambridgeport Problem Center, where Hirschman was interning, was run by volunteers and a small professional staff of lawyers and therapists. The first rape speak-outs and rape crisis centers in the country started at this time. Women from Herman's clinical consciousness-raising group opened Boston's first rape crisis center in 1970, and a second grew from the Cambridge Women's Center, which opened in 1972. Women volunteers began to counsel victims on the phone and accompany them to exams, interrogations, treatments, and trials, because at the time many rape victims experienced police and hospital emergency rooms as stage two of the rape—shaming, blaming, callous retraumatization. When these mostly college-educated, white middle-class young women decided they deserved better, they fixed it themselves, like Lisa Hirschman in her Andean backyard, rather than wait for somebody else to do it. Restricting truth to personal experience, which Mary Belenky and her colleagues were later to write about in *Women's Ways of Knowing*, was part of the Zeitgeist that made it easy for Herman and Hirschman and other young therapists to believe their patients who reported incest, and to doubt the authorities who specifically told them not to believe such reports. But in another way, despite all their movement commitments and credentials, this very same kind of personal, almost solipsistic empiricism made it hard for Hirschman, at least, to take on the subject of incest. Incest hadn't happened to Hirschman or Herman, and the movement they were part of was so distrustful of received knowledge that "in order to write a book about anything, it had to have happened to you," Hirschman recalled. "That is where we were coming from."

But they did believe that the politics that created incest had happened to them, Herman says. "When we started listening to our patients who told us that they were being beaten or that they were being raped or that they had been molested or talked about the shame they felt, we knew what that shame was. We felt it ourselves—not in such extreme ways, but we felt the same shame that whatever we did was wrong, whatever our bodies were was wrong, whatever we felt was wrong, that the people we loved and cared about often exploited us sexually, took advantage of us, shamed us for our desire for relationships. We knew that. It wasn't hard to transpose ourselves into the dynamics of rape or the dynamics of incest, because we lived that—in a lesser form with our brothers in the Movement, with our fathers, with our teachers."

So they saw the blackout. They discovered that almost since Freud had retracted his notion that women hysterics were suffering from memories of incest, and replaced it with his notion that a myth of mother-son incest was the primary driving force in men's development, "no one had written anything on it," Hirschman remembered. It was as though psychology and psychiatry had a negative hallucination about incest. And now Herman and Hirschman saw the not seeing and decided to keep their own eyes open. And as soon as they did, what they saw made them feel worried about their own sanity.

"We went through this period of wondering whether we were

crazy," Herman says. "How come we were seeing all this and nobody else seemed to be? Was there something about us in particular that attracted so many incest survivors? Or is this really an epidemic?" And yet, despite the current Freudian line, "when we started to ask therapists, a lot of them had cases and believed them," Lisa recalled.

Their first research was really to answer that question, Are we crazy to notice incest when no one else seems to? "We began asking therapists, and everybody had cases," Hirschman said. When they asked their friends, their clinical consciousness-raising buddies, "four out of the first ten therapists we questioned reported that at least one of her clients had an incest history."[6]

That answered their question about whether they were somehow tilting the population so that they got more incest cases than other therapists they knew. Seven of their own patients reported incest. It was easy to turn up a score of others, just by asking around. By then, Herman says, "we felt like, 'Well, yeah, this really is an epidemic, but nobody seems to be talking about it. Somebody ought to say something about it.' And eventually it came to be, 'Since nobody else is saying anything about this, I guess it had better be us.' "

She began digging in the library. "I went to Widener and there were six references," Herman says. "A couple of them had to be gotten from the Library of Congress because [the Harvard libraries] didn't have them."

Six references, two of which were famous: Freud, and Alfred C. Kinsey's *Sexual Behavior in the Human Female*. In addition, "there were maybe a dozen articles in the psychiatric literature. That was it." The *Comprehensive Textbook of Psychiatry* dismissed incest with its estimate of one case per million. "So that was the baseline" when they started their research, Herman says. "Five years later it was completely different."

The 1970s, the decade in which the women's movement made real political gains in the United States, was also the time when women who had managed to become sociologists, psychologists, and psychiatrists did major research on violence against women, especially rape. The most influential of these was probably the sociologist Diana E. H. Russell, who was later the first to track the incidence of incest in a random sample of women.[7] The statistics about rape that Russell and other feminist researchers amassed "were chilling," the feminist historian Flora Davis writes, though they mirrored the percentages that women in consciousness-raising groups all across the country had been finding. "An American woman stood one chance in three of being sexually abused before the age of eighteen—usually by a relative or friend of the family. When she reached college age, the chances were one in five that she'd be raped on a date. Nine female employees out of ten had been sexually harassed on the job. Every year, about 7 percent of American women were kicked, punched or choked by the man they lived with," Davis writes.[8] These first confirmations of the endemic sweep of violence against women convinced a few foundations and other grant makers to sponsor more research. When Herman and Hirschman needed small grants to do their first study of incest, a private entrepreneur who wrote mystery stories helped them find support, even though they had no academic affiliations, Herman says. Later they got five thousand dollars from a new rape center that had been created at the National Institute of Mental Health.

By 1975, they were writing.

Herman and Hirschman wanted to describe what incest actually turned out to be for people who suffered it, but they also had to investigate why their disciplines of psychiatry and psychology dealt with incest as myth or fantasy, or as a mother-son problem, or as a problem of seductiveness in children—in other words, as many things it basically was not. Herman's grounding in anthropology got them started. They looked at incest as a cultural constant "generally considered by anthropologists to be the foundation of all kinship structures." They cited the anthropologists Claude Lévi-Strauss and Margaret Mead. Then they skipped right over psychiatry, the field that essentially said there was no incest worth bothering about, and found the social workers: they cited the Children's Division of the American Humane Association, which provided them with an estimate that at least 80,000 to 100,000 children were sexually abused every year and that about a fourth of these were abused by kin. These estimates, they wrote, were based on social workers' experience with "poor and disorganized families who lack the resources to preserve secrecy." They summoned evidence to support the idea that most incest took place in families that were intact enough to keep incest invisible to child protection agencies. Kinsey and his staff had interviewed eight thousand mostly middle-class women. One in sixteen of those women said they had sex with a relative during childhood, and most of them said they had kept it a secret, they noted. Today, after a couple of decades of child-abuse hotlines and sexual-abuse scandals, most sociologists would find these estimates far too low. But in 1975, compared with that one-in-a-million psychiatric baseline, these figures seemed high and shocking—and yet they had been around for decades.

So the first thing Herman and Hirschman demonstrated was that this universal taboo was actually violated a lot. But the taboo meant violators tried to keep it a secret and usually succeeded. Then Herman and Hirschman showed that as far as anybody could determine, almost all of these secret violations were by men. The myth of incest that Freud had judged to be the key to Western family structure and all human development was emphatically not its common form: the mother-son incest of the Oedipal story was in fact rare. In the few studies Herman and Hirschman could find of proven cases—one in Chicago, another in Germany—mother-son incest constituted between 1 and 4 percent of reported cases. In most of the cases where boys were the victims, adult males were the perpetrators. "Incest appears to follow the general pattern of the sexual abuse of children, in which 92 percent of the victims are female and 97 percent of the offenders are male," they wrote.

Incest was common. Most perpetrators were men. Most victims were girls. Why? Why did fathers commit incest between twenty-five and ninety-nine times more often than mothers? And most important—especially in a field dominated by a theory that put the incest taboo at the heart of psychological development—*why had nobody noticed this huge discrepancy before?* Once again gender was marking an enormous cultural rift. "We believe," they wrote, "that a feminist perspective must be invoked in order to answer these questions."[9]

Patriarchal culture gives fathers ample power to commit incest even if it technically denies them the right. Here is the late classical historian

John Boswell's dry but chilling summation of the right of the paterfamilias, the original patriarch established in Greek and Roman law:

> At Athens and in the Roman Republic, legal heterosexual matrimony was essentially the transfer of power over a woman, who had been under the control of her father (or brother, or uncle, or some adult male), to that of her new husband (or his father, if the husband was not head of his own household), who then stood in this role as her controller/protector. Romans called this marriage cum manu [the Latin phrase means "with hand" or "by the hand," and Boswell's note asks us to compare the European idea of "asking for her hand" in marriage]: the basic idea was that all persons in a household were subject to the adult male, the paterfamilias; this included his wife, children, servants, clients and slaves. The word familia, from famulus, "servant," described this unit, and was significantly different from its modern English derivative, "family," which generally applies only to kin and does not denote ownership or control. (Note, for example, that any member of the familia would be considered available to the paterfamilias for sexual purposes, whereas in the modern family it is only the wife.)[10]

In pure patriarchy, where rules about incest are rules about how men regulate ownership of their women, father-daughter incest insults and robs not the daughter but the son-in-law or his father. However, as long as the daughter is unmarried, it's a hypothetical theft, a problem of futures, since there is no husband or father-in-law.

"Family" comes from "servant" in the ancient history of our language. Herman and Hirschman saw their work was important for culture and civilization, not just for psychiatry and psychotherapy, because it measured the distance between contemporary family values and the early tyranny of the pagan patriarch. They could begin to assess how often and how easily a twentieth-century father could act like a Roman paterfamilias. They could ask whether fathers still had the power to commit atrocities at home. And if they had that kind of power, when did they use it?

Herman and Hirschman couldn't have made this kind of assessment if they hadn't had another idea of family that they liked better than the Roman one, a democratic concept that grew out of the Enlightenment tradition that had meant so much to Herman since her school days. Then the reactivated women's movement of the 1960s and '70s made the reorganization of family a hot topic. Juliet Mitchell, a brilliant young British feminist, had published a manifesto for this movement in the *New Left Review* at the end of 1966. She called it "Women: The Longest Revolution," and Herman bought a copy for fifteen cents as a newsprint pamphlet published by the New England Free Press.

"Women are essential and irreplaceable; they cannot therefore be exploited in the same way as other social groups can," Mitchell wrote.

> They are fundamental to the human condition, yet in their economic, social and political roles, they are marginal. It is precisely this combination—fundamental and marginal at one and the same time—that has been fatal to them. Within the world of men their position is comparable to that of an oppressed minority; but they also exist outside the world of men . . . women are offered a universe of their own: the family. Like woman herself, the family appears as a natural object, but is actually a cultural creation. There is nothing inevitable about the form or role of the family any more than there is about the character or role of women. It is the function of ideology to present these given social types as aspects of Nature itself. But they can be exalted paradoxically, as ideals. The "true" woman and "true" family are images of peace and plenty: in actuality they may both be sites of violence and despair.[11]

The currency of ideas like Mitchell's, about revolutionizing families, made it easy to imagine alternatives to a patriarchal family that had already seen patriarchal power diluted by the rise of bourgeois capitalism and by movements for men's, women's, and children's rights. By the 1960s and '70s, many people, including Herman for a time, experimented with communal living, creating nonhierarchical "families" of choice. These were groupings of equals held together by the quality of their relationships. And Herman and Hirschman were to discover from their very first study that nothing discourages father-daughter incest like an active, strong, protective mother who treats her husband as her equal, not her master.

Psychiatry had blown it, they suggested. The profession had not been very scientific when it came to incest. Psychiatric investigators had failed to make much of incest because something less than science had been going on when they had looked at it, and the something less was dominance, marked by gender.

Freud had been the first and most famous psychological investigator to deny that incest happened. Herman and Hirschman quoted the letter of 1897 in which Freud explained to his odd professional confidant Wilhelm Fliess why he had stopped believing his female patients when they reported incest: "There was the astonishing thing that in every case blame was laid on perverse acts by the father, and the realization of the unexpected frequency of hysteria, in every case of which the same thing applied, though it was hardly credible that perverted acts against children were so general."[12] "Hardly credible" is hardly credible as a standard of scientific proof, and, as we will see, a great deal of attention was later very usefully paid to the state of Freud's own culture and psychology while he allowed himself this lapse. It is also worth noting that a recent judge as distinguished as Freud's biographer Peter Gay has no difficulty calling Freud's reasoning in this letter "good and sufficient" and doesn't find any lapse in it at all.[13] Herman and Hirschman, taking on Freud's backpedaling in 1975, kept it simple. Freud had theorized that sexual abuse caused hysteria because virtually all of his hysterical women patients told him they were seduced by their fathers when they were *girls*; but when he retreated from this theory, he wrote about "perverted acts against *children*." Herman and Hirschman argued that Freud was misled by a gender difference that was the same in 1897 as it would be in 2007. "To experience a sexual approach by a parent probably *was* unlikely for a boy: Freud concluded incorrectly that the same was true for girls," they wrote.[14] Starting in 1897, Freud allowed his wakening half knowledge of the psychological impact of power on gender to lapse back into ignorance. But in the 1970s, supported by an American women's movement that was making very large political gains, Miller, Herman and Hirschman, and Gilligan and her colleagues stayed with this reemerging insight until they got it.

And once they got it, it was easy to see bias in the way the psychiatrists who followed Freud continued to focus on the powerless child instead of the powerful adult. Even in cases where incest was known to have occurred and could not be dismissed as a child's fantasy, psychiatrists and psychoanalysts often saw the child who was a victim of incest as an equal or even primary instigator, even when they knew threats of physical violence had terrified the child into submission. These adult clinicians did not see "Eve made me do it" as an evasion of responsibility cloaked in a lie about power. "Thus," one pair of psychiatrists wrote in 1937, in a paper about incest, "it was not remarkable that frequently we considered the possibility that the child might have been the actual seducer, rather than the one innocently seduced."[15]

Most of the six books about incest Herman and Hirschman found had been written in the 1950s and shared the heavily editorialized science of Alfred C. Kinsey that "further cemented the oppression of women because they were so pro-offender, pro-pornography, and pro-rape," Herman says. Kinsey presented himself as an "objective," Harvard-trained scientist who moved almost without a blink from entomology to human sexuality. It was no surprise to discover in 1997, from a new biography, that he was a bisexual masochist who liked to masturbate with a toothbrush stuck up his penis while pulling on a rope tied around his scrotum, a procedure he demonstrated to his staff and had them film. All through his career as a sex researcher, *the* sex researcher of the 1950s, Kinsey pressured interviewees and members of his staff to have sex with him, each other, and their wives in endless variations, and hired a professional to film them in his basement, all sworn to secrecy. "Their view of sexual liberation was unrestricted access for penises," Herman commented in 1993. "It wasn't necessary to know these grotesque details about his personal behavior to realize that his ideology was sexist to the core," she added in 1999. "The later revelations merely confirmed the obvious." Forty years after Kinsey did his work, Herman could see through the research disguise of his campaign for penis liberation because she read with an active women's movement behind her. "They didn't even ask about male victims of incest," she says. "Their editorial comment was, 'Why should a boy mind? There really probably isn't any harm. The damage, if there is any, is caused by making a fuss.' They were very offender-oriented." Kinsey's actual words: "It is difficult to understand why a child, except for its cultural conditioning, should be disturbed at having its genitalia touched, or disturbed at seeing the genitalia of other persons, or disturbed at even more specific sex contacts."[16] Eighty percent of the women in Kinsey's study who said they had been sexually abused as children (though he didn't call it abuse) also said they were hurt or frightened by it, but Kinsey wouldn't call that harm. Instead, he called it cultural conditioning, and he limited what he would call harm to "a very few cases of vaginal bleeding" that "did not appear to do any appreciable damage."[17] No one outside his staff knew just how cruel his standards for appreciable genital damage were.

So for Kinsey, as for other post-Freudian investigators Herman and Hirschman dug up, the supposedly empirical criterion for determining the harm incest might do was completely circular: these researchers concluded that incest was not harmful because they believed from the outset that it was not harmful. Sixty years before Kinsey, when Freud stopped believing his young bourgeois women patients who said they had been damaged by incest, it was not because he didn't think incest would harm them. Freud simply couldn't believe that incest was commonly committed by men of his own class. The reasoning that Freud employed to discount incest was different from Kinsey's, but it was just as circular and just as dependent on prejudice: he didn't believe incest happened because he didn't believe it happened. Freud's later mission to make the world frank and unashamed about sexuality changed the world. His somewhat wishful theory about infantile sexuality, which replaced his theory about the harmful effects of paternal sexuality, conveniently shifted the blame for incest from fathers to children.

Other researchers had other ways of looking at incest without seeing it. A study of incest among working-class Irish treated it as a sort of side effect of isolating overcrowding that did no harm. Others found harm but, like Kinsey, said the incest itself didn't cause it. One article Herman and Hirschman found was confidently called "Children Not Severely Damaged by Incest with a Parent"; but when they read it, they discovered the authors made their judgments without naming any criteria for deciding if incest was harmful or not.[18]

Even decades later, it is astounding to read these references, a historical culture shock. A few researchers found plenty of harm in incest.

But their articles were published in the same professional journals as the ones who said incest was fine or who blamed the child victims. No one mentioned power.

Herman and Hirschman knew they, too, might be tugged away from the attention to facts that they were striving for by the same "defensive reactions such as denial, distancing or blaming" that they found in the researchers who had looked at incest before them.[19] Citing Freud, Juliet Mitchell on Freud, and the New York feminist psychologist Phyllis Chesler, they called incest a political agreement among dominant men about how to regulate their possession of women. In the Freudian version of boys' development, they paraphrased, "the boy learns that he may not consummate his sexual desires for his mother because his mother belongs to his father, and his father has the power to inflict the most terrible of punishments on him: to deprive him of his maleness. In compensation, however, the boy learns that when he is a man he will one day possess women of his own." The boy also learns something Freud doesn't talk about: this code comes with an escape clause. He may not have sex with his mother, because she belongs to his father and his father would punish him if he tried. But when he grows up and marries and has daughters, his wife and his daughters will all belong to him. He is supposed to keep his daughter for the man he will give her to in marriage. But who will punish him if he takes her for himself? Incest is forbidden, and the prohibition is enforced by fathers. Herman and Hirschman saw a big loophole in this cultural arrangement: *"There is no punishing father to avenge father-daughter incest."*[20]

The girl in Freud's theory, on the other hand, learns that she will never possess anyone. "Her best hope is to *be* possessed by someone like her father" when she grows up, or maybe, given the wrong father, while she is still a child. But even if she avoids actual incest, as most girls do, her culture encourages her, as Chesler wrote, "to commit incest as a way of life"—to marry a bigger, older, more powerful, wealthier father figure who will protect and support her.[21] This asymmetry helps to explain why fathers might find it relatively easy to break such a strong taboo. But why did mothers—who "neither make nor enforce the incest taboo"—break it so rarely? Having found a political answer for fathers and daughters, Herman and Hirschman found a relational answer for mothers and sons: for millennia, women had very commonly been victims of sexual crimes. So women could see all too clearly both "the harmful effects of introducing sex into a relationship where there is a vast inequality of power" and, from the role men assign them as the primary caretakers of children, "the needs of children, the difference between affectionate and erotic contact, and the appropriate limits of parental love."[22]

Without any announcement or analysis, for a moment Herman and Hirschman switched into a relational mode, but only for women. The men they described acted from power; the women acted from love. And of course this is the row Gilligan and Miller were hoeing in separate gardens across the river in Brookline, none of them knowing more about each other's work than the fact that it was being done, yet all of them inspired and encouraged by knowing they were part of a movement of women psychologists who cared about women and saw power. Though women's relations with men are often clouded by coercion and fear of coercion, the fact that women only rarely commit incest with children "has much more to do with the relational theory as propounded by Jean and Carol," Herman said in 1999. "If you actually know what it is like to nurture a younger person, to have the practice of relating to a developing child, if you have empathy for that child, you understand that imposing adult desires on a child who is unready to respond to them is exploitive and damaging, and you don't do it. That's one thing. Two is you don't get your jollies from imposing sex on someone smaller and weaker than you. You don't think that's sexy. You don't think that's exciting. It doesn't make you feel manly and strong. So you're not suffering from what Catharine MacKinnon calls the eroticization of dominance and subordination. You don't get off on having your way with a smaller, younger, weaker person. I don't think the fear of retaliation plays a part at all." On the other hand, for fathers incest can only be a temptation "if you are in fact relationally challenged and what gives you a hard-on is weakness and submissiveness in another person—you know, if assertiveness makes you droop and submissiveness and obedience and weakness make you excited," Herman says.

The women in their study were "ordinary." They were all white, like most women in psychotherapy. They were from all classes, aged fifteen to fifty-five, evenly divided between single and married. Seven of them talked about incest as soon as they entered therapy. The others only spoke about it "after having established a relationship with the therapist," as long as three years after they started treatment. Their stories were as strikingly similar as the women were otherwise both ordinary and not particularly similar. Most were oldest daughters. Most were between the ages of six and nine when the incest started, and it went on for a long time, three years or more, rarely ending in intercourse and never involving physical force, though sometimes ending as a trade for physical force: "He gave me this rationale about preparing me to be with boys. He kept saying I was safe as long as I didn't let them take my pants down. Meantime he was doing the same thing. I split. I knew what he was trying to do, and that it was wrong. That was the end of the overt sexual stuff. Not long after that he found an excuse to beat me."[23]

All but two of these women kept their experiences of incest secret. So they had secrecy in common, but the rest of their lives cut across class and professional lines in a way that previous studies hadn't. In almost all of these cases the victimized daughter was estranged from her mother, and the mother was frequently absent, alcoholic, or ill. Many of the fathers already abused these mothers, and the daughters were afraid that if they told their mothers about the incest, their mothers would tolerate the news the same way they tolerated their own abuse. "The message that these mothers transmitted over and over to their daughters was: your father first, you second. It is dangerous to fight back, for if I lose him I lose everything. For my own survival I must leave you to your own devices. I cannot defend you, and if necessary I will sacrifice you to your father," Herman and Hirschman wrote.[24]

This message is a concise formulation of the deal that white mothers had been making for themselves and preparing their daughters to make for generations: I put your father first, you second, and in exchange for that he gives me—and you—safety and status that I can't get for you or for me any other way. So I can never put you first, or even call it a tie, but I can teach you how to get a man who will protect and keep you, too, if you put him first.

In the families of the women Herman and Hirschman studied, the fathers didn't make good on their side of the deal: they didn't protect their wives or their children; they abused them. But the mothers couldn't walk away, because there was nowhere to walk, no other way to get the respectability, assets, and income that men could give them. In one of the two cases in the study where a daughter told her mother what her father was doing, the mother immediately supported the daughter and filed charges. But when the mother realized that the result of a court proceeding would be that her husband would be found guilty and go to jail (and that she and her children would lose their income), she reversed her testimony and called her daughter a liar and a slut.

Daughters whose mothers offered this deal to them in the 1960s and '70s often saw economic barriers falling and realized they could say no deal. They had a chance to make marriages on completely different political terms from their parents. But for the women in this early incest study, at least until the time they sought therapy, the deal was still on. Even though their fathers had molested them, these women had followed their mothers' examples, giving up their relationships with their mothers and putting their fathers where their mothers and the whole culture put them: first. These victims of father-daughter incest were angry at their mothers, not their fathers. And though most "expressed feelings of fear, disgust, and intense shame about the sexual contact and stated that they endured it because they felt they had no other choice," half of them also said there was some pleasure in it for them.[25] "The whole issue is very complicated," one woman said. "I was very attracted to my father, and that just compounded the guilt."[26]

Where *was* the harm in incest? Kinsey had said it was in the needless fuss adults made about sex with kids. Other, later researchers said it was in the victims' failure to marry—to make the deal—or in their above-average representation in the pool of prostitutes, dealing sex. With her book *Against Our Will: Men, Women, and Rape*, Susan Brownmiller jumped on the second bandwagon of feminism early with her theory that rape—and all other dealings between men and women—was about dominance; incest was "father rape."[27] The harm of rape was the harm of being overpowered, disempowered, kept down; like rape, incest was political terrorism against the have-nots by the political haves.

The women Herman and Hirschman interviewed, women who had

experienced incest, didn't confirm any of these theories. They felt chronically and definitively put down, but that wasn't the only pain. "The father's sexual approach is clearly an abuse of power and authority, and the daughter almost always understands it as such. But, unlike rape, it occurs in the context of a caring relationship," the young clinicians wrote. "What is involved here is not simply an assault, it is a betrayal."

Of what? What does incest betray? What bond, what promise, does it break?

In the Roman family, the father had the right to have sex with his daughter because she was dependent on him. She would betray him and their bond if she refused. In the American family, incest could be seen as a betrayal of the *daughter* for the same reason. In the twentieth-century United States, it was assumed that the one with more power, the father, was constrained by some kind of democratizing noblesse oblige. He owed his daughter consistent care. "The daughter who has been molested is dependent on her father for protection and care. Her mother is not an ally. She has no recourse. She does not dare express, or even feel, the depths of her anger at being used. She must comply with her father's demands or risk losing the parental love that she needs," Herman and Hirschman wrote. The consolation prize for daughters who became incest victims was that they could borrow power through their illicit relationship, knowing that "as keepers of the incest secret, they had an extraordinary power which could be used to destroy the family."[28] They tended to replace their ill or absent mothers not only as sexual partners but also as caretakers of younger children. Herman and Hirschman found no current cultural assumption that fathers should step in when disabled mothers could no longer play the role of primary parent. Instead, they found a rule straight out of ancient Rome: the father's role in these families was to be served; when the mother was unable to serve him, then the daughter he selected, generally the oldest, took her place, in every way.

And the problem, the harm? "I'm dead inside," one woman explained. "I have a problem getting close to people," another said, putting it mildly. "I can't communicate with anyone," said another. Their therapists agreed.

They called themselves "witch," "bitch," and "whore." They had not made these names up. "My father called me a 'big whore' and my mother believed him," one woman said.[29] Desperate shame and no trust drove them to extreme isolation. They were afraid they couldn't feel anything. But they could feel fear. They were afraid they couldn't love. The ones who had children were afraid they would lose them, or afraid they wouldn't be able to protect them from incest. Several of them had used self-induced numbness and immobility as a way of turning off their fathers or at least blocking out the experience. "Passive resistance and dissociation of feeling seemed to be among the few defenses available," Herman and Hirschman wrote.

The women longed for heroes and saviors who would rescue them sexually and every other way, and perhaps rekindle that special sense of power they got from being "Daddy's girl." But many of them "became intensely involved with men who were cruel, abusive, or neglectful, and tolerated extremes of mistreatment."[30]

When incest was discovered while it was going on, "the most common social intervention is the destruction of the family," Herman and Hirschman found.[31] If the only alternatives to incest were sending their fathers to jail or being sent away themselves, most victims, like their mothers, chose to keep their mouths shut.

And when incest victims finally made their way into psychotherapy after suffering years of the despair, distrust, and self-hatred that followed incest, male therapists often had a hard time working with them, Herman and Hirschman dared to suggest; male therapists often identified with and excused incestuous fathers and blamed the daughters. "It was obvious that she was not all that innocent" was the way one man they quoted saw his patient. "Not suprisingly, the client in this case became furious with her therapist, and therapy was unsuccessful," they wrote.[32]

The women therapists they interviewed admitted that it was too easy for them to identify with the victim. They often avoided exploring the incest their patients talked about, not because they didn't believe them but because incest sounded all too plausible and the topic felt personally overwhelming to the therapists. Some strongly feminist women therapists tried to push their patients into feeling angry at their fathers rather than their mothers. At bottom, whichever gender the therapist might have, all psychotherapy was problematic for incest victims: therapy was secret; so was incest. Confiding sexual secrets to someone who promised to keep them secret was too much like being Daddy's girl. Finding ways to transform an incestuous family by making it safe and honest was far more healing than diagnosing and treating women who were still dependent on incestuous fathers and still forced to lie about it outside of therapy. Herman and Hirschman found one program that took the father out of the family and required him to tell his daughter he had been wrong. But the people who ran this program would only work with fathers who pled guilty to a felony and entered the program under court order.

Incest was finally about power. That old Roman patriarch, who owned his *famuli*, his servants, still breathed and reigned in the incestuous home. He only let up when someone with more power made him stop or when the risks of getting caught and punished were too great. Families that came closest to fitting the ancient patriarchal model were the ones most at risk. The best way to prevent incest was to "strengthen and support the mother's role within the family." Where women and children had rights at home, incest couldn't get started. As psychotherapy, Herman and Hirschman recommended political involvement with the first of what would become a national movement of incest survivor groups. Public speak-outs about rape and incest (first held in New York in 1971), free child-care centers, safe houses for abused women, strict enforcement of existing laws against child abuse, isolation and reeducation of father-offenders, and education for all fathers about how to raise children without treating them as sex objects—these were the treatments of choice for incest. The two clinicians concluded, "Father-daughter incest will disappear only when male supremacy is ended."[33]

Essentially, they prescribed family democracy as a cure for incest. They could never have done such a thing in a professional psychiatric journal, and they never even considered submitting their article to one, even though their study was a psychiatric breakthrough. They sent it to *Signs*, a new journal in the new field of women's studies, another child of the women's movement. "We were really taking the path that seemed open to us," Herman says.

Even before their paper appeared, in 1977, the word got out, and Herman and Hirschman were *not* what they feared—not derided as crackpots like Freud and his colleague Josef Breuer when they published their clinical work on incest in the 1890s. The two women had done something Freud and Breuer hadn't conceived of. They had called a perennial bluff when they listed the dominant political beliefs that were part of the fabric of psychiatry and its treatment of incest victims. And they addressed their work to women.

"We wrote this stuff up in '75–'76, and the thing circulated in manuscript for a year before it was published, because there was a long lead time. And that's when we realized that this was part of the surfacing of unconscious knowledge," Herman says, "because we started getting letters from all over the country.

"Way before the article was published, the letters started pouring in. People xeroxed this thing and just handed it. It went hand to hand. It was the women's underground. That's when we knew that this was real, and this was an epidemic or was endemic, and the prevalence was staggering. It was an amazing moment, because it really was very affirming to have gone through that period of questioning and wondering, saying, 'Can I believe my own perceptions?' And then, because we had each other and we had the women's movement, saying, 'Yes, we can. The fact that no one's talking about this doesn't mean that I should shut up and doubt my own perceptions. It means I'm the one to speak out.' And then as soon as one person did, more people were ready. It kind of snowballed. It really was kind of a privileged moment. When something surfaces into public consciousness, it releases tremendous energy. By 1977, we knew it was a big deal." To many women, Herman and Hirschman were suddenly heroes. And to many men and women, they were suddenly experts.

4.

Free Space

On a misty April Saturday in Waterville, Maine, the Colby College campus, groomed and somberly gray-green, is jangled awake by golden busloads of Girl Scouts from all over the southern part of the state.

Lyn Mikel Brown, a developmental psychologist and associate professor of education at Colby, has worked for months with Maine scout leaders and with her own students to put this program together. We are in the mid-1990s. Banners emblazoned with "Girls are Great!" hang from the red brick building where it's held. And as the girls file in, Brown promises them a day of inspiration and encouragement and a chance to meet scouts from other troops. She has already promised her undergraduate students, who are studying girls' development, scores of willing subjects for the "exhibitions of mastery" they have to put on to show what they have learned about girls' development in her course.

The big day begins with a mob scene in which women leaders corral girls behind tables to hand out name tags. First the girls clown around with them: "Can I put it on my head?" "I'll put mine on my stomach." But then they notice that the name tags have colored dots in the corners. Seeing this slows them down; the rippling, inquisitive energy of these eleven-to-thirteen-year-old girls sweeps them briefly backward, away from the tables and the leaders with the name tags.

"What do the colored dots mean?" one girl asks. The girls know instantly that the dots mean *something*. They smell it. They also know they have only a few seconds to temporize while they try to figure out how to use these dots and make a choice about them, instead of becoming passive dottees and getting dotted at random, which they see is the adults' goal for them. The girl's question gets no answer. But it tells the leaders that the girls are figuring out that something is going on and need to be instructed, as schoolchildren are so often instructed, to ignore what they are learning.

"Don't worry about the color," a leader tells them. But by this time most of the girls have realized, or heard in terse murmurs from other girls, that they're going to be split up for the day according to the dots on their name tags. So girls are picking or trading for the blue or red dots that will keep them with their friends, and friends are high-fiving each other and shouting "All right!" The undergraduates who tell them that the girls with the blue dots are to step this way, and the girls with the red dots are to follow over here, find plenty of not-at-all-random groups of friends in their somewhat "randomized" groups.

I have permission to look in on all of the demonstrations that Lyn's students are to run this morning, so I have no dot. But of course I am not invisible. The girls see me just as they saw the dots, and I introduce myself, in the blue-dot room first, as a writer. On a few faces I see signs of conflict: Should they think it strange or good that I am interested in writing a book about them and about work like this? They agree to let me stay.

The blue-dot room is a large, carpeted classroom with all the chairs taken out. There are four undergraduate leaders, two women and two men, and the women hand out green pinnies, little half aprons for their upper torsos, to half of the girls. Separation on separation—first dots, now pinnies. But of course there is nothing at all strange about that; these middle-school girls are very used to being told to group and regroup all day long in different configurations that they have far less power to shape than they have here. After half of the girls have put on pinnies, one of the young men explains that "the green pinnies are the boys in the class" and the girls without pinnies are to stay girls. It's time for gym, he says, starting with ten jumping jacks.

"Come on, boys, get your arms up!" "You guys getting tired? You're not tired," the young men urge the girls in pinnies.

Then it's the shuttle run, a race across the room and back, done in two trials. "Boys, it should take you around seven seconds. Girls, it may take you a little longer." The young men yell "Great job!" or "Great time!" as the girls in pinnies finish. Then a girl without a pinny asks a question. Her "teacher" answers, "What's the matter with you—you've never done the shuttle run?" The girls without pinnies get no response when they run. The times of the girls in pinnies improve by about a second from the first to the second trial. The times of the girls without pinnies stay the same or get slower.

Then the undergraduates teach the girls without pinnies to do push-ups from the knees, the easy way, and they teach the girls in pinnies to push from the toes, the hard way. A "coach" explains the difference: "Boys are stronger, so they can do that."

The two young Colby men do all the active teaching. The two young women carry clipboards, keep records, and stay quiet, except that once in a while they cheer for the girls in pinnies. When the girls in pinnies struggle with push-ups, the coaches praise them and push them to try harder and do a few more. When a pinniless girl says she can't do any more, the coach says, "Okay. You can stop." Neither of the young men looks at the girls without pinnies while they do their push-ups. All of the girls in pinnies do more push-ups than the girls without pinnies, even though the girls in pinnies do them the hard way.

For the broad jump, the teachers affectionately chaff the girls in pinnies, "You boys sweating a little bit? That's what you're supposed to do in gym class." They have a colder question for the girls without pinnies: "You girls getting tired?"

At the end of this exercise, the teachers grade the class. The girls in pinnies have consistently outperformed the girls without pinnies. The teachers give the girls in pinnies As. They give the girls without pinnies Bs.

Then the young man who's been doing most of the talking asks all the girls to sit on the rug in one big group again. He asks about the class he's just taught. "Did you notice anything that was a little unusual?"

Long silence.

Long, long silence.

Long political silence.

These girls want to play; they want to stay connected; they have seen everything that has gone on; but they don't want to get hurt. They are thinking, in this silence, about what they are being asked for. I know this, because I was once a girl myself, and at this moment I am flooded with remembrance of what it is like to be treated this way and then pointedly asked not to notice it. So I know this word "unusual" presents a problem. Actually, what these girls have just gone through, a textbook example of the effects of differential encouragement and expectation on achievement, is not at all unusual in their experience. But this was so gross, so obvious. There weren't even any boys around, so these young men and women made some up, and then taught the usual way. Could it be that they actually want them to talk about it? But why would they want to talk about it? No other adult ever has. And if they don't want to talk about it, to say what you noticed about those kinds of differences in the wrong place could bring on intense humiliation, shaming, angry denial. Too much of a risk.

Compromise. Put your little toe in. Show you notice difference, but not *that* difference.

"You gave out apples after the race and oranges after the broad jump," one girl says. Another girl turns to each of the two young men in turn. "*You* taught the broad jump taking off from both feet, and *you* taught it taking off from one foot," she tells them.

This is the girls' coded comment on the word "unusual." No, nothing unusual, but if you really want to talk about difference, we are extremely observant.

More silence. Vibrant silence, silence we have all felt before and recognize as silence that is right on the edge of speech about something that is known but not spoken. We recognize this moment as a door that can swing toward risk, common discovery, and trust that isn't there one minute and the next feels as though you could cut it with a knife. Or the door can stay so shut that the people here would never even remember that there was once this chance to open that door. What we don't know is who decides. Who or what decides this moment in a classroom full of Girl Scouts in Waterville, Maine, this moment in a roomful of renegade philosophers in seventeenth-century England, this moment in a seminar room at the Harvard Graduate School of Education, in an interview room at the Laurel School near Cleveland, Ohio, or in a conference room at McLean Hospital in Belmont, Massachusetts? The space is not free. You sense no possibility of speaking what you know. What is in your mind, what fills your consciousness, should not even affect your voice. No one has actually made a threat about what would happen if you let your knowledge show. But you have seen no proof that these leaders do not intend the same unfair and negligent things as the powerful people who have threatened and hurt you in the past for speaking up, so you feel it's the same space, same culture, same danger in speaking.

Gilligan uses a lot of words and metaphors from music because they are not very judgmental, unlike so much of the language of psychology. "Higher" and "lower" in music are about pitch, for instance, and not about good and bad. So she calls environments that set thinking and feeling free "resonant"; she calls supportive comments and gestures "resonant" and says they are a necessary part of the process of opening up when someone begins to talk about something that has been in the realm of the known but unsaid. Borrowing from her research colleague and voice teacher, Normi Noel, she compares this process to the way the sounding board of a cello amplifies and gives resonance to a bowed string. Noel and Gilligan call this kind of support "cello-ing."[1]

For instance, now someone breaks the silence. One of the Colby women, who has not spoken before, asks a question: Did the girls notice any *differences* in the way they were treated?

This time the silence lasts half a breath. "You were pushing more for the boys," a pinniless girl says. "Yeah," says another. And we hear a cello concerto:

"The boys are expected to do more than the girls."

"A lot more."

"Girls have to do 'girls' ' push-ups."

"They think the girls are wimpy."

"Like the boys in our class—they think they're so much better in sports."

Yes, the girls saw everything the teachers did to help the "boys" and slight the girls, but they also need to talk about another difference that didn't get addressed in this class: in real gym classes, boys are not just encouraged to play better; they are also encouraged and pressured to be rougher, to hurt people, and to ignore the pain they cause and the pain they feel, even serious pain. Many of these girls say they are happy not to be asked to make sports a world of aggression and pain. "We're playing lacrosse now, and the boys are pretty rough, so sometimes the girls play separately from the boys. They're pretty rough with their sticks, so it's all right," one girl says.

The girls see that this separation isn't fair to boys, because boys are pushed to be more aggressive and take more risks, while girls get to choose whether they want to play hardball, quite literally: "Girls can play baseball, but boys can't play softball," as one scout says.

"Girls without the pinnies—did you feel anything about being treated differently?" one young man who played gym teacher asks them.

Silence again. Several bars of silence. Who *is* this guy? How could he not know that treating you badly would make you feel bad? Play it safe: talk about results, not feelings. "You gave the boys higher grades," a girl says. The annoyance in her tone says everything she needs to say about how she feels, but she lets the feeling ride the words and doesn't describe it.

And again, the girls bring up a difference that this experimental class didn't address. "A lot of the boys in our class get bad grades because they mouth off and say bad things to girls," a girl says. In a real gym class, some of the boys would have been rougher, and some of them would have been putting girls down much more rudely than the teachers—even at the cost of the good grades those boys might otherwise expect.

Now that the girls feel free to speak, and even to teach these four undergraduates, the undergraduates bring out some independent evidence. Exhibit A is a collage of pictures of men cut out from *Sports Illustrated*. Exhibit B is a collage of pictures of women cut out from *Sports Illustrated*.

First they look at the photos of men. "Most of the guys are really strong. They're all doing something physical. Some of them have their mouths open like they're saying, 'Oh, we can do it! We're the best!' " a girl comments.

The collage of women is a third or a fourth the size of the collage of men. One of the Colby women explains, "We got these out of the same magazines. We didn't just pick out certain pictures. We cut out everything. We couldn't fit all the men."

"The girls are barely doing anything," one of the girls observes.

"Makes us look like we're babies," another says, identifying and not liking it.

"I play all the boys' sports," one girl declares, wanting to add something that counters the pictures in front of them.

"Why are they 'the boys' sports'?" an undergraduate asks.

" 'Cause they make it seem like only boys can do it," another girl answers.

"They're funner."

"They're harder."

"The boys get hard footballs, and we get these little soft things," another girl says.

"Some of these girls are so afraid of the ball it's pitiful."

"Why do you think that is?" the other man asks.

"Because they never had a chance."

"They're not really boys' sports. They're everybody's sports. But they say the boys can do them better."

"They mostly show boys' sports on TV."

Another girl comes back to the collage of women athletes: "They're smiling or crying, so it makes it seem like we're soft."

"Boys—they have these macho pictures, and girls have these pictures like they're not really that good," another girl sums up.

They're right. All of the women athletes are pictured sitting down, resting, or dressed in evening clothes. One of the Colby women backs the girls' observations: "There was an article about women tennis players, and there are no pictures of women playing tennis," she says, letting her own anger ride her words, "cello-ing" for the girls.

"The girls are wearing all these skimpy clothes," a scout says. "They're pretty. And the boys are wearing sweaty, icky clothes. Girls look like that, too, but they don't have any pictures of that."

"The boys have sweat pouring off them. They look like someone just poured a bucket of water over them," another girl agrees.

"They have the boys always fighting and the girls never fighting. I fight," another girl says, refusing to let go of the subject of aggression and the way boys are pushed to fight and girls are assumed to be nonviolent.

After about ten minutes, these girls' consciousnesses are audibly rising. They have integrated into their own experience everything these undergraduates wanted to show them. And they have integrated it in a way that teaches the undergraduates subtleties and subplots of the gendered culture of physical education. The undergraduates drew the boys as favored and better taught. The girls agree with this picture but add their opinion that girls are protected in ways that boys aren't, and they say that aggression, fighting, and hurting are a gendered part of sports, too.

So much for truth. Now justice: "How would you design a gym class?" one of the women asks.

"I would tell the boys they can't be rough and they have to play with the girls." This girl's immediate answer is about aggression and integration, not about encouragement and attention. She says sometimes boys are allowed and even encouraged to rough up girls as a way of getting girls to give up on sports.

But sometimes what girls are taught to think of as rough play is just all-out, very active play. When she was six, my daughter concisely described the pedagogy of physical education in the United States: "They teach the boys, and they let the girls play." And some of these Girl Scouts know that changing the content of what gym teachers are supposed to say won't change the situation if the teachers don't change their attitudes about girls and boys. Simply instructing boys not to be rough can be just another put-down for girls, they say: "Our gym teacher always teaches the boys to be 'easy.' It makes it sound like the boys are so strong, and the girls are so weak they could just break all your bones."

These are middle-school Girl Scouts talking. They are at the ages of early adolescence when most girls are having the growth spurts puberty brings and most boys are not yet. At this age, most of these girls are bigger, taller, and stronger than the boys in their gym classes. Yet during these years, gym teachers regularly turn up the pressure on boys to play rough and to hurt and to hide their own hurt, at best to test themselves and learn endurance, and gym teachers start giving girls "special" treatment and allow or encourage them to make excuses for sitting out or not playing hard—as though the boys were stronger and the girls were more delicate at a time when precisely the opposite is true. To these girls, this timing is evidence that the different ways middle-school boys and girls are treated in gym class are lessons about political power and not about physical power or "natural" aggression. "We might not look so weak anymore if we had our fair share. And the boys might not look so macho," one Girl Scout says.

"The boys have more teams than the girls do. We only get, like, two coaches, and they get three or four."

"When we were undefeated, the boys were like, 'Oh, my gosh, I don't believe you could win.' "

"My brother was saying, 'It's because you have easier teams.' "

"We played against the boys, and we beat them. Because we were undefeated, we were allowed to play them."

But they looked shabby. And always getting boys' castoffs hurts. "When we get the old uniforms, it makes me feel discouraged, and I don't want to do it anymore," another girl says. "I just don't feel equal."

"The pants are old, grass-stained."

"They think that the guys should look better."

At one Maine middle-school tournament, "the girls played first and no one was there for them, and then the guys played and everybody came," another girl says. Their anger about magazines that treat women athletes as though they were Barbie dolls wilts into the discouragement of realizing that they themselves are treated like sports pariahs.

"If you girls got together and spoke about it, do you think the coaches would do anything?" one of the Colby women asks.

"Probably not" is the immediate reply.

"They just kind of say, 'Don't worry about it. It'll be better someday.' It's like, when's someday going to be? We can't wait till the year 3000."

The psychology demonstration ends with a pep talk. The undergraduate leaders do not leave these girls despondent by pretending to be neutral or objective about unfairness. They say they want the girls to learn and go on learning about gender stereotypes in sports, and they encourage them to speak out about the unfairness they see. "You don't want to wait till the year 3000," one of the women says, "cello-ing."

But the last word belongs to a girl, a realist who knows the forces she's up against: She says she spoke to a coach about how worn the girls' team uniforms were, and he told her they didn't have money for new ones. So "last year," she says, "we did fund-raising for new uniforms. And we're not getting new uniforms. We're getting old uniforms." The coaches decided to use the money for other projects.

Sometimes speaking up, organizing, and raising money don't change anything. On the other hand, getting on a bus and traveling to some college where you're not sure what they're going to do can give you and your friends an experience of freedom that you've never had before, one you'll be able to remember together for a long time. Maybe now when these girls learn in civics class about free assembly and free speech, they'll have a better idea of what the founding fathers were so excited about (an idea that middle school itself may not do much to promote): the experience of a free space in which to think and speak with people who are your equals and treat you that way.

In half a lifetime of interviewing, I have never talked to anyone who didn't know something I didn't know. Everyone sees and hears in a different place from everyone else. There is no objective standpoint that we all somehow occupy, contravening all the laws of physics.

"We're always somewhere," Gilligan tells a graduate proseminar, introducing her methods. "What we see is related to where we're standing." And what we say is related to how we are being heard—sympathetically or antagonistically, supportively or critically. "The more I feel resonance," from listeners who communicate their agreement or their understanding, their attunement, "I will start to speak differently," Carol says.

"Descartes tried to take the I out of the body and thought out of feeling—you know, 'I think, therefore I am,' " Carol says, quoting the seventeenth-century French philosopher's most famous dictum. Why wasn't it "I feel, therefore I am," or "I dance, therefore I am"? Because Descartes was building a conceptual wall between thought and feeling so convincing that scientists have been walking around the nonexistent thing for centuries, Gilligan says. She wants to cut through it. "I am trying to put the I back into the body, back in relationships, back in the culture, back in the natural world," she says, "and that leads to an immense difference in theory and in method of working in psychology."

Because we all stand in different places, Gilligan says, everyone sees and hears something more clearly than anyone else. Sometimes it is just a little thing, but DNA is a little thing. So in a way, the biggest, most important question is not any single what or why about superconductivity, hyperspace, light, DNA, HIV, peace, racism, or fresh water. The biggest question is how to keep creating spaces, climates, and relationships that invite all kinds of people to tell all the truth they know, instead of forcing them to narrow their vision or even to shut their eyes and just imagine what they are supposed to see from an impossible, imaginary, universal, or ideal standpoint, which somehow always turns out to support or match the opinions of a small group that has the most political power. Everyone who has ever had an idea in a group of supportive listeners knows the breakthrough quality of the inspirational freedom she's talking about, whether we call it bull session, rap, gossip, consciousness-raising, or brainstorming. It happens on every deck, stoop, and street corner and in every classroom, kitchen, car, conference room, and office on the best days. But it is hard to stop looking at the world of ideas as the product of a few great minds and Nobel Prize winners who somehow do it on their own. I remember my first American history teachers exclaiming about what an amazing coincidence it was that all of the founding fathers were alive at the same time. When I obediently memorized Ben Franklin's famous line "We must all hang together, or assuredly we shall all hang separately," it never dawned on me that the words meant those guys hung *out* together. In classrooms where talking to other students was a worse offense than anything but walking out, how could I conclude that what made the founding fathers effective was talking to each other, corresponding and convening? Yet later, after I had the opportunity to do some consciousness-raising, I could no longer ignore the fact that the founders did not treat all men, far less all humans, democratically. The founders may have talked to Indians, slaves, and free women, but for the most part Indians, slaves, and free women were not at home, not heard as equals, in the assemblies where the founding fathers framed their ideas about how a republic should make democracy work.

Now I think the whole history of ideas can be told as a history of more or less free spaces. I began on this line of thinking when I listened to the women I'm writing about in this book and started asking myself, how did they do it? How did each of these women find and enter a space where she could think these things: incest is common; women and men may be acculturated so differently that they actually construct different senses of self; women have strengths; there is a kind of relationship that is necessary for development; separation is not a developmental necessity but a coercive tactic; people go crazy because other people, often people they love, abuse and lie to them; people go sane because other people, who respect and trust them, become their friends and allies and listen to the truth they have to tell. Many of these ideas already seem psychological commonplaces, and yet a little more than two decades ago they were totally unscientific. Artists might say these things, but not psychologists or psychiatrists. And even now, intriguing discoveries in psychobiology and neurochemistry are being seized on as reductive solutions to all psychological problems, as though the fact that nerve synapses have various electrochemical routes allows psychiatry and psychology to treat thought, feeling, relationship (and of course politics: gender, race, and class) as synaptic situations that can be made optimal through drug therapy, without ever mentioning them—although, as we will see later, many neurochemical discoveries support a relational way of seeing.

Relational psychology does not ride easily in the mainstream of psychology, since conventional psychology for so long treated most people as the objects that kept the synapses of white middle-class men firing. Relational psychology has women and children in it, as subjects. It acknowledges power imbalances and treats them as political rather than natural. It underlines the huge role that force and the threat of force played in twentieth-century psychology and culture, and it details another way of living, a culture and tradition of equality, mutuality, and freedom that has come into existence and focus as sporadically, imperfectly, and blurrily as any other child of the Enlightenment.

But relational psychology has one very good answer to my question—how did they do it?—and that answer is, of course, together. It wasn't so amazing that these women were in the same town, part of the same political movement, and linked by profession and friendship when they began to build a body of knowledge about the impact of relationships on people's lives. It was the sheer necessity that is the pattern for every intellectual or cultural breakthrough. These women did not invent their free way of working. The whole intellectual hit parade of dead white men and their great ideas is a succession of free spaces, usually created arduously and on the fly in times of great political ferment, that inspired great truth telling. We just don't usually hear about the relational part. Many of the great men of science did see that they were in a relational process, but the history we hear about them often leaves the relationships, the "cello-ing," out.

In 1670 or so, the political philosopher and psychologist who invented and first defined the phrase "personal identity" told a story at the beginning of his *Essay Concerning Human Understanding* about how he came to write it:

> Were it fit to trouble thee with the history of this Essay, I should tell thee, that five or six friends, meeting at my chamber, and discoursing on a subject very remote from this, found themselves quickly at a stand by the difficulties that rose on every side. After we had awhile puzzled ourselves, without coming any nearer a resolution of those doubts which perplexed us, it came into my thoughts that we took a wrong course; and that, before we set ourselves upon inquiries of that nature, it was necessary to examine our own abilities, and see what objects our understandings were or were not fitted to deal with. This I proposed to the company, who all readily assented; and thereupon it was agreed, that this should be our first inquiry.[2]

John Locke was describing consciousness-raising. If we updated his language a little, Locke's prologue could be the four core theorists of the Jean Baker Miller Training Institute writing about the origin of their book *Women's Growth in Connection*.

What has changed for these women is that they no longer have to be in the business of making excuses for the system of dominance. In the past, great ideas have been the answers to scientists' heartfelt questions, *and* they have done a handy political job of work that the system, the culture that upholds dominance, needed done. In the free spaces that past scientists have created, thinkers have not been free to see dominance. John Locke, for instance, sat down with his friends to examine what human beings could do and be—*and* Locke was one of the original shareholders in the Royal African Company, which held a monopoly on the British slave trade until 1690.

Charles Darwin, perhaps the ultimate great man of science, is perhaps the ultimate example of this kind of trade-off. Darwin was practically preordained to "have" the idea of evolution by natural selection. His father's father, Erasmus, wrote *Zoonomia*, a long poem about evolution as a kind of learning, at a time when people had noticed fossils but didn't understand much about how evolution might take place. The potter Josiah Wedgwood, Charles's maternal grandfather, had been a prominent abolitionist in the years before Britain ended chattel slavery in its empire, and Darwin took on an antislavery attitude as a family trait. But unlike the other right-thinking members of his family, Darwin had a friend and teacher who had been a slave. This man, John Edmonston, was born a slave in the West Indies and traveled with the British naturalist Charles Waterton throughout South America. Later, after he was freed, Edmonston settled in Edinburgh and lived at 37 Lothian Street, about a block from the apartment at 11 Lothian Street where Darwin lived while he studied medicine for two years in his late teens.[3]

Darwin liked Edmonston immensely, admired his intelligence and skill, paid him to teach him taxidermy, and played hooky with him instead of attending the university medical lectures that he found deadly dull. Edmonston was clearly, for a short time, a mentor for Darwin. When I read about this relationship, which Darwin describes briefly in his autobiography, it struck me as so extraordinary—such a remarkable exception to the intellectual segregation that white racism still often maintains at the highest levels of scientific work; I found myself wondering if any other celebrated white scientist had had a paid black teacher of any subject that he used in his scientific work. When Darwin later spent five years sailing around the world on the British navy survey ship the *Beagle*, making the voluminously detailed observations he later used as evidence for his idea of natural selection, collecting and stuffing specimens, he wasn't following in either grandfather's footsteps. He was following his mentor the Afro-Caribbean freedman John Edmonston.

Stephen Jay Gould was an evolutionary biologist who found the place where Darwin wrote "Never say higher or lower" in the margin of a book. In a letter written toward the end of his life, Darwin made his position even clearer: "After long reflection, I cannot avoid the conviction that no innate tendency to progressive development exists." So Darwin knew full well, as Gould says, that "the real success stories of mammalian evolution" are not human beings but "rats, bats and antelopes" who outnumber people and can live in more places. And among living things, mammals are by no means the fittest, since more than half of all vertebrates are fish, and vertebrates are certainly less fit than the ultimate survivors, who will bury us all, beetles, bacteria, and viruses.[4] "I believe Darwin's views contain an unresolved inconsistency," Gould writes. "Darwin, the intellectual radical, knew what his own theory entailed and implied; but Darwin, the social conservative, could not undermine the defining principle of a culture (at a key moment of history) to which he felt such loyalty, and in which he dwelt with such comfort."[5]

Darwin did both of his jobs—in biology and in ideology—in a very relational way: after he thought of natural selection and really had the whole scheme of evolution worked out, he spent about twenty years talking it through with the most important and respected scientists in England before he published one word about it. These men—Charles Lyell, Joseph Hooker, and Thomas Huxley, among others—became his best friends and the godfathers of his children. And eventually these scientists became his converts. When he finally described his theory in a joint paper and then in *The Origin of Species*, it was because these men begged him to publish—since a younger man, Alfred Russel Wallace, had by then come up with the idea of natural selection on his own, and Darwin's friends wanted Darwin to get the credit.

More than forty years ago, the historian of science Thomas Kuhn, in his book *The Structure of Scientific Revolutions*, tried to describe how scientists create, discard, and then create again big theories like Newtonian mechanics or quantum physics that become the basis of how we are taught to see and know the world. Kuhn called these comprehensive theories paradigms, and he was the first to acknowledge that paradigms are not built up or broken down according to some impossibly superhuman criterion of objectivity—a point of view no one can ever have but that is nonetheless supposed to be based on sense data that only a person can ever have. "As in political revolution so in paradigm choice," Kuhn wrote, "there is no standard higher than the assent of the relevant community." Kuhn concluded that theories in science change because young scientists see phenomena that the old theory leaves out, think of a theory that explains both what the old theory included and what they see that it left out, and start converting other scientists, usually also young, to their way of seeing. He recognized that these paradigm shifts, truly new ways of thinking and seeing, are never complete until the generation of scientists who grew up learning the old way is dead.[6]

Darwin, who saw all life as a web of kinship *and* did the handy job of making dominance a "natural law," put himself on the scientific map in a very relational way. He simply waited for those older scientists to die while he made friends with the finest scientists of his generation. Then privately, at home, in the lively give-and-take of the private conversation of public people, he spent twenty years convincing these contemporaries. He made his home a free space in which winning and losing could take second place to thinking and discovering because there was no authority or official audience, no one to bow to or grandstand for. Darwin's father, a popular doctor and astute investor, left him independently wealthy, and Darwin was acutely aware that his inheritance was a key to his freedom to do his work; in fact, he insisted that the class of independently wealthy people was essential for independent research and the advancement of knowledge—without realizing, of course, that independent wealth may make some things very hard to see. In Darwin's case it took money, class, expensive education, world travel, lifelong friendships, and profound apprenticeships, both to Edmonston and later to the Cambridge University naturalist who recommended him for the *Beagle*, to make a free space in which he could think his great thoughts.

But "never say higher or lower," one of his most revolutionary thoughts, gets marginalized—literally jotted in the margin of a book—or entrusted to a private letter. Even after decades of relational preparation for his theory of natural selection, he simply knew he did not live in a world that would support the notion that hierarchy is a political construct and not a biological feature.

Darwin is not just a convenient example. His political work on behalf of the British Empire, combined almost seamlessly with his description of a relational biology, still influences how we see men, women, competition, cooperation, emotion, thought, and maturity. Darwin's vision had a lot to do with the picture of life that the women who invented relational psychology were given to start with. It was a picture that mixed relational and dominant brushstrokes in a striking and yet typical way. Darwin identified so intimately with black experience that his wife's nickname for him, the name he wanted to be called in his most private and mutual life, was Nigger; he and his children called his wife Mammy.[7] He wrote, "The American aborigines, Negroes and Europeans are as different from each other in mind as any three races that can be named; yet I was incessantly struck, whilst living with the Fuegians on board the *Beagle*, with the many little traits of character, shewing how similar their minds were to ours; and so it was with a full-blooded Negro with whom I happened once to be intimate."[8] But his personal quest to make biology include John Edmonston's experience as human experience didn't stop him from naming his big book *On the Origin of Species by Means of Natural Selection; or, The Preservation of Favoured Races in the Struggle for Life*. Later, in *The Descent of Man*, the book he wrote ostensibly to place man firmly in the family tree of life, he gave genocide his scientific blessing and foresaw the happy ending of evolution with the victors of the last genocidal battle.[9]

Everything we write
will be used against us
or against those we love.
These are the terms,
take them or leave them.
Poetry never stood a chance
of standing outside history.
. . . .
We move   but our words stand
become responsible
for more than we intended . . . [Adrienne Rich][10]

It may be slightly easier today to see how power relations bias science, to hold on to what we see, and to say it. The psychologist Beverly

Daniel Tatum—in *Why Are All the Black Kids Sitting Together in the Cafeteria?*, a book that applies relational theory to racial identity development—cites the research of John Dovidio, Jeffrey Mann, and Samuel Gaertner in their essay "Resistance to Affirmative Action: The Implications of Aversive Racism." Tatum quotes their definition of aversive racism as " 'an attitudinal adaptation resulting from an assimilation of an egalitarian value system with prejudice and with racist beliefs.' In other words," writes Tatum, who has worked and taught at the Jean Baker Miller Training Institute, "most Americans have internalized the espoused cultural values of fairness and justice for all at the same time that they have been breathing the 'smog' of racial biases and stereotypes pervading the popular culture."[11] This combination of ideology and custom allows people who vow they believe in freedom and justice for all to cross the street when they see a black man approaching, for instance, or hire a white woman because they intend to pay her less than they feel they would have to pay a white man. Darwin's story shows us how dense this noxious mixture of principles and prejudice was 150 years ago in the birthing room of evolutionary theory.

Nearly a century after Darwin wrote about how essential his friendships were to the birth and development of his ideas, the California feminist Pamela Allen described a gathering of the sort of private think tank he created. The difference is that there was no great man in Allen's group, which had the sixties whimsy to call itself Sudsofloppen. "We" did it, Allen wrote. "We have defined our group as a place in which to think: to think about our lives, our society, and our potential for being creative individuals and for building a women's movement. We call this Free Space," Allen wrote in a pamphlet in 1970.[12] She and other "middle-class white women in our 20s and 30s,"[13] many of whom were friends and all of whom knew at least one other member, formed their group in San Francisco in 1968, that year of protests and assassinations, and set themselves "to understand not only the ways this society works to keep women oppressed but also ways to overcome that oppression psychologically and socially."[14] They found they couldn't succeed if they were cut off from other women's groups—"growth stagnates if isolated," Allen wrote.[15] So they joined a network of women's groups. "It seems so clear to us now that relationships do not grow in a vacuum but through experiencing the whole of life together, and that a human politics will not grow from people who fear honest human relationships but through ones who are willing to share their total selves."[16]

The women got together for three hours a week and tried to analyze their experience of being subordinate. Then they would make what Allen called "a synthesis of the analyses."[17] For instance, by generalizing from their own experience, they concluded that "physical and psychological brutality" was the basis of male supremacy.[18] They called this generalizing process "abstracting." And they felt that while they did it, "we come to understand what we could be if freed of social oppression. We see this abstracting experience as the purest form of Free Space."[19] They were clear that "the total group process is not therapy, because we try to find the social causes for our experiences and the possible programs for changing these."[20] They developed tremendous respect for the insights oppression had brought them—wisdom they didn't know they had till they came together and deliberately focused on it. And they deduced from this new self-respect that other, more oppressed people probably had more of this wisdom: they felt the women's movement ought to take directions from "poor women, and especially black and other nonwhite women for they are the most oppressed of our sisters."[21] They made a short but comprehensive enemies list—"capitalism, men, ourselves and the State"—and then said, "The fifth enemy, racism, is all pervasive, and internally, probably our most dangerous enemy for it has historically separated women from each other, allowing white women to seek privileges for themselves rather than making their cause with all women."[22]

By discussing the political evidence as well as their personal experience of subordination, they accomplished what Locke and Darwin hadn't: they observed their own dominance, and they heard how it had deafened them. "Our enemy is our arrogance," Allen wrote.[23] "This group has had a radicalizing effect on us. Now we understand in our gut something we used to give only lip service to: that there is no personal solution to being a woman in this society."[24]

What Pamela Allen and her "sisters" in the Movement were doing was regarded outside the Movement as politics or even more dismissively, she notes, as therapy. Whatever it was, it wasn't taken seriously, wasn't empirical philosophy or science. But all around them in the early 1970s, women were being admitted into the professions and the sciences in greater numbers than ever before. They were being handed knowledge that women before them had been denied, and yet the existence of a women's movement gave them the courage and the freedom not to shut their eyes, not to dissociate from their own experience as women but to bring it to the science they were taught.

Carol Gilligan and the Harvard Project on Women's Psychology and Girls' Development; Judith Lewis Herman, Emily Schatzow, and the Women's Mental Health Collective; Judith V. Jordan, Jean Baker Miller, Irene Pierce Stiver, and Janet L. Surrey at the Stone Center— all of these groups used the same method women had used for fomenting political change in the salons of prerevolutionary France and in the kitchens and parlors of the United States during the independence movement, the abolition movement, the temperance movement, the suffrage movement, and the women's club and civil rights movements. The engine of change was the small group, usually gathered at home, where women met to think about what they wanted and how to get it— and where they also could work in affectionate, equal relationships in which they could move and challenge each other to think and to act. When it swept the nation in the 1960s and '70s, it was headlined as new, new revolutionary politics, but this kind of revolutionary politics is an old tradition not just for Western women but for the whole Enlightenment movement. This is where women and men have given each other so much of the "unpaid for" kind of education that Virginia Woolf knew was so vital that she wanted to plan a new kind of university around it. "Surprisingly often, change began with half a dozen women, sitting around a kitchen table, defining a problem and figuring out what to do about it," Flora Davis finds in her history of the second wave of the women's movement that the first relational psychologists rode to maturity.[25]

When Mary Belenky and Carol Gilligan first laughed about the "kitchen-table research" they were doing for their groundbreaking abortion study thirty years ago, they were simply making the small group into a methodology for psychological research. Later, when they collaborated across state lines to write *Women's Ways of Knowing*, Mary and her co-authors graduated to what they called "the pajama-party model of research."[26] Still later, for her Listening Partners project, Belenky talked of "invisible colleges," and, finally, in *A Tradition That*

Has No Name, her study of women's ways of thinking and working together, she writes of "public homeplaces."[27] Three decades later, Belenky, too, is still thinking about this way of working, and still working
this way.

Of all these women, Herman is the one who explicitly links her
work with the European Enlightenment tradition in which John Locke
and the authors of the U.S. Constitution and later Darwin and Sigmund Freud have starring parts. This allegiance was and still is not always easy for a feminist: because women have often been excluded
from the movements and institutions that enlightened men began,
many women have been reluctant to place themselves in the cascading
history of rights and free thought. Herman says she took some flack
from the women in her clinical consciousness-raising group for sounding like a Eurocentric intellectual. She remembers Schatzow "doing a
sort of trip on me for being an intellectual. And I said, 'Damn straight
I'm an intellectual, and I'm proud of that. Do you really want our
movement to be ignorant?' And she sort of went, 'Oh.' And we've been
very good friends ever since, and of course she's no mean thinker herself." "Endless, endless talking" in their therapy consciousness-raising
group grew into the Women's Mental Health Collective, Herman says.
The young clinicians' dream clinic shared a storefront with the
Somerville Women's Health Collective. The health collective belonged
to an overarching "collective of collectives," Schatzow remembers. This
super-collective connected the Boston Women's Health Book Collective, the authors of *Our Bodies, Ourselves*, and three other, similar
groups. So the mental health clinic was really a collective in a collective
in a collective—nested in three boxes of group process that were all
dedicated to changing things for women, including themselves. And
they were far from being the only women's therapy collective in town.

"In five years, there were, like, fifteen women's therapy collectives"
around Boston, Schatzow remembers. Their Women's Mental Health
Collective was really "a shared fantasy," she says, that came out of
weekly meetings, mostly in people's homes, of about a dozen women
who were being trained in every kind of setting for psychotherapy.
When they compared notes, they concluded that there was no adequate training for psychotherapists even in the most prestigious graduate schools and medical schools, because they found that the theory,

the practice, and the training worked as political policies that aimed to keep the system of dominance in place, even when that political motive meant disregarding or condoning suffering. Afflictions born of the worst abuses of power were ignored or blamed on the victim or the victim's mother, whether the afflicted were rape or incest victims or Vietnam veterans.

The women decided the first way the collective would change things would be financial. The bottom line would actually be the bottom line for these women, and not every line, as it became in so many other health-care institutions. Money could come last—not because these women were independently wealthy, like Charles Darwin, but because they were not in debt. Low tuitions, scholarships, cheap rents, and low mortgage rates made easy possibilities for creating free space—for saying, as Emily and her group could say, "Maybe we don't have to do this other thing; maybe we can do our own thing." They finished their graduate training mostly without debt, which left them free to choose to cast their lots together, invent a new kind of clinic, charge no fees at first, and later, when they realized they had no talent for fund-raising, charge on a sliding scale, and pay every staff member the same fee, regardless of training. And the Commonwealth of Massachusetts licensed them as a clinic on this basis. So they had practically no money, but they also had practically no overhead. And they had freedom and official status. They could find out, as Emily says, "what it was like to be in a free space where we really created the structure and the rules."

For instance, coming out of a psychology that judged the source of psychological symptoms to be personal flaws or weaknesses that clinics were supposed to fix, they noticed "that when we were taught about how to do assessments, we were never supposed to ask what somebody's strengths were. So we included that, and we didn't have to run that by anybody," Schatzow says. Their innovative assessments began with the discovery of strengths on which recovery could be based instead of simply focusing on what was wrong.

In her formal training, Schatzow says, like every female psychotherapist I have ever asked about it, "I lied to my supervisor when I did my thing." But now, in the collective, they met in marathon peer supervision groups or with senior volunteer supervisors like Jean Baker Miller. "Suddenly we weren't lying," Schatzow says.

"From the very beginning, the conviction we had was that women's psychological problems or intrapsychic problems were also the result of the social, economic, and political context of their lives," she says. Politics and economics had to be dealt with in therapy, too. "It seems so obvious now," she says, "but at the time it was radical."

At the time, for instance, psychiatrists generally failed to notice that many patients had suffered physical or sexual abuse, or both, in childhood. No one had asked. In the Harvard doctoral program she eventually dropped out of, Schatzow had been expected to learn an orthodox theory that didn't work well in practice and then improvise by trial-and-error makeshift methods that did work but had no theoretical basis. But after Schatzow worked with Herman, and later at the Victims of Violence program, she and Herman made the consciousness-raising behind their own new clinic a solid theoretical basis for the treatment method they developed.

At first they went a little overboard with collectivity, Schatzow says. They were so committed to group process that they sent two therapists to work with each and every client they took in. She laughs as she remembers how bewildered, and perhaps slightly ganged up on, their first clients felt till the staff collectively realized it would be all right to send one therapist to individual therapy sessions and save their work in pairs for group and family sessions. In 1980, Herman and Schatzow started their first incest survivors' group. The idea of the healing power of small groups was sweeping the globe as the basis of a self-help movement in psychotherapy, which began to use the free space of the small group to heal sexual abuse. Survivors' groups were different from traditional group therapy, because the listening, witnessing, and solidarity of the members were considered the agents of healing. Seeing how similar the "plots" of the crimes against them were and how abuse of power was always part of sexual abuse, and at the same time learning to trust and root for each other, led to political awakening and personal change. As Schatzow says, "The idea of helping people together in groups wasn't an accident—because we had been able to do so much more as a group than we would have been able to do as individuals." Since the conventional sources of psychotherapy still officially denied that sexual abuse took place or that if it did it had much to do with mental illness, survivors' groups, whether led by professionals or organized as leader-less groups of women, spread almost as quickly as consciousness-raising groups had. Those first, inventive years set a high standard for collabo-ration on research, theorizing, and community and professional advo-cacy that the collective itself couldn't meet as time went on, Herman says. "Later on, when everyone had children, they kind of went into a pattern of maintaining what we had built rather than building further," she says. In 1994, Herman and Schatzow, by then involved in the Vic-tims of Violence program, finally left the collective. Both continue in private practice, and they share an office suite.

By 1978, Jean Baker Miller was a psychiatry professor at Boston University, and Judith V. Jordan and Janet L. Surrey were junior mem-bers of McLean Hospital's psychology department, which Irene Pierce Stiver directed. Stiver had made the almost-unheard-of switch from ex-perimental to clinical psychology—from Gestalt and learning theory to psychoanalysis—and Jan and Judy had come to McLean largely to work with her. Judy says two things convinced her to stay at McLean: the great oaks and maples of the McLean campus and "Irene's eye con-tact." Judy and Jan were disappointed when Irene told them she was too busy to think about joining another group. "That's when Jan told me I only had to come once," Irene says, smiling, nearly twenty years later.

Across the river—three towns away from the urban storefront where Judith Lewis Herman and Emily Schatzow learned to work with traumatized individuals and families—sitting under a nineteenth-century patchwork quilt in Jean's living room, looking out big windows past the shrubbery to a quiet, dark suburban street, Jordan, Miller, Stiver, and Surrey patched together a theory about how people, espe-cially women, grow up. They did their work by hanging together so tightly that after a decade or two, the four of them were thinking to-gether—not debating, not engaging in serial monologue or station identification.

It's hard to take notes when I'm with them all. Once, they were talking about the old model of therapy—the patient who was supposed to become autonomous and the therapist who was supposed to be neutral about everything, withholding any insights he or she might have about the patient. They were saying this method was disastrous for women. They talked paragraphs, in which each one took a sentence or part of a sentence—1, 2, 3, 4—without skipping a beat.

"Withholding men made women feel dependent. That's a power trip," Jan said.

Irene chimed in instantly with the keynote for this neutral father figure: "I know best."

Jean: "But I won't tell you."

Judy: "You've got to find it out for yourself."

For the first decade, there were five or six of them. Early on, Sarah Greaves, a social worker who had invited Jean to join, dropped out and moved. The psychologist Alexandra G. Kaplan joined after Jean became director of the Stone Center in 1981, and Jean started pushing the other members to write papers that the center later published in its series Work in Progress. Sandy Kaplan remained what the women called a core member until early Alzheimer's stopped her in the 1990s.

They say they started meeting because they felt that as conventional therapists, they were in the awkward phase that Emily Schatzow talked about. "We felt we'd done all this work personally but it hadn't broken into theory yet, and we were still using the old theory," Jan explains.

"Everything I learned never seemed right," Jean says simply. Jean's book, out two years before, had begun to move the women's movement into psychology. But by the time these four or five women decided to look together at their own abilities and experience, psychology had slipped a long way from measuring itself by empirical criteria: for these women and, they saw, for their patients, the standard psychological explanations of mind, feeling, love, hate, desire, and distrust were simply not true to their experience.

"Our roots are in the women's movement," Jan says. When they started meeting with Jean and Irene, Jan and Judy were already in a women's group and wanted to bring some of the empirical rigor of consciousness-raising into psychological theory building, just as Jean did. They trusted Irene because they worked for and with her, and they trusted Jean because they had been inspired by her book. In their consciousness-raising groups they had found words for their experience, their ambitions, and their desires: "connection," "relationship," "caring," "cooperation." These words also fit what they wanted for and with their patients and what their patients wanted, what made them better. But the theory they'd been taught called these experiences "dependency needs," "merging," "manipulation," "fusion." The psychology they knew was telling them to pretend their patients fit a mold they knew didn't fit at all. The women's movement was telling them to be empirical: What, exactly, did they see, hear, feel?[28]

Jan says she kept going to the meetings at Jean's because she wanted to be in a group that would help her keep asking what she calls "the questions of my life." These questions started, when she was about five, with the question of how her mother could be so brilliant and powerful and count for so little in the world's eyes, she says.

"I said when I was five years old that I was going to be a feminist, which meant I wasn't going to take money from my husband," Jan says. And she was going to alleviate suffering; she knew that at five, too. "When I was five I remember being driven out of the temple parking lot in Albany, right next to the Girls Academy, and saying, 'I want to be a psychologist, and I want to go to people's houses and make things better and then leave.' And I remember people saying, 'How do you know that?' "

When she got to Jackson College, then the college for women at Tufts University, she studied philosophy, particularly phenomenology. But she remembered her early sense of vocation and entered the doctoral program in counseling psychology at the Harvard Graduate School of Education in 1967. There she learned that psychology didn't necessarily mean making things better and then leaving. It could mean leaving a client long before things got better. "I started at Harvard and quit because I didn't feel I could be a psychologist," she says.

"I did this testing of a kid," she elaborates. She typed the first line of the test report and couldn't write the second line. "It still sits there in my imagination," she says, along with her memory of feeling that she was being asked to chloroform and pin up her relationship to a child like a specimen butterfly. She says she left Harvard with a master's degree, feeling, "I can't do it—there's something wrong with me."

Two years later, she entered the doctoral program in psychology at George Washington University, because, she says, the women's group she had joined in the meantime insisted that she reapply. They were sure she could be a psychologist and that psychology needed her. This time she looked for a program she thought would teach her to help before she had to leave, one that would help women especially. She wrote her dissertation on depression in women.

Then, two years after she started her internship at McLean Hospital, Surrey was making friends with Jordan and trying to figure out a way to get closer to Irene Stiver. It wasn't long before she was in Jean Baker Miller's living room on a Monday night, "sitting on the edge of the chair." She remembers a sense of "something being lifted that you'd covered, some incredible energy liberated—just a wonderful mixture of excitement, anger, humor, and creative energy." Trying to make a psychological theory that included some of the political insights of the women's movement was a way of "trying to stay alive myself," she says.

Jordan, too, remembers an "awareness of girls' and women's pain from the beginning" of what looked on the surface like a picture-book upbringing in the small town of Stroudsburg, Pennsylvania. "I remember from my childhood a sense of being excluded—being excluded from crafts classes, being excluded from the safety patrol," because she was female. Supported by her mother, a physician and an active feminist, "I chose to fight it," Jordan says. Jordan was six feet tall by the time she was thirteen, so one reason for fighting was that she didn't fit the image of the cute little adolescent girl; she was big enough to fight. Girls were supposed to be popular with boys, whom she towered over, and girls weren't supposed to be smart, but she was always thinking, Jordan says. Her sisters teased her for talking to herself, so she shut up, and her mother, a dermatologist who respected psychology enough to believe that most skin problems were psychological in origin, didn't pick up on her youngest daughter's silence. Jordan says the most painful event of her childhood was being sent away from home to boarding school, supposedly a middle-class privilege. Her parents sent her to Abbot Academy, a school for girls in Andover, Massachusetts, because she was an excellent student and they felt she deserved better than Stroudsburg High. Unfortunately, they omitted themselves and their home, as parents so often do, from their assessment of where Judy was being educated and why she was doing well. She did well at boarding school, too, academically, but she had such a violent case of homesickness that after six months she was still sobbing inconsolably every day, calling home and telling them she couldn't stand it. Her mother assured her that she could come home, and eventually both her parents insisted that she come home, but her new teachers gave her the sense that her homesickness was pathological and that if she failed to separate from home, she would never succeed at anything. "They decided I should see a therapist," Jordan says, so she stayed and started therapy, and that was her introduction to what became her own profession: therapy was what she got instead of home. It worked. Only years later, after she had begun to find a voice in which to praise the role of connection in adolescent and adult lives, did Jordan realize she had been talked into the idea that unless you could get along without the people you needed most, you couldn't be normal. Now she thinks of adolescent homesickness as "a testament of attachment and love," and she teaches that therapists' freedom to let their eyes fill with tears as they listen to their patients is one of the keys to movement and healing in psychotherapy. But at fourteen, "I had internalized so deeply the message that this was a sign of weakness. It also felt like a danger. I think I felt if I didn't separate, if I didn't do it the way the world said I should do it at that time, I would never be able to do it."

So she did it at Abbot Academy and then at Pembroke College, then the college for women at Brown University. After college, Judy got the same lecture Carol Gilligan had gotten from the head of the psychology department at Harvard, about how the place she had won in the doctoral program was wasted on a woman. Judy knew that her mother, too, had been told to "go home and forget her dream" when she got to medical school. Judy didn't accept the department chairman's invitation to leave, but the experience didn't allay her "feeling I don't fit and it's right that I don't fit." When she left her home, she lost her sense of belonging, lost even her sense of possessing her own talents and achievements. "I went underground in terms of any sense of competence and strength really until this group," she says. She looked competent and strong—her Harvard doctorate came with a commendation for outstanding performance, and her internship at McLean was followed by a job offer—but "it didn't feel like me," Jordan says.

Once again, as a young clinician the model she was supposed to follow—of the distant, neutral, impersonal therapist who offered mind-altering insights when he or she judged the moment to be right—made Jordan feel she didn't fit. The kind of therapy she did "felt deviant," she says. Like Jan with her unfinished test report, Judy couldn't bring herself to abandon her patients in order to please her supervisors. "When I would laugh with a patient, when I would tear up, when I would answer a personal question, usually with some thought, I would sometimes think, 'Oh, this is going to have a bad impact on my patient,'" Jordan says.

After her new friend Jan Surrey talked her into joining a consciousness-raising group, Jordan began to realize that *not* connecting, *not* being honest, *not* being responsive might be what had a bad impact. She began to connect her own refusal to disconnect emotionally from her patients, even at the cost of doing what her teachers taught was the wrong thing, with other kinds of feminist political resistance. After that, finding Miller, Stiver, and the others in the Monday night group was "a tremendous relief," she says.

"When I got together with this group of women, whom I respected enormously, seeing that they were living with the same kind of uncomfortableness in this position, and they were making the same kinds of changes in what they were doing, was incredibly validating," she says.

The meeting at Jean's house burst into truth like the Girl Scouts in Maine. The women planned all of their trips and vacations so they could be in Brookline every other Monday night. The Monday meeting became an intellectual and emotional home—the first Judy had known for decades—where they could tell the truth about the cases they would have had to lie to conventional supervisors about, and where they could think of ways to make their consulting and teaching closer to what they began to work out together about healing. They met outside of work, outside of the established professional conference scene. And for the first ten years, none of them missed one meeting.

Like the consciousness-raising group that became a clinic, the meeting at Jean's house took on a life of its own. "How did this group become revolutionary? I don't understand that," Jordan says, years after the group had propounded its own psychological school of relational-cultural theory and had started its own teaching arm, the Jean Baker Miller Training Institute at the Wellesley Centers for Women.

"I remember how I would struggle, before I got involved in this, and always have trouble, really isolating myself in a way," Stiver says. After majoring in math at Brooklyn College, Stiver got her doctorate in experimental psychology from Cornell, where she was surprised to find that the major influences on her were a couple of other graduate students rather than any faculty members. She moved to clinical psychology after she began to do testing and assessment on the side at McLean Hospital while she was teaching at Wellesley College in the 1950s.

What kept her at McLean was the innovative "milieu therapy" she learned under the chief psychiatrist, Alfred Stanton. Stanton, a Quaker, taught that when staff members had good, clear relationships with each other, patients got better. "His position was that whenever any two people did not agree and it went underground, the patient went crazy. And when they started talking about it, the patient stopped being crazy," Stiver says. But the theory that was supposed to guide what happened between patient and therapist at McLean, even under Stanton, was still the distant, neutral Freudian model. The less dogmatic training Stiver got as a therapist on the job at McLean still included self-condemnation for forming good relationships with patients. Stiver's instincts, too, rebelled. Whenever she found herself forming a caring, close, listening relationship with a patient, she would think, "I'm right to do it, and I feel I shouldn't do it," she says.

"We all know how hard it is, even now," Stiver says. "If I were alone, I don't think I would have done it, because it's *too* alone. It feels too uphill." Debriefing cases in the new Monday night group—including arguments with supervisors and colleagues about cases—"was very important for me, to sort of stand firm and talk up, and it gave me courage," Irene says. "I just know it was such a relief to me to have a place to talk."

In the beginning, she explains, "all we did was talk cases and ask, Do the current theories help us understand women?" What did the theories mean, and what did they themselves mean by ego, enmeshment, separation, relationship, growth, connection? They wanted their answers to be clear, direct, and yet complete. They wanted to include political realities about healthy development, suffering, and therapy that were never named in the prevailing theories. They spent the first five years or so talking about normal development, mostly for women:

What were women like when they turned out well-balanced and vital—and how, and in spite of what, did they get that way? Then they began to outline new techniques for treating women. And after Stephen Bergman (also known as the novelist and playwright Samuel Shem) began working with Jan and presenting with all of them, they talked about treatment for couples and men. Here, about fifteen years after they started, they were asking a basic question as a kind of parenthesis in a much longer discussion.

IRENE: "What's 'limit setting'?"
JUDY: "You can't do this."
JAN: "For the good of the patient."
JEAN: "Supposedly."

These snippets of conversation are a handful of still frames from a decades-long film. They suggest trust, excitement, quickness, and inventive camaraderie. "We've always done this on our own time. It's not our job, and everyone has had full-time work going on," Jean said once when the four women were all together talking to me about their collaboration. "We're always doing this on top of that." But this extracurricular work they do together "feels like my life," Jean admitted.

Jan remembers a dream she had sometime about 1985. In the dream she was talking to Steve on the phone, asking him to pick her up somewhere in New York City. But, she recalls, "the place I was at was not on the map." How could she give directions? "Here's this map of the city that's supposed to have everywhere on it, and it doesn't have where you are."

The city of Jan's dream was like the range of human psychological experience and ability, and the map was like psychological theory in 1985. The women knew they were in the city, but they couldn't tell any other psychologists how to find them. First they had to figure out where they were. What were women like, not as theoretical mirror images, contraries, or obverses of men, but in their own experience from their own point of view? They had to draw a map that showed where they were in reference to all the things that were on the old maps—egos, defenses, drives, selves, complexes. And they had to get copies of their map to other people who were both on and off the map and persuade them to use their new map instead of the old, incomplete map. Only the map that showed where everyone was could work as a tool to bring people together. Any other map would keep some people isolated and invisible.

It had taken the accident of studying only women to bring Carol Gilligan to realize what was wrong with drawing conclusions about all of humanity from studies of white men and boys. Her department hired her to teach the adolescent psychology course in 1971, "because I had excellent credentials," she says, "and nobody else wanted to do it." Ten years later, she was not surprised to open the big *Handbook of Adolescent Psychology*, the standard textbook for psychologists, and learn that the psychologist assigned to write about girls had not found enough research to fill one chapter. But at least in this case, the textbook writers themselves saw the absence of girls as a problem in theories about how human beings grow up. "Inattention to girls and to the processes of feminine development in adolescence . . . has produced a psychodynamic theory of adolescence that is both one-sided and distorted," the handbook declared in 1980. This imbalance meant that adolescent psychology was completely focused on issues that fit stereotypes of boys' behavior: "impulse control, rebelliousness, superego struggles, ideology and achievement." Meanwhile, adolescent psychology left such critical issues as "intimacy, nurturance and affiliation" off the official map of the adolescent psyche. Psychologists ignored these issues because they were stereotyped as girls' concerns and girls' concerns were assumed to be of no importance. The history of social science reveals no higher motive for the way girls were left out of research on adolescence until the 1980s.[29]

Gilligan decided to try to remedy this imbalance and study girls. But it was hard to find an agency to pay for studies of girls. Private girls' schools—first Emma Willard, in Troy, New York, starting in 1981, then the Laurel School near Cleveland five years later—were the first institutions Carol could find to back her belief that girls were important enough to study.

Lyn Mikel Brown is the Colby professor who teaches her students to create free spaces with Girl Scouts while the students design these exercises for academic credit. She learned how to teach while she worked with Carol Gilligan, earned her doctorate, and wrote her first book, *Meeting at the Crossroads*, about the Laurel School study, with Carol.

Gilligan, Brown, and other graduate students began their research on girls with the old methods that Gilligan and her early colleagues Nona Lyons and Sharry Langdale had used "to distinguish a voice of justice from a voice of care, a separate from a connected self," Gilligan says. But when she and her student researchers started listening to girls and boys, Gilligan realized these methods were too crude. Listening and coding or grading for a care voice or a justice voice, or a separate or connected self, they couldn't pick up all the other voices they began to hear in children, and they couldn't hear a just voice *and* a caring voice—it had to be either-or. "We could not go further with these binary coding systems," Carol says. "It's like Audre Lorde: 'The master's tools will never dismantle the master's house.' "[30] Standard psychological methods for coding responses about responsibility and rights and the whole methodology of quantifying moral values and beliefs were supposed to be an unbiased way of sorting out information that would guarantee "objective" results—results that could not be dominated or distorted by anyone's opinion. But these "objective" standards had built-in opinions. They required scientists to leave out women and people of color; they put things in an either-or mode, and then quantified things like care and justice: Are you a one or a three? Quantifications inevitably made the qualities they were trying to study more or less, better or worse, higher or lower.

"We decided that we would go to try to learn from girls about girls' development—that if we went with the categories of psychology, we would be slotting girls into categories that had been developed from listening to boys or, for women, from listening to men," Gilligan says. The current standards were based on beliefs about how one strand of thought could be floated out of a complex knot of thinking and feeling in a way that could tell scientists something useful. Gilligan began to feel she needed a more flexible, less reductive tool—"a method that was not bound by either-or categories"—in order not to lose the baby with the bathwater. She already knew how to listen. She could hear complexity with the ear of a novelist or a playwright—in fact, she would eventually start a theater company and write fiction—but she didn't know how to write about what she heard in a methodical way that she could teach others and call social science. Her students—especially Dianne Argyris at first—pressed her to make her own method of listening explicit, and Gilligan "began to meet with a group of students (women and men, more diverse in age, culture, race, class, and sexuality than the Ed School was) every Friday, to develop a method that could register complexity of voices and gender—a voice-centered, relational method that became a listening guide," she says. Because their subject matter was regarded as unscientific and unimportant, few of their colleagues noticed that their agenda was huge—much bigger than the little pieces scientists usually work on. By 1981, Carol and her students and co-workers had set out to trace women's psychological development, by studying girls, and to create a new way of studying all psychological development. The old methods tended to divide and oppose women to men and girls to boys; the women and men of the Harvard Project worked on new methods that would show the links between girls and women. "This led us into studying dissociation and using more clinical methods, and more relational ways of working, to understand what we were seeing and experiencing. We traveled together, a group of us, over a period of roughly ten years, going back from adulthood into adolescence and then from adolescence into girls' childhood," Gilligan says. "It was tremendously encouraging for us as women to be in relationships with girls, and we resisted at every single turn, not effectively always, the tendency to turn it back to 'How can we help girls?' And people kept saying, 'How can we help girls find their voices?' And I would say, 'Listen, girls have their voices. They may not always choose to speak. But they have their voices.' And it was the girls who were helping us, really, find our voices, and to find our voices in the sense of voices that really would come from the inner world into the outer world."

Their question was simple: How do girls grow up? The facts that they were women and somehow both knew and didn't know how girls grew up, and that they couldn't read any kind of an answer in a standard text, led them to the edge of what they began to feel was a chasm between women and girls, "a chasm that opened at adolescence when girls became young women," Gilligan says. The name they chose for themselves as they began the work at the Laurel School was a bridge across the chasm: the Harvard Project on the Psychology of Women and the Development of Girls.[31] "In one sense, one of the most innocent questions—how does it happen?—led to what most of us feel is our most radical work, because in connecting women with girls, it led us to see into a critical intersection of psyche and culture: girls were naming and resisting a culturally sanctioned initiation that was psychologically damaging, that involved losing voice and losing relationships, paradoxically for the sake of having relationships with others but also with school, and possibly for social and economic advancement. The girls work was like a window: there was this moment when the girls were saying, 'Ouch!' " Gilligan would say later, talking about the book she and Brown wrote about working at Laurel. "We were not a research group. We were not a group doing our inner work. We were a group of voyagers. We were on a journey together, and the journey was to connect women with girls, meaning each of us with our own history." It was a voyage without a map, or with a map like the one in Surrey's dream, a map that never had where they were on it. It led to what Carol calls "the incredible accomplishment of relational psychology— to get the map of development." They got it by realizing "that until you brought in the women, you couldn't get the map of development. The Harvard Project work was really putting that map together."

They met every Friday, when they weren't traveling, first to Troy, then to Cleveland and to other schools and organizations around Boston—a coed private school, then public middle and high schools, and Boys and Girls Clubs. Every Friday the researchers, most of whom were also teaching fellows in Carol's courses, would come together. "I remember that so vividly," Brown says, "sitting in Larsen, in a windowless room." Around the room in the red brick, almost completely windowless HGSE high-rise, Larsen Hall, sat the whole group that was working on the project's study at Laurel: Carol Gilligan, Lyn Brown, Annie Rogers, Steve Sherblom, Jill Taylor, Elizabeth Debold, Judith Dorney, Barbara Miller, Deborah Tolman, Janie Ward, and Mark Tappan.

Tolman, a Harvard graduate who had spent a couple of years working for Planned Parenthood on issues of adolescent sex, had arrived full of questions about sex, race, and class to work toward an Ed.D. Now a professor in the Center for Research on Gender and Sexuality at San

Francisco State University, Tolman says she "bulldozed" her way into the Harvard Project by immediately offering to look for sources of funding. She also carried the free space of the project into her research interviews with adolescent girls, whom she asked about sexual pleasure and desire. The girls Tolman studied told her no one, not even their girlfriends, had ever talked to them about the pleasures of sex. The Harvard Project group became a second family for Tolman. "I was the baby. It was the one time in my life I wasn't the oldest child," Tolman says. "Being part of that group was one of the most intellectually stimulating experiences I have ever had, and also emotionally very sustaining."

Jill Taylor, trained as a physical therapist in her native New Zealand, and, like Gilligan, a mother of three boys, took on a multicultural project with low-income teens—the "poor relation," she calls it—when she joined the group. The project followed forty-eight black, Latino, Portuguese, and white girls and boys who had been labeled "at risk" in local public elementary schools and reported on the twenty-six girls. Taylor and half a dozen other interviewers listened for differences in the way these students talked and felt about relationships and tried to link those with positive or negative outcomes, like dropping out or going to college, or early pregnancy and motherhood. Now an associate professor in the departments of education, human services, and women's studies at Simmons College, Taylor says her "at-risk" project was much harder to fund than the first projects on more privileged private-school girls.

Almost as soon as Gilligan started reporting about her research on girls, critics had taken her to task for only writing about white girls and women. In fact, she hadn't just written about whites. In a Different Voice just didn't say she hadn't, and the general assumption was that she must have. "But even when I said it clearly—with Lyn in Meeting at the Crossroads, and in the three co-edited books that preceded it—critics didn't listen, and the accusation continued," she says, "despite the fact that more than 30 percent of girls quoted in Meeting at the Crossroads were identified as of col   ʾss but attending private schools."

Critics who demanded research about girls of color and low-income girls had nothing to do with the funding process, and no agencies were demanding research on such girls or even grudgingly willing to pay for it. Taylor and her colleagues often worked on the multicultural project, called the Understanding Adolescence Study, without pay. But she stayed with it and pushed the Harvard Project to stay committed: low-income white, black, Latina, and Portuguese at-risk girls had a lot to teach the researchers, they learned. Taylor also pushed the group to realize that if they wanted to get at the girls' working knowledge of race and gender relations, "then we had to have other races as part of our interpretive community." Listening to these girls the same way they had learned to listen to private-school girls, the researchers also tried to form interpretive communities among themselves that would be free spaces for work and reflection about race as well as gender.[32]

Janie Victoria Ward, a social worker with a history of civil rights activism, was drafted into the group early and wrote "the black chapter in the white book," *Making Connections*, that the Harvard Project put together about their work at Emma Willard. Ward, who directed the project's work in Boston Boys and Girls Clubs and co-edited the project's book *Mapping the Moral Domain*, entered the group of otherwise all-white women at the almost all-white Ed School at a time when "race meant other race, somebody else's race," not yet the white race, Ward says. Like Beverly Daniel Tatum and later Yvonne Jenkins, Robin Cook-Nobles, Maureen Walker, and the Stone Center group, Ward worked with the Harvard Project researchers putting racial identity theory together with the gender-based relational work they were already doing. Ward, who with Taylor is now an associate professor of education and human services at Simmons College, grew up in Cambridge as one of the few black students at "a mostly white upscale private day school," she says. At Laurel, she could ask questions about racial identity that black students were waiting to hear (but that confused and stymied white students), and she could listen to the minority of black and "other" students who were living lives much like the one she had led as a student.

In the first year of the Laurel study, the Harvard Project researchers used two interviews. They had noticed in their work at Emma Willard School that the girls they interviewed using questions they designed ended up in leadership positions. Now, at Laurel, they wanted to test whether their interviews by themselves were effective interventions in helping girls develop. So half the girls got a Kohlberg ego-and-ethics test, and half got an imaginative, open-ended interview Gilligan and her students designed, where girls were asked to speak about their own experiences of moral conflict and choice. The interviewers asked half the girls how they knew what they knew, how they learned, how they thought about themselves and their relationships. The researchers asked this experimental group, "Were you ever in a situation where you had to make a decision and you weren't sure what was the right thing to do?" and "How would you describe yourself to yourself?" This division into a control group and an experimental group was "based on the assumption that girls didn't talk to each other," Gilligan says. But "the girls, of course, talked to each other," Brown says. Within days, the girls knew all about the two interviews—"the good one and the one with the little stories," Gilligan says. "And they had the good one pegged, and they coached each other in the bathroom. You set up a hierarchy, and you create an underground."

When the control girls found out how much more fun the experimental girls were having in their interviews, "they really felt offended," Brown recalls. The researchers came on saying they really wanted to know what the girls thought and felt, but then gave half of them structured ego-development tests and asked impersonal, hypothetical questions about moral dilemmas. "And we started to see the connection between what we were doing and what the school was doing with the honor code, because on the surface the girls were saying, 'Gee, I had my interview today. It was really wonderful, and this is really going well,'" Brown says, imitating the voice of the girls who pledged allegiance to what the Harvard Project would call "the tyranny of nice and kind."[33] "And in the underground, we're hearing that they're pissed," Lyn says. "In hindsight, I would say that that was one of the wonderful mistakes," she says with the scientist's love for the oversight that leads to insight. "It was because they responded so seriously to the standard measures and the interviews that we saw the distinction between being in relationship and using the girls for data."

They began to realize that the so-called objective tests and methods they were using to look at and measure relationships made relationships impossible, made them disappear, or go "underground," as they saw it. "When research gets good," Carol explained to a graduate proseminar in 1994, telling this kind of story about her work with girls, "is when you reach an impasse. You don't know everything. You come to a place of not knowing. You come to a place where you're going to have to work."

The Laurel experiment started to boil over in 1987, its second year. The girls the Harvard researchers had interviewed in 1986 "had responded to the hierarchical structure of research by forming an underground," Carol says. When the researchers asked the girls about the school's honor system, for instance, "the girls on the surface were saying the honor code was working, and the teachers were saying, you know, the honor code's really great here because people can leave their bags around, and we've only had one or two violations of it in any one year," Lyn says. But beneath this surface acquiescence, some girls were angry. The honor code meant they were supposed to inform on each other as a way of keeping the school honest. That did not feel like honor to many of these girls. And the carefully worded questions that the Harvard Project interviewers were asking some of them sounded as though the researchers were playing along with the system and merely wanted to know the girls' cover stories, as it were. One woman pointed to this surface-versus-underground tension when she asked Carol in an earlier study, "Do you want to know what I think, or what I really think?"

Like the girls, the researchers themselves began to regret losing relationships whenever their science required them to take up an "objective"—distancing, unresponsive, impersonal—approach again. Just as the girls they were studying had begun to hope that they could have real relationships with the researchers, now the researchers began to hope that they could find a way to do research on girls' relationships that wouldn't make it impossible for them to have relationships with the girls. "I've come to think of hope as the most dangerous of emotions, because it creates such vulnerability—to imagine that things could be different," Carol would say later.

The researchers brought to the school's almost all-female faculty and administration their hope that girls might voice disagreement openly and stay in real relationship with the school and their regret about losing their relationships with girls in order to study girls' relationships. Carol framed her plea for girls to be encouraged to voice disagreement as "preparing girls for citizenship in a democratic society." She recalls that one teacher responded, "How can we help girls to voice their disagreements when we can't do that ourselves?" So, scouting out the chasm between girls and women they were there to explore, the researchers reported that the girls had confided in one or two of them about the complex, creative cultural juggling they had to do to make the honor system work both as a way of holding on to adult approval (keeping bags safe) and as a way of holding on to their own values (keeping friendships safe, and keeping their school from turning into a school for spies). Because informing on a friend would interfere with friendship, girls found ways of solving honor-code violations without telling on their friends. The girls' way of policing themselves without ratting "made the staff believe that the honor code worked, when in fact it fostered an active underground of resistance," Brown says.

Wanting to tap into this underground creativity, rather than the superficial compliance, the Harvard interviewers told the girls in the second year of the study that they would all be having long, open-ended confidential interviews once a year. They would all be in the experimental group. The girls took them at their word. A few of them confided bombshells at these interviews—plans to run away from abusive or alcoholic homes, for instance. Now the researchers had a moral dilemma of their own. Should they stick with science and just move on to the next question? Should they stay with these girls and help them think and plot their way to safety? Or should they inform on these girls and involve school and state officials? How could they both stay with the girls who were confiding in them and be responsible to the school that had been generous enough to give them access to these girls?

If the school was really going to be "a democracy in which you have the full participation of the girls," Brown asked the teachers, could the school find a way to incorporate the "underground" wisdom girls used to resolve serious difficulties completely outside—or underneath—the school organization? "How do you include that knowledge in the life of the school? How do you create spaces for it—even modifying the honor code if you have to, but to create space for it?"

Brown faced this difficulty herself when she wrote the first draft of her dissertation as Carol's student. "I saw the nice and kind, because that's what I thought I was looking for: how wonderful girls were, and da-da-da-da-da. I also saw the places where girls couldn't speak or refused to speak, the girls' resistance, the not knowing, or what they were doing to each other that was not so nice. I knew something was going on for these girls. I was more than willing to name the nice and kind, because that's what I thought people wanted, but it was when Carol said, 'Look what they're doing. Look what they're saying'—that was the moment when I had permission to make these observations. It's the same thing the girls were going through. The experience for me was of permission, of empowerment. Someone of Carol's stature gave me permission. That really was very powerful, to have someone say, I trust you to say what you know—rather than say, I need you to support what you think I want to hear," Brown remembers.

As the administrator of the Laurel project, Brown began to realize she knew from her own working-class background that the code of nice and kind was about class and race as well as gender. "Class emerged for me while I was directing the Laurel project," Brown says. "I would go into meetings with the upper-class female administration, and they would make suggestions, and I would leave confused. I would ask my colleague Elizabeth Debold, who also grew up working-class but had more experience in the business world, to help me translate." As an interviewer, she also found another ally: "My class background connected me with Anna, a white working-class scholarship student at Laurel," Brown says. "For the five years of the study, Anna became my interclass guide, an outspoken critic of the school and class and race who articulated what it felt like to be an outsider in such a privileged place." Anna's anger moved Brown into anger of her own, and Anna's clarity "brought class difference to the surface of my work," Brown says. "Once I named it, I saw it wasn't her problem and it wasn't my problem." Brown's insights about class and anger led to research that produced two books. In 2003, decades after Anna helped her start working on the problem, she could describe her book *Girlfighting: Betrayal and Rejection Among Girls* this way: "Fundamentally, it's a political story about battling the surveillance and control of girls' bodies, minds and spirits; a story that varies with social context, with race, class and sexual orientation. It's a story about containment and dismissal that gets acted out by girls on other girls because this is the safest and easiest outlet for girls' outrage and frustration."[34]

In 1991, the last time Gilligan taught her big adolescent psychology course, she told a powerful story on herself. It is really the story of why she stopped doing research on girls, though I think when she gave this lecture she didn't yet know that she would be taking a long sabbatical from research and then taking up research on boys and adult couples. It is also part of the story of why this was the last big lecture course she taught at Harvard, but she didn't know that yet, either. In fact, and she tells this, too, at the time she did some harsh or blind things, and she didn't notice them—in much the same way that she didn't notice that all the psychological research she was first taught couldn't lead to accurate conclusions because it left most people out.

She says she only heard what she had done when she listened to the tape of what was to be her last interview with a girl she can't name because of promises to keep the name confidential. It's a story she will tell over and over again, for years, until she finally realizes it's the story of why she can no longer do research the old way, research that ignores relationships while ostensibly studying them.

Carol tells the story in the present tense, just as I am telling her story here. She says because she had interviewed the girl several times in the three years before this last interview, as part of a research project called Strengthening Healthy Resistance and Courage in Girls, she went over the rules with the girl quickly.

"Now, the interview is confidential, meaning that it's just between you and me—"

But the girl interrupts. "And she says, 'And your tape recorder.' "

Carol agrees. "And my tape recorder." But then she reminds the girl that no one will listen to the tape except members of the research team, and they will never reveal the girl's name to anyone.

So the girl asks, "Then why don't they all just come in here?"

The girl is talking about relationship. The researcher on relationship is talking about separation, role, protocols, rules. "And I say, 'Oh. Well'—because I'm going to fudge now," Carol warns her class. She means she's going to cheat a little, be a little dismissive of the girl she's interviewing. But she didn't realize she was fudging, didn't strategically decide to pooh-pooh the girl's concerns when she was interviewing her. She wasn't thinking about what the girl was actually saying, wasn't really listening. Instead, she was thinking that the girl seemed to get more depressed the longer they talked. She knew the girl's mother had just had a baby, and that might make the girl feel displaced, "and so I had a good psychologist's reason for thinking that she was depressed when the year before she had been so lively.

"But here she has taken me right to the edge of naming this relationship. What is this relationship between her and me? And my sense is that I could read the whole interview through this initial conversation."

Carol tells the girl that the relationship with her and with the other researchers is not really a relationship, but is some sort of commodity or datum that can be studied, and would she play along with Carol and pretend it's a relationship? And the girl starts getting depressed. "I tell her I'm going to fudge, and would she fudge with me?" Would she pretend that it's just the two of them talking and that every word she says is not going to be examined by a study group, because "I need her to be in relationship with me in this way so I can practice my psychology." Will she stop "really speaking what she sees and knows" in order to have this interview that has the look of relationship without the listening or trust that would make it real? Will she pretend there's no tape recorder and no research team?

"And she agrees basically to do it," Carol says.

But none of this crucial transaction, which sets the tone for the whole interview that follows, is discussed. Instead, Carol tells the girl that though she can't get rid of the tape recorder or bring in the research team, she can allow the girl to pick out whatever name she wants to be called by in the study, as long as it's not her real name.

The girl wants a real relationship. She has real relationships with the other girls in the study, who have been meeting every week with each other as well as individually for these interviews, and in those weekly meetings "again the conventions of research are contested by the girls," Gilligan says. For instance, when they learned at their weekly group meeting that the project was to end, one girl asked, "Why would you end this?"

"We've run out of money," Carol had to say.

"We'll set up a toll on Appian Way"—the street that runs through the Ed School—one girl suggested. "We'll have a bake sale," another said. None of them thought there should be any reason not to continue their meetings and interviews every week. Why would you end a good relationship, or a good bunch of relationships?

The girl Carol is interviewing for the final time at the end of this three-year project wants to have a real relationship with her interviewer until the tape recorder goes off for the last time. But that's not an option. She can only choose from among the things Carol puts in front of her—names that aren't her own. And she goes along, even though it's not what she wants.

"She's going to choose now, within my framework, 'Elisa.' And then I say, 'What's it been like to be involved in this project?' And she says, 'Odd.'

" 'In what way?'

" 'All ways.'

"Now she's still staying with the truth of this oddness of this relationship. I say, 'Can you put more words to it?'

"And she says, 'Peculiar.' "

Carol feels a little stymied and thinks that this girl is not very forthcoming because she's really depressed about this new baby. Carol is not seeing that the girl is squeezing into a very straitened kind of relationship with this researcher, telling the truth but not pushing it. The framework of the interview *is* odd and peculiar.

"And she says, 'Strange.' And she says, 'I don't know.' And I say, 'Can you tell me what parts feel strange to you?' And she says, 'I don't know.'

"Until Kate O'Neill brought me this transcript on Tuesday morning, in my mind it was that 'Elisa,' as she would 'like' "—the word drips with irony as Carol pronounces it—"to be called, was beginning to be depressed in the third year of the study, for reasons that were very easy to attribute to what was going on in her family and so forth, or I could go back and talk about her early childhood or something like that, but here's the text of her in a sense naming the relational fudge that I'm asking her to come into with me, and her doing it."

So here is the researcher, pushing the subject into dissociation—

from knowing to not knowing, from "Odd" and "Peculiar" to "I don't know." This story of relationship has returned and returned and returned through the history of civilization, Gilligan says. "As long as there's been civilization, there have been girls' voices speaking about a problem of relationship. And anyone with good ears—Chekhov, Shakespeare, Sophocles, Euripides, Apuleius, Freud at the beginning, Virginia Woolf, you can go on and on," she says, "can hear it. So psychology isn't such a mystery. The mystery is why hasn't it been heard—or when does it get heard, and then when does it not get heard, and then *how* does it get heard and not heard, and then the question *why? Why* does it get not heard?"

To find the parts of themselves that hadn't obediently become good, nice, and perfect when the culture told them to, Brown and several of the other Harvard Project investigators started a "twelve-year-old group" for themselves. They met regularly and tried to remember and revive the girl in themselves together, the girl who had spoken candidly about tape recorders or honor codes or gym class or the emperor's clothes. "We started with twelve and went back" to eleven, ten, nine, the age of the clear, big voice of the girl who is left to speak her mind even if, or quite possibly because, no one but her eleven-year-old friends pays much attention. Elizabeth Debold, who came to the Harvard Project from a career in a New York law office and intense experience in a New York women's consciousness-raising group that was still alive and well in 1985, says she was fascinated to find herself wondering, as part of her research for a Harvard doctorate, "What would a ten-year-old say about this? What does she know that I've forgotten?"

Like the women in the mental health collective, who asked their volunteer supervisor, Jean Baker Miller, to help them talk about their relationships with their mothers as an essential part of their training, the graduate and postdoctoral students in the Harvard Project realized that they couldn't make out the developmental dilemmas of the girls they were studying if they didn't recover their own political and personal history of facing the same dilemmas. So much of girls' developmental story had been left out of the discipline called developmental psychology that the young psychologists who began to try to trace it had to start with their own experience. There were no better data. And even their own memories were evasive, hard to keep hold of.

Carol did this personal recovery work with them while she supervised their research and advised them on their dissertations. Lyn, who became the director of the Laurel project, remembers this apprenticeship as an arduous and exhilarating search for both student and teacher. "I remember sitting in Carol's office and going through interviews together, the two of us, and starting to see what the younger girls were saying and doing and *being*, really—I mean, as she said, actually, the voices were both familiar and really startling."

Gilligan and Brown were trying to pick up the differences between the ways girls were thinking and expressing themselves at eight and at eighteen. That mouths-of-babes, darnedest-things combination in the younger girls, familiar wisdom that was so clear it was shocking, was strangely hard to assess.

Diana, for instance, at the age of eight, told a Harvard Project interviewer that she had found a way to stop her family from interrupting her and teach them how she felt when they cut her off: "One night Diana's response to this problem was to bring a whistle to the dinner table. When she was interrupted, she blew the whistle. Mother, brother, and sister, she says, abruptly stopped talking and turned to her, at which point she said, 'in a normal voice, "That's much nicer." ' "[35]

Marianne, in second grade, took clear, honest, direct action to deal with a bossy new girl in the neighborhood: "I just played with her a lot. [At first I didn't like her] because she always was like the boss, but then I told her, 'Hey, I don't like you being the boss' . . . 'And I know another friend who played with you before, and she doesn't like you being the boss.' And then she stopped being the boss and I liked her."[36]

Jessie found herself being shut out in second grade when a friend invited her over but then ignored her and played with another girl. Jessie took her friend aside and said, "Can you please play with me, too? . . . I will go home if you don't, 'cause this isn't any fun for me. Just sitting here." But her friend didn't feel like playing with her anymore and bluntly told her, "Just go home." Jessie said she didn't like being left out that way. But when she went home, she started trying to understand how her friend felt and what she could do to repair the relationship. "It took me a couple of weeks to understand" that the way to make it better would be to make them "even," she told Lyn, "because if we're even, then we could start being friends again. And um, being friends is better than just thinking about what you've done, and feeling down."

"How do you get to be even when you're uneven for a while?" Lyn asked her.

"Well, you start, you start, um, realizing that that friend was special to her and so she wanted to—she hadn't seen her for a long time, and so that friend, she wanted to play with a lot."

"And how does that make you even, by understanding that?"

"Well, I would get a chance to do it to her also probably, and after that I would have a friend over, and also have her over . . . I would show her how I felt."

"Okay. And that's how you would get even?"

"Uh hum."

"And that would allow you to be friends again?"

"Uh hum."

"That's the part I'm not sure I understand. If she did something that hurt you and you did something to hurt her, how would that make you friends again?"

"Well, we would be even, and I would just tell her that I was just trying to show her how I felt . . . an example of how I felt, and so I would ask her to be my friend again."

Understanding why her friend had hurt her wasn't enough. Jessie had to understand and then do something to reestablish the balance of power and pain in the relationship. Once her friend felt that Jessie, too, had the power to hurt her, because she cared about Jessie and because Jessie, too, had other friends, Jessie believed this friend would feel "even," too, neither more powerful nor less vulnerable nor less committed to staying in a relationship that had cost them both some heartache to hang on to.[37]

Lily, an eight-year-old from Afghanistan, wrote a book about friendship. Carol read it at a lecture she and Lyn gave about *Meeting at the Crossroads*.[38] The dedication of Lily's book read, "To My Friends," Carol says.

CHAPTER 1: MAKING FRIENDS
You have to be careful because anything can happen and you will have to cope with it.

CHAPTER 2: FIGHTS
Don't worry, because it's normal.

CHAPTER 3: RACE
When you want to make a friend, do not worry about race.

CHAPTER 4: THE END OF FRIENDSHIP
There is usually no end of friendship.

CHAPTER 5: MY OPINION
Good luck in making good friends, but remember never judge someone by race.

How did eight-year-old girls know that chapter two of friendship is fights? How did they know that the joy and difficulty of relationships are that "anything can happen" or that needless worry and racism, personal obsessions and cultural divisions, are equal obstacles to relationships? How could they know that after some disconnections, understanding isn't enough and it takes getting even to make respect and empathy kick in again? How could they learn so much about conflict, anger, love, and power from dinner-table interruptions and school-yard squabbles? And what was it again that they knew? The researchers say they would know and then not know what these girls were telling them, like Jean Baker Miller thinking about the strengths of housewives, or Judith Lewis Herman thinking about the incidence of incest—or Charles Darwin thinking about no higher or lower. "That was hard to hold on to," Lyn says, "and that's the piece I don't think either one of us could have done individually, because, you know, the desire is to cover that over real fast. Other people have to help you with that interpretation and help you hold on to it."

Carol says she sees her students gain and lose their own best thoughts this way again and again. Women, and men, come to her because they've read her books and heard that she allows her students to ask the questions—about love, about power, about race, about betrayal, about healing—that can become a kind of life purpose for the best psychologists. And of course these students want to become the best psychologists. They are excited about working with Carol and yet afraid other psychologists will think the questions they're burning to ask are unprofessional and will treat their work dismissively.

"People's papers start with 'I'm scared, I'm scared about writing this paper.' They write a psychology that reads more like fiction, because it's so voiced," Carol says. "In working with individual women students, I just work at that place. They tell me their idea, and what I do is I just hold that while they get very scared about it and tell me a lot of reasons why they have to abandon it, start voicing-over people's voices by saying what everybody means, not believing you can really learn from listening to people. And I just stand there and say, 'The inspiration of your work is brilliant, and this is a very creative place you've come to, and I'm staying here. I've heard it. I'm not panicked and scared about it. Go further.' "

Students repeatedly suggest topics Gilligan finds outstanding, and then write papers or dissertations that bury or omit the outstanding part. Finding herself in this position time and again—and remembering her own determination to bury "In a Different Voice"—Gilligan anticipates "a tendency for women to cover and retract what is most brilliant and creative about their work," knowing it's a move that makes sense for people who are used to being given shabby uniforms to play in—or who have been abused or lied to.

"And that's where I would join them, and I would hold the piece that they were trying to give up, and then they would fight," she says. "You know, we would struggle around that together, about what would it mean not to give that up—and their feelings around that were so powerful, so intense, so telling about what had happened in these women's lives, that they had had to give up what they most loved and what they most believed was most true and real to them." Years after she discovered this pattern, Carol says, "I can go through with every individual woman student the moment where she begins to feel that to survive she must abandon the creative part of her work, and I know that I can stay there, and I can hold it, and wait for her, you know, and struggle with her over what that's about, not join her in the denigration and abandonment of that, and actually on the individual level I find that always very, very moving, because the win is a win for creativity and life. It's like choosing life, at that moment."

Later, after they married, Lyn and Mark Tappan would write about how people who are trying to observe something for the first time need to be part of an "interpretive community" (a phrase they borrowed from the literary theorist Stanley Fish) that creates consensus for their new knowledge, or they just can't hang on to it. "We believe the process of interpretation is essentially a *relational activity*," Brown and Tappan wrote: interpreters inevitably have relationships with each other and with the authors of whatever data they are interpreting. Good science ought to require that interpreters have good, responsive relationships, with their colleagues and their subjects.[39] Judy Jordan, too, talks about how hard it was to interpret or even accurately observe infants and mothers enjoying their own effectiveness when she was looking at them at Harvard in the 1960s for a study that downplayed relationship. "When that support isn't there, you just can't get clear," she says. Not until two decades later, when she was part of a group of women who wanted to talk about the effects of empathy first, not last or never, Jordan says, could she put together the pieces about mother-infant empathy she had registered but not understood so long before.

This need for consensus before you can sense something is one of the most difficult things for science to admit about its own method. Scientists often want to pretend that new observations are possible simply because people look harder or look in places they haven't looked before. Readiness to see—and the fact that politics and personal psychology play a part in that readiness—is harder to acknowledge. And yet the truly exemplary scientists, who love the discipline, are among the first to acknowledge this mystery. It is no surprise to find that Charles Darwin, who made science his life, wrote perceptively about how easy it is for the best-trained and most highly motivated scientists to look at things and not see them: Reflecting on his location in science near the end of his life, Darwin remembered a walking tour he went on the summer after he took his bachelor's degree at Cambridge University. Perhaps as a way of taking his mind off the embarrassing fact that he hadn't yet decided what he wanted to do when he grew up, young Charles ambled through Wales with Adam Sedgwick, a senior Cambridge geology professor. So here were not just one great scientist but two, walking along through glaciated valleys, paying special attention to one called Cwm Idwal, looking very hard at crystal-clear evidence that the valleys had once been filled and were partly carved by massive glaciers. Decades later, after both Darwin and science had seen into the vast age and glacial prehistory of the earth, Darwin remembered this walk as "a striking instance how easy it is to overlook phenomena, however conspicuous, before they have been observed by anyone.

"We spent many hours in Cwm Idwal," he recalled,

> examining all the rocks with extreme care, as Sedgwick was anxious to find fossils in them; but neither of us saw a trace of the wonderful glacial phenomena all around us; we did not notice the plainly scored rocks, the perched boulders, the lateral and terminal moraines. Yet these phenomena are so conspicuous that, as I declared in a paper published many years afterwards in the *Philosophical Magazine*, a house burnt down by fire did not tell its story more plainly than did this valley. If it had still been filled by a glacier, the phenomena would have been less distinct than they now are.[40]

Darwin knew empirical observation is not a simple skill. Sometimes scientists look and they don't see; sometimes they look and they observe. And even if a scientist manages to be the someone who makes that first observation, after many others have missed it, the first observation doesn't necessarily start a chain of recognition that builds consensus. In letters he wrote toward the end of his life, Darwin acknowledged that at least two English scientists had worked out his idea of evolution by natural selection years before he did. One published a paper about it as early as 1818, when Darwin was nine, forty years before Darwin and Alfred Wallace published their famous joint paper. But nobody really heard what the earlier writers were saying, and the writers themselves had no notion of the implications of their work (in one case on trees, in the other on mulatto women). Lyn Brown and Mark Tappan would say the pre-Darwinians had no interpretive community to help them know what they were seeing—no consciousness-raising group, no Harvard Project, no private circle of scientific friends intent on making sense of the fossils and other evidence that were being noticed.

"I went to my version of the Galápagos Islands with a group of colleagues including Nona Lyons, Sharry Langdale, Lyn Mikel Brown,
Janie Ward, Jane Attanucci and Kay Johnston," Gilligan writes, listing
colleagues who joined her research before and during the Harvard
Project. "We travelled to girls in a search for the origin of women's development," she writes in a paper about her relationship and conflicts
with Kohlberg and the academic psychology he came to represent. "It
was essential to work collaboratively because the research into girls' development led us through a massive dissociation on a cultural and personal level. It was impossible, we used to say at the time, to do this
work alone; we had to stay with each other and build strong resonances
in order to know what we were coming to know."[41]

Brown remembers how hard it was to hear girls' honesty beyond
the nice and kind at Laurel because really hearing the girls' mastery
of two worlds—the relational underground and the official nice-girl
surface—brought Brown herself a personal challenge. In order to understand the Laurel girls' clear, sophisticated grasp of political and
moral reality, Lyn says, she had to make "a real breakthrough not only
in the work I think but also in myself."

After the first year of their study, the researchers realized that by
introducing themselves to the girls with standard pencil-and-paper, fill-
in-the-blank measures of ego development, "we had potentially sabo-
taged ourselves, because they were so angry and felt so used by those
measures that they were resisting during the interview," Lyn remembers. But the researchers had also heard how generous and forgiving
these girls were in their relationships, and how good they were at noticing and responding to being listened to. So like the new girl who
stopped trying to be the boss after Marianne told her she didn't like it,
the researchers met in that windowless room in Larsen Hall to design
an interview that they hoped would let them into the girls' "underground"—their name for the free spaces where the girls were at home
with each other.

They worked with questions that Mary Belenky and Blythe Clinchy
had helped them make up, to get at girls' ways of knowing, the way Belenky and Clinchy and their colleagues had gotten at women's ways of
knowing in their empirical study of how women think. The Harvard
Project researchers sat in a circle and struggled to put the concept the

girls themselves had taught them into words: there was an official way of behaving that put many things—honor, data, psychology—ahead of relationships, and there was an underground way of behaving that kept girls sane by putting relationships first; to remain both legitimate and sane, girls had to act both ways. Eventually, Annie Rogers worked out a wording for a question they hoped would turn the key to the underground when they put it to the girls.

Annie read the question: "Has there ever been a time when what you were thinking and feeling was different from what people around you were saying and doing?"

"All the time," replied Anna, one of the first girls they asked back at Laurel. "That's my life."[42] They had found a question that invited students to describe a divorce between experience and expectation, for-real and for-show, the thought they pretended to think and the thoughts of their hearts, what they were supposed to know and what they knew.

"That's what got us into the underground—that question and questions about what they knew, what they felt," Lyn says. "We'd had a lot of stuff about thinking, using reason in that old cognitive form. We added a lot of questions about feeling." But the most important change "was a real clear attitude shift, so what we said was, 'We're going to go with the girls,' " Brown remembers. No longer would they just march down the list of questions they had prepared for a standardized interview; instead, when a girl let them in on her underground experience of making decisions to protect relationships in a world that required girls to be too nice and kind, too perfect, to have healthy relationships and honest conflicts, they would follow the girl's lead and let the interview go where she went. "We felt like these girls knew things that there was no place for them to think about or elaborate. I don't think we knew what our resistance might be to hearing it," Lyn says.

They spent hours teaching and catching each other as they tried to move beyond their own often involuntary, reflexive complicity in what they began to see as a kind of cultural etiquette whose repressive effect was to keep girls nice and quiet. And the girls, for their part, started trusting the interviewers' promise of confidentiality; they started confiding in them about how they dealt with dilemmas—not only about whether or not, or how, to run away from a well-to-do but abusive home, but also about how they thought, how thought felt in their bodies, about how they caused and coped with crises in friendships and love. The interviewers began throwing their prepared questions out and listening, following the girls "underground" to insights about the relational world and staying with them, Debold says.

Meanwhile, teachers and administrators at Laurel began to form an underground resistance of their own—to the stifling, surface niceness they began to realize they themselves had been practicing and teaching. "We were not open with each other in public settings and, like the girls, had silenced ourselves beyond the walls of our classrooms or offices or in the presence of authority," Patricia Flanders Hall, a psychologist and the dean of students at Laurel, wrote. "We did not publicly disagree with policy, with each other, with men, with the Head of the School or the lunch menu. Above all, we began to fear that we were teaching girls to do exactly the same thing, and were perpetuating the same feelings of loss and inauthenticity that we recognized had colored our lives at the school. Clearly, how could we address questions of silencing without acknowledging and understanding our own silencing?"[43]

Hall and fifteen other Laurel staff members began going on retreats with Harvard Project researchers, who let them hear some of the girls' interview responses. "It was first with a sense of shock and then a deep, knowing sadness that we listened to the voices of the girls tell us that it was the adult *women* in their lives that provided the models for silencing themselves and behaving like 'good little girls.' We wept," Hall wrote. "Then the adult women in our collective girlhoods came into the room. We could recall the controlling, silencing women with clarity and rage, but we could also gratefully recall the women who had allowed our disagreement and rambunctiousness in their presence and who had made us feel whole."[44]

These administrators and teachers also had the experience of knowing and not knowing, recognizing and then denying their roles as silencers, as they moved between the mutual risk taking of their informal retreats and the hierarchical order of the school, which pushed all their nice and kind buttons and sometimes pushed their new self-knowledge out of their minds, or at least out of their voices. "We recognized that this is frightening work that cannot be done alone by a single woman but can only be successful in the supportive bonds of community," Hall wrote. "And we agreed," she added, acknowledging that there would be resistance to this kind of honesty and community, "that we could not bring this knowledge back into the school effortlessly or without pain."[45]

After the interviews, the researchers read the transcripts, using the four-layered "reader's (or listener's) guide" that they hammered out in their Friday meetings over five or six years and that Brown wrote up to replace more simplistic coding manuals. They read four times: for the sense of story; the sense of self ("the I, the speaker's voice," Carol says); the sense of relationship or care; and the sense of justice. They heard "a voice of resilience, a voice of despair," Carol says, and they created a way to read and listen in which these voices weren't pitted against each other, allowing only the loudest to achieve the status of data. Instead, they could hear four voices blending and interplaying like contrapuntal voices in a quartet.[46] "Reading the interviews over and over again— their words, their struggles—works in us very, very powerfully," Debold said in 1992, when she was using the data to finish her dissertation. Project members would arrive at their Friday meetings inspired and moved by their reading and listening. "They were such a combination of intellectual rigor and real community. You'd come out of those meetings flying—like, 'Wow! So much happened today, how am I going to hold on to it?' " Brown says.

"It was like tapping into what was most creative about me. What attracted me to psychology was the idea of relationships and understanding people." And here she was, using relationships—with girl "subjects" and with women and men researchers—to understand people. Lyn was actually sitting in a meeting at Harvard University asking the questions that had brought her into psychology, and that had led her as a working-class girl from northern Maine to dare to write "psychologist" in the futures line of her high-school yearbook entry. "I remember feeling at times in the group meetings, I can't believe I'm doing this. This is so great. I remember this as a conscious thought: God, this is so great. I hope this never ends. This is what I want to do," Brown says. "This was a time when people were being the very best of themselves. People would come into those meetings and say, 'I'm on fire.' "

5.
Relationship

If you kill for knowledge, what is the name of what you have lost?

—MARY OLIVER, *BLUE PASTURES*

There's a relational reality. It's like the sky. It's like the water. It's like the sun. You know, you can stop seeing it or you can see it. And we're going to try in this class to be artists, in the sense of to keep seeing it—and, if I can use this double negative, to not not see it," Gilligan tells an audience of graduate students.

As she begins speaking, her voice sounds all too grown-up—confident but somewhat passionless and defended. She has said this before, been attacked for it, and is still saying it, her voice declares. As she goes on, she becomes more passionate and compassionate, persuasive, ironic, moving—not louder or histrionic, but more personal, as though she were talking to a friend.

Three people I know are taking this course—all women, all writers. They have no intention of becoming professional educators, counselors, or developmental psychologists, which is what the Harvard Graduate School of Education, where Carol is giving this lecture course on adolescence, is designed to train people to be. The women I know are taking this course because they want to hear Carol talk about relationships, and they tell me that each week they see the same metamorphosis as she speaks. She starts out sounding almost wooden—uninterested, uninvolved—and she looks exhausted and old beneath her long dark brown curly hair, as if standing in the big lecture room in Longfellow Hall and trying to talk were a life-and-death struggle. At the end of an hour, her voice is vibrant and she looks twenty years younger—all, she might say, from having allowed herself to know what she knows and say it to her students.

All human beings swim in a relational sea, Carol is saying. We die without it. We thrive in it, body and soul. And on an infinite scale between death and thriving, we find ourselves doing worse or better according to how distant or close we are to people and other living things who swim with us in this sea.

"Human development takes place inexorably, inextricably in relationship, in a medium that is always moving, a tide of change," she declaims. And all writing and thinking about human development take place in the very same conditions.

This marine metaphor breaks down, however, because relationships are not places or things. They do not take up space, even in the invisible way that sound waves do. You don't have to be in the room with people, or even in sight or in earshot, to be profoundly affected by relationships with them. And yet relationships bring with them a quality of presence and immediacy that holds our attention like nothing else. Relationships are as completely dependent on us as we are on them. In fact, it is not too much to say that we are in some way the tangible, audible, visible aspects of the relationships we are in.

Is this love? Possibly, but even if it is, what do we know about love? We can answer that we know quite a lot about love if we read novels or listen to gossip. But we can't even show love exists if we turn to psychology much before Carol and her colleagues and the Stone Center theorists started to talk about women—about why and how the women they knew did so much good and yet often felt so bad about it, or were seen as deficient, or were mistreated.

The Stone Center women, too, realized right away that the proper psychological words for the twists and turns in women's lives—"enmeshment," "dependency," "merging"—didn't fit the reality they encountered in women patients, students, experimental subjects, and themselves. And not only the words but the molds and models of what women were or should optimally or normally be were wrong.

These psychotherapists lived and worked in a scientific and professional world where the official pictures of what people were and how people worked were pictures of individuals or selves, or parts of individuals and selves. But their experience as therapists, and as mothers, daughters, friends, sisters, aunts, spouses, writers, theorists, was always of relationships, never of unrelated selves or individuals. So they decided to alter a basic assumption in the science that underlay their work. They decided to assume that everything is connected and that the connections between and among everything and everyone are at least as important as what they connect.

Immediately, they found themselves describing a ground state of human being, experienced through relationships, that connects us to everyone we love, everyone we know. They explored a psychological and physical state that is completely connected: you can only swim in water; you can only move people and be moved in relationships, and we are all, always, in relationships. They began to see "the development of an enhanced capacity for relationship and the desire to be in connection as the central intention in people's lives."[1] "A change of perspective on what constitutes the basic human motive, from being gratified to participating, represents our central shift from traditional approaches," Miller and Stiver would write decades later. "It's not a question of *getting* but of *engaging* with others."[2]

They had been taught that healthy people outgrew relationships and became separate individuals. But in the context of the civil rights movement and the women's movement, the current version of the separate self started to look like a political idea that worked to divide and rule people who often courageously fought to stay connected. The theorists certainly knew that wherever they found healthy women, they found strong, lasting relationships. Why? What did good relationships provide?

"At least five 'good things,' " Jean wrote in a classic Stone Center paper.[3]

1. " 'Zest.' I don't think I have the right word for this."[4] Miller has never felt right about any single word she's come up with for the increase in "vitality, aliveness, energy" that she says any intense or even not-so-intense episode in a good relationship brings. This is not euphoria, not head-over-heels, not cloud nine, not an "up" with any taste of mania in it. It is a spacious, clear, and clarifying sense of more life, simply turning up the volume of life. This vibrancy can go along with feel-

ings of great sadness or fear, or with joy, courage, anger, or resolution; it accompanies whatever people feel whenever they can confide in someone they trust, someone who is really listening, and they know for certain, from the response, that their listener "gets it." The connection doesn't make sadness or any other painful emotion go away, but it moves sadness, or perhaps it is the pathway on which sadness moves; it gives sadness meaning not as a static bad feeling that you're stuck with—depression—but as a message, as the content or story that is flowing between at least two people and connecting them. Maybe Miller feels "zest" is not quite the right word because it's a word that's been used for hype, to advertise things: it's a brand of soap, for instance, and it's also a quality that we might say some people have no matter what kinds of relationships they're in or out of. The intense liveliness Miller talks about is the special emotional marker of every healthy connection, no matter what the people who are connecting are doing or talking about. People who hear Miller describe this kind of zest usually nod their heads while she's talking, and then say they remember times that fit her description, times when they felt an almost visible shimmer of life with someone else. Or they start at the other end and remember a time when people really moved them or heard them profoundly in many different kinds of relationships or encounters—at work, at home, at school, on a plane, at a party, in a therapist's office. What people notice about these connections is how alive they feel, with an unmistakable relational impetus that seems to pour them into action.

2. Power and effectiveness. At first Miller talked about this second characteristic of healthy relationships as "action." And then she and her colleagues began to use that Movement word, "empowerment." In a good relationship, you feel "empowered to act *right in the immediate relationship—in this interplay, itself*,"[5] Jean wrote. She often uses the example of a friend who comes to you in a crisis and scared because she may have a terrible disease or she fears her husband may leave her or she worries that a possible promotion will sever her from her workmates and isolate her so that, at worst, she will fail and, at best, she will lose her closest allies. As her close friend, you hear the feeling behind what she says, hear her fear and her hope, and you push her right then

into spelling out how she feels even more clearly, and you make it clear you won't stop listening to her because she has difficult or unpleasant things to say. Miller calls this kind of action within a relationship "the *key* form of action," because "it is the way we play a part in augmenting or diminishing other people—and the relationship." Action in a relationship is the only way people affect other people's psychological development, she says. "I'm assuming that babies are born with a basic ability to act, or energy. From then on, the amounts of zest and empowerment which each person goes on to develop depend on the interactions in life," Miller writes.[6] The sense that we have the power to move people in relationships and the desire to use that power often spread from one good relationship into other relationships, either as direct action or as resistance. Your response to your friend's appeal has a way of turning into a decision to talk to someone else who is also involved or to someone who isn't involved but who you know needs to feel your closeness and solidarity about something else. This is "power with others," as Surrey puts it, "power in connection or relational power," rather than power over others. It is not personal power, doesn't belong to an individual, but is power created by the movement of relationship, power that belongs to everyone in the relationship. In situations where people allow their relationship the power to change them, "neither person is in control; instead each is enlarged and feels empowered, energized, and more real," Surrey writes.[7]

3. Knowledge. People in relationships explore and learn more about how they feel; good relationships increase both self-knowledge and knowledge about others, and they bring people out of confusion into very particular and detailed clarity. This clarity does not come from standing alone and not being impinged on, but comes from immersion in relationship. Jordan quotes a client who described the causes of her newfound sense of personal clarity this way: "I connect with myself through connecting with you. I know myself partly through your knowing me."[8]

4. A sense of worth. Because people feel more alive, effective, and powerful in a good relationship, people feel that they are worth

more, too. "We cannot develop a sense of worth until the people important to us convey that they recognize and acknowledge our experience," Miller writes. "Adults often do this for infants and children, of course. If a child expresses distress, adults try to figure out what the matter is, and to respond. Is the child afraid or tired or hungry? Or, if a child is joyous or just 'hanging out,' they join the child in that mode or mood, and the child feels attended to and recognized. This attention and recognition are just as vital to adults and must be present all through life."[9] There is no other source of self-esteem, Miller writes. "We all develop a sense of worth only because another person(s) conveys attention to, and recognition of, our experience."[10] Whenever we are convinced that someone really sees and knows who we are and wants to be connected with us, whenever we see and hear someone liking and accepting exactly who we are after we have felt free to express all of our thoughts and feelings just as they come to us, we feel more worthy, Miller says.

5. A sense of greater connection and a desire for even more connection. Maybe because we feel more alive, more powerful and effective, more knowledgeable, and worth more after any good encounter, we also feel that we care more about anyone we share a healthy relationship with. "This is an extraordinarily wonderful feeling," Miller writes.

> It is different from being the recipient of the other's concern, or being loved, and very different from something like feeling "approved of." It is much more valuable. It is the active, outgoing feeling of caring about another person because that person is so valued in our eyes. It leads to the desire for more and fuller connection with that person and also to a concern for that person's well-being. We cannot will this feeling into existence. It comes along as a concomitant of this kind of interchange. And it leads to wanting more relationship with the person whom we value and care about.[11]

In fact, the momentum of a good relationship pushes people even further, into wanting to form good relationships with people they don't know or don't know well yet, so that the idea of being connected to lots of people becomes more attractive and isolation, even for protection, has less appeal.

These are five good things in motion, Miller says. Each of these gifts of good relationship moves between the people in the relationship, moves outward beyond that relationship to other relationships, and moves inward to the most intimate well of self-knowledge in each person. Although we speak of them as gifts to individuals, these five good things are always given to both or all of the people in any healthy relationship.

And they are always experienced as both thoughts and feelings. While Miller was coming up with these five characteristic benefits of good relationships, she was also finding her way past Descartes and the echo of his seventeenth-century mind-body split to her own conviction, shared with the other women in her group, that no one normally has thoughts *or* feelings; instead, we all have thoughts *and* feelings, or "feeling-thoughts," as she put it. No normal feeling is just raw, with no thought content; we always feel good or bad about something, and it may be something very interesting. Feeling never supplants thought; it accompanies it. Or, as an eighth-grade girl in a workshop with Surrey and Bergman said she wanted the boys in her class to know, "Just because I show my feelings doesn't mean I'm not smart, too."[12] No idea is utterly without feeling. "Nothing is *just* emotional; there is always content." Every feeling is part of a thought that is part of a feeling. And no feeling or thought is disconnected from relationship. "Most of the time we don't know our feelings fully until we try to put them into interaction with other people," Miller writes. "I think that 'feeling-thoughts' in reality don't come to us so clearly because of the very nature of what they are. We get to know them as we put them into interaction and we simultaneously keep changing them as we express and know them—and would keep changing them more if we had more mutual interactions, because feelings are very much a response to the immediate. That's how they are."[13]

In a horrific experiment in the early thirteenth century, the German emperor Frederick II proved that babies die without love. That is not what he set out to prove. He wanted to learn about language. So Frederick ordered the nurses of a number of foundling babies never to speak to them, in order to discover what language the babies would speak if they had no language to imitate. He thought it might be Hebrew, since he believed Hebrew was the oldest language. "But he labored in vain because the children all died. For they could not live without the petting and joyful faces and loving words of their foster mothers," wrote Frederick's contemporary the historian Salimbene, supplying an explanation that seemed as evident to him at the time as it does now.[14] Eight centuries later, when democracies require scientific experiments to meet ethical standards that forbid the denial of relationship, scientists are only beginning to pay attention to the specific ways that babies thrive as they are loved, cuddled, and prattled to. And until the last decade or so, scientists have ignored the way that primary caretakers, who are almost always mothers, thrive in relationships with infants, or how good relationships move development in children and in parents. But what is by now widely influential research on infants and mothers tends to confirm what the Stone Center women deduced from their clinical work with adults. Daniel Stern, a physician and psychoanalyst who became the pioneer of research about babies and relationships, writes that he undertook his work to recapture an ability to relate to infants that he believed he had lost around the age of seven.

Stern and his research colleagues observed mothers and babies and tracked the feeling-thought-acts that went on between them.[15] They concluded that babies are always working in and on their relationships. Relationships are the medium of all infant learning, and they are a good deal of what babies spend their time learning about. "The infant's life is so thoroughly social that most of the things the infant does, feels, and perceives occur in different kinds of relationships," Stern writes. Human connections are "permanent, healthy parts of the mental landscape that undergo continual growth and elaboration" from the very beginning of life, he finds. And he says making relationships is the primary task of infancy.[16]

When he asked mothers why they performed thousands of little "attunements," as he calls them—coos, pats, and rhythmically babbling "conversations"—with their infants, "the largest single reason that mothers gave (or that we inferred) for performing an attunement was 'to be with' the infant, 'to share,' 'to participate in,' 'to join in.' "[17]

"What makes us humans rather than just apes is this capacity to combine intelligence with articulate empathy. But all humans develop this empathic component in the first months and years of life as part of a unit that involves at least one other person. This is what the psychoanalyst and pediatrician D. W. Winnicott meant when he said, 'There is no such thing as a human baby; there is a baby and someone,' " writes the sociobiologist Sarah Blaffer Hrdy. Hrdy, who also calls herself an evolutionary psychologist, was inspired by the British theorist John Bowlby's early work on human attachment and by her own mothering to look for the roots of human caretaking in natural, sexual selection. "No matter how sophisticated the in vitro technology, or even the capacity to clone one human organism from another, the DNA of *Homo sapiens* does not develop these uniquely human capacities without the intervention of other humans, sustained interactions between a genetically engineered baby and its interacting caretakers," Hrdy writes.[18]

By 2000, Renee Spencer, a Harvard Project psychologist and social worker now at Boston University, could focus on infancy research in a long section of a qualifying paper the Stone Center published comparing relational psychologies. Evidence of empathic communication soon after birth, gathered from more than a dozen studies she cites, has led to growing acceptance of the idea that relationships "are the mechanism through which psychological development occurs," Spencer writes.[19] "We are born to form attachments," says Allan N. Schore, who explores the neurology of connection in studies of infants and children at the University of California at Los Angeles School of Medicine. "Our brains are physically wired to develop in tandem with another's, through emotional communication, beginning before words are spoken."[20]

Jordan, too, working just out of college as a research assistant for the Harvard psychologist Jerome Kagan's infant research project in the late 1960s, saw that the zest of connecting with an infant was enough to keep mothers coming back for more and more—and powerful enough to motivate infants' growth, so that infants, too, learned to act on what they learned through empathy. "I remember vividly when I was doing mother-child observational research an incident that convinced me of early empathy," Jordan writes. "A mother inadvertently jammed her hand in the door of the playroom and was in obvious pain. Her 18-month-old daughter immediately picked up a soft, cuddly toy with which she had been comforting herself earlier and took it to the mother, standing close to her, looking worried and rubbing it against her mother's cheek. When the mother smiled and said she was all right, the child's face lit up."[21] But of course, some caretakers—and some caretakers' children—are more like Frederick II than the mothers Stern and Jordan studied.

"You can never have too much of a good connection," Miller has said.[22] But what about all the bad connections, in which people don't listen to each other deeply and as equals and don't respond with honesty that calls forth more honesty? The relational-cultural theorists of the Stone Center are asked constantly, and have been for as long as they have been presenting their work: How can they say that human growth hinges on relationships when so many relationships are destructive traps that block development? But the relational-cultural theorists say that only good relationships can teach you to limit the damage from bad relationships or, if need be, end them. "You don't just leave a bad relationship; you need good relationships to help you leave bad relationships," Jordan said at a colloquium in 1999.

Almost from the beginning, Miller has said that the good connections she means are "growth-fostering relationships." Her idea is that as those five good things about relationships work in our lives from birth to death, the result is psychological growth. Miller, Stiver, Surrey, and Jordan all talk about psychological growth as a process that never stops as long as good relationships are present.

As far back as 1973, when she was still working more or less solo in New York, Miller was calling growth the distinguishing mark of psychological health—rather than some more widely used standard, such as autonomy, adaptation, or achievement, or something trendier at the time, such as Maslow's self-actualizing peak experiences.[23] A quarter of a century later she writes, with Stiver, "The goal of development is not forming a separated self or finding gratification, but something else altogether—the ability to participate actively in relationships that foster the well-being of everyone involved."[24]

By growth, "what I mean is an enlargement or expansion of your psychological experience and then abilities," Miller says. "What makes people grow is being engaged with what's really happening." Jean imagines a child who is sad but having trouble being sad—afraid of being sad, trying not to feel it. You, an adult, realize the child is sad, and "you have the motivation to be with that child," Miller says. So you just stay with the child who is feeling sad—not condemning, not trying to talk the child into or out of the feeling, but just listening and accepting and accompanying the child in her sadness. Because you are there, the child can grow, Jean says, "can find out it's not so bad, it's not so terrible or terrifying or even that there's a certain fulfillment—that you can actually feel good in a certain way to be able to experience a feeling, even if it's very painful." And on the other side, on your side, the adult side, "with even a young child, with trying to engage with the child, the adult can be expanded.

"I call that growth," Miller declares. "Whenever that happens, that can bring great joy and fulfillment, and that's what makes you really care about or love the other person," she says. "And then, because you care about the person, I think you're even *more* motivated to care for that person, because that person is so much more valuable to you" than she was before you sat down and were sad with her and saw her feel less squeamish about feeling sad because you were there. And so relationship makes for care, which makes for more relationship, which makes for more care, and the whole relational process enfolds or supports growth. First you're sad and don't want to be; then a friend, teacher, parent, aunt helps you just by staying with you and listening to your story while you're sad, and then, having had that experience, you are more able to cope with sadness the next time you feel it, and you become more likely to turn to other people when either you or they are sad. That episode is one movement—one "attunement," to use Stern's word—of psychological growth; we all experience thousands of such moments, in relationships with dozens or hundreds of people, in the course of growing up. And part of what makes us human is that we need never stop growing up, never stop growing in relationship.

"I think that the central activity of human beings could be said to be growth-fostering relationships, which then allow each person to develop to the fullest," Miller says. And "growth fostering involves both people," says Jordan: the person we would probably say is giving—the parent, the doctor, the teacher—and the person we would say is getting—the child, the patient, the student—"are both growing" in a healthy, honest relationship, according to Jordan. Because human psychological growth is tied to relationship, and because it has no end, no apex, no final stage, "increasing the sense of relatedness is intrinsically good," Jordan said in 1996, at a meeting with business and labor experts to talk about women and work; it is always better—healthier and more productive of growth—for people to feel connected to the people around them than to feel separated from them.

Empathy gets us there. Empathy is the sense of connection and the connector. The sense of touch often serves as a metaphor for empathy, and touch works the same way. Touch is a way of feeling and a way of doing; we say we are touched, or we reach out and touch someone, but in truth we can't touch someone without being touched. And we don't have to learn to touch and feel; we come with the capacity. In the same way, Stern and later researchers have found evidence of empathic responses in newborns; babies cry when other babies cry, for instance. Clearly empathy becomes much more than the spill of tears at the sound of crying, just as language becomes much more than baby talk; but, as Surrey writes, "almost no attention has been devoted to the topic of *teaching* and *learning* empathy."[25] Empathy—"so ignored in our culture, so not valued in our society," Miller says—was the first topic Miller, Stiver, Surrey, and Jordan took up when they started meeting.

They knew empathy was pivotal in women's experience, and they knew it had never been adequately described. If relationships were the "central organizing feature" of women's experience, as Jean said, then empathy had to be the central organizing agent of women's experience of themselves and others. Or was "empathy" the right word for the relational sense they meant? The word had come into the language at the turn of the century, imported into English from German psychology of art by the Anglo-European aesthete Violet Paget, who used the pseudonym Vernon Lee. Lee's version of empathy—translated from the German word *Einfühlung*, "feeling at one"—described an act of projecting oneself onto a work of art, so that you imagined that the artwork carried all your own feelings and kept you company in your sadness or joy.

So at first, empathy described a kind of self-mirroring, a viewer's version of the "pathetic fallacy" by which poets and artists supposedly invented feelings in nature that mirrored their own. Half a century later, the German psychoanalyst Heinz Kohut borrowed this aesthetic notion of empathy and applied it to his concept of mothering or being a good therapist; Kohut thought of empathy as a kind of didactic mirror or echo playing back the feelings that a child or patient expressed. But this emotional echolalia was not at all what the Stone Center women found themselves talking about on Monday nights.

"I don't think people grow if one person is 'mirroring' the other," Miller said at a Stone Center colloquium in 1986.

> Moreover, I think it is impossible to mirror the other with the exact "feeling-thinking" content. There will be inevitably a difference of connotations and meanings. But it is possible to be closely attuned to the feelings and thoughts of the other person. That is not really so hard as many of us have been led to believe; it can be "learned" if it is encouraged in people's development. Most especially, we can "attend" to the other person and convey that we are trying to do so. The "trying" matters a great deal.
>
> The combination of emotional responsivity and yet difference allows each of us to add something to the interplay; that's what makes possible the movement, the flow which makes for growth, change. If you attend to me and respond with feelings and thoughts which connect and convey recognition of what I've just expressed—but which are your authentically different feelings and thoughts—I have the chance to see and feel and think something a little different. I'm "stretched" a little in my actual "life experience," enlarged in that way. And then if I do likewise, you are, too.[26]

"Difference is inevitable and actually contributes to personal growth; there can be an exciting 'back and forth,' a mutual enhancement and enlargement of each other and of the relational field," Jordan said after she spoke at another colloquium. "Empathy is never perfect attunement; it is in the approximations and reaching toward 'feeling-understanding' of the other's experience that we develop and expand."[27]

"Kohut (1971) emphasizes the importance of empathy in a more one-directional parent-to-child phenomenon. I am broadening this to a more two-way *interactional* model, where it becomes as important to understand as to be understood," Surrey wrote. "All of us probably feel the need to feel understood or 'recognized' by others. It is equally paramount, but not yet emphasized, that women all through their lives feel the need to 'understand' the other—indeed, desire this as an essential part of their own motivating force."[28]

The empathy they were talking about was first of all "not I with a big I," Jordan says. Instead, "it's a big WITH," she says—a common experience of being with someone or with several people, where the emphasis is on the with, not on the you or the me. "It's a kind of knowing," Jordan says, that "also is a way of being with—and that alters your experience of being. It alters you." Empathy is a "responsive, open, changeable process" of being with people—"an embracing responsiveness," Jordan calls it.

You can be empathic when you are listening or when you are talking. It is a powerful process, but it is not about dominance. Dominators want to have control and avoid being controlled. But empathy demands change on both ends of a relationship—"power with" rather than "power over," Jordan says. If you are listening empathically, she says, "you shape things when you listen; you shape things and you change." But the you that's involved is not "the self with a little *s*, the self-conscious self," Jordan says. Empathic exchange is "beyond the content—it's not about the object" of a relationship, she says. It's about the relationship. And the relationship, rather than anyone who is part of the relationship, is in charge. "It's about the way we are together, and it's about the way we are with the people we're talking to. The message gets through in the way we look at each other, the way we stay with each other in uncertainty."

What does she mean? And why do we hesitate to admit that we know? Jordan is talking about an ordinary human experience that is essential for life, like breathing or drinking water. And yet, coming at it along the pathway of psychology rather than fiction, art, gossip, music, or spirituality, we may approach it and ask, "What's that? *Folie à deux*? Religious ecstasy? Narcissistic mirroring? Oceanic fusion?"

When she introduces the idea of empathy, Jordan often quotes a letter John Keats wrote to his brothers at Christmastime in 1817. On a long walk with a friend, Keats felt he had come up with words to de-scribe "what quality went to form a Man of Achievement especially in Literature and which Shakespeare possessed so enormously—I mean *Negative Capability*, that is when a man is capable of being in uncer-tainties, Mysteries, doubts, without any irritable reaching after fact and reason."[29] Jordan's idea of empathy is the connection made when two people put their "negative capability" to work with each other at the same time. It is no accident that she finds support in a Romantic poet. Somehow, because of the rules of Cartesian objectivity—rules that say you have to kill something or at least make it hold still in order to get to know it—psychology, the science of the soul, the study of live hu-man experience, grew up to leave out love, the experience humans die without, and creativity, the inventive responsiveness to difference and change that relationships die without.

"To have confidence in the process of unfolding, to welcome the relational, contextual meaning of things is to surrender our armored self-control. Keats' notion of living," Jordan continues, "exemplifies the courage to be open, vulnerable and related. Therein lies the capacity for empathy, and therein lies the capacity for creative connection."[30] Vulnerability is essential for empathy to operate, Jordan says. Your heart has to be open enough to be hurt if you are to be open enough to let love in and out. She laughs when she talks about a conference in Southern California where she and the other Stone Center theorists appeared in the mid-1990s with Robert Stolorow, a psychoanalyst who has developed a polysyllabic psychological language for talking about what he thinks of as empathy. The trouble is, Jordan says, that Stolorow wants to be in charge of defining this language, just as he holds that the therapist controls empathy in a healing way the patient doesn't.[31] So there was Stolorow expounding about "intersubjectivity," and there were Judy, Jean, Jan, and Irene, who would "get to a certain point and we'd say, 'It's not this' "—Judy points to her head. " 'It's this,' " she says, pointing to her heart.

People already know what empathy is. We use it and start learning it before we use or learn language. As adults, we use empathy every day and we have ways—usually confined to the complex but informal lan-guage of gossip—of describing its infinite permutations quite clearly. The Stone Center theorists began by trying to make a language psychologists would approve of for the ordinary experiences of love and care that they were including for the first time in their idea of psychological development. "Intersubjectivity" crops up in Jan's early writing, too, for instance. But the theorists' language has become simpler and more ordinary as they have come to realize that the informal word in general use or even a finger pointed toward the heart is often "a better representation of reality," Jordan says.

Kaethe Weingarten, a family therapist who has written about mothering with Surrey and others and who shares their passion to move empathy into the official, professional kit of psychologists, has a videotape that shows what happens when people who are left cold by psychologizing are encouraged to work on their hearts instead of their "dysfunction." Weingarten showed the tape, of the last fifteen minutes of a two-hour session with two mothers and two daughters, during her keynote talk at a psychotherapy conference on mothers convened by the child psychologist Jessica Henderson Daniel at Children's Hospital in Boston. It is an old tape. Weingarten appears in it with her hair longer, dressed in the casual slacks of an apprentice in a "hang-loose" era. In the session, Kaethe had interviewed two white low-income mother-daughter pairs, because both teenage daughters were doing badly in a state residential foster care program, a jail/clinic/home for wayward girls. Both girls, Maryann and Tara, were deeply into a rebellious yet repressive adolescent age of poker faces and mute or mumbled monosyllabic responses to adult questions. Weingarten's job was to find a key to the silent deadlock between these mothers and daughters. She asked the daughters when they had noticed something was wrong. Maryann said she was eleven; Tara said she was four. Their evidence was drinking, drugs, and thinking about suicide. Maryann also said that no one had noticed she was in trouble until she dropped out of school at fourteen. One reason these mothers hadn't noticed their daughters were in trouble was that they were in trouble themselves. Roberta, Tara's mother, had been drinking and drugging since she was nine, when her stepfather started abusing her. Bonnie, Maryann's mother, had been drinking and using drugs since she was fifteen, the year after her mother died; her father, "drunk all the time," hadn't noticed.[32]

At the outset, Weingarten's taped session looks and sounds as though it is going nowhere. She cannot engage either daughter, and the mothers speak only perfunctorily to her and to them. Weingarten is the only one who seems able to speak freely, but no matter what she says, the mothers watch her as though she were speaking another language. Nothing clicks, and no one picks up on anything. Weingarten tries again and again, getting softer and softer. You get the sense from the poker-faced mothers and daughters, who are all also dressed in jeans or casual slacks, that lots of professional types have asked them questions before, and, like Kaethe, a few have even tried to get them to talk to each other before, but none of that went anywhere, and they're convinced that someone like Kaethe can only get them into more trouble, or blame them more because their daughters have gotten into trouble. Maryann is looking down and sitting crumpled in a chair and not responding. In a completely stymied, opaque moment, when you can only imagine Weingarten's next move will be to walk out of the room muttering, Kaethe stops and asks the girl if she didn't get what she was asked. The girl grunts that she understands. "So you understand, but it doesn't matter," Kaethe tries to translate the grunt of assent, the refusal to engage. And Maryann grunts yes again, and then turns inward on herself. Kaethe sees her closing in around her heart and asks, "Is your heart cold?" The effect is electric. The girl nods again, and Kaethe says, "I'm going to draw a heart here [on a whiteboard], and I'd like you to come up and mark what part of your heart is feeling and what is not feeling." Weingarten walks over to the board and draws a large heart— not an anatomically correct heart but a Valentine.

Kaethe holds out the marker, and without a word the girl walks up and draws.

As Maryann hands the chalk back to her, Kaethe asks which is the part that doesn't feel, and the girl points to the smaller part.

Solemnly, Kaethe draws another big heart.

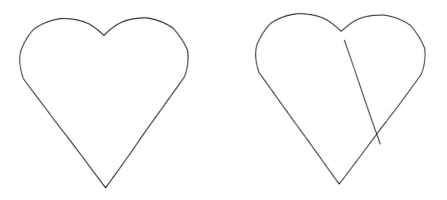

She holds out the chalk to Tara, who takes it and draws her line.

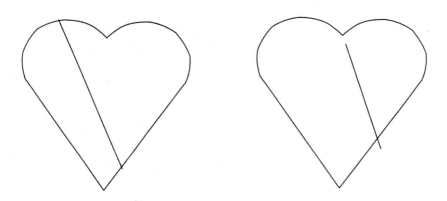

Tara points to the smaller part as the part that feels, and she hands the chalk back to Kaethe.

"I think if they feel nobody cares, that's where the not feeling comes in," Bonnie says, looking at these pictures of two divided, partly numbed hearts.

And yet it is hard for these women to show their feelings to their daughters, they say. "Our way of caring as mothers is almost a cold caring because of the way we were brought up," Bonnie says.

They speak quietly, and there are still long silences. But as they witness the problem of disconnection and shutdown drawn so graphically in front of them, the silence in the room is transformed: a moment ago it was the closed silence of stalemate and self-stricture; now it is the wide-open empathic silence of tender respect for silent pain. Watching the tape, you know this transformation takes place, because you feel it take place in you as your own empathy for these girls and their mothers melts frustration into compassion. As they draw their hearts' truth, the girls know that Kaethe has listened to them carefully enough to realize that, paradoxically, with the simple logic of a fairy tale, they can only speak in silence, which is a refuge they can't leave, like the state residential program where they've been more or less sentenced to treatment. And after the girls finish, when they stand back and watch Kaethe and their mothers taking in their diagrams, the girls see that their mothers and Kaethe are moved by what they have shown them.

Now the adults can find ordinary words that fit. Kaethe hears that phrase "cold caring" and knows at last which words will help. She asks the two mothers if they think they could form a group to help them learn to show "warm caring" to their daughters. She also says she was scared at the beginning of the meeting because she didn't know what it would be like. She cries as she says it has been one of the best sessions she has ever been part of. "You really taught me a lot. I feel really both sad and touched," Kaethe says.

The mothers are relieved. "When you put it down on the board, I can really see that I'm not to blame, because all these years I've been blaming myself," Roberta says.

In a way, the long-term effects of this intervention don't matter. Whatever came of it, the episode shows empathy unfreezing four women as though they were the statue people at the end of the witch's reign in Narnia. The movement of empathy is self-evident as you watch it—as an auditorium full of caring professional women watched it in 1994, many of them with tears in their eyes—because your own empathy is touched into movement; you know very well what must have happened to these women, because it happens to you. It is the sort of miracle moment that makes you realize how relational "craft," left to women for millennia, could be taken for witchcraft, and how at certain climactic moments empathy can work for love like a wand or a magic word breaking a spell.

In this case, simply by being in the situation and paying so much empathic attention, Kaethe found the right words for the feelings the girl was trying hard to hide because she was distrustful of the judgmental, jargon-spouting professionals she'd met before; they had not listened to her long enough to be able to speak her language about her pain. Kaethe's relational craft went on working for these four mothers and daughters, and they spread it to other people just as Miller's list of five good things predicts they would. On the Monday after the taped session, the two mothers began meeting to talk about how to care warmly for their daughters, and they invited the mothers of other girls in the state residence where their daughters had been confined. This group continued to meet every week. After showing the video at the conference, Kaethe read a letter she wrote the two mothers after their daughters graduated from the program. She remembered the language she had learned from them and congratulated them on all they had learned and taught about "warm caring."

Empathy listens, sometimes a long time, for its moment. Often the listening *is* the moment. Jordan remembers taking care of her mother, who was fading and then dying of Alzheimer's disease in the late 1970s, when Judy was developing her ideas first about empathy and then about what she and Jan began to call "mutual empathy." Judy and her mother had returned to a state in which only one of them was verbal, and in which the action of the relationship was "sitting in that room, feeding her, diapering her, bathing her, and sitting and holding her hand." Judy found herself talking to her mother, who could no longer reply in words, just as her mother had prattled to her when Judy couldn't speak. "People would say to me, 'I could see your doing that if it were for a child,' " Judy remembers. She herself had grown up enough by then to know that empathy would expand and regulate this relationship just as it had when she was the nonverbal one and her mother was the talker, and she learned that the empathy was mutual. "I had no question that the spirit was there and intact and beautiful in spite of the fact that the self-organization was decimated by the disease," she says.

Surrey psychologizes the Buddhist notion of "dependent coarising," the idea that everything comes to be in relationship with everything else. Everything emerges in relationship, she says; relationships are present and necessary for the birth of everyone, every encounter, every decision. There is no first cause. Nothing comes first. Nothing can be understood in isolation because nothing is in isolation. It doesn't make things simpler to try to understand them as if they were unrelated; it makes things unreal, inauthentic. Treating human beings as unrelated individuals whites out the mutuality in which empathy operates, making a basic human sense seem like some kind of magic trick or circus act, the way a compass or the migration of birds looks to someone with no knowledge of the earth's magnetic field.

How can people know what another is feeling even if they don't really share those feelings and wouldn't react the same way if they were in the other's shoes? How can people cry tears of joy or sadness for each other, just hearing a story of love or loss? The answer is simple, elemental, built in to our existence: we are related; we are in relationship all the time; we come with a "capacity to participate with another person," Miller says at a meeting of a study group focusing on gender and work, and we can choose to commit that capacity to a specific person or group of people; we are psychologically well equipped from birth to understand and respond to relationships; a great deal of our early upbringing, especially in infancy, is training in how to use this equipment.

Because each of us is equipped with a sense of empathy, empathy is always potentially mutual, always both felt and thought about, and always both active and receptive, the way musicians play and listen together. "Empathy always involves surrender to feelings and active cognitive structuring," Jordan writes.[33] And except in the reflexive case of "self-empathy," which makes solitude of what would otherwise be isolation and brings us into relationship with ourselves, empathy always involves at least two people who are being empathic at the same time. The Stone Center theorists find this mutual empathy embedded in a normal psychological attitude of mutuality, which Jordan defines as "openness to influence, emotional availability, and a constantly changing pattern of responding to and affecting the other's state." In a sense, mutuality is the we, the "self" of the relationship. A mutual relationship is "a relationship where neither person is at the center. *Relationship* is," Jordan said at a colloquium in 1999.

Human development is the development of relationships, and every relationship "comes to have a unique existence beyond the individuals" in it—an existence that needs "to be attended to, cared about, and nurtured," Surrey writes.[34] "Frequently the capacity for empathy develops slowly and over time," Jan told an audience of therapists at a lecture series on women's psychology at McLean Hospital in 1993. "But sometimes people experience it as an 'aha!' One client talked about the moment when she first noticed her mother as the daughter of her grandmother." And though it has gotten bad press as a potential destroyer of balanced perspective and common sense, empathy sends and receives both intimacy with someone else's feelings *and* clear and particular insight about those feelings, she says. A common worry about empathy is "that if you're empathic to another person, you're going to lose yourself." But in fact "being attuned to the other builds healthy connections," Jan says. "Empathy should lead to greater flexibility and choice in relationships," because it's always unscripted and improvised. Empathic insight is free from individual biases, because empathy brings insight from the perspective *of the relationship*, she says.

Even as she was discovering the importance of empathy, Jan says she was experiencing it in her one-on-one discussions with Jean, who was more senior and might have been expected to want a younger therapist to sit at her feet. What stood out "was the mutuality," Jan says. "She would sit and listen to me as much as I would sit and listen to her."

In empathy, "you're saying, 'I'm going to be with you in your experience so you don't have to be alone in that experience.' And if somebody's with you, all things can evolve," Stiver says. "What Judy says describes it best, when she talks about being moved by someone being moved by you." The golden rule only hints at what Stiver calls "the ethics of mutuality" that guide this responsiveness. Jordan cites as a kind of empathic mantra Stiver's idea that the work of empathy in impasse is finding "one true thing" to say, without hurting anyone and yet without fudging, that will move the relationship toward reconnection—exactly as Weingarten did in her taped session with the mothers and daughters.[35]

Mutuality in a couple keeps both members as awake to the life of their relationship (what Surrey and Bergman call "the we") as they are to their individual needs and wants (the you and the me).

Mutuality in a friendship creates a reservoir of trust that may be lifesaving even when life is ending. Surrey tells the story of two friends, whom she calls Laura and Marcia. Laura was a client of Jan's, and Marcia was Laura's friend. Even though Marcia was dying of leukemia, fear of death and the guilt and resentment implicit in a situation where one is to live and the other is to die failed to divide Laura and Marcia, who stayed mutual and authentic right to the end. "This relationship taught me what it means to be there, I mean really *there as myself*. I can recognize this in myself now in other situations—not disappearing or withdrawing because I'm afraid to say what I see or think, or feeling it's hopeless, or just getting angry," Laura said afterward. Marcia was angry sometimes; she was dying and Laura wasn't, after all. But she expressed her anger in an open way that served the relationship and helped to move the friends to new tolerance and respect for their differences. "The most important thing was that I always felt that Marcia would want to hear my experience," Laura told Jan. "We had some big disagreements and learned the ways we usually disagreed. This helped me to know myself better. The space and trust I felt developed into a faith in the power and endurance of the relationship."[36]

Mutuality in the workplace is played out in distinct relational practices that Joyce Fletcher, a professor of management at the Simmons College Center for Gender in Organizations, outlined at a Stone Center colloquium in 1995. Fletcher "shadowed" and then interviewed six women design engineers as part of a study, funded by the Ford Foundation, of gender equity in the workplace. She saw these engineers perform and heard them describe relational work that she labeled "preserving," "mutual empowering," "achieving," and "creating team."

"Preserving" meant doing whatever it took to keep a project alive:

it meant doing low-status jobs once in a while because they had to be done right now and no one else was free to do them; it meant working weekends or overtime to maintain quality; it meant "scanning the environment for information that needed to be passed along and then passing it along"; it meant making sure that people essential to a project felt recognized and thanked; and it meant "rescuing"—seeing emerging problems and doing what it took to get a problem recognized, even if it meant convincing someone higher up that there was a problem and standing aside to let him or her sound the alarm because that would be a more effective way of dealing with the problem.

The "mutual empowering" Fletcher saw was "empathic teaching—a way of teaching that took the learner's intellectual or emotional reality into account and focused on the learner (what does s/he need to hear?) rather than the teacher (what would I like to say?)." It included a sense of what Fletcher calls "fluid expertise," a teaching style that projects equal willingness to learn and teach: "skill in empowering others (sharing—in some instances even customizing—one's own reality, skill, knowledge, etc., in ways that make it accessible to others) and . . . skill in *being* empowered (willingness to step away from the expert role and/or minimize status differences in order to learn from or be influenced by the other)."

Fletcher called the desire and ability to reestablish a sense of mutuality and equality after disagreements or hurt feelings "achieving." Another part of achieving was what she called "relational asking, or asking for help in a way that made it likely you'd *get* the help you needed. That is, in a way that called forth responsiveness in others." Mostly this meant asking for help as a team member who was going to pass that help on to others instead of demanding service or obedience. "This ability to use emotional data seemed to come so easily to these engineers that they were amazed when others didn't do it," Fletcher wrote. "One said: 'These are smart people, they're engineers . . . and yet some of them don't seem to realize that they are never going to get that person to say what they need him to say because two hours earlier they made him look stupid in a meeting. They can't seem to figure out that the way to get someone to support you is not to call them stupid!' "

Fletcher saw the use of language "to create an environment in which the positive outcomes of relational interactions can be achieved—outcomes like cooperation, collaboration, trust, respect and collective achievement"—as "creating team." This is where she put the cello section, what Gilligan calls "resonance"—in Fletcher's words,

> all kinds of verbal and non-verbal interactions that acknowledged people and seemed to be intended to communicate a sense of "I hear you" or "I see you." It included things like nodding and smiling when others were talking, maintaining eye contact with speakers in meetings and chuckling at their jokes, or making encouraging comments like "right," "good point" or even just "uh-huh." It also included listening and responding to others' feelings, preferences or unique circumstances.

And it included acknowledging and adding to people's ideas and comments rather than ignoring or assimilating them without comment— "for example saying things like, 'What I like about Dave's idea is . . .' and then going on to add to it. As one engineer notes: 'I like to talk about things, explain why I think something, hear about what the other person thinks about something. But I know there are some people who like to operate in a state of conflict . . . with voices raised, like, 'That's not a good idea,' instead of 'Why do you think that's a good idea?' "

The relational practice these engineers embodied in these four skills was not just some kind of rote nice behavior, Fletcher writes. "*Its use was strategic.* The engineers in this study made a conscious decision to work this way because they believed that operating in a context of connection was more effective, better for the project, better for getting the job done."[37]

Mutuality between teacher and student leaves a memory of a relationship, Surrey says, rather than of "conceptual things" that have been deposited in one's mind like money in a bank, to use Paolo Freire's analogy. Gilligan builds this kind of memory with her teaching style of holding on, holding with, while her students gain and lose their own best thoughts again and again.

"Love, like empathy, is not something *in* me which I give *to* you," Jordan writes. "People move into relationship, not simply to 'get for the self' or as a *means* to develop the self, but to contribute to the growth of something which is of the self but beyond the self: the relationship." And this motive of giving to the relationship is neither selfish nor un-selfish, because " 'being in and for the relationship' . . . includes being for the other *and* for the self," she writes. "Increasing the experience of connection through empathy involves some sense of 'loss of self,' if by self we mean the self-contained, self-sufficient, in-control self of West-ern psychology," Jordan writes. But when we disengage the "control-self" and expand into "relational awareness" or empathy, we do not lose the inner experiences we most associate with being ourselves: on the contrary, paradoxically, "we experience an expansion of our sense of in-tegrity, realness, and freedom," she writes.

The cliché moment many Westerners recognize as containing this simultaneous expansion of relationship and authenticity—being true to oneself, being real, being the best one can be, and being with someone else so powerfully that it feels as though you are part of each other—is the moment of falling in love. But falling in love can involve inflation and projection that really have little to do with the other person. We can fall in love with someone we make up. We can fall in love with an image or an idea of someone else. But we can't have a good relation-ship with an image or an idea. Besides, most of us don't fall in love very often, but we may move from a dominant or subordinate posture into mutual action in relationship, or back, several times a day, depending on what Herman calls the "relational field."

For instance, almost everyone argues for victory sometimes. Com-petitive debate—lawyer talk, campaign rhetoric—is conversation in a non-relational, "power-over," control mode. But when the jury goes out to make its decision, when the party caucuses, and when legislative leaders meet to compromise, our culture closes the doors and leaves the relational way open. Almost everyone can recall letting go of the drive to win an argument, and feeling empathy begin to light things up, so the talk becomes heart-to-heart instead of something a political re-porter might use boxing metaphors to describe. That little dawn is a common shift from a dominant mode to a relational one. And no mat-ter which side we're on, our experience of freedom and authenticity— of being ourselves—sharpens as soon as any interaction moves into real mutuality, these theorists say.

When you win an argument, you have an intense experience of dominance: you're the king of the castle. When you join a serious, heartfelt conversation, you have an intense experience of personal identity and authenticity: you're "being yourself." School bull sessions and other conversations that go on into the middle of the night, or arguments with loved ones, especially children, often involve this kind of shift. The counterpoint becomes one full melody woven of two or ten melodic lines, instead of two or ten melodies fighting. What we remember from these intense relational moments—once we give up the goal of being the only one left standing—is somehow being made more genuine, more ourselves, just more, as though the listening we are doing adds to us.

As Jordan writes:

> Here we move beyond the paradigm of altruism versus egoism. Both people contribute to, and both are sustained by, grow in, and depend on the relationship. People do not just come together to "give" or "take" or trade off dependencies. They create relationships together to which they both contribute and in which they both can grow. At its best, this kind of relationship goes beyond the duality of self and other and describes true community and relational interdependence.[38]

When Gilligan began to look at her work as an answer to a question about self and other, she says it transformed the way she wrote and did research. In a 1988 paper called "Psyche Embedded," she, Lyn Mikel Brown, and Annie Rogers wrote:

> What language, what words will we choose in speaking about Psyche—currently known as "the self," the modern heir to the soul, the sense of an I, the sense of a center of feeling, of consciousness, of being in life, of appearing, of taking part, of standing in the human condition, of living in connection with others by virtue of having a common sense, or perhaps sensibility, or perhaps a common spirit—a breath, a wind, what once might have been called the hands of a living god?[39]

With Brown and Rogers and the others in the Harvard Project, she carefully began to return psyche, the center of experience, to a body with a certain look that placed it by age, gender, maybe even class, depending on the clothes worn, and with a certain voice that spoke of gender, race, class, region, and politics—an embodied voice always embedded in culture as well as in relationship that moved it and moved with it.

When the Stone Center group first started talking about what Gilligan calls "relational reality," Surrey came up with the phrase "self-in-relation."[40] The modern concept of the autonomous self, the self made much of in the theories of Freud and his followers, was a self that reached the apex of development despite relationships that might tie it down or hold it back. But the sort of development the Stone Center theorists were noticing didn't have an apex. And they began to realize that the elaborate Freudian construct of the self—complete with id, ego, superego, defenses, drives, and self-objects—was totally unnecessary.

Once you thought of a relationship as real, a something, then the subjectivities in the relationship could simply be thought of as streams of experience being lived more or less consciously, depending on how safe it was for each person to express everything he or she authentically thought and felt. "For Ann, as for all of us," Miller wrote about one of her many composite examples, "her feeling-thoughts *are her*."[41] Unconscious thoughts, images, memories, and feelings, Miller saw, were the part of people's inner experience that they could not tell anyone about, even themselves. She came up with a phrase, "being-in-relation," that blurred the line between noun and verb in exactly the way that human experience does. Mental health was relational health.

If a person has healthy relationships, the Stone Center theorists realized, the person is healthy; you don't have to work with, worry about, or even mention a self at all.[42] "A focus on 'the self' is central to almost all of modern psychodynamic thinking," Miller and Stiver were to write. "We believe this reflects the individualistic bias of Western European and North American cultural concepts. The term has become so reified it's worth remembering that there is no such *thing* as a self. It is a *concept* made up by psychologists and sociologists."[43] "The goal of development is not the creation of a bounded entity with independent internal psychic structure that turns to the outside world only in a state of need or deficiency," Jordan wrote. "On the contrary, in the ideal pattern of development, we move toward participation in relational growth rather than toward simple attainment of personal gratification."[44] "The essential feature of good, that is, growth-fostering, relationships is that they are in motion. There has to be a flow. If relationships are static, they are usually bad for the people in them, not fostering growth," Miller wrote. "Another way to put this is to say that emotional development for children and adults occurs basically in the context of relationships where there is a possibility for us to be moved by another person or persons, and for us to affect them. The relationship changes along the way. It moves with us."[45]

What was important, Surrey had decided by 1990, was not that a self was in relation but that there was *movement* in relation. In fact, to think of a person and all of his or her experiences and relationships as a kind of movement, the way we speak of a social movement, is much more interesting and descriptive than the Freudian notion. The earth moves around the sun, not the sun around the earth, and these movements make no sense until we understand the forces that relate them. Relationships, not selves, are the forces that move and guide human development. The concept of self that extrudes self-objects, benign but inescapable narcissism, and "separation issues" becomes as superfluous as the notion of planetary orbits with Ptolemaic epicycles.

When they talked about people in relationships, instead of about selves with defenses, images, objects, and other isolating and self-serving components, the Harvard Project and Stone Center theorists began to describe human development with the kind of simple elegance that science prefers. People grow in healthy, mutual, caring relationships and stop growing in unhealthy, non-mutual, uncaring relationships: their formulation leaves out unnecessary complexity in describing human experience and includes political complexities that psychology had ignored until then.

So when we talk about being ourselves—"I am being myself"—what does that tautology mean? It doesn't mean that my mind and personality have a certain trinitarian structure. It means that I feel and know I am being genuine, real, honest; even if it is only safe to tell myself what I think and feel at the moment, I know what that is. Or as Anna, the Laurel student who taught Lyn Brown so much, put it at the age of twelve: "You can be yourself when you think of your opinion."[46]

Margaret Bullitt-Jonas, a literary scholar turned Episcopal priest, writes about Overeaters Anonymous, a twelve-step program modeled on Alcoholics Anonymous, as an experience of the way good relationships intensified her experience of being herself:

> I slowly took in the presence and companionship of these new friends. I began to experience myself not as an autonomous individual who lives over and against everybody else, not as an isolated monad, not as a self-sufficient individual who goes out into society but then withdraws into the "real" world in which she is fundamentally alone, but rather as a person whose basic identity is relational. I discovered that I was most truly myself when I was open to relationships with others, when I knew that I belonged to a community. I was most truly me when I felt my participation in a web of relationships that extended far beyond my own little life, my one little self.[47]

The Stone Center theorists call this experience of being oneself "authenticity," which Jean has defined as a person's "ability to represent her experience as it arises."[48] In other words, they say this primary experience of being who we are is an experience of confirmation. I feel I am most myself when someone is listening to me and really taking in and believing my account of what I am thinking and feeling and doing—or when I am really listening to someone else. Sometimes we are on both ends of the listening, talking to ourselves, reflecting in a journal, or just thinking about our lives. Jordan describes a form of "self-empathy" to explain how we can have growth-fostering relationships with ourselves. To her and her colleagues, authenticity is not the Lone Ranger doing it his way—not the self, standing alone and fully developed, having kicked away supportive relationships it no longer needs. They consider such a defiantly solitary stance not as a stage of development but as an aberration, an abandonment of development for an isolated position in which growth is next to impossible. To them, authenticity is relational honesty, not some interior construction that stands on its own. In this theory, it takes at least two to be authentic, just as it takes at least two to be empathic.

Authenticity is determined not just by some innate or achieved disposition to be exhaustively honest but by outer political realities, too, these theorists believe. Being oneself is a political, relational act. It depends on caring listeners and political circumstances that allow honest, passionate speech and listening to go unpunished. You are authentic when you can represent your experience to someone—to yourself, to trusted friends or family, to the readers of your book—who will listen generously to what you really think and feel. In the poorest, most coercive conditions, it isn't safe even to rehearse to yourself what you know about what you are going through or about your past—in other words, about your own human development. In the richest, healthiest, most fertile relational conditions, it is safe to talk honestly about what you are thinking and feeling to virtually everyone. When these theorists say that they couldn't have made their discoveries, couldn't have seen how people grow, without the civil rights movement and the women's movement, they are saying that political reality had to change in order for them to be authentic and to see through the old, isolative politics of "self."

"The word *self* has its own problematic connotations. It continues to suggest structure, containment, separation, and reification," Surrey wrote to revise her opinion of self-in-relation.

> I no longer feel that anxiety I felt originally when Jean Baker Miller (1984) raised the questions: Do women have a self? Do men *really* have one? Is there a cultural illusion of self-possession, self-reliance, independence, and autonomy? Is this such a healthy and valuable thing after all?
>
> The concept of self-in-relation represented an early attempt to get through some of these questions. The hyphen suggested connection, but still held some of us to what we all had been taught. Today I have become more ready to question and let go of such language. As self recedes as the primary object of study, we are trying to describe relational processes which enlarge and deepen connections that empower all participants. Thus, I have moved from *self* to *self-in-relation* to the *movement of relation. Connection* has replaced self as the core element or the locus of creative energy of development.[49]

It's not that self isn't "a useful construct," Surrey says. She laughs when she remembers how as a toddler her daughter Katie invented a chant during a Buddhist retreat Jan and Steve took her to with the Vietnamese monk Thich Nhat Hanh. At the end of a morning of silent meditation or a talk about Buddhist concepts of no-self, the monk would pick Katie up and lead the group off to lunch or a break, and Katie would loudly start singing, "Self, self, self, self, self, self"—because she wanted to pour her own milk and serve her own food herself. Even in the Stone Center theory group, "we always get back to using self," Jan says. "It's like Katie at the Thich Nhat Hanh conference singing, 'Self, self, self.' " The problem is almost one of transition. "Self" has been such a buzzword in the development of the West for the last five hundred years or so, it's hard to just drop it. "I don't think we've found a good enough language yet" to dispense with "self," Jan says. But to believe in its usefulness as a reflexive pronoun is not "to believe in its existence and to glorify it, when the concept is the root cause of so many painful moments in our lives," she says. The notion of self does harm "if it becomes the center from which everything is seen, and the ability to be part of the whole gets lost."

Later, Surrey would use the term "self-in-diversity" to "emphasize the capacity to work with difference in relationship without the filter of self-reference that is seeing the other as 'different from me,' which still places 'me' at the center." This "capacity to 'decenter' " means not so much to put yourself in someone else's shoes as to see your own shoes embedded in a particular cultural position and to listen to and learn from other people who might, especially if your position were dominant in some way, see you better than you could see yourself. Surrey thinks this ability is essential for making relationships across differences that are politically important, like gender, race, and class. As an example, she quotes a man at a gender workshop she and Bergman led. The man refused to be stereotyped. "If you see me as a white male, you don't see me," he said. A woman at the workshop disagreed: "If you don't see yourself as a white male, you won't see yourself; and if you don't see yourself, you can never see me as a woman, and we can never make a real connection." "With this," Surrey writes, "they began to struggle together with this paradox of authentic connection, which works through and not around personal, cultural and historical power differentials to create a new 'we' emerging out of the struggle for mutual relationship."[50]

When they are felt as part of a good connection, emotions—"movement out of," in the Latin root—carry and signal the larger movements of relationship like flutes and cellos carrying the movements of a symphony, the Stone Center theorists believe. Every emotion can be solo or orchestral—can play its music with other instruments, other feelings, or can honk alone—and every emotion is about something, means something. So it is always *this* feeling, with *this* thought, about and to this person or these people or things, that moves us, continually.

Relational happiness, contentment, and joy are what a good relationship feels like when it is pushing the people in it toward new, desired growth. Nursing mothers and babies, and lovers, live this kind of happy, open, inventive connectedness in the most obviously integrated mind-body way. But relational contentment is part of any group whose members feel free to talk about and act on their inner experience, their thoughts and feelings, and who feel the kind of love for one another that makes them want to know the feelings and thoughts of the other members. Relational joy is that unitary, integrative zest that signals how life is pouring into and out of you in a good relationship that's working well right now, and clarity is the way we know that joy intellectually or cognitively. "Joy often accompanies clarity and characterizes the empathy/love mode. We feel a sense of well-being, pleasure and delight in knowing and being known. Joy seems 'contactful' and outreaching and not comparative," Jordan writes.[51]

Every healthy relationship feels good. "People experience pleasure if they can respond to another person's feelings with feelings of their own, regardless of what the feelings themselves are," Miller and Stiver write. "We experience pleasure in this, *per se*—the feeling of being in the flow of human connection rather than out of it."[52] Even when friends argue or bewilder each other, if they stay with their difficulty until the relationship resolves itself, so that they feel attuned, though they may still disagree, "through their interaction, they have created something new together. *Both* are enlarged by this creation. Something new now exists, built by both of them. This is what we call 'the connection between.' It does not belong to one or the other; it belongs to

both. Yet each feels it as 'hers,' as part of her. She contributed to its creation, and it contributed to her, to what she now 'is,' which is more than
she was a few moments before."[53]

The pleasures of sex in particular expand and intensify when sex is
part of a mutual, mutually responsive relationship—in just the same
way that the pleasures of speaking expand and intensify when we move
from debate to heart-to-heart talk. "Sexual intimacy, literally becoming
naked physically and psychologically with one another, can provide the
most incredible arena for exploration, discovery of self and other, and
pleasure," Jordan writes.[54] It seems a fairy tale to discuss relational sex
without talking about the omnipresent political pressures that endan-
ger, mock, co-opt, commodify, and corrupt it. On the other hand, the
Song of Songs is a very old book: there is an ancient tradition and culture of healthy relationships in the West, a tradition in which sexual
pleasure is a common form of relational pleasure, reflected in the fact
that an ancient, intensely erotic poem is included in the Bible among
its most sacred texts.

Jordan's only paper about sex appeared after the Stone Center
group had been meeting for a decade, and it shows. We hear a voice
that has been listened to and feels part of a consensus. Jordan writes
with confident authority and makes her views persuasive and authentic
by speaking personally, rather than sticking with imitative psychological
jargon. She wrote about the kind of confidence she was feeling. Confidence is not just an inner attitude but a relational quality, she wrote.
Relational confidence means a trust that the people around you—or
the people you carry around with you in your heart and your memory
as your allies and friends, whether or not they are actually in the room
with you at the moment—will keep faith with you and with one another. "Unlike entitlement, confidence does not involve a 'right' or
'claim' to something because of one's achievements or inherent worth.
It is trust or faith in oneself and/or others, a clearly relational concept.
Both joy and confidence stand in marked contrast to narcissistic praise
as a basis for good feelings about oneself," Jordan writes.[55]

"If I want something from or with you, an empathic awareness of
you will alter the experience of how and what I want. You are not just
an object to me," she writes. "My sexual pleasure is a function of my
own intense sensate experiences, joy in joining with and exploring your

experience, excitement in having fun, pleasing you and knowing you want to please me, feeling 'abandoned with you'; but there is a larger, synergistic sense of the pleasure of both, the mutual surrender to a larger union, a diminished self-consciousness and decreased awareness of the other as a separate person," she writes. "Desire in the larger sense affirms connection and being 'a part of' rather than 'apart from.' It leads to *expansion* rather than *satisfaction*; the former suggests growth, life and openness; the latter suggests stasis."[56]

Jordan tells me that when she read this paper in the big lecture hall at Wellesley where Stone Center colloquiums are held, she was burning with shame—"absolutely exposed, frightened, alone"—and the experience pushed her away from writing about sexuality and spurred her to realize "how much shame functions to take people out of connection." The experience was so stark and intense that Jordan began to study shame instead of sex. It was one of the experiences that moved the four theorists from their early focus on normal or optimal relationships to the effects of disconnections and bad relationships.

In the late 1990s, Deborah Tolman reviewed the literature on teenage girls and sex and found that most of it was "epidemiological rather than psychological" and focused on behavior that raises or lowers the risk of pregnancy rather than how and with whom teenage girls feel sexual pleasure and desire. But Tolman notes that one researcher, Sharon Thompson, found that the 25 percent of teenage girls who reported "desire, agency, pleasure and entitlement to protected sex in their stories of first sexual encounter" also said they had "mothers who spoke to them in positive ways about female sexuality, telling them about the pleasures and possibilities of masturbation, orgasm, a sense of connection to another person through sex and the responsibilities that accompany such active sexuality."

In other words, when teenage girls had open, trusting, authentic relationships with their mothers, and this openness and trust didn't change when the subject of sex came up, they were moved toward open, trusting, and safely pleasurable sexual relationships. "Thompson also found that friends played an important role in how girls organized, learned about and made sense of their sexual and relational experiences. They told about learning from their girlfriends, through observation and through discussion, both good and bad ways to manage relationships and to regulate their emotions and their sexuality."[57] In her own research, Tolman found that for teenage girls who felt at home with it, "sexual desire became a compass for making decisions about relationships" that could keep them feeling "happy to be alive, connected to themselves and to others through their embodied feelings."[58]

In the 1980s, Surrey and Bergman decided to bring their own relationship with each other more frankly and vividly into their work. They began teaching gender workshops together. They wrote a play about the origins of Alcoholics Anonymous in the friendship of two men, *Bill W. and Dr. Bob*, with the idea that community groups could put it on. And they began working together with couples, so that by the late 1990s Jan could say, "The work supports the relationship, and the relationship supports the work." In their book about couples, *We Have to Talk*, Bergman (as Shem) and Surrey write about a therapy group they ran for six couples who agreed to violate the culture's taboo on frankly discussing current personal sexual practices and specific experiences with other couples. By the time the group stopped meeting after about a year, each of the six couples had moved into relational sex. One sign of this movement was that the women were talking about sex and the men were talking about relationships:

"*Big* changes. I've really felt with you. Speaking through our bodies," the composite woman Surrey and Shem call "Liz" told her partner, "Paul," at the concluding session of this couples' group.

> One night I set up the bedroom with music, and candles, and we spent hours together—and it was an ecstatic sexual experience. It wasn't dependent on what Paul did or didn't do, but what we did. He moved in some very different—not antagonistic—ways, and we kept moving together, sometimes gently, sometimes wild. It was full of who we both are. I couldn't sleep half that night, it's way richer a sexual experience than I've ever had before. Paul has really been *in it with* me, both of us saying and expressing the tough, straight things in the relationship, and it all kind of clicked. I walked around feeling the heat flowing, flowing all through my body all the next day too. Incredible.

Paul responded that the insights that led him to this enhanced sexual relationship with Liz hadn't "been particularly about sexuality, but about the relationship." He focused on his decision to connect with Liz, which he said has to come before foreplay, and he talked about his own need for support from other men:

> It used to be I'd come home from work overwhelmed and Liz would take one look at me and march into the other room. I said to myself, you can get overwhelmed by this or that, or you can just stand up and decide to go into the "we," and march forward toward her. That's what I've been doing. And the other thing I realized: I've got to be on my personal journey to find a community, maybe of men, to help. I'm way too alone. I *admire* her with her friends—which is of course why I was angry before.[59]

It takes a special courage to make this kind of change—to move when the relationship says move. Both Annie Rogers, Gilligan's colleague at Harvard, and Judith Jordan, searching for words about human wholeness and interconnection, went to the dictionary and discovered that the word "courage" wasn't always as militarized as it is now and "encouragement" wasn't always so wishy-washy. Courage was about integrating heart and mind a millennium ago, Rogers writes, and she restores it to an older meaning, "to speak one's mind by telling all one's heart."[60]

Rogers writes about Helen, a nine-year-old who told Rogers during a Harvard Project interview about a time when her parents argued and her mother walked out. "No one was doing anything about it, and so I knew where she was and I called her up and said 'why did you leave us like that?' I told her to come home. I said, 'I am mad at you for leaving us. You can talk to Daddy now . . . so please come home.' And she did."

Though she is certainly not debating or talking for victory, the girl doesn't hesitate to use the power of her relationship to move her mother. "In straight-forward terms, Helen tells her mother what she thinks and feels, and effectively brings her home," Rogers comments. "She describes this phone exchange in the same matter-of-fact tone of voice she uses to tell me about playing croquet with her dog: 'I usually win and she doesn't like that, but what can you expect?' "[61]

Rogers discovers among girls, before adolescence, "a practice of courage" that "occurs moment by moment in the art of being playful and outspoken, a vulnerable and staunch fighter, someone who transgresses the conventions of feminine goodness to invite, in fact to welcome, a struggle for real relationship."[62]

"Courage involves bringing our truth into relationship," Jordan writes. To encourage is "to seed and sustain courage in another human being." People who seem to be acting from a solitary, self-starting, bootstrap courage are in fact almost always either with or thinking about other people who have encouraged or inspired them, she writes—especially when they act to make relationships more mutual or honest. "En-couraged people act with feeling and passion; they transcend separate self, isolation, inaction, and stasis. It often takes courage to 'move toward' and engage with others, to act from a place of authentic and strong emotion. We do not achieve courage once and for all, but we re-create it."[63]

These good relational feelings are not "nice." Nice, as Gilligan heard girls struggling with it in her work with girls and women, "can be oppressive, a means of controlling and being controlled," Brown and Gilligan write. As boys are being teased and pressured to dominate more openly—to speak out, to go for it, to fight, to win—older women and other girls are pressuring girls to conform daintily to the control mode, a white middle-class code of "nice behavior" that regulates conduct by means of " 'whispering,' 'telling secrets,' 'making fun of,' and 'laughing at' others."[64] This kind of niceness achieves the look of relationship without the risk that "anything can happen," as eight-year-old Lily's book cautions. But emotions that move between the people in a healthy relationship are intensely connecting, with a tendency to cauterize this controlling niceness out of the experience of authentic connection.

And many feelings that go along with good or healthy relationships do not feel good at all. "Waging good conflict," which Jean put forward as an indispensable skill for people who want good relationships in her first book, always feels dangerous, because good conflict does—it must or it isn't authentic—put relationships at risk. It would really be more accurate to say that good conflict allows the risk that's inherent in all relationships to express itself even at the riskiest times. The Harvard

Project researchers and the Stone Center theorists insist that the greatest risk of all to good relationships is the idea that they should be without conflict—that peace is a soporific, changeless hum of contentment and concord instead of a creative, agile, often infuriating, heartbreaking, and dumbfounding struggle to keep up with difference and change, to stay connected with actual growing people and not substitute an ideal or some other static idea about them. Seen relationally, conflict is "an invitation to engagement which can bring closeness and resolution," Shem and Surrey write.[65]

Conflict "arises when a difference between two (or more) people necessitates change in at least one person in order for their engagement to continue and develop," Jordan writes. "The goal in *good conflict* is not to eradicate difference but to move beyond mere tolerance of existing difference to the creation of new opportunities" for being in relationship. Good conflict opens the relationship to new territories in each of the participants and convinces them, after a struggle, that it will now be safe to be authentic in new ways with each other. "Good conflict creates change in the relationship so that both people experience growth," Jordan writes.[66]

The disconnected, dominating, control-mode forms of difficult feelings feel worse than the relational forms, because whether they're "nice" or not, they are dead-end: the feeling arises but doesn't connect, either because it's never "sent," never communicated, or because it's never received honestly or taken seriously. That difference—between relational feeling and feeling that has been withheld, ignored, or bullied out of relationship—is the difference between sadness and depression, regret and shame, fear and panic, anger and rage, interest and obsession or denial, doubt and paranoia, not knowing and confusion. Almost none of these feelings feels good, but the first member of each pair visits every good relationship and often moves it to a new balance point where a good relationship feels more stable and good again.

In a healthy relationship, whenever sadness, regret, fear, anger, or doubt comes up, it is an emergency message from the relationship to and from the people in the relationship. These feelings point out what or who is at risk of being put down or left out, and they push people to express them, to treat them as important, and to make the adjustments they push toward so that the relationship becomes balanced, mutual, and comprehensive again.

Sadness, Stiver and Miller write, is a "feeling state." The depression that sometimes follows sadness is a "nonfeeling state" in which hidden feelings about loss cannot find their way into expression or relationship. "Genuine feelings of sadness enhance the experience of connection with others and increase self-esteem. Sadness, unlike depression, allows for more direct awareness of the meaning and importance of lost relationships or disappointments in existing relationships."[67] Depression is the masked face not of anger but of sadness or sorrow, the emotional response to losing something precious like a relationship, an opportunity, or a right.

Unlike sadness, which is a response to a loss that feels as though it can't be reversed or changed, anger is "an emotion that arises when something is wrong or something hurts and needs changing," Miller writes.[68] Any experience of anger "is inevitably a social encounter; it occurs in interaction with other people," Miller writes. "The trouble comes when powerful people surrounding you say that you cannot react that way—and, more importantly, that you *do not have* the emotions and the perceptions that you, in fact, have."[69]

Anger is almost always part of a feeling-thought we might call anger-injustice, both Miller and Brown suggest. People's beliefs about justice are behind what makes them angry, and what makes them angry is behind their ideas of justice, Miller said at a Stone Center workshop called "The Movement of Conflict and Anger" in 1993. For instance, if a white woman has been taught and believes that it is just, right, or natural for her to have more power and wealth than someone of another race but less power and wealth than white men, then she will be angry or take it as a challenge if she sees that she has less wealth or power than people she doesn't see as white. But she may not be angry when she sees that a white man has more than she or treats her as inferior. If a black male judge believes he should have every right that white male senators have, including the right to exploit women in private, then he may feel indignant if some senators try to deny him that right.

On the other hand, an idea of justice can follow a feeling of anger: because people are psychologically equipped for mutuality—to partici-

pate in life with others as equals—anger erupts whenever one participant in a relationship is treated as less powerful and less equal than the
other. Anger in unequal relationships is a shout for help by the relationship, because such a relationship can't be fully alive or honest—can't be
authentic—for either member. The person who feels this anger is usually the less powerful one. Sometimes the dominant group exerts extreme pressure—the threat of violence, loss of a job or status—on
anyone who hints that what the dominant group is doing could make
anyone angry. That kind of pressure may keep subordinates from recognizing that they feel the anger that inevitably arises from being
treated as inferior. And since the system of dominance is a pyramid of
ascending power, all but one of the people in dominant groups are actually subordinate to someone.

As Gilligan often points out, everyone has felt the relative powerlessness of being a child in a world of adults who say they do not want
to hear about it when the child complains about almost anything in an
angry tone. So pressure not to express anger that is aroused by perceived injustice falls on almost everyone. Both women and men in our
culture are taught to misdirect anger, though in different directions,
Miller says. Boys are taught to move anger into aggression or to suppress it, and women are taught to express anger only on behalf of others or to suppress it. Girls, it appears, are allowed to get away with
anger, at least for a while.

During the question-and-answer period after an early colloquium
at the Stone Center, Miller imagined what another culture of anger
might be. She had

> a vision of people just reacting straightforwardly when something
> hurts, or is bad, or is wrong. The reaction would be emotional and
> could be made without fear of hurting anybody. The problem now
> is that most of us have a lot of trouble giving an honest, straight-
> forward reaction when we're angry, and we also have trouble ac-
> cepting it when someone else tries. We tend to get embroiled in
> complicated, indirect messages and actions that leave both parties
> feeling bad. I'd prefer a scenario where, instead, the angry person
> could let another know her or his feelings without embarrassment
> or hesitation, then the other person could react directly, conveying

real feelings. Some of us might consider the interaction to be impolite or rude or "not nice." I say fine, let's get on with it—get even the impulsive or "unreasonable" notions out, understand them in this light, be honest and hear each other. I believe it would be ever so much better than no expression—with a resulting gradual, corrosive buildup of angry feelings that eventually can lead to intense explosions, including violence. Now this notion would not work for all situations—for example in situations of real structural inequality which gives some people real power over others. But for many of the ordinary, day-to-day conflicts we face I think it would be a great relief. Parents who allowed such honest expression among their kids could view intense interactions as normal and appropriate instead of getting upset over "bad" behavior and wondering what they did to make the situation go wrong.[70]

In 1983, when Miller had her vision of good conflict, Gilligan and her colleagues were just beginning to do the research that eventually showed that girls know how to get angry in a way that makes relationships better. But to do it, the researchers discovered, girls often have to go "underground"—and wait until their parents and other adults who might pressure them to be "nice" are not around.

Noura, at age eleven and in the sixth grade, reports a four-way fight that she says "was big":[71]

Well, I think it was last weekend when [my friend, China] was over to my house, we were talking to [Mia on the phone] . . . and then we heard that [Heather] was like on her three-way phone, and she was just listening. And they didn't tell us that she was on, and we got into this huge fight . . . And then like, first China started crying and then, I don't know why she started crying, but I guess I just felt like I had to, so I started crying, and then we kept hanging up the phone on each other and calling them back . . . and China wanted to spill her guts to them, but I wouldn't let her . . . I didn't want her to yet, because I knew that they would hang up and never talk . . . First I was asking them all these questions because I wanted to know why they were doing it, that . . . and then in the end I said, "I've got an idea, why don't we just go around and start with

Heather and she can say what bothers her the most about what China and I do," and then we went to Mia and then China and then me. And we just did that . . . and we decided that we would always be friends even if we got really mad.[72]

During this big fight, this good conflict, anger is far from the only emotion Noura and her friends feel. She says they cried; they were defiantly unrepentant ("We are not going to feel sorry for her if that is what you want us to do"); they screamed at each other; and they just screamed. "I was like screaming on the phone even when they were off. I was like, 'I don't care,' you know. And then we were, like, laughing a little, too, and then we got upset again."[73] We don't even have to know all the ins and outs of exactly why they were angry and hurt and also amused and just exuberant during this particular conflict. It is enough to learn from Noura's description that they listened to each other until all the elements of their conflict were out in the open and not so much resolved as fully heard, accepted, and experienced together. They could not have gone through all they had to say and feel either at school or at home with "adults who would only want to control their emotions and quiet them down," Brown and Gilligan write. But at home with her friends and no one else, "I felt like we could make as much noise as we wanted and I could take a long time," Noura says. "If they hadn't had the time and space to work their problems out, Noura explains, 'nothing would work out and somehow the whole class would end up knowing and our teacher would get into it and say well, how can we solve this,' " and their teacher's solution, Noura implies, would be a quick and quiet sweep under the rug, not rededication to a revitalized relationship.[74]

Regardless of the race or class of the girls in the Harvard Project's first studies, at private schools, most of the youngest girls had no trouble "experiencing and expressing anger as a natural part of their relationships," Brown writes. The capacity of most seven-to-nine-year-old girls "to be openly angry—'really mad'—to be disruptive and resistant, gave them an air of authority and authenticity, and revealed a simple desire to speak and to be listened to."[75] But as the girls got older, the researchers found this capacity began to get diverted into outright aggression or "nice" suppression.

The researchers were a little surprised to find that the girls who seemed able to hang on to the ability to let anger cleanse and rebalance relationships without suppressing it or letting it explode into aggression were the least privileged girls, who did not fit the "nice" white middle-class image: the girls of color, the low-income girls, and a few others. Nearly two decades later, Lyn Brown worked with working-class and middle-class white girls in Maine and came to the same conclusion. As Brown sees it, most working-class girls don't have an idea of justice that conflicts with their feelings of anger or contentment. What makes them angry—a teacher refusing to let a girl wear her coat in a classroom where the teacher keeps the windows open in winter; another teacher who makes an agreement with a girl, and then forgets it and yells at the girl for acting as though they had an agreement; beatings in their families; or "stuck-up" and "two-faced" middle-class girls who won't give them the time of day—also strikes them as unjust. " 'You want to know something that really makes me mad?' asks thirteen-year-old Rachel. 'When teachers think that they can do and say anything they want to us and they don't care how it makes us feel, but we have to be so careful what we say to them. It's really stupid.' "[76]

Justice is such a big part of anger to young girls or to girls who are not in the middle or upper class that they identify getting angry with speaking out. "We don't bite our tongues for anybody," Anita, an at-risk African-American tenth grader from a low-income family, tells Jill Taylor. These girls think of anger and conflict as ways to protect relationships, fighting not against but for relationships. "If they don't agree with what I am saying, or telling them, then I would get a little mad because no one would listen to me, but at the same time I would fight to get [them to listen]," Anita tells Jill.[77]

The closer to the ideal of slender Aryan beauty, unobtrusive intelligence, placid and accommodating temperament, and middle-class wherewithal that a girl and her mother actually are, the harder it is for them to trade the affectation of perfection, in which conflict and difference are suppressed, for an authentic and truly mutual relationship—to trade "nice and kind" for "close but we fight." As Taylor, Gilligan, and Amy Sullivan write:

> Girls whose voices are socially marginalized because of their class, race, ethnic background, or sexual orientation may also be more

difficult to listen to than other girls because they are often more willing and able to speak painful or difficult truths. Whereas most girls in the Laurel School Study felt reluctant to portray themselves, their school, or their families as less than the ideal or other than they "should" be, many of the [at-risk, low-income] girls in the Understanding Adolescence Study evidence little hesitation in acknowledging the presence, in these areas of their lives, of anger, betrayal, sexual desire, unfairness, wanting power—all the thoughts, feelings, and experiences that girls are expected to cover over or deny.[78]

Brown, noting that mothers of working-class girls defend their daughters and offer them hope when their teachers have given up on them for not fitting the ideal, sees mothers fighting alongside their daughters through the conflict between an ideal that the girls don't match and the satisfying future that they really can have.

"Anger is a mode of connectedness to others and it is always a vivid form of caring," the theologian Beverly Harrison writes. Surrey borrows a phrase from Harrison to describe the difference between relational anger and aggressive anger: "the power of anger in the work of love."[79] The example Surrey gives is Mothers Against Drunk Driving, the activist group of mothers whose children were killed by drunk drivers in a culture that treated even homicidal drunk drivers with a permissive "boys will be boys" attitude. Starting in the 1980s, these MADD women used their anger—which was acceptable because it was about protecting their children—to mount a campaign that pushed police, legislatures, and the general public to begin responding to drunk driving as a deadly act of aggression, with less tolerance and more severe penalties for drunk drivers and the people who serve them alcohol. "The acronym, MADD, sounds especially relevant here," Surrey writes.

It represents the mothers' shared anger—but also hints at the possibility of anger leading to feelings of insanity under conditions where anger isolates and separates and when constructive arenas for action are not possible. When people can share anger and build connections that allow ongoing movement and interplay around feelings of great intensity, the power of such experience can lead to deeply passionate and constructive, long-term action.[80]

"I think many of us come to feel that where there is anger, there is a loss of love," Miller writes. "We need to learn to place anger as a part of relationships, as part of love and, ultimately, of building better connection."[81] Adults are often more frightened of anger—including their own, perhaps especially their own—than children are, because adults have seen anger used too often in service of aggression, to keep a system of dominance operating. For children, anger is still often simply the feeling that comes when they want to change something that hurts them. "It makes a very big difference to see it as a reaction, often very justified, to something that is wrong, rather than the expression of an aggressive instinct that is linked with a need to destroy," Miller says.[82]

Gilligan writes about Tessie, an eleven-year-old living in a Boston suburb who says she thinks it is important to fight things out when you feel in conflict with someone, because then both people voice their stories, their sides of it, so they have to *"hear* the [other] person's point of view." Even when you report an argument to a third person, if you listen to the he-said-she-said-I-said of your own account, you have to hear from your own mouth what the other people said, Tessie explains: "When you are having an argument . . . and you just keep it inside you and don't tell anyone, you never hear the person's point of view. And if you are telling someone about it, you are telling it from both sides and so you hear what my mother said, or what my brother said. And the other person can say, well, you might be mad, but your mom was right, and you say, yeah, I know. So when you say it out loud, you have to listen." Because it makes people voice their differences, "fighting is what makes relationships go on" despite, or through, conflict, and "the more fights you get in and the more it goes on . . . the stronger it gets because the more you can talk with that person," Tessie says. As long as people who are in conflict make themselves keep talking, fighting is better than "just saying 'I'm sorry'" because fighting makes you learn "how that person feels" and "how not to hurt their feelings" the next time. The danger in conflict comes when you stop talking in order to avoid or quash conflict, Tessie says, because "then you seem to grow apart."[83]

Carol started thinking about voice almost as soon as she started interviewing women in the early 1970s. By 1981, she felt that the difference she was hearing in men's and women's voices wasn't really about voice or gender but about "two modes of thought."[84] She talked and wrote about what she heard in the voices of the first women she interviewed like a literary critic schooled in the New Criticism that she'd been taught as an undergraduate—the idea that a very close reading of texts could turn up "all ye know . . . and all ye need to know," to quote Keats again, and that biography and other information about the context of a writer were much less telling.[85] She concluded that the different voice was really a different way of knowing, one that changed the framework of knowledge and "the basic constructs of interpretation" that were commonly taught and used in universities.[86]

In 1986, Gilligan's former student-colleague Mary Belenky and Belenky's colleagues Blythe McVicker Clinchy, Nancy Rule Goldberger, and Jill Mattuck Tarule finished their research project on how women think and reported on four typical ways of knowing. They called one of the ways "connected knowing." Connected knowers learn by empathy, believing that "the only way they can hope to understand another person's ideas is to try to share the experience that has led the person to form the idea."[87] Belenky, Clinchy, Goldberger, and Tarule also found that the women they interviewed "commonly talked about voice and silence: 'speaking up,' 'speaking out,' 'being silenced,' 'not being heard,' 'really listening,' 'really talking,' 'words as weapons,' 'feeling deaf and dumb,' 'having no words,' 'saying what you mean,' 'listening to be heard,' and so on in an endless variety of connotations all having to do with sense of mind, self-worth, and feelings of isolation from or connection to others."[88] These researchers, too, treated the talk they heard about voice and speech as a metaphor for mind, one that they contrasted with a "mind's eye" point of view that they said was more common in traditional academic thinking, which used metaphors of seeing and being seen to describe the workings of knowledge and thought.

It was in her own experience and in continuing to listen to girls and women, with a trained dramatic teacher of voice, that Gilligan came to change her mind. She came to believe voice was not a metaphor for a way of thinking and knowing, but that certain tones and uses of voice actually embodied the different way of knowing and thinking that she had stumbled upon. Unlike thought, voice is intrinsically relational, she realized. No one has to know what you are thinking, but everyone within earshot knows what you are voicing. By the time she was offering a short course in her work and research methods at a Harvard graduate proseminar in 1994, her answer to the student query "What do you mean by voice?" was, "By voice I mean voice. You know—listen." Later she amplified: "When you hear yourself, you don't need a mirror to hear yourself, but also, you take in other people's voices, not in some idealized state but just as another way life goes." The quality and timbre of your voice are constant monitors of what you have heard in the voices around you about how safe it is to express what you feel. So "when your voice starts to sound weird or stupid or crazy or too loud or too sexual," you know that you are picking up some judgmental or critical tone from someone else's voice that says it's no longer safe to be honest. "Then you start hearing your voice, and you say less and less, and that changes the resonances" for everybody else in the conversation.

"If you have a place where your experience is re-sounded"—a friend who talks back to you in an understanding voice in the low, relaxed or high, exuberant tones that tell you you're free to express what you feel—then you can speak and feel that you can stay connected to the whole world at that safe place. But "if your experience is not re-sounded, you start to feel like you're not part of the world and you can't talk in the world," Carol says. A voice has to be listened to. Relationship, listening, empathy, are built into it. But a self requires no other, no listener. So the concept of the self allows the illusion that it is possible to live without relationships. "I think that 'the self'—that to speak about 'the self' and to feel one has a 'self' instead of speaking of a voice and knowing one has a voice"—supports the dissociation of inner experience from experience that is talked about in relationships, Carol says. "What you get when you take yourself out of relationship is 'the self.' And 'the self' is the culturally sanctioned strategy for maintaining yourself outside of relationship."

Carol tells a story about being part of a lecture series that Harvard Ed School students set up in the early 1990s. The idea was to get professors who seemed to speak different languages to talk to each other. The series was called "In Tandem," and the big draw was the lecture that Carol was to share with Howard Gardner, the Ed School's prodigious theorist of intelligence. "We begin by doing our colleague act, you know, how collegial we are, how much we like each other—like parents do for the children. Then, at a certain point, I realized that I was speaking and every time I spoke he was overriding my voice," Gilligan says. "I said, 'Voice,' and Howard said, 'The metaphor of voice.' And I said, 'Voice,' and he said, 'The notion of voice.' " He didn't say he was translating Gilligan into Gardnerese. But Carol says she felt that way. "He wasn't listening. He wasn't hearing me. There was no way I could be heard," she says. So she acted.

"We're sitting like this"—Carol moves her chair right next to mine—"on this stage, you know, very chummy? Colleagues? So on the front of the stage, I move my chair like that." She moves it about six feet away. "And I said, 'Howard, there's a huge space opening up between us now, because when I say "voice," you translate it into your terms and speak about "the metaphor of voice" and "the notion of voice." And when I say "voice," I mean voice. So why don't you speak and name your work, and I will speak and name my work, and let's try to listen to each other,' " Carol says. " 'And then we can explore: What is the relationship between your work and mine?' "

One of her students saw this demonstration as a revelation, Carol says. When Gardner started listening and naming Gilligan's work in her terms, she says, "Then I moved my chair back close to him—you know, just did it, visually." For the student, "that you could keep your voice when somebody, a man, appropriates and disagrees and renames it, was a possibility she hadn't imagined." In Gilligan's class the next day, all the students knew the story, she says. "The students heard it. They heard me not being heard by Howard, and that he wasn't even hearing that he wasn't hearing me."

Howard Gardner isn't the only one who has found it hard to follow Gilligan from the "different voice" of her early work—an approach to life or a way of thinking—to her current emphasis on the embodiment of psyche in relationship that is the actual human speaking voice. I remind Carol of the question she got in the class she's just finished teaching: "What do you mean by voice?" And her answer: "By voice I mean voice. You know—listen." The questioner came right back: "But what do you *mean* by voice. I don't understand. Aren't you just talking about socialization?" Many of Gilligan's admirers and critics have not moved with her from her interest in voice as metaphor to her interest in voice itself.

If she'd had more than three meetings with these students, Carol says, she would have started to teach them to observe voice, starting with their own: "Listen to your voice. Where is it coming from? How are you breathing? Notice when you stop breathing," she says she tells students who are voicing things that are hard for them to say—or all too easy—in seminars and even in her big lecture classes.

"When I work with students, I ask them to put voice every place they put self," Carol says, "to write 'voice' every place they would write 'self' and see what happens. And immediately it puts it in relationship instead of out of relationship. I really have decided—I mean, it occurred to me this week that the self is what you get as a kind of consolation prize for giving up relationship. Because in relationship you have voice, which is not imagined in the discussion of self and relationships. It's not something you have to get. You have it. You have it right from the beginning. But to develop it, you have to be in relationship. And it's really wonderful if you think about it because you're in relationship with yourself. You can hear yourself. You can hear when your voice changes, follow your own shifts in your body and when you breathe and when you don't. I can tell. I've started sort of guiding my movements in the world on that basis. You know, just watching what happens in my voice, what happens in my body, what happens to my breathing," Carol says. "It's a very reliable guide."

In the winter of 1987, Gilligan met Helen Epstein, a critic and biographer who had recently written a book on the British actress Tina Packer, founder of the American repertory company Shakespeare & Company. Packer had told Epstein that when she read *In a Different Voice* she finally understood how she ran her company—"meaning relationally, rather than top-down," Carol remembers. Epstein took Gilligan to see Packer teach an intensive acting workshop at Wellesley College with Kristin Linklater. Linklater is a Scottish-born actress who had become the teaching heir to the "natural voice" method of acting in England and had brought it with her first to New York and then to Lenox, Massachusetts, as a founding member of Packer's company at its first home, the Mount, once Edith Wharton's summerhouse. Gilligan was just out of what she calls "the straitjacket" of tenure review at Harvard. She had been granted tenure in the fall of 1986, and in the next year she did two things that, she says, returned her to sanity and "took me completely out of the world of research": she took a fiction-writing workshop on Martha's Vineyard in the summer of 1987, and that winter she met Linklater. Suspecting that "Kristin's work on the natural voice gives me the physics for my psychology"—a physical grounding for her discoveries about psychological development—Gilligan agreed to take the monthlong intensive acting workshop at Shakespeare & Company in the winter of 1988–89. Rebecca De Mornay and Keanu Reeves were in it with her. Carol was the only non-actor in the group. "And you know, where I work, nobody spoke with their feelings in public. I mean maybe you do in therapy."

The workshop "was like coming home," Carol says. "That world was so resonant to me personally, and it gave me a way of understanding where I was going, and, I will say, it gave me the physics underneath my psychology, instead of my psychology floating around with some metaphysics," she says. Instead of working on an actor's ideas about the words she or he had to say, "Kristin would start on all the ways that you were not saying what you wanted to say, in your body. She was doing it with where you're holding in your throat, or where you're tensing in your shoulders, and you'd end up in tears or end up screaming at your father and your mother. And you were in this group of six or ten, and Kristin was with you there in this moment of release and exposure, too. And it was tremendous," Carol remembers, maybe a little like Noura and her friends.

After that workshop, "it was on a much deeper level that I understood what voice was," Carol says. "Body, psyche, self, relationship—voice connects them all. Or if they're disconnected, you can hear that in the voice." She had reached this understanding by changing the community of understanding around her, from an academic one—where "nobody spoke with their feelings in public" and many people think of voice as a metaphor for literary or moral style—to the theater.

And "in the theater," Gilligan found, "everybody knows voice means voice."

Voice travels back and forth through Descartes's imaginary wall between mind and body without a hitch; in fact, voice resides right in the middle of the incarnated, integrated junction of feeling-thought-act that theories based on Descartes's ideas say cannot exist: voice is physical and it carries the most abstract meaning. Voice is also more than "*my* voice," more than an unlistening, bombastic entitlement to make noise. " 'This is my voice.' That feels like the old model"—of self and development toward psychological isolationism, Jordan says. "It feels too cut off. It feels like that isn't really the way we operate in the world." If you listen, Jordan says, you will hear that voice listens, too; the way we speak is profoundly affected by the voices around us. "The listening is incredibly important," Jordan says. "You speak in a context. Your voice is totally contextual," she says. "How we speak depends on who is listening," she said at a colloquium in 1999. "It's the listening into voice—or out of voice."

Surrey describes listening to clients in psychotherapy this way: "I have to be transparent, to be real, to be vulnerable, to be focused on my experience and to share it, and to be open to hearing if it's not feeling right to that person—even the leaning over to really hear, to be on the edge of your seat, interested in what's going to happen next, and that sense of giving over your authority to listening for the real voice, and really responding when it's there, and really responding when it's not there, in some way that says, 'I know when it's there.' "

Voice is often simply one dancer in a whole ballet of voices that is being danced or spoken in relationship, and just as the spaces between dancers are as much a part of the dance as the dancers, so silence is a part of speech—often a shared part that belongs to both or all of the people who are speaking. One of the things that has impressed Jordan about the way her work and the work of other relational psychologists is received or heard is the resonance that Gilligan talks about—or the lack of it. There is a kind of communal silence that holds all voices. When it's about things that aren't all right to talk about, sometimes that silence is polite, no more than mildly shaming; sometimes it is quite impolitely coercive, sets your nerves on edge, and gives you the sense that one false move could cost you your life; and sometimes it signals a shift in what the community can hear and becomes receptive or, as Carol says, resonant. This relational silence that holds people's voices or holds them back can harden, shift, buckle, or melt and turn empathic depending on who is speaking where and when. Often, Jordan says, "we speak what is right on the verge of being spoken by others."

During a question-and-answer period that followed a 1991 collo-quium where all five Stone Center theorists talked about relationships, Jordan and Stiver took a question from a woman who wanted to hold on to the old idea of autonomy. How could they insist that the concept of psychological autonomy should be jettisoned because it is basically used to isolate and control people and keep them out of relationships? How could they hold up relationships as a panacea when so many rela-tionships were unhealthy, unmutual, and destructive and ought to be kept out of? Didn't people need autonomy, precisely a way of manning the borders of the self to keep out invading relationships, when so many relationships were used to dominate and control?

"There certainly are power differentials which interfere with the development of mutuality," Judy answered.

> Dominant groups do not want to hear the authentic experience of the subordinate group if it conflicts with their needs. They find all sorts of ways to silence that group. It is very difficult but very im-portant for the less powerful groups or persons to try to gain clarity and to find a way to represent their truth in the relationship and to continue to function effectively outside the relationship. Some might call this autonomy. Where there is a power differential, there is a suppression of real conflict and of the authentic voice; that's an incredible problem. In such a situation, where a more powerful person is destructively impinging on you, you will often have to move out of connection. This takes a lot of courage and confidence, which is most often engendered and encouraged by having other connections.

"I would like to elaborate on that a little bit," Irene said.

> I think, as Judy has said, the concept of autonomy can be translated in various ways, in terms of the relational model. Finding one's own

voice, to use Gilligan's words, feels to me like another way of talking about autonomy. I think we find our own voice only when we have a network of support. When faced with that power differential, the more we can find others who are also in subordinate positions, who are able to join together to validate our experiences, the stronger our voices become. In the face of power imbalances, we do feel in some degree of isolation, but it can be countered by a relationship to a network of support. That's how empowerment happens, which makes for the possibility of bringing about some changes in that imbalance.[89]

The October morning was clear as a bell, a rainbow of blue sky, blue river, falling and rustling leaves of red, gold, yellow, green. The yellow shingles and blue shutters of Carol Gilligan's Cambridge house were almost camouflage. Up from the flagstone path, between the big wooden outer door and the big glass inner door, I shared the wood-floored foyer with bottled water, mail, logs, sand for the front walk in the winter to come. Carol opened the inner door, dressed in a black skirt and white sweater, her very curly dark brown hair just at shoulder length. She greeted me warmly, but I wasn't there to see her. I was there to meet with Normi Noel, the actor, director, and voice teacher who is Carol's personal voice trainer.

My reason for interviewing Normi, whom I knew only slightly, was that she worked with Carol and Annie Rogers, Carol's colleague at Harvard, on their last major piece of research, the Strengthening Healthy Resistance and Courage in Girls project we first heard of when we met Elisa, who thought Carol should turn off her tape recorder and have all her colleagues come into the room. The room that the researchers came into, before and after they met with the girls as a group, once a week for three years, was this room, in Carol's house, or Carol's kitchen. It was still a place for a community of relational thinkers.

Normi was using Carol's house as a sort of daytime base when she had to commute to Boston from Shakespeare & Company in Lenox, Massachusetts, where Normi was living in Tina Packer's house and working on a project about women Vietnam veterans—nurses—which she sold to the BBC in 2004. Tina was a fellow at the Bunting Institute of Radcliffe College, now the Radcliffe Institute, just a few streets away, and was living at Carol's. Carol was also keeping Normi's fluffy calico cat, Carolina, also known as Weenie, who led us a bit stiffly, stretching, into the small sitting room by the front door.

Tina, her short auburn hair eternally tousled and her whole face a smile, offered to make me coffee and toast before she ambled out to her office at the Bunting, but I wasn't hungry. As I set up my tape recorder on the coffee table by the pale yellow silk-covered couch, Carol said she couldn't stay long but wanted to be in on a few minutes of this interview, since her relationship with Normi is so important to the development of her work.

Two hours later, Carol left. In those two hours we made and defined a lexicon of Carol's ideas about relationships: especially the state Normi calls "To Be."[90] Carol, Normi, and I found ourselves in a long, wide-ranging conversation about the healing, staying, quickening power of the world of relationships, using Carol's terms. And we ended up *in* that world with each other.

We talked as women often talk, chorally or orchestrally rather than taking turns in a debate or dialogue or an alternation of monologues. At times we all talked at once or added a sort of walking bass—Normi would say a "cello-ing"—of affirmations that let one of us know she wasn't shouting or whispering into a void. I find myself wanting to leave a number of these purely relational yahs and yeses in my account of this conversation, even though they are almost always edited out. I am tempted to leave them in because in speech they encode some of the regular, constant work of keeping relationally attuned, but I have to admit they look silly on the page. "Yes" and "right" and "umm," written down, do lame the pace and stupefy the level of conversation, even though I know that when we were saying them, the conversation sped and sparkled. The constant relational monitoring—are you with me? yes, I'm with you—that these monosyllables add so efficiently to dialogue was part of what took us into an experience of relationship; without them we would simply have been lecturing each other.

On this October day, we also talked about what Normi and Carol called the "little voice," and we used it. Called in as the theater consultant, Normi worked with Carol and Annie Rogers for all three years on their project with middle-school girls in urban public and private schools. The three women spent virtually all day every Tuesday during the fall semester meeting to plan what they'd do, then met after school with the dozen or so girls in what they called the Theater, Writing, and Outing Club. After the club met, the three would meet again to talk about what had happened. They taped these post-club sessions for the first two years and have let me listen to them. They had a way of becoming inaudible—moving into the "little voice," Normi might say— when they were talking about crucial turning points in the games, skits, talks, and outings with the girls that moved them into memories of their own girlhoods or drove them to examine the clarity and honesty of their relationships with each other. But I heard enough when I listened to the tapes to know the three women were trying to find a way to be with these girls very openly, so the girls would not hide their feelings because the adults were putting up some kind of facade or communicating an expectation that the girls should behave in a certain way. And the women were trying to find a way back to their own knowledge of living in a girl's relational world, remembered from their own girlhoods.

The rest of the week Normi lived in New York at first, then in the Berkshires, where Carol had also rented a house as a writing retreat. During the time they were working with these girls, Normi and Carol had a lot of important talks driving the 150 miles between Lenox and Cambridge on the Massachusetts Turnpike.

"We called it 'piking,'" Normi says, laughing. And while they "piked," she and Carol talked about the normal world of middle-school girls that the researchers were finding "so alive and vivid," she says.

In the winter of 1990–91, the second year of their study, their talk on their "pikings" turned to *Hamlet*. Tina Packer was prodding Normi to direct the play, which would be performed at Shakespeare & Company that summer. Kristin Linklater, who taught Normi to be a voice teacher, suggested directing the play from Ophelia's point of view, and that suggestion piqued Normi's interest. She says she decided to follow the feminine voice in Shakespeare and found that in *Hamlet* it fell to Horatio, in whom Normi says she heard "one of the strongest feminine points of view" in the play. She cast a woman as Horatio and had Horatio and Hamlet do "To be or not to be" as a dialogue rather than a soliloquy.

Normi pauses in her recitation of the relational history of "To Be" to check on whether I'm understanding her. What have I heard on these tapes of Carol, Annie, and Normi that touches being and not being? She is asking for resonance, so she can register where I am before she continues talking, and immediately I remind her of a moment on a taped discussion of an afternoon when Carol, Annie, and Normi had played games with the girls. At one point Annie started to recount a dream or an insight she had had, and then she seemed to lose courage and said, "I'm not sure I can do this."

"We dare you! We double dare you!" Carol called out to her, loudly and playfully.

Listening to this exchange on tape, "I thought, they're there!" I tell Normi. "That's how girls use that playfulness"—to give each other courage to stay in the girlhood world of authentic relationships that Normi, on the tapes, calls "wild and safe at the same time."

"That's what I started to see as, 'Ah, that's "To Be." That's living in the moment. That's being in the moment,'" Normi says. "And then 'Not to Be' became the patriarchal world. I mean, those are very bald terms. And then I thought, Oh, *Hamlet* is talking just about that: if I live in that vibrant, alive world, or if I don't—if I stay in some kind of relationship to myself or if I don't. And it was like magic. I had no idea whether it was in there or not, but it tracked like a map, and Horatio was the leader. Horatio kept telling how to stay in 'To Be.'"

"When we came back into the research in the third year," Carol says, "Normi provided me with the resonating chamber I had been looking for."

With her idea of "To Be," Normi found a way to see to the bottom of relationships and repair them or let them go, Carol says. But first the three investigators found a way to move their own relationship to a middle-school standard of vitality.

"We had a screaming fight one day," Normi says.

"We had a *screaming* fight," Carol italicizes, "about trusting women and what it would take to turn away from 'Not to Be'"—"a.k.a. patriarchy," Normi adds—"and to go in the company of women and start to stay in 'To Be.' We had this screaming fight."

Carol reflects: "There were moments in that work with the girls when I would just be amazed. You know, I would hear myself—" and here she laughs, almost giggles, for pure pleasure, and we laugh with her—"I mean it was the quality of voice and movement, and just being in my body. We all did that. And it was so, 'Oh my God, I remember this.' And it *wasn't* extraordinary."

Carol wants to talk about the difference it made in her ability to follow what the girls were doing, and to remember and return to their free way of acting, when Normi was working with Annie and her. Normi is not a psychologist, not an academic, and the research she was interested in was about the natural voice, as Kristin Linklater calls it, and ways to leave the speaking voice free to express thoughts and feelings as they arise.

"Carol and I keep saying to each other over and over: you need a resonating chamber," Normi says. "If you do it just by yourself, with another person, it creates a sweet vibration that begins to strengthen, and then you need more of the symphony—then you need more of the instruments coming in: more strings, more—because it begins to build and redouble and they can't go back on what they said, nor can you."

Normi says she couldn't find much literature to study about voice. "Kristin's book was the only book about the speaking voice," she says.[91] The other books she read were about singing, or music.

"All I could do was actually go in the most mundane way, to physics, to try and understand the nature of sound—the nature of reverberation, and what it needs in order to grow, and what gets drowned out," Normi says. She says she made a breakthrough while reading about the physics of sound "on this cold winter day, with a fire, up in the woods." She was trying to understand what they were hearing in the shrinking speaking voices of some of the older middle-school girls. "I burst into tears, because it said in a room full of nine tuning forks, eight can be tuned to one pitch. The ninth can stop the eight if it's not tuned to the same pitch." She slows it down: They had been trying to understand how girls pressured each other to shut down, to leave the clear and open world of "To Be," when Normi read that eight tuning forks all vibrating on one note can be stopped by one that is dissonant. "So I thought, Where does the vibration of the eight go when it picks up the ninth?" Normi says. "It's the exact same thing that's happening in these classes" with the middle-school girls.

But she also realized that sometimes a girl found a way to hold out against the pressure to conform that other speaking voices conveyed by not resonating. "I have also seen, with the courage of lions, one little voice saying, 'But I think . . .'" She says that if "someone else picks it up and resonates, that will be the beginning of the idea, and the growth will start" for the little voice. But if no other voice offers that little voice a "yes," or an "um-hmm," or a "right on," "if someone doesn't pick that voice up, then when you watch the person who went, 'But I think . . . ,'" you hear the little voice just go dead or disappear. Going dead—stopping the vibration—is different from having it diminish into silence. Or you could say there are two kinds of silence—the silence of "Not to Be," when dissonant voices stop a voice, and the silence of "To Be," which we might call a resonant silence, the silence of the heart. This is a dramatic voice teacher's take on the poles of the "communal silence" Jordan speaks about, that ether of peace or ice that holds voiced relationships. The deadened and faded-out silences Normi speaks of are the silences of Weingarten's tape before and after she found "one true thing" to say to two troubled girls and their mothers. A voice that diminishes into silence when it hears no resonance may be able to "go back inside again to this world inside themselves of vibration," a sort of inner "To Be" of remembered community, Normi says, where people who try to speak up without finding resonance can store inner strength to hold on to their resistance or opposition and save it until they are with people who will resonate, support, or help them with it. But without hope or memory of resonance, of supportive voices, that lone voice, that vibration of one's own, "can be wiped out, it can be stopped, it can be—you can think you're crazy because you're having it and no one else is," Normi says.

Our most trusted, most daily experiences of relationship are constantly backed by the resonance of people who feel with us. "We do this with each other all the time; we tune each other all the time. No one else is agreeing with me, and I'll say, 'Carol, I think . . . ,' and she says almost exactly what I'm thinking," Normi says. But "To Be" is not a world where the resonance is all on one note. Sometimes what she hears from Carol or anyone else who is speaking with a voice that's attuned to her own relational openness is a new idea, perhaps even a painful truth, that she is able to consider deeply because it is spoken with honest vocal resonance, which sounds inherently trustworthy. And the silences that punctuate this kind of speech lead to the most powerful experiences of "To Be," she says.

Carol kept a journal while she was working with these public-middle-school girls, and also with a dozen girls from a private school. After an outing with them to Plum Island, a wildlife refuge north of Cape Ann, she wrote:

> This morning in the shower I began to remember what it was like on Monday, that intense experience of pleasure, seeing the girls at the beach—their bodies, their freedom, minnow-like bodies darting in and out of the water. Running on the sand. Dancing, turning. I began to remember an eleven-year-old body—I began to remember my eleven-year-old body and to enter that body. Without thinking I began running, unencumbered, fast like the wind.[92]

In the paper that Carol, Normi, and Annie wrote about this work and read at a Harvard Medical School conference called Learning from Women in 1992, Normi describes the girls' voices as they drove back from a country outing in three cars: "The girls bellow to each other, calling from car to car. Voices are huge, bellies responding effortlessly to greater and greater demands to reach across traffic, wind, space. Raucous laughter: the girls are wild, contagious. Their voices are not damaged. These voices do not need my 'help.' " And about a later meeting of the club in a classroom after school Normi writes:

> Rachel in a rage calls her teacher Ted "pig," for not taking them on an outing with him. Her voice is clear, direct, coming straight through the middle of her face. Her feelings are powerful, fly through her body and voice. Eyes are darkened in pain and anger, thunderclouds. This is a living, breathing, upset, unrestricted girl. The room is changed. She excites and awakes all of us, me. The circle grows quiet, attentive, alive to her. My senses are jangled. I begin to remember.[93]

The girls they worked with kept asking about relationships—starting with their relationships to these researchers—tracking the authenticity Jean Miller talks about: "What was the nature of our relationship with them, did we really care about them, did we prefer other girls to them? Girls were especially persistent in their efforts to establish what is real in relationship, who really listens to them and who are real friends."

"Listening to girls talking about relationships," the three researchers wrote, "we get the sense that what care means to them is someone who will stay with them, including someone who will struggle with them in the face of conflict and will voice and listen to strong feelings. Care means someone who cares enough to work things through."[94]

Lately our culture applauds the judge who sentences felons to long jail terms, or the principal who fires teachers he thinks are incompetent. And that is the traditional, rights-oriented notion of care. I am right—about terrorism, perjury, campaign finance, abortion, education, art, whatever—this way of reasoning goes. You are wrong. Even though I feel this punishment hurts me more than it hurts you, because it makes me go against my fellow feeling and condemn you, I express my care for the whole system of justice and your place in it by condemning you.

But we also applaud the mother who visits a condemned son in jail, the wife who sticks by her justly fired husband and helps him find a new career; most Americans didn't want to remove their president from office for lying to a judge about an unconsummated affair, or for lying to them about reasons for going to war. There are times when we miss people we've condemned more than we condemn them. At those times, we feel that jail, failure, segregation, and isolation hurt us all equally, because they destroy relationship, unless we work very hard to hold on to it.

The effort to hold relationship across disagreement, to stay with someone in unknown territory, comes out of another kind of care, a kind of care that keeps relationship going when there isn't any apparent common judgment, common experience, belief, or reason to keep it going.

"Holding with people. That feels very important," Jordan says.

She is talking about the times when empathy feels like holding on—holding the relationship like a sheet you're getting ready to fold or spread, except that the object isn't to do anything but just to hold it. At good times, the holding may be a rich, warm, basking silence. Jan Surrey and Steve Bergman have a framed picture of themselves taken in Arizona at Canyon de Chelly the summer before they adopted their daughter. In it, they are facing the camera with their arms arced toward each other, as though holding an invisible medicine ball between them.

"That's the relationship," Jan says with a smile.

At hard times, holding the relationship may look more like a mother or father going through a list of twenty things to do when the baby's crying and starting over when none of them works, or sitting in sadness with someone who is in great pain, or not fleeing when someone you are with says or does something that feels unbearable or crazy. Like conflict, holding may move the relationship closer, but it's a kind of opposite of conflict. Conflict erupts when something happens or a difference arises that the relationship can't tolerate, usually something that makes the relationship unequal or not mutual. And where the conflict is allowed to take its course, the relationship bucks and kicks as its participants struggle to stay authentic and in relationship, until the troublesome difference has been accepted or changed and the relationship is back on a mutual footing.

People notice that they are holding when something happens that one or all of the individuals in a relationship can't tolerate—often some kind of loss or hardship, or the appearance of a kind of difference that we've been taught is unbridgeable—but the relationship *can* tolerate it. In her relationships with her students, Gilligan holds their ideas while her students lose and regain the courage to explore them. The example I always think of is Job, who endures fabulous losses: his children die; his herds die; his servants die; he gets covered with boils from head to foot, and his wife tells him to give up and die himself. His three friends hear about these catastrophes and come to see him. And when they set eyes on him, they immediately feel how far his grief has taken him from them; they weep and tear their clothes, and they sit down beside him, in the ashes where he has settled to mourn. "So they sat down with him upon the ground seven days and seven nights, and none spake a word unto him, for they saw that his grief was very great."[95] Job's friends spend a week holding his grief in silence, letting him know that their relationship can hold his misfortune and his agony, letting empathy go where words cannot.

"Mutuality is when differences add," Shem and Surrey write. Good relationships do not choose between voices and do not privilege one difference and ignore another. "Both or all voices are heard and responded to. In dialogue or group process something else is created, larger than anyone or all, which helps all."[96] And that helping agent is a relationship, which holds all the differences, all the voices, all the silences. So the experience of a potent relationship is not agreement but enlargement—by the addition of all the differences a relationship bridges or encompasses. And this sort of holding, staying attentively in relationship to people while aware of their differences, has the effect of encouraging people to be even more themselves, because they feel assured that they will stay in relationship even when they show all their differences.

Using "the we" to mean the mutual relationship in a couple he worked with, Shem writes, "My faith is that if she feels Tom 'holding' the we *with* her—especially through disconnections—she will be more herself"; that is, she will be able to express more of her authentic thoughts and feelings to Tom as they arise.[97] "Each person can be more him or herself by being held in relationship," Shem and Surrey write. At the same time, every relationship can also become closer—more itself, so to speak—when the people in it suspend their "irritable reaching after fact and reason," as Keats has it, and just hold what they know in an open way that allows them to learn more. "To feel the feelings together and do absolutely nothing—no 'fixing' them, no 'analysis' of them, not 'Xanaxing' them or 'Zolofting' them—invites a certain kind of shared understanding," Shem and Surrey write.[98]

This is not holding back; it is holding emotions and thoughts the way one person physically holds another. And in a culture where divisions are power points, and pointing out opposites is perhaps the most common way of seeing things, holding is very hard. For instance, Jan says, "How hard it is for women to see that they're oppressors; it puts them in the position of questioning their relationship to patriarchal culture, to men." But white women can't make honest relationships unless they can hold the way they may be one up and one down in the same relationship—to a black man, for instance—and hold other people's reactions to that oxymoronic, down-up status.

People often have to hold two roles that try to pull them apart: a woman might be both the mother of a victim and the wife of a perpetrator in the case of father-daughter incest, for example. Or she might be the mother of a weeping child and the wife of a man who drove the child to tears because he felt she failed to treat him with deference. Surrey says the women in her relational-cultural theory group are trying to feel and hold the way race, class, age, and gender affect them from within and from without.

One of the first in a continuing series of interracial dialogues at the Stone Center on the Wellesley campus was a public dialogue between Carter Heyward, a white lesbian who was ordained a priest at the first "outlaw" ordination of Episcopal women in Philadelphia in 1976, and Katie G. Cannon, a black feminist Presbyterian minister who was on the faculty of Episcopal Divinity School, across the river in Cambridge, with Carter in the early 1990s. Cannon, who attended retreats on women and race with the Understanding Adolescence Study researchers, cited Gilligan's "wonderful, energizing stories of how preadolescent girls name, claim, and flow with the push-pull power of rage and anger." And then she asked Carter if they could have a mutual relationship, despite the white women's fear of black women's anger that Katie found so commonly derailed relationships between white and black women. Could Carter really take in everything Katie had to say, including her anger?

"Can you hold the anger?" Cannon asked.[99]

"In essence she is saying, will you be with me in this process? Will you share this experience with me?" Robin Cook-Nobles, director of counseling at the Stone Center, commented at a colloquium a year later. "To hold somebody else's anger involves being able to hear and to listen without being defensive," Cook-Nobles, an African-American psychologist raised in the segregated South, continued. "Since a great deal of Black women's anger is directed at white women, both past and present, this can be very hard for white women to do. Also given the history of slavery and oppression that Black women carry with them every day, including white women's historical role in it, and the current privileges that white women still have as a result of this historical oppression of Black women, holding the anger is no easy task," Cook-Nobles said. Even fairy tales polarize white and black women, making the pale, fair heroine "passive and submissive, waiting for someone to take care of her or to rescue her," while the dark villainess is "evil and assertive and powerful." When women who live with these different stereotypes come to make relationships, "conflict is inevitable," Cook-Nobles said.[100]

"Katie, I can try to hold your anger if, in giving it to me, you can try to hold my honest response—be it remorse, confusion, or anger," Heyward replied to Cannon.[101] Heyward's response seemed to come a little too fast and to return the focus too quickly to her own needs, Cannon said, but it was a beginning.

"I believe very strongly that for colleagues or peers who hold different status with respect to class, race, ethnicity, religion, sexual preference, physical difference, etc., these differences and the accompanying social, cultural and political realities must be addressed if one is to establish a truly mutual cross-cultural relationship," Cook-Nobles writes. This work of exploring differences has to be "experiential and interpersonal," much more emotional than intellectual. And the motivation for it has to be personal, Cook-Nobles asserts. "Each person in the relationship has to believe that she will be getting something personal out of the time, energy, and risk-taking that is necessary in order to look at the truth and own one's own 'stuff.' " Most of the time, the reward is "a personal re-working of some injustice that one experienced or witnessed in a very personal way," Cook-Nobles believes.[102]

Holding their own cultural histories as they gathered each other's, Cynthia García Coll, Cook-Nobles, and Surrey met together for several years so they could form trusting relationships that would make a healthy context for doing clinical case studies and other research that would reveal something about making relationships across cultures.

"Throughout our regular meetings, we have experienced miscommunications and passionate arguments; we have also experienced sadness and exhaustion from sharing very personal, painful experiences," wrote García Coll, a Puerto Rican native who was then the director of the Stone Center and is now a professor of education, psychology, and pediatrics at Brown University. "We have become aware of our own misconceptions and prejudices about each other's experiences and have found some commonalities in areas that were quite unexpected. It has been hard work. Going from the personal to the political, the process has also evidenced very clearly to me that the notion that when women acknowledge their differences, the solidarity among them will be lost—is a misconception."[103] Cynthia talked about growing up in a multiethnic majority in Puerto Rico and arriving in Florida at the age of twenty-two to become part of a "so-called minority"—and winning fellowships because of it. "I have been granted a lot of privileges," she said, "just because a lot of my people have been so oppressed." Her way of asking the question about holding anger was this: "Can we be different and not alienated?"

Robin talked about growing up in segregated Winston-Salem, North Carolina, "in an all-Black neighborhood of hard-working, honest families," taught by black teachers and served by black businesses. "Our Blackness was a nonissue. Our teachers told us we could be anything we desired, even President of the United States, if we tried hard and got a good education. And we were sheltered enough, and naive enough, to believe them," she said. Robin learned about racism one day when her parents were driving with her to visit relatives in Charleston, South Carolina, and Robin told her parents she needed a bathroom.

> What followed was very interesting and new for me. My parents began to discuss tactics of gaining access to a restroom. My mom and dad disagreed on the tactics. My mom's strategy was to approach a filling station that appeared "hospitable," to ask whether we could use the bathroom, and if the answer was yes to buy gas. My father had a different strategy. He wanted to go up to any filling station, be pleasant to the owner, buy gas and then ask whether we could use the restroom. This resulted in an argument. I heard my mother saying, "Roy, why do you choose this filling station with all those crackers hanging around?" I did not know what in the world my mother was talking about. I looked out of the car on the ground and did not see any crackers.

But after her father, who was driving and so got to choose, stopped at a station and had the car filled with gas, she did see the meanness her mother's reference was really about. It came from "the owner, who initially seemed nice" but then, when asked the crucial question, "turned with a cold, stony face and said, 'We don't have restrooms for niggers.' "[104]

Jan talked about being raised "in a very white, middle-class, semi-suburban city in upstate New York, where my Judaism and my white privilege were fairly invisible to me." Though she knew "the shadow of the Holocaust and the dangers of anti-Semitism encircled my birth," the bias she felt most strongly was sexism. And at sixteen, she said, "I had an argument with the rabbi of our temple who claimed that the central fact of the lives of all Jews was the presence of anti-Semitism. I told him that the discrimination and prejudice most salient in my daily life was related to my being female." The rabbi dismissed her talk of sexism, telling her that anti-Semitism was worse no matter what she felt. "The rabbi refused to listen or take my experience seriously, and I subsequently left the temple," Jan said. "As a white, Jewish woman coming of age in the '60s, my own immediate experience of confusion and injustice centered around the issue of gender, and this issue was not validated within a liberal, deeply patriarchal religious system."[105]

What Jan didn't see until much later, really until after adopting an Asian daughter, she says, was whiteness, her whiteness. "White Middle-Class women have to do the work of coming to terms with our own internalized domination and our personal and collective history of exposure to, and participation in, power-over relationships," Surrey wrote then. "We have learned to see the white experience as normative and all others as other. We must learn to see our own particularities as simply part of the spectrum of cultural diversity and not the measure by which others are judged." White women may be prisoners of the stereotypes about them, she wrote.

> It is especially hard for many of us as women to confront the ways we may be participating in destructive or harmful actions partly because of the strength of our identification with the victim and the difficulties we have in thinking of ourselves as hurtful, especially as we try so hard not to hurt others. Among women, there is also a kind of hierarchy of pain, where women feel they must give up their own feelings when someone else's pain seems more intense or deserving of attention. We need to learn to hold our own and others' feelings simultaneously.[106]

———

"How can these two people live in the same world with each other? How can one person hold these two things?" Carol asks a class in which two students, a gay man and a Catholic seminarian, have passionate, opposite opinions about a text. She is most interested not in who is right but in how two kinds of experience can coexist. "Most of the most troubling things in the world, violence in the world, are done in the name of somebody's truth, or somebody's belief that this is the way," Gilligan says. She touches on a theory that became important for her in the mid-1980s, when she was fighting for recognition and tenure, and she found support from an economist at the Institute for Advanced Study in Princeton named Albert O. Hirschman, who wrote a book called *Exit, Voice, and Loyalty.* Hirschman had supported his daughter Lisa when she and Judith Lewis Herman took on the taboo subject of father-daughter incest, and he invited Gilligan to link her theory to his when she was struggling for academic acceptance. In the senior Hirschman's theory, voice—speaking up—changes systems; but the possibility of exit—packing up, walking out—makes people listen, and that empowers people to talk, just as loyalty makes people stay some-place they don't like and try to speak up and change it.[107] In the case of a priest at a Jesuit seminary and a gay actor who was abused in a parochial school, for example, "how is it possible not to exit in the face of such relational conflict? What would it mean to stay and talk in the presence of differences that are that powerful?" Carol asks her class.

"When voice is associated with messiness and heartbreak, this is what this means. It's so much easier to say, 'I'm leaving. I'm out of here.' Or to say, 'I'm just going to eliminate all those people who challenge what I know to be true and my view of the world, by trying to gain more power than them, or'—and you know psychology has been used in the service of that—'by labeling them lower stage, by diagnosing them, by explaining that it's because of this and this and this that they haven't yet (developmental stage theory) come to see the light which I see.' That's so easy for the person in the dominant position, so easy." And then she brings up her ally Jean Baker Miller and says Miller's book *Toward a New Psychology of Women* introduced the idea in 1976 that political dominance was what gave force to men's definitions of women as weak, enmeshed, too dependent, and that these same qualities could be looked on as strengths—nonviolent, supportive, connected. "As Jean Baker Miller explicates in the passage we read from her book, the people who have the capacity to institutionalize truth (the universities), goodness (the churches), and the use of thought force (the state, the army) can impose a vision of the truth on other people and call it the good, the right, and other people have a very hard time believing in what they know through experience. Now, if you get rid of the psyche, you get rid of the problem, because the subordinates then are socialized" and forced into believing the vision of the dominant. But the fact of political resistance complicates this picture. The existence of an inner psyche is proved by "that human psyche's capacity, even in the face of enormous oppression, to say, you know, 'this is my experience.' "

Gilligan cites Jamaica Kincaid's novel *Annie John*, a book about the knowledge of a black girl on a tiny island in the Caribbean, the sort of island Columbus landed on in 1492. Carol paraphrases Annie telling her teachers, "This is your view of Columbus, but my experience is that Columbus did not discover the West Indies." "And what happens?" Carol asks. "She gets punished in school; she feels herself going crazy."

Carol returns to the disagreement in her class. "How can these two people have a conversation which is not abusive, offensive? It's the essence of education. How can you educate voice so people don't have to exit at that point?" she asks. "The problem with the exit option is that it denies, as Hirschman says, the reality of interdependence." But voice has its problems, too: "Voice depends on the belief that one will be listened to, because voice makes you vulnerable. It's the relational option. It involves messiness, speaking, and also heartbreak—that is, speaking and having somebody say, 'I don't get what you're saying, sounds crazy to me.' " So voice takes patience and a love of engagement that our society actively discourages these days. I think of Jimmy Carter and Bill Clinton being mocked by their political opponents for trying to listen to them instead of shooting from the hip. "That's what's happened in our society," Gilligan says. "We don't like the voice option, because it's messy, because it takes too much time."

Later she says, "What I like about Hirschman's exit, voice, and loyalty analysis is that in the presence of either strong experiences of relationship, or in a cultural and societal world, it's possible not to feel that one's relational wishes and desires and thoughts are in themselves shameful and humiliating," which is what she thinks the culture pressures boys, and later girls, to feel. Knowing that voice is the way to make a system respond may make it "more possible to work through conflicts in relationship without breaking relationships," she says. "But this doesn't say that the presence of the exit option isn't very helpful. When divorce became more acceptable in this society, a lot of problems in marriage were revealed, not because divorce created the problems in marriage, but because once it was possible to leave, it was possible to speak. Once it was possible to pursue something that felt like relationship, it was possible to say, 'This is not relationship' or 'This doesn't feel like relationship.' "

But now, in the lecture hall, with that forceful preface, making it clear that in this impasse they are touching the essence of her discovery of voice as the music of human difference, and difference as the key to psychology, Carol listens to the offended students again.

"How about breathing and feeling what you're feeling?" Carol asks the whole class, and I hear her breathing, fully and evenly, on the tape. Carol speaks to both sides and asks if they can listen to each other without abandoning their own feelings. "Now, is it possible to stay with your feelings *and* hear what you said, too, and you, without negating or your not having to feel the strength of what you feel about this?"

Another student raises his hand and says he knows it's hard to go against what's "politically correct." Gilligan jumps in: "Politically correct according to . . . ?" He backpedals. She underlines the assignment: "I'm specifically asking, 'Can we talk about difference without one side being named the truth?' It's not just different opinions," she says. It's different experience, different people, different lives. "These are not about abstractions. These are about relational reality," what it feels like to live in the world, she says.

"I'm trying to hold the full tension of this problem for at least five more minutes," Carol says. "There are institutions in this culture—" But then a burst of laughter from the whole room swamps her, and the laughter is still swelling when the tape ends. Apparently five minutes of holding these differences without saying that one is better or right or true is too much to ask. But at least the tension breaks with a laugh instead of a war or a spray of bullets, and Carol says the laughter led to a lasting friendship between the gay student and the Jesuit.

Surrey says she had to study Eastern philosophy before she really understood what it meant to hold differences and even opposites the way she knew that she and other people, especially women, actually did. "I realized you had to study Eastern philosophy in order to understand non-Aristotelian logic," she says. The Western, Aristotelian logic she had learned says, "A is A and not B." I am I and not you. Self is self and not other. "There was something about 'A and not B' that was really wrong for women," she says. Then, she says, she came upon Hinduism, Buddhism, and "the idea of paradoxical logic—that A is A and B." I am I and you. Self is self and other. Thought is thought and feeling. Or even, women are victims and oppressors. This was more like it—more like the way she herself thought and felt, more like the way she was and worked with other people.

This is the land of Keats for Jordan, "the Edge" for Gilligan, the frame of mind you enter when you are holding many different, even opposite facts, feelings, and ideas, and instead of trying to sort through them and come to a conclusion, you open your mind and wait to think, feel, and listen your way to finding more—perhaps a synthesis, or perhaps simply one more item to hold in mind. In relationships and in research, the Edge is "the place from which you can honestly speak. That's the place where you can ask anything, because it's a real question. When you shift the dynamics of the research relationship to make it truly relational is when you come to someone, and you come with them into their not knowing and your not knowing, to a place of really true learning, true discovery. That's when you can say, 'Is that how you really feel?' That's when you can say, 'Is this true?' because you don't assume you know it," Carol says. "You're really there with them. And it frees your own voice in your own research." The Edge asks for an attitude of total listening, like Jan's sitting on the edge of her chair, leaning forward into whatever she's hearing, whether she's with a client or Jean Miller. "I really always like to work on the Edge," Carol says. "I love not knowing."

Our culture often plays up differences between parent-child, teacher-student, couple, friend, work, and community relationships. But these researchers say that all healthy relationships share an openness that allows empathy to operate and mutuality to be at least a goal, and at least some of the time they live in "To Be," on the Edge. They are, in other words, inventive and surprising while being sources of trust that are intrinsically devoted to the growth of their members—in Normi's phrase, "wild and safe at the same time."

When they first tried to map human relationships, the Stone Center theorists spent a lot of time talking about relationships between mothers and daughters, because they all were daughters, and so were many of their clients—and because the bond between a mother, who is assigned the role of primary parent, and a daughter, who will be schooled and expected to take care of relationships in some ways all her life, is indispensable for civilization. In 1978, Nancy Chodorow had begun moving the women's movement into psychology with *The Reproduction of Mothering*, her book about the huge cultural impact of the fact that mothers and not fathers were the primary parents of both girls and boys. But even by the century's end, motherhood "hasn't been really—I think even yet—fully described accurately and hasn't been seen as a basis of our culture. In fact it's been, probably more than most occupations, almost really looked down on," Miller says, even though every mother is "vitally connected with the survival and growth of another human being."

Some of the Stone Center group's first clues about the importance of these relationships came from work with mothers and daughters themselves. For instance, in one early study of Wellesley students, the theorists found that while current theories said college-age women should be trying to separate from their mothers, most of the undergraduates in their study considered their mothers friends; these young women reported that they were struggling not to separate from their mothers but to stay connected—to maintain close, honest relationships with their mothers while they developed into adults and then as adults. "Most students still saw their relationship with their mothers as one of the most important relationships in their lives," Surrey writes.[108] Just as the synergy of the five good things predicted, but contrary to the Freudian notion that girls need and want to separate from their mothers, these Wellesley undergraduates wanted to move from apprenticeship to friendship with their mothers. Their god was equality, not separation.

"They often described their mothers as one of their best friends. They expected this to continue throughout their lives," Surrey and her mother, Rosalie G. Surrey, wrote in a paper they presented at Ball State University in 1991. "They wanted to be more authentic in the relationship, bringing their own new experiences and personal growth into the relationship, to talk *more* not less," the Surreys wrote. "One said, 'I want my mother to talk to me like I can talk to her. I want her to be able to share her real feelings and experiences.' "[109]

They cited a larger study of older daughters by Rosalind Barnett, then at the Wellesley Center for Research on Women; the daughters were aged forty on average, and most of them said they had a positive relationship with their mothers, and having that positive relationship was correlated with "high 'well-being' and low distress." More black women than white reported having good relationships with their mothers, but race and class made no difference in the correlation between good relationship and good mental health in the daughter.[110] In fact, Wellesley therapists came to learn that undergraduates who reported strong and close relationships with their mothers were more likely to report other strong relationships with peers—again, as the five good things would predict.[111] Stiver found an early study that showed this pattern—of strong attachments spreading or generalizing from a strong attachment to mothers—begins in infancy.[112]

"Give me an example of what you look forward to as being the sweetest thing about freedom?" an interviewer for a Stone Center study asked a woman inmate of a Massachusetts prison.

"Taking care of my children," the woman said. Her reply sums up the study's main finding, which is that for the 75 percent of female prison inmates who are mothers, even if they feel they have been negligent or blameworthy mothers, "motherhood remains the central focus of their lives."[113]

Mothers yearn for connection with their children and for the growth and pleasure that these relationships mean for them, the mothers. "Healthy development of the mother-daughter relationship involves increasing and *not decreasing* the possibilities of connection based on mutual empathy and mutual authenticity whenever this is possible," Surrey wrote. Problems in these relationships represent "the need to change relationships, to attempt to build mutuality and to accept and act on relational needs and desires" as they change during growth.[114]

Talking to girls about their development, the Harvard Project came up with similar data about mothers and daughters. In one book that Gilligan, Rogers, and Tolman edited, Minnesota researchers reported that a feeling of "family connectedness" was the strongest predictor of a lack of emotional distress in both girls and boys, in a survey of more than thirty-six thousand Minnesota adolescents.[115]

Gilligan writes about Rosie, for instance. At fifteen, Rosie knows that she and the "close to the perfect child" her mother believes her to be are very different, as are the way her mother sees herself and the way Rosie sees her. But she doesn't see these differences as evidence that she should separate—or that she has separated—from her mother. Instead, she wants to admit and use these disparities to move into a better, truer, and more honest relationship with her mother. As soon as her mother found out Rosie was having sex, Rosie says, "I hunted her down and made her talk to me, and it wasn't like a battle or anything. I just wanted to see what she had to say."[116]

Eleven-year-old Amy has a clear and direct relationship with her mother that weathers storms and calms equally well. Asked if she and her mother disagree, she says, "Oh yeah. What usually happens is we'll scream and yell at someone. I mean, at each other, then I'll go and walk away, and then later I'll say 'I'm sorry,' and she'll say, 'That's fine.' And then we'll feel better about everything." For Amy, the important thing is that anger is something that comes and goes, something she and her mother move through for the sake of a relationship that can honestly hold anything, and that "she'll listen to me whatever I want to say." "Can you tell her how you feel and what you really think?" Carol asks. "Um, yeah," Amy says. "I can because she really listens and she understands, and she'll give me advice if I need advice, but sometimes I'll say things like: 'Just don't tell me what to do. Just listen.' "[117]

The Harvard Project researchers were somewhat surprised to see that mothers who maintain good relationships with their daughters teach imperfection—in a culture that begins to pressure and bully girls with an ideal of perfection that includes semi-starvation, teetering on awkward shoes, and always being nice and kind. "I think it's important to be honest with my children, to let them make mistakes and feel disappointment and to see that I am ambivalent about things and I make mistakes, too," one mother told them.[118]

"The girls in our study who keep their strong voices direct our attention to their mothers, but their mothers do not fit conventional images of good women," Brown and Gilligan write. Nawal, an Arabic girl at the Laurel School, told them her "big realization" came from putting her dark, curly-haired Arabic mother, wearing sandals and laden with jewelry, next to the ideal image of the demure blue-eyed blonde Nawal felt pressured to fit, and thinking and feeling until she sided with reality. Her mother actually asked her, "Do you really want me to be like everybody else?" Nawal's first impulse was to say yes, she did want her mother to affect the understated Waspy look of her friends' mothers. But "then I was like, 'Wait.' I thought about it and I tried to picture my mother like that. And I just couldn't," Nawal said. "It makes me shudder, because that's not her." Seeing how valuable her mother's authenticity was helped Nawal assert her own. "Devoting her senior speech to this subject, she voiced in the school's open assembly her resistance to American standards of beauty," Brown and Gilligan write. "Nawal cried after her speech, and her friends cried with her, and she felt, 'this weight was lifted and I finally said what I had to say to this school.' "[119]

Mothers and daughters in good relationships learn to see, hear, and love each other as they are, and not as approximations of an ideal or a stereotype, negative or positive. Asked to describe the ideal mother, Diana, an African-American eighth grader who has been labeled "at risk" by her public-school administrators, simply refuses: "I don't know. I don't know how I would describe an ideal mother. Nice . . . I don't know. I don't know what I should say about an ideal mother. Be like mine . . . she's not perfect, but she does the best she can . . . That's all I'd say, to do the best that they can do . . . No one's perfect."

What these girls value is not an approximation to an ideal but a real commitment to remaining authentic. "There's nothing we keep from each other," Diana says, "like if I was to like a boy, I could talk to her about it. Or if she was having trouble at work, she could talk to me about it, things like that. But we're real close . . . She always told me if I had anything to say, that I could come talk to her, and that's about how mainly we got to being so close."[120]

Barbara, a white ninth grader with an Irish background, also labeled "at risk," explicitly calls the idea of the ideal mother false. "Maybe I should describe the 'Leave It to Beaver' mother. The high heels, dressed up . . . That she is all perky and that, you know. She's happy when anything is wrong and she always has the answer for everything," Barbara tells her interviewer, describing an unreal TV sitcom mom who always has a smile on her face. "That's not true though, that's on a show," she explains. Her own mother is not an ideal but they are close, she says. "We get along good. We're like sisters, like. We tell each other everything, you know. Tell her, I tell her everything. Like I tell her the truth like, 'Oh Ma, I went out there.' And she'll like, 'Well, as long as I know where you're going,' you know, because she knows, like, wherever I am, I'm safe and all that, I'll call her wherever I am or something. So we have a good relationship, but we do have fights sometimes."[121]

Speaking at a Stone Center colloquium in 1998, Jessica Henderson Daniel, a child psychologist of African ancestry, names "the three Ps" of African-American mothering: "Praise, prepare, and protect." Black mothers need all three, she says, because "after you praise and you prepare, somebody's going to tell them that they're not smart." Black children need protection against the racist teachers who will insist that their black students live down to their prejudices. "It's almost raising children for warfare, psychological warfare," Daniel says.

Mothering, too comes down to holding, Surrey writes, in a relationship that is held or embedded in other relationships. The capacity of a mother and daughter " 'to act in relationship' . . . leads to the capacity to 'hold' the psychological reality of the other as part of an ongoing, continuous awareness beyond the momentary experience and to 'take the other into account' in all one's activities."[122] Ultimately, from this foundation in the very first relationship, holding becomes the basis for a new way of doing science, a standpoint that is a true alternative to objectivity—or subjectivity—in which the object of interest has the respect, attention, and luminous love due a subject.

Explaining her voice-centered method of doing research to second-year doctoral students at Harvard, Gilligan writes on one side of a blackboard:

autonomy

and on the other side she writes

> *dependence*
> *subjectivity*
> *intuition*

and draws a vertical line between them. She says this is one "axis." Then she puts up another axis:

connection	*disconnection*
living in community with	*dissociation*
	living out of relationship

with a vertical line between them.

"What is called connection in one framework is called dependence in the other. What is called autonomy in one framework is called disconnection in another," she says. "The question is not 'Can I be out of a framework?' but 'Which framework will I be in?' There's no way not to be in a framework."

She goes on writing. A traditional psychologist who wants to "impose a condition of non-relationality on your psychological inquiry" has an axis that looks like this:

relational	*non-relational*
nonscientific	*scientific*
subjective	*objective*
biased	

A relational psychologist who is studying the effects of relationship, never forgetting to include her own relationship to the people or groups she is studying, is on an axis that looks like this:

relational	*non-relational*
openness	*suspicious*
vulnerability	*guarded*

trust	*mistrustful*
	self-protective

The relational, voice-centered method that Carol and her students and colleagues have worked out begins with four questions about relationship, which they put to every theory, journal article, interview, or lecture they encounter, she says.

First, "Who is speaking? Whose voice is there? Every human being has a distinct voice, whether it is Freud or Erikson or Toni Morrison or Carol Gilligan, it is a person who has a distinct voice."

Next, "To whom?" Who is meant to receive this communication? Viennese doctors, all middle-class men? Psychoanalysts? American intellectuals curious about race?

"In what body?" Carol continues, "Which brings in the relationship of the voice to the body—is it speaking as if disembodied?" Is it mimicking Descartes or the latest scientific journal? Or does it admit it has feet of clay? And are they size five or ten?

"Telling what story about relationship? From what vantage point and what perspective? In what societal or cultural framework?"

"These are somewhat abstract questions," Carol admits. But the answers to them aren't, and "you can also hear the sound of the voice" in any piece of discourse, written or spoken, and know immediately, "is it speaking as if from a society and culture, or is it 'from nowhere,'" pretending it's no voice at all but just *the* truth.

"Objective" science uses relationships to gather knowledge about the participant who is not the scientist. "Objective" scientists draw conclusions from this knowledge, and then ignore the relationships and hold on to the conclusions, which are seen as the goal and product of science. The object of this science is to see or present information about something as though the knower had no relationship with the something, and as though the knower were not a particular person with a particular cultural history and bias. "Objective" science also assumes that the only other point of view is subjectivity: you can pay attention to another or you can pay attention to yourself. But the practice of "holding" represents a third standpoint: Bergman and Surrey's "we," the relationship.

On the relational axis, "to hold" as a scientific attitude, a way of knowing, means to stay in relationship, to hold the link between subject and object and assume a standpoint there, in the connection. Instead of experimenting and then concluding that something is or is not true, the "holding" scientist holds on to her or his experience of relationship with the subject and makes deductions in the context of that relationship. That scientist understands his or her experience to be rooted in the scientist's actual, unidealized, unique life history and point of view, and in one particular relationship between subject and object. No "held" conclusion is ever absolute or final because no relationship is ever finished or still. Knowledge comes out of a relationship that is changing and moving, and the scientist holds the knowledge for the sake of that relationship and uses it to foster growth on both sides of that and other relationships. In this sense, "held" scientific knowledge is always tentative, always recognized as a premature abridgment and simplified encoding of a highly complex experience of relationship.

Nonjudgmental, relational thinking moved into the sphere of science in many fields at once; the German philosopher Jürgen Habermas and his Frankfurt school call it hermeneutics and critical theory, and it can be found thriving in history, law, literature, and even biology and anthropology. Like Gilligan and the Stone Center theorists, critical theorists emphasize the political force of "objective science" that makes "social patterns such as extreme individualism, competitiveness, and poverty appear to be inevitable or natural," the feminist sociologist Joyce McCarl Nielsen writes.[123]

This new kind of political, relational thinking comes especially easily to Western women because of the way culture and politics treat women at this moment in history, the sociologist Marcia Westkott adds.

> The idea of grounding inquiry in concrete experience rather than in abstract categories is reflected in women's historical identification with the concrete everyday life of people and their survival needs. The idea of knowledge as an unpredictable discovery rather than a controlled outcome is reflected in women's historical exclusions from institutions, where planned rational control is the mode of operation, and in women's historical identification with domestic spheres which have been less rationally controlled or predictable.

Joyce Fletcher and the relational-cultural theorists of the Stone Center would add that women's readiness to "hold" knowledge and let their knowledge change comes from women's training in relational creativity and their excitement and expertise about uncovering the unknown and being able to handle surprises in relationships, which they are trained to approach as adventures that are healthy when they are moving and changing, and sick when they are static or stuck. "Holding" as a style of doing science is really about making empathy a part of empiricism.

"And finally, the idea of knowledge emerging from a self-other dialectic is reflected both in the historical exclusion of women from educational institutions where knowledge has been transmitted through books and lectures and in women's participation in societies and friendships where social knowledge has emerged from dialogue, a practice recently exemplified by women's consciousness-raising and support groups," Westkott wrote in "Feminist Criticism of the Social Sciences," an article that was published in the *Harvard Educational Review* two years after "In a Different Voice" and became a feminist classic in sociology as Gilligan's article did in psychology.[124]

Approaching psychological questions in an empathic way, with a community of fellow inquirers, brings the inquirer not into an objective standoff with an alien Other but into the relational state Carol and Normi talk about as "To Be." "The information is here amongst us in our relationship with each other in a way that it does not exist" when a subject tries to observe an "object" as if the subject had no relation to it, Normi Noel says that golden October day when we talk about her work with Carol and Annie Rogers. Using this relational way of learning by "holding," "the mining of this, the potential for it has been so profound, and the places I have come to thus far have been so extraordinary, I can't bear leaving it," Normi says. "When we leave each other on that deep, deep—it's like everyone's sort of waiting around for the other one to get back so we can start work again. I mean . . . as Carol would say, it's the Edge."

Normi reiterates how much better she thinks artists are than academics at finding the Edge and staying there and how lucky it is that Carol is so much of an artist. "If psychology didn't have an artist that entered in in that way, the world wouldn't have changed on its ear the way it has," Normi says. "But it's time—I mean—to beware what that world can do, and I'm really glad that Carol's out of Harvard."

There is a long silence here, the longest of the whole conversation. It touches the knotty issue of Gilligan's relationship to the institution that gave her work legitimacy while deeply opposing it. Year after year as I interviewed Carol, her feelings about Harvard ran from excitement about her students to distress about disparaging colleagues and their distress about her. She worked in "an often-toxic atmosphere" and got academic tenure in a Kafkaesque process where she found herself having to justify her work "in the very terms my work had revealed to be problematic" and to face review committees that were plodding and uncomprehending at best, malign and scheming at worst.

The university gave her a place to work and supported good research, and her students were her colleagues. "I love the students. I love the process of teaching," she would say. But for years she felt "completely isolated" by faculty members "who accepted me personally but taught psychology as if my work or even the problems addressed by my work did not exist." The message she got was "to stay because I drew so many students but not really to be part of the program" because she "wasn't doing 'psychology.' " I cannot remember a year when she didn't tell me at least once that she had decided to leave Harvard and plant her work in "a more resonant setting"—right up to 1998, when she settled into the endowed chair in gender studies at HGSE, Harvard's first, an endowment she had initiated, and then left for a year of writing at New York University.

"Why Harvard?" she asked herself once. "There's a deep ambition in me," she said. "I deeply, deeply care about the issues at the center of my work—whose voices are listened to and heard, the costs, collectively and personally, when people have to choose between having a voice and having relationships. It goes to the heart of democracy—and psychologically it is an incoherent choice. You can't have a voice without having relationships, and you can't have relationships without having a voice." She had taken on the questions of whether listening to women and girls or anyone else who has not been seen and heard in the dominant culture can count as psychological research, and whether a researcher can have an honest relationship with a research subject "rather than lying to discover 'the truth,' " she said.

"You have to repair the world," she said, speaking almost religiously. "You have to heal the world," and you have to do it in a place where you can change things. "If you're going to change things, you have to go where there's power," Carol said.

Carol found two kinds of power at Harvard: the dominant kind and the relational kind, in which she and her Harvard Project colleagues worked together so closely that "we left the culture for a while," Carol says, and made a community in "To Be." "Jerome Murphy, my dean, told me that I was 'running a school within a school,' " she says. The conflict between these two kinds of power, which are dedicated to almost opposite ends, has preoccupied all these relational psychologists since they started thinking together.

"My own working definition of power is *the capacity to produce a change*—that is, to move anything from point A or state A to point B or state B," Jean Miller wrote in 1982. "This can include even moving one's own thoughts or emotions, sometimes a very powerful act. It can also include acting to create movement in an interpersonal field as well as acting in larger realms such as economic, political or social arenas."

The relational world always operates in the same universe as the non-relational axis, the one on which power is aggression or a capacity to limit other people's capacity to change things. "There is enormous validity in women's *not* wanting to use power as it is presently conceived and used," Miller wrote, because it is not yet common or easy "to be powerful in ways that simultaneously enhance, rather than diminish, the power of others," outside of the private sphere of child rearing.

Using power to spread power "is a large and difficult prospect," Miller wrote. "It can appear naive or unreal even to talk this way. But the fact that it sounds unreal must not stop us! Once we recognize the undeniable truth that the world has been explained so far without the close observations of women's experience, it is easier to consider that seemingly 'unreal' possibilities can become real."[125]

"What's always stunned me about Carol is," Normi told me on one of those days when Carol kept herself going at Harvard by telling herself and her friends that she was going to exit, "I mean different women who've been heard in our world in our voices in different ways do this, but Carol, going in and out of 'To Be' and 'Not to Be,' she's like translator supreme. I've never heard translation like that before—

into patriarchese, from patriarchese. Being able to track jump, like a ballet dancer almost, but I could never understand how she did it, how she could sort of gird her loins to go back into that place again."

Asking her four questions about psychology—about its pioneers and heroes, and about its oversights and anomalies, realizing that she herself was an oversight and an anomaly—and holding her growing knowledge about the unseen and overlooked girls and women she has used as experiential subjects and asked to think about how they develop, Gilligan came up with what she calls "five true things." "Five psychological truths" she called them when she first wrote them down in her essay "Joining the Resistance."

The fourth one is really the basis of relational psychology: "The logic of the psyche is an associative logic—the free-falling logic of dreams, poetry and memory—as well as a formal logic of classification and control." Psyche is about "with": what goes with what, who goes with whom, what time or place is like what other time or place. Psyche is built on relationships and works by relationships.

Gilligan's fifth axiom is about psychological inquiry and is a kind of answer to the question implicit in her or Habermas's drawing of two axes of human knowledge: Which is better? This fifth rule is "One learns the answers to one's own questions." Cui bono? The question that Anne Forer, Kathie Sarachild, and the original radical feminists had asked as they started the first consciousness-raising groups. The question of who benefits and "who sets the terms of the debate," as the Boston activist Kip Tiernan puts it, has a huge shaping effect on what questions scientists ask.[126]

But Gilligan's first three psychological truths are not about good relationships at all. They concern another chapter in the story of relationships, one that is less fundamental but attracts much more attention—the one about broken relationships, separation, disconnection, dissociation, violence, and trauma.

6.
Disconnection

1. What is unvoiced or unspoken, because it is out of relationship, tends to get out of perspective and to dominate psychic life.

2. The hallmarks of loss are idealization and rage, and under the rage, immense sadness. ("To want and want and not to have.")

3. What is dissociated or repressed—known and then not known—tends to return, and return, and return.

—GILLIGAN, "JOINING THE RESISTANCE"

Once we begin to see not only the 'things' in the world but the 'connections' in the world—from defining and locating atoms by their relationship to each other to seeing the rain forest as the lungs of our planet; once we start to see not only the people, the men and boys and women and girls, but the relationships between them; once we start to shift our seeing from separate 'I's' and 'you's' to 'we's,' our whole world changes and we can never go back," Shem and Surrey write in *We Have to Talk*.[1]

One of the things we can't go back to is the notion that trauma is simply an injury to an arm or a leg—or a vagina or a cerebral cortex. Trauma is an injury to a relationship. Once you see—or, as Carol says, once you stop not seeing—that relationships are real, then you can see that psychological trauma is about breaking, betraying, hurting relationships. When relationships are broken or wounded, the wounds have common characteristics, and the healing of the wounds follows a certain pattern. Dissociation—the ability to sever thought from feeling, memory from conscious control, and even one aspect of personality from another—is part of that pattern. On a spectrum that ranges from absentminded "spacing out" to "losing time" and the disjunctions of dissociative identity disorder—"multiple personalities"—dissociative phenomena announce that psychological trauma has taken place and that a psyche is trying to get better. To psychological science, this is recent knowledge; but to poets and girls, it's common lore.

Before Jean Charcot, Pierre and Jules Janet, Josef Breuer, Sigmund Freud, and William James, people knew about the anguish doctors called hysteria because they suffered it and saw other people suffer. People made and appreciated art about it. In the sixteenth century, Shakespeare identified the cause of dissociation as traumatic psychological overload; Shakespeare's Gertrude describes Ophelia, singing and floating to her death, "as one incapable of her own distress."[2] Emily Dickinson, writing in about 1862, described dissociation unmistakably, almost diagnostically:

> *There is a pain—so utter—*
> *It swallows substance up—*
> *Then covers the Abyss with Trance—*
> *So Memory can step*
> *Around—across—upon it—*
> *As one within a Swoon—*
> *Goes safely—where an open eye—*
> *Would drop Him—Bone by Bone.*[3]

Dickinson knew the pain of dissociation starts with isolation. Dissociation is something you may have to do when you are left alone with pain. Jessie knows about that, too, or at least she knew when she talked to Lyn Brown, in the Harvard Project's Laurel School study, near the end of the twentieth century, at the age of eight. Something can happen that makes you feel disconnected both from the person who does that thing and, at least for the moment, from other people, too.

"Can you tell me about a time when something happened to you that you thought was unfair?" Brown asks Jessie.

"Sometimes my friends have friends over when I'm playing with them and they play with *them* and I feel left out, and I don't think that's fair," Jessie says.

We have met Jessie before, when she told Lyn how hard she worked to make friends again—how she realized that getting even, getting the same amount of power as her friends, was an essential part of making up. But the first part of Jessie's story was about feeling bad when her friends left her out. Jessie told her friends she'd just go home if they wouldn't play with her, and one of them told her, "Just go home."

"When that happens, do you continue to play with them anyway, or do you say . . ." Lyn speaks slowly, waiting for Jessie to fill in the blank.

"They don't really care," Jessie answers. "They don't really care. They just leave—they just don't talk to me. They whisper in each other's ear, saying things about me. I just don't like it."[4]

This kind of realistic paranoia is an old feeling, an old knowledge. A hundred years before Jessie, another voice we have heard before describes the crushing feeling of being apparently included but really, deliberately shut out: "Not long ago, Breuer made a big speech to the physicians' society about me, putting himself forward as a convert to sexual aetiology. When I thanked him privately for this, he spoiled my pleasure by saying, 'But all the same, I don't believe it.' "[5]

Sigmund Freud, a young Viennese neurologist, a Jew whose father was an unsuccessful wool merchant, had decided to take on what was seen as the major research challenge of his field at the time—hysteria, perhaps the most common and commonly misunderstood mental affliction of nineteenth-century women. He was writing to his friend Wilhelm Fliess—a physician who, it turned out, didn't really support him, either—about the fickle support he was getting from his senior colleague Josef Breuer, a popular and respected family doctor, on their joint work on the causes of hysteria.

Richard von Krafft-Ebing, the chairman of the psychiatry department at the University of Vienna and the man Freud most needed and wanted to impress, presided at the meeting, in late April 1896, when Freud declared the problem of the age was solved and he had solved it. Sexual trauma was the cause of hysteria! A few days later, Freud wrote to Fliess again. He wrote with bravado, bluffing cavalierly that having discovered the truth from his own clinical experience was enough for him and he could do very well, thank you, without the support of the dolts who refused to believe his epochal discovery because it was so socially embarrassing: "A lecture on the aetiology of hysteria at the Psychiatric Society met with an icy reception from the asses," Freud wrote, "and from Krafft-Ebing the strange comment: It sounds like a scientific fairy tale. And this after one has demonstrated to them a solution to a more than thousand-year-old problem, a 'source of the Nile.' They can all go to hell."[6]

Less than two weeks after telling Fliess that his colleagues could go to hell, Freud wrote his friend in a very different tone: "I am as isolated as you could wish me to be: the word has been given out to abandon me, and a void is forming around me."[7]

Nearly thirty years later, Freud wrote that he stopped going to medical society meetings at this time. "For more than 10 years after my separation from Breuer I had no followers. I was completely isolated. In Vienna, I was shunned; abroad no notice was taken of me," he wrote.[8] Although this isolation was painful, it allowed him to take credit later for being the lonely giant on whose shoulders his followers stood, since he could claim that in the beginning of psychoanalysis, "I stood alone and had to do all the work myself."[9]

This other side of the story of the discovery and description of dissociation is the side of the doctors, the side of psychiatry and nosology, the science of naming and classifying pain. It took psychiatry a couple of decades longer than it took Emily Dickinson to begin to see and name the psychological aftermath of trauma. And the doctors, who did the observing, listening, and naming, were no more immune to the relational politics of you're-my-friend/you're-not-my-friend than Jessie, the second grader, or than the patients, almost all young women, whom these nineteenth-century doctors tried to treat.

In the mid-1880s, the French psychiatric diagnostician Jean Charcot publicly theorized that traumatic events could produce hysterical symptoms. Charcot taught both Pierre Janet and, briefly, Freud at the huge public mental hospital in Paris, the Salpêtrière.

By 1886, ten years before Freud's speech to the doubters in Vienna, Janet recognized that traumatic events themselves didn't cause hysteria, since people often lived for years after a trauma before developing symptoms. Janet realized that the memory—or rather, the *lack* of controllable and integrated memory—of trauma caused hysterical symptoms. Janet said some people who had been traumatized experienced "a genuine inability to cognize what is going on in the mind and express it to oneself," so these people couldn't call up memories of what had happened. Amnesiac victims might experience symptoms—paralysis, blindness, muteness, fainting fits, trancelike repetitive actions, or the prostrate arching of the back commonly seen as typifying hysteria—instead of memories, Janet found.[10] By 1889, he had theorized that his patients produced their hysterical symptoms in a way that "bypasses ideation" and produces "psychological automatism." Janet called this automatic, involuntary response to trauma "psychic disaggregation," or dissociation, and said it separates traumatic memories from other, accessible memories so that traumatic memories cannot normally be recalled.[11] Traumatic memory could become disease-producing or "morbific because it was dissociated," Janet wrote. "It existed in isolation, apart from the totality of the sensations and the ideas which comprised the subject's personality: it developed in isolation, without control and without counterpoise."[12]

Unlike Freud, Janet never gave up his conviction that psychically segregated, dissociated memories of trauma produce mental illness. He never stopped listening to the stories of trauma his hysterical patients invariably had to tell once they understood that this doctor was actually listening to them. Janet came to believe that memories of trauma had to be integrated into a whole life story to cure a dissociating patient. But he never really understood how important betrayal and broken relationships were in trauma, and how important intimacy and trusting relationships were in healing.

As early as the 1890s, when Freud came up with his theory that traumatic memory caused hysteria, Freud insisted that the severity of the trauma, and not, as Janet argued (like Charcot before him), some inherited tendency to mental degeneracy, made the difference between traumatized people who became hysterical and traumatized people who stayed sane or recovered. But neither the Janet brothers, nor Freud, nor Breuer wrote about the part relationships played in the genesis, onset, treatment, and cure of hysteria—relationships to people who caused traumas, relationships to witnesses and intimates, and relationships to the doctors who tried to cure it.

These psychiatric pioneers never publicly talked about their work on hysteria as political, but their work was part of a political process of liberation and democratization that moved from Europe to the United States and back again from the eighteenth-century Enlightenment to the twentieth-century civil rights movement, the anti–Vietnam War movement, and the second wave of the women's liberation movement. As children, Freud and Breuer experienced political subordination that they expected to continue all their lives, and then they saw their subordinate legal status just dissolve. In 1848, when Breuer was six, male Jews in the Austrian Empire were first allowed to own property, to forgo harsh special taxes, and to hold office, including university professorships. In 1867, when Freud was eleven, male Jews in the Austrian Empire attained full civil rights. It was not hard for Breuer and Freud to sympathize with other powerless people—with women, for instance. They had been there. On the other hand, they weren't there any longer, and women were. As men, they had been admitted to a class women couldn't enter—a class whose members had the privilege of learning and ultimately practicing medicine, for instance. By the 1880s, half the doctors and lawyers in Vienna were Jewish men—a far greater proportion than would be graduating from professional schools in New York with Jean Baker Miller sixty years later, for from the 1880s on, the liberal tide receded, and European Jews began to feel the backlash that became Nazi genocide in the 1930s.

So Breuer took Freud under his wing in a world that had only just started accepting Jewish doctors. But Freud, fourteen years younger than his mentor, played the role for Breuer that Jean Miller played in her group: Freud pushed Breuer to publish a record of his remarkable work with Bertha Pappenheim, whom Breuer disguised as "Anna O." in his case study of her.

Diagnosed hysterical at twenty-one because she showed several of the kinds of psychosomatic symptoms associated with hysteria, Pappenheim threw things when people told her she was lying, complained of "losing" long periods of time, spoke in four languages, and didn't remember when she was speaking English what she had said when she was speaking French or Italian. She lost her voice entirely, focused so narrowly that she could only make out one flower at a time in a bouquet, and failed to recognize the most familiar people. "I was the only person whom she always recognized when I came in, so long as I was talking to her she was always in contact with things and lively, except for the sudden interruptions caused by one of her hallucinatory 'absences,' " Breuer wrote a decade later. "Absences" was the word that Charcot and the Janet brothers had chosen for the blank states in which hysterical patients sometimes seemed to be sealed off in another world.

Breuer treated Pappenheim by asking her when her symptoms started. She could not remember or often even respond to him at first, but he found that in her self-induced trance states young Bertha could remember. While she was telling the story—under hypnosis—of how each symptom started, the symptom would get worse. But each symptom disappeared after she finished recalling to him and to herself the shock that started it.[13] Partly because hypnosis seemed to be the key to helping patients in and out of "absences" at will—at least at the doctor's will—Breuer chose the phrase "hypnoid states" for the waking trances in which hysterical patients could remember things they could not remember during normal waking awareness. His idea was that trauma might push anyone into such a state and that when it did, patients produced symptoms like Pappenheim's instead of memories. *"A tendency to such a dissociation, and with it the emergence of abnormal states of consciousness (which we shall bring together under the term 'hypnoid') is the basic phenomenon of this neurosis,"* Breuer and Freud wrote in the mid-1890s.[14] The trauma that caused this "splitting of consciousness" might involve physical injury. But it was the emotional reactions to trauma that caused hysterical symptoms and had to be recalled in order for the symptoms to disappear, Breuer found. "Each individual symptom in this complicated case was taken separately in hand: all the occasions on which it had appeared were described in reverse order, starting before the time when the patient became bed-ridden and going back to the event which had led to its first appearance. When this had been described, the symptom was permanently removed," Breuer wrote.[15] Pappenheim told him the story of her symptoms, and the symptoms went away.

Freud became a doctor in 1881, as it happens on the very day Bertha Pappenheim got out of bed for the first time since Breuer and she had begun inventing the treatment Freud would later claim as the first psychoanalysis. Pappenheim saw Breuer for the last time more than a year later, on the day she revealed to her beloved and trusted Dr. Breuer—who had visited her so frequently that his wife had become jealous—her delusion that she was carrying his child. Although he had treated her intensively for two years, making house calls as often as three times a day, Breuer never went near his patient again. He completely dissociated himself from the patient who helped him discover dissociation and made her famous under a pseudonym of his choosing. Pappenheim suffered a grave relapse after he cut her off. She became a morphine addict, thanks to the methods of the doctor who treated her after Breuer stopped. Freud later said that when Breuer heard she had been admitted to a sanatorium, he told Freud he hoped she would die and be released from her suffering.[16] But whatever we may think of Breuer's scandalized flight from Anna O., it was Breuer, not Freud, who "got" psychological dissociation and who seems to have been the better clinical listener. Freud's nephew Ernst Hammerschlag explained the difference in the two men's self-presentation this way: "When you saw Freud, you felt awe. When you saw Breuer, you felt warm and confident."[17]

Breuer did not mention his sudden abandonment of Anna O. in the account of the treatment Freud persuaded him to write ten years later. In fact, Breuer lied. He insisted that, unlike in all of Freud's hysterical patients, who had developed their symptoms after sexual traumas, "the element of sexuality was astonishingly undeveloped in" Anna O. and she never showed any signs of sexual interest or history.[18] So even though he put his name on the book in which Freud described sexual trauma as the cause of hysteria, Breuer said in *Studies on Hysteria* that he had found no sexual trauma at the bottom of his prize patient's hysteria. Fifteen years later, he was telling the same story, still insisting that Pappenheim's case "proves that a fairly severe case of hysteria can develop, flourish and be resolved without having a sexual basis."[19] Breuer could never acknowledge that Pappenheim had had sexual feelings about him, far less observe those feelings and her imaginary pregnancy as signs of a troubling, sexualized relationship she might have had with someone else.

Freud, for his part, had come to believe that memories of sexual traumas, mostly from childhood, caused hysteria, but he didn't go along with Breuer's ideas about dissociation. And after Breuer dissociated himself from Freud, because he couldn't bring himself to believe that sexual abuse was common enough to cause all hysteria, Freud dropped both hypnosis and Breuer's ideas about "hypnoid states" or dissociations. Working alone, Freud began to reconceptualize consciousness, what we know we think and feel. He stopped thinking of consciousness phenomenologically, as a stream of accessible or inaccessible memories and experience, and reconceived it as a mental machine that protected itself from trauma by erecting various "defenses," which could then "resist" the intrusion of reminders or questions about trauma or memory and "repress" any painful knowledge that had managed to slip by the defenses. So even though he put his name on the book in which Breuer described it, Freud actually said in *Studies on Hysteria* that he had never seen "hypnoid" hysteria.[20] Freud also lied in this first book about hysteria, written with Breuer. He asserted that the trauma that began hysteria was always sexual abuse, and he named as the perpetrators nannies, governesses, uncles, and occasionally older siblings. But he admitted something quite different to Fliess in a letter of 1897, and he repeated it in his autobiographical essay of 1925: all of the women patients who lost their hysterical symptoms when they told him about sexual trauma had named their fathers as perpetrators, he wrote.[21] According to Freud's first patients, traumatic memories of father-daughter incest caused hysteria, but Freud did not mention this etiology in the book that he hoped would solve the riddle of the illness.

Like Jean Baker Miller and Judith Lewis Herman with their first women patients—and like Carol Gilligan and Lyn Brown with the first girls they listened to, or like Mary Belenky and her colleagues and the women they interviewed for *Women's Ways of Knowing*—Freud, Janet, and Breuer collaborated with the young women who were their first patients and research subjects. With them, Freud could begin to know things about suffering that the methodology he was trained to use as an up-to-date psychiatrist near the end of the nineteenth century made it all but impossible to learn.

"We recommended the continuation of systematic kneading and faradization of the sensitive muscles, regardless of the resulting pain, and I reserved to myself treatment of her legs with high tension electric currents, in order to be able to keep in touch with her."[22] There is

Sigmund Freud's voice—or not quite his voice, since this is Freud writing to colleagues again, but a bit earlier, in the Vienna of 1893. He had left neurology for psychiatry because he thought he would make more money in psychiatry. He had a young family to support. Before that switch, he had switched from animal to human neurology for the same reason. In his notes about faradization, Freud writes about one of the only ways a psychiatrist could "keep in touch" with a patient in 1892. He had guilty dreams about these machines, which dealt electric shocks to any part of a patient except the brain, where psychiatrists deliver them today; Freud felt that faradization wasn't effective, and yet he was charging his patients—a sad pun—for it.

Freud called this particular patient "Elisabeth von R." in the case study he wrote about her. He was thirty-six and she was twenty-four when he began treating her for hysterical pains in her legs in 1892, ten years after Breuer dropped Bertha Pappenheim. "In particular, she seemed to take quite a liking to the painful shocks produced by the high tension apparatus, and the stronger these were, the more they seemed to push her own pains into the background." He stopped shocking her legs soon after he started. But when he wrote about her treatment the following year, he claimed great things for it, calling it "the first full-length analysis of a hysteria."[23]

"I want to talk about Freud": Carol Gilligan's voice now—on the tape of her adolescence course that I am listening to, a hundred years after Freud wrote about how much Elisabeth von R. enjoyed the pain he administered to her. "I feel like that's an *F*-word," Carol says. "There are two *F*-words not usually said in the same place—that's 'Freud' and 'feminism.' I'm really concerned when the world—the intellectual world, the literary world—becomes cordoned off."

Gilligan says that for a brief, shining moment—the moment that some of Freud's colleagues never forgave him for and that Breuer backed away from him for—the young, impecunious, but enormously ambitious Sigmund Freud listened to women, listened to Elisabeth von R., and heard "relational truths which are . . . fundamentally upsetting," truths about incest and thwarted ambition.

"To listen to women's voices is going to make it impossible for Freud to be in connection with the culture he lives in. It's an incredible thing to read this history and come back a hundred years later, because we're here again." Once again, our culture is saying we can't talk about the epidemic of incest and family violence, or we can only talk about it out of relationship, as though it has nothing to do with power or culture but is something like a virus that can be isolated and cured in a petri dish. "But Freud discovered that whatever is taken out of relationship, whatever becomes unspeakable, goes out of knowledge and dominates psychic life," Gilligan says. And to let the unspeakable back into relationships, back into knowledge, "means the world has to change," she says. "Freud gets caught in exactly the position that women are in—and other groups"—today, Gilligan says. "And he solves it by giving up relationship with women for the sake of relationships."

Here, telling a story about Freud and Elisabeth von R., whose real name was Ilona Weiss, Gilligan introduces her class to the paradox that Jean Baker Miller and she have seen at the heart of relationships in a culture that idealizes the non-relational. Freud later saw the story of Oedipus and the riddle of the Sphinx, desire versus power, at the heart of human misery. For Jean and Carol, the riddle at the heart of pain is "giving up relationship for the sake of relationships." By relationships, Carol means some idealized or conventional form of relationship that actually has no life or honesty but has the form, the look, of relationship. And this is what she says Freud eventually did in his relationships with his first women patients: he stopped listening to them, gave up honest and equal relationships with them, gave up the mutuality Carol feels was the healing factor for Elisabeth von R., and started telling *them* to listen to *him*. He traded listening for instructing so that he could preserve his relationship with the Viennese medical establishment, go on practicing psychiatry in Vienna, get his coveted professorship, and support his growing family in a world where his wife could not possibly work for payment, first of all because he would never have allowed it.

But when Freud was treating Ilona Weiss, his treatments were still relational, Carol says. In fact, early on, she says, "Freud makes an incredible decision. This is 1892. He decides that her physical symptoms have a psychological cause," a cause that lies somewhere in the history of her relationships and her reactions to them. It took one hundred years to come back to it. "It's very interesting to ask why this turned out to be an idea that basically disappeared" and is under assault yet again,

Gilligan says. And then she indicates one reason why the idea of psychological, relational causes is so hard for professionals trained in the Western tradition that began in Greece. Freud himself, writing in 1892, complains that it was difficult to get into a conversation with his patient about her feelings and memories.

"All he's doing now is sitting with somebody, and he's saying, 'This is one of the hardest things I've ever done.' Basically what he's saying is that to stay in relationship with someone is far harder than to treat them with all this machinery and so forth and so on. Relationships are not cost-effective, except that they work. It takes a long time. They're not replicable"—you can never repeat them exactly or know exactly what is going to emerge from them because they have to be created one by one, each different, at every moment. No one can control a relationship because "it involves two people," Gilligan says.

"So you can't package it," and you can't know beforehand what is going to come out of any relationship or guarantee results like a chemist repeating an experiment with known elements. "Freud had to not know. He had to stay in darkness. So all this training that says, you know, 'Know it. Know the answer. What's this? What's this?'—all the need for control and everything else. He had to let go and stay in a process of relationship, which I think Freud sustains for this one case, and then it really is too hard, and his voice changes, and the voice of psychiatry changes, and so forth, and a century goes by before we come back to this place." After Elisabeth von R./Ilona Weiss, Freud moved on to Dora, and there we see him firmly telling his patient what she is experiencing, rather than listening to and with her, Carol says.

Freud admired Ilona Weiss. And after he lists all the machines he used on her as a way of convincing his colleagues that he was as hard-nosed as any of them, he admits he admired her—which is revolutionary for a doctor talking about a hysteric. Jean Charcot, in France, had already revolutionized the understanding of hysteria by anatomizing it into types and showing men as well as women had it. But Freud bucked Charcot and Janet to insist that his patient shared "the features which one meets with so frequently in hysterical people and which there is no excuse for regarding as a consequence of degeneracy: her giftedness, her ambition, her moral sensibility, her excessive demand for love, which, to begin with, found satisfaction in her family, and the independence of her nature which went beyond the feminine ideal and found expression in a considerable amount of obstinacy, pugnacity, and reserve."[24]

Gilligan says Freud's first question about the patient he calls Fräulein Elisabeth is crucial: "Is Fräulein Elisabeth aware of the precipitating cause of her illness?" The question is important because his relationship with her will be very different depending on the answer. "And in this instance he says yes," though in later cases he says no and moves back into a more dominating, doctor-knows-best mode. After listening to her intently, he comes to believe she knows, but he has to infer the answer, since Freud, like the psychiatrists of the 1970s, does not include a direct question about sexual or physical abuse as part of his intake interview. In this case, Freud realizes that Fräulein Elisabeth knows something she can't admit she knows—even to him or perhaps to herself. Knowing it by herself would be too painful. She needs a companion, someone in relationship with her who can come to know with her the things she cannot bear to know in isolation. And Freud, as the doctor, has to depend on this need of hers, because he "can only know as far as she comes to know, and she comes to know because he is with her, as opposed to a subordinate-dominant psychology, where the subordinate comes because the dominant possesses greater knowledge and so forth"—Carol takes a big breath—"which is much easier to do."

Gradually, Carol says, Freud begins to listen for Fräulein Elisabeth's voice, just as Gilligan and her colleagues listen for voices when they're interviewing girls or replaying tapes of interviews. Freud notices that "her painful legs began to 'join in the conversation' during our analyses": when they would discuss painful memories, the pain in her legs would get worse, adding its two cents, and when they finished the conversation, the pain would subside.[25]

He realizes that her memories are coming up in an order that is leading to a secret she is keeping from herself and him. "He follows her associations," Gilligan says. "Her associations, he begins to think, will lead toward what has been split off or separated, toward what she knows. The human psyche wants to be in relationship, so what is split off moves toward relationship." As it happens, Freud thinks he realizes what Ilona knows and doesn't know she knows before she realizes this knowledge herself. "Her love, Freud says, had become separated from her knowledge. She could not know that she loved her brother-in-law," Gilligan explains, because that seemed to her a betrayal of her dead sister, who had been his wife.

It is hard, listening to Carol's lecture and sorting through the volumes of Freud, to be sure that Freud really got it. It is hard to believe that his idea that Ilona loved her brother-in-law was right. Too much of the work of this relational movement in psychology has gone to show that our bodies encode memories as physical symptoms in a fairly simple language: that if Ilona's legs really hurt, then someone—and not just an idea about loving her dead sister's husband—may well have really hurt her. Perhaps it was her father, who died of heart failure shortly before her sister died and left her nephew motherless. Years later, Ilona Weiss herself told her grown daughter that she remembered Freud as "just a young, bearded nerve specialist they sent me to" who tried "to persuade me that I was in love with my brother-in-law, but that wasn't really so." It's hard to dismiss Ilona's own words, even though they come thirdhand, through her daughter and through Freud's biographer Peter Gay.[26] On the other hand, at the time of treatment, Freud recorded her saying, "Now he is free again; now I can be his wife," Carol reminds us.

And it is not hard to feel, reading Freud's affectionate summary of his work with Ilona, that his relationship with this young woman healed her, even if he didn't get everything right. When she denies his suggestion that she loves her brother-in-law, he tries to tell her that she's not responsible for her feelings; the fact that she put herself through so much pain on account of them certainly says she's moral, he tells her. Then he goes to see Ilona's mother and asks if her relationship with the brother-in-law might not be supported somehow, but because this brother-in-law has been less than brotherly to Ilona's other brother-in-law, in addition to reasons of health and finance, her mother says the match is impossible. Freud then encourages Ilona's mother to be to her daughter the kind of confidant he has been. When her mother tries to begin this new relationship by telling Ilona what Freud has told her, Ilona is furious that he has let her mother into their doctor-patient relationship, and her pains begin again. But Freud, as Gilligan says, has confidence that the relationship will hold, and he is right. Later Ilona sends him a message that she is better and will return to him, but she never goes back. "From Freud's point of view, this is a loss," Gilligan says. The young psychiatrist allows himself to feel sad that this intelligent and vital young patient has moved on into her life, away from his. And when he gets a chance to go to a dance he has heard she will attend, he takes it. "I did not allow the opportunity to escape me of seeing my former patient whirl past in a lively dance," he writes.[27] This pleasure—aesthetic, affectionate, relational—is a far cry from the pleasure they began with, when the young psycho-neurologist introduced himself by zapping her pain-filled legs and she liked it.[28]

Studies on Hysteria was well reviewed in England. In France, Pierre Janet welcomed it as a confirmation of his own findings. In America, William James remembered it a decade later as one of a handful of studies in French, English, or German that revolutionized psychology at the end of the nineteenth century.[29] But in Vienna, Freud and Breuer's book simply disappeared. In their own country, the prophets were shunned. Breuer ultimately dropped Freud, too—much more gently but no less finally than he had dropped Pappenheim. And Freud, famously now, dropped his scandalous idea that memories of sexual trauma caused hysteria. The young Freud was just making his way in his new profession, convinced he was destined for greatness; three years after he got his medical degree, he burned some of his papers to tweak his image for the biographers he was sure would want to immortalize him. A man with such ambition could not get along in isolation any more than a second-grade girl can. When his professional colleagues sent him to Coventry for saying that sexual abuse caused hysteria, his voice changed, and gradually so did his position, and so within a few short years he came to a conclusion his colleagues could accept: women's stories of sexual abuse were fantasies, not memories. Women had made these fantasies up as children because they secretly desired incest. Ostensibly, many of his colleagues didn't like this formulation any better than the first one: Why talk dirty at all? they seemed to wonder. But now they let Freud get ahead.

Seventy years later, Jeffrey Moussaieff Masson, a young Freudian analyst whose high ambitions, like Freud's own, were more for research than for clinical work, rediscovered Freud's trauma theory and the story of its abandonment. And the same thing happened to him. Masson set out to conquer the psychoanalytic world with his discovery, and

that world turned on him as a traitor and cast him out. The acknowl-
edgments in *The Assault on Truth*, the book Masson wrote about his
discoveries, are a catalog of broken relationships. He thanks his former
wife, his former employers, his former colleagues, and his former
friends.[30]

Masson's take is that Freud was a great man who betrayed women
for the sake of his ambition. But Judith Lewis Herman takes a more
understanding, relational view of Freud:

> Freud's . . . retreat from the study of psychological trauma has
> come to be viewed as a matter of scandal. His recantation has been
> vilified as an act of personal cowardice. Yet to engage in this kind of
> ad hominem attack seems like a curious relic of Freud's own era, in
> which advances of knowledge were understood as Promethean acts
> of solitary male genius. No matter how cogent his arguments or
> how valid his observations, Freud's discovery could not gain accept-
> ance in the absence of a political and social context that would sup-
> port the investigation of hysteria, wherever it might lead. Such a
> context had never existed in Vienna and was fast disappearing in
> France. Freud's rival Janet, who never abandoned his traumatic
> theory of hysteria and who never retreated from his hysterical pa-
> tients, lived to see his works forgotten and his ideas neglected.[31]

Freud listened to women, as Gilligan puts it, early in his career,
when he was still more a son than a father; he began to listen to his
colleagues when he was more a conventional Viennese patriarch than a
son.

Medicine only "discovered" child abuse—bone-shattering, con-
cussing, sometimes fatal physical abuse—in 1962, when C. Henry
Kempe and four other American doctors published the article "The
Battered-Child Syndrome" in *The Journal of the American Medical Association*. Part of the syndrome, the doctors said, was doctors' "reluctance" to read X-rays showing signs of repeated trauma and see signs of
possible abuse. Here was Darwin not seeing signs of glaciation in the
ice-scarred valley; here was Freud believing and then not believing stories of incest in the hysterias of his first patients. "This reluctance stems
from the emotional unwillingness of the physician to consider abuse as

part of the child's difficulty," the American doctors wrote. "Physicians have great difficulty both in believing that parents could have attacked their children and in undertaking the essential questioning of parents on this subject. Many physicians find it hard to believe that such an attack could have occurred and they attempt to obliterate such suspicions from their minds, even in the face of obvious circumstantial evidence. The reason for this is not clearly understood."[32]

It was only in the 1970s that historians of childhood like Lloyd DeMause realized that the history of American childhood contained a history of child abuse. In the 1970s, the sociologists Murray Straus and later Richard Gelles, working at the University of New Hampshire, learned from some of their earliest studies of American family violence that most Americans received their first physical punishment—usually from parents or close family members—at a very young age. Almost a generation later, the 1998 National Violence Against Women Survey of sixteen thousand women and men documents that more than half of the women and two-thirds of the men had been physically assaulted, almost all by men. (Six times as many women as men had been raped.)[33] Violence enters the lives of most Americans before they can talk, most often at home, from the source of food, love, warmth, and protection, and it remains a feature of life at all stages. Only in the twentieth century did psychiatrists and psychologists actually think to trace the mental and emotional harm that lingers after the physical wounds of violence have become scars. The terrible casualties of World War I made it almost impossible not to see this lasting damage.

The front lines of the Great War, as it was called in Europe, presented European doctors with deaths and wounds on a mass scale that evoked the century's revolutionary manufacturing technique, the assembly line. And the emotional carnage was as shocking. "According to one estimate," which was suppressed at the time to keep morale up, Herman writes, "mental breakdowns represented 40 percent of British battle casualties" in World War I.[34]

The British psychoanalyst W.H.R. Rivers wrote in 1919, "Perhaps the most striking feature of the war from the medical point of view has been the enormous scale upon which its conditions have produced functional nervous disorders, a scale far surpassing any previous war."[35] Rivers, who is celebrated in the contemporary novelist Pat Barker's *Re-*

generation trilogy, picked up the thread of post-traumatic dissociative mental illness and followed it where Freud and Janet never went. Men were sent back from the trenches to Rivers's psychiatric wards lame, mute, blind, racked with exhaustion they clung to in terror because sleep might bring another dream. "The nightmare of war-neurosis generally occurred at first as a faithful reproduction of some scene of warfare, usually some experience of a particularly horrible kind or some dangerous event, such as a crash from an aeroplane," Rivers wrote.

> A characteristic feature of this variety of dream is that it is accompanied by an affect of a peculiarly intense kind, often with a special quality described as different from any known in waking life. The dream ends suddenly by the patient waking in a state of acute terror directly continuous with the terror of the dream and with all the physical accompaniments of extreme fear, such as profuse sweating, shaking, and violent beating of the heart. Often the dream recurs in exactly the same form night after night, and even several times in one night, and a sufferer will often keep himself from sleeping again after one experience from dread of its repetition.[36]

Rivers's wounded patients were clearly dreaming, often exactly replaying, traumatic events that had happened to them very recently. "Moreover, it has become clear that in the vast majority of cases the morbid processes which have been set up by shock or strain are not connected with the sexual instinct, but depend on the awakening of suppressed tendencies connected with the still more fundamental instinct of self-preservation," Rivers wrote.[37] Rivers, who famously and successfully treated the poet Siegfried Sassoon's shell shock, was a humane scientist who had the courage and empathic skills to connect with traumatized soldiers and the learning and intelligence to make a careful clinical study of their disabilities. Fascinated by anthropology early in his career, he published and taught both as an anthropologist and as a psychiatrist. Like Freud and Janet, he didn't understand the importance of his own relationships with patients and felt that once a patient understood what was wrong or remembered during daytime the trauma that had been causing his nightmares, his problems should be over. But unlike Freud and Janet, who encouraged patients to suspend other relationships during treatment as a way of increasing their own influence, Rivers was the first psychiatrist to understand and teach that a patient's relationships with comrades—a soldier's trench-mates or the soldiers of his own unit—could be healing. He also assumed but never especially noted that much of what created mental trauma for the men he saw was relational: for instance, a pilot who had witnessed other deaths from a distance without breaking down became unable to function after he was injured in a crash in which his co-pilot was killed, and a physician broke down after weeks or months of having to see and attempt to treat horrific wounds in a field hospital where he knew most of his patients could never recover, and came to feel that rather than go on practicing medicine, even on civilians, he would have to kill himself.

By World War II, American psychiatrists had recognized that shell shock was neither a physical reaction to exploding shells, as its first observers had thought, nor a cowardly collapse due to some learned or congenital weakness (like the weaknesses and defects nineteenth-century psychiatrists looked for in hysterical women), but a psychological trauma that was the direct result of exposure to combat. Given long enough exposure, shell shock was inevitable:

> A year after the war ended, two American psychiatrists, J. W. Appel and G. W. Beebe, concluded that 200–240 days in combat would suffice to break even the strongest soldier: "There is no such thing as 'getting used to combat' . . . Each moment of combat imposes a strain so great that men will break down in direct relation to the intensity and duration of their exposure. Thus psychiatric casualties are as inevitable as gunshot and shrapnel wounds in warfare."[38]

Military psychiatry rediscovered Rivers's two main teachings: relationships with troop-mates could help heal and reintegrate victims of combat stress; and recalling memories of combat trauma, often involving the death or mutilation of buddies, and making it part of a soldier's known life story about himself could cure disabling symptoms. Military psychiatrists used these insights and quick interventions—hypnosis or drugs like Amytal—to speed recovery of traumatic memories and send soldiers back to their units fast. It was as though psychiatrists were only interested in seeing the truth about combat stress in order to keep soldiers active in an ongoing war. Once the war was over, "the familiar process of amnesia set in once again," Herman writes.[39]

Psychiatry seemed to have the same kind of recurrent amnesia about women and sexual trauma. "Throughout the history of psychiatry, there have been many male liberators—Pinel, Conolly, Charcot, Freud, Laing—who claimed to free madwomen from the chains of their confinement to obtuse and misogynistic medical practice," the feminist historian Elaine Showalter writes. "Yet when women are spoken for but do not speak for themselves, such dramas of liberation become only the opening scene of the next drama of confinement."[40]

"I am not aware of a single account of sexual abuse by a woman published during the nineteenth century. Who in the nineteenth century would permit its publication?" Masson resonates. "It was not until the rise of the women's movement in the 1970s that such cases could be openly discussed."[41]

But in the 1970s, the widely popular antiwar movement backed up the experience of soldiers, and a women's movement supported the experience of women. Now, for the first time, women who had been traumatized by rape, incest, or domestic violence and men who had been traumatized in combat began to create spaces that were free from the old way of seeing shell shock as cowardice, or physical abuse as education, or sexual abuse as something akin to—and indeed training for—prostitution. Mass movements for human rights were at last able to budge the conventional resistance to seeing the diseases of subordination that Freud, Rivers, Abram Kardiner, and the authors of "The Battered-Child Syndrome" found so pervasive and yet so hard to grasp. Vietnam veterans who came home and organized against the war formed "rap groups" that raised their consciousness about combat stress around the same time that women were getting at the very first data about the pandemic of rape, incest, and child sexual abuse in their own consciousness-raising groups. "The US Army [in Vietnam] was like a mother who sold out her kids to be raped by [their] father," a veteran told Jonathan Shay for his study of combat stress *Achilles in Vietnam: Combat Trauma and the Undoing of Character*.[42] And the nurses and sociologists who set out to study the effects of rape noticed that the symptoms they saw in rape victims were like the symptoms that veterans returning from combat complained of.

Bessel van der Kolk, a young Dutch psychiatrist working at Veterans Administration hospitals in Boston, listened to Vietnam veterans and realized, as Rivers had fifty years before, that the trauma they had suffered in combat was "a process of rupture of relationships between men," van der Kolk, now a professor at Boston University, says. In 1980, Vietnam veterans' postwar battle to get treatment for the terrors, addictions, depressions, and other agonies that the atrocities and betrayals of the war had left them with finally moved the American Psychiatric Association to make "post-traumatic stress disorder" an official diagnosis. PTSD, as the diagnosis quickly came to be called, was now something a hospital could treat and an insurance company could pay a hospital to treat, even in peacetime. Van der Kolk found himself describing the same kinds of phenomena that Herman addressed in the book about incest she was compiling at the Bunting Institute in Cambridge. "We very shyly started to talk to each other, because politically we came from very different angles," van der Kolk says. But they had arrived at the same place.

Herman writes:

> Only after 1980, when the efforts of combat veterans had legitimated the concept of post-traumatic stress disorder, did it become clear that the psychological syndrome seen in survivors of rape, domestic battery, and incest was essentially the same as the syndrome seen in survivors of war. The implications of this insight are as horrifying in the present as they were a century ago: the subordinate condition of women is maintained and enforced by the hidden violence of men. There is war between the sexes. Rape victims, battered women, and sexually abused children are its casualties. Hysteria is the combat neurosis of the sex war.[43]

Herman was among the first to see a connection between incest and prostitution. In the first edition of the book she wrote based on the research she and Hirschman continued to do on incest, Herman saw that the relational trauma of father-daughter incest was a rite of passage that prepared victimized daughters for prostitution. In committing incest, "the father in effect forces the child to pay with her body for affection and care which should be freely given. In so doing, he destroys the protective bond between parent and child and initiates the child into prostitution," she wrote.[44] Herman's theory was shocking. But over the next decades, as researchers began to compile social and psychological data to test it, her theory held up. "Men appear to be selecting previously victimized females for further . . . victimization," the sociologist Diana Russell concluded in 1986 from the results of her careful survey of 930 randomly chosen women and their histories of sexual abuse.[45] Writing in 2000, in an essay for a new edition of *Father-Daughter Incest*, Herman quotes one of the many researchers now studying incest; the researcher interviewed a pimp, who told him incest victims made the best prostitutes: "Beauty, yes. Sexual expertise, somewhat. That can be taught easier than you think. What is important above all is obedience. And how do you get obedience? You get obedience if you get women who have had sex with their fathers, their uncles, their brothers—you know, someone they love and fear to lose so that they do not dare to defy."[46]

Herman published *Father-Daughter Incest* in 1981, reporting on a study of forty incest victims. Her informants said they felt like outsiders, always abnormal. They married early—nearly half were pregnant as adolescents—but almost all of them didn't like marriage, and most didn't like sex. Most of them idealized men, but a fourth married men who beat them. Most were depressed as adults, and more than a third had attempted suicide. Herman saw incest as a hidden force creating the look and feel of gender in the West. "Thus did the victims of incest grow up to become archetypally feminine women: sexy without enjoying sex, repeatedly victimized yet repeatedly seeking to lose themselves in the love of an overpowering man, contemptuous of themselves and of other women, hard-working, giving and self-sacrificing," she wrote. "Incest represents a common pattern of traditional female socialization carried to a pathological extreme. Covert incest fosters the development of women who overvalue men and undervalue women, including themselves. Overt incest fosters the development of women who submit to martyrdom and sexual slavery."[47]

Eventually, Herman and other researchers discovered that most psychiatric inpatients and many outpatients reported that they had been physically or sexually abused as children, or had experienced both kinds of abuse. Jean Miller conceived of and worked on an early study that found sexual or physical abuse, or both, in the childhood histories of nearly three-fourths of a group of women mental patients. More than 85 percent of the women who had been diagnosed with border-line personality disorder, until then a diagnosis believed to reflect some intrinsic defect of personality formation, had been sexually abused as children. The study also showed that for almost every psychiatric diag-nosis, the women inpatients who had been abused had more severe symptoms than the women who had not, and the women who had suf-fered both sexual and physical abuse had more severe symptoms than the women who had suffered only physical or sexual abuse.[48] Like the women Russell had studied, almost all of these patients said they had never talked to anyone about their histories of abuse before. No one—no doctor, no nurse, no therapist—had ever asked them about it.

Getting therapists to ask was a political task, Herman knew. She compared two studies: One study was of a psychiatric clinic where the standard intake interview did not include a question about incest; there, 4 percent of patients reported incest without being asked. In an-other study, a psychiatrist had no patients who spontaneously reported an incest history; but when he asked the question, he discovered that "one third of all his women patients had an incest history."[49]

Gradually, backed by the women's movement and new women's in-stitutions born of consciousness-raising—rape crisis centers, incest sur-vivor support groups—women began to feel enough social support to reveal traumatic histories to their therapists. Around Boston, some of these women were lucky enough to be working with therapists who be-lieved them, even if the therapists felt they didn't know what to do. In her small private practice in the late 1970s, when the Monday night meetings at Jean's house started, Judy Jordan recalls, "Two of the four people I was seeing were sexual-abuse survivors. I hadn't been taught a thing about it." The other group members were surprised Jordan had those two patients. "It was unknown. It wasn't in the field," Jordan says. But she heard from Jan about a young psychiatrist, Judith Lewis Herman, "who believes that this stuff is much more prevalent than people think."

With van der Kolk and another psychiatrist, J. Christopher Perry, Herman wrote a series of medical papers that appeared not in a women's movement journal but in *The American Journal of Psychiatry*, the flagship journal of the American Psychiatric Association. "Why preach to the choir?" she asks. Their choice of this journal meant not that Herman had abandoned her politics of writing for women but that she wanted to reach and convince the medical establishment. And she succeeded. "At the time that the borderline study came out, I gave a grand rounds at Cambridge Hospital," Herman says. "A lot of the senior honchos were there. I had expected that I would get a lot of challenges or hostile questions. Instead, they stood up and said, 'We've always known this.' It was a sort of Orwellian moment: 'We're at war with Oceania. We have always been at war with Oceania.' "

But Herman continued to remember that the ability of senior honchos to see the relationship between trauma and psychiatric illness had a political history. "In my own training, there was no mention of sexual assault, and I think that is true in most psychiatric training," she told an audience during a talk on sexual violence at the Stone Center in 1984.

"The reality is we were all taught Freudian ideas," Miller expanded later in the presentation.

> I never heard of incest in my own training—except for learning that Freud made that mistake, then recovered a year later and reconstructed his theory. Because we were well-trained, we never believed stories of incest when we heard them. In other words, one does not have to be malevolent to hold such attitudes. With that in mind, the changes that have been made in the past decade are phenomenal! Fifteen years ago we would have all been declared incompetent professionals for holding this kind of discussion! The change has come from women pressing on the profession, and from a few heroines within the profession. They struggled hard—often with a lot of courage—to challenge their colleagues and question longstanding theories which everyone honored.[50]

In 1989, Herman, van der Kolk, and Perry embarrassed the field of psychiatry by documenting that 81 percent of a group of patients with so-called borderline personality disorder "gave histories of major childhood trauma," and that the more "borderline" they were, the more abuse they had suffered or witnessed.[51] This study found that patients who had been labeled borderline were responding to traumatic events that took place in relationship.

Herman knew she had another book to write, both for therapists who were being confronted with people asking for help with problems that still officially did not exist and for traumatized women and men whose therapists wouldn't read such a book. The photographer Jerry Berndt, then her husband, sat down with her to help her get ready to write. "We watched all nine hours of *Shoah*," Herman says. Claude Lanzmann's searing documentary about the Holocaust moved her "into the mind-set that was needed to write this," she says. "The book is as much a product of the Holocaust as anything."

"Psychological trauma," she writes in the beginning of the second chapter of *Trauma and Recovery*, "is an affliction of the powerless." The chapter is called "Terror." The cause of trauma is "overwhelming force," she writes—disaster when the force is natural, atrocity when the force is human. Much as we would like to think so, atrocities and disasters are not rare. But they are extraordinary, because "they overwhelm the ordinary human adaptations to life."[52]

Y. was seventeen. She lived in a suburb of a major city, in a house in a neighborhood her parents felt safe in, safe enough to let Y. stay in their house alone while they went out of town. They were wrong.

"The most terrifying part of it was the initial moment of having someone at the door and fighting for my life," Y. says now, more than a decade after her rape. "I was just more violent than I ever knew I had it in me to be." Y. stopped fighting when the man took out a knife. Then "I just started to negotiate with him about how much I would submit and how much I wouldn't," she says. She was white. He was black. She had never seen him before.

Afterward, she went to a neighbor's, and then stayed with her sister till her parents got back. "I became really paranoid, just scared all the time. I couldn't sleep. I started to drink to sleep," she says. Living in her suburban house in terror as a high-school senior, Y. felt "very mistrustful, extremely alert, and I felt also very, very much alone with it. My faith in people plummeted because I was just aghast at how unavailable people were."

Her parents didn't want to talk much about it. They read the police report: an unidentified black male had raped their daughter. Y. misidentified him in the police picture file, but he was arrested on another charge six months later and confessed. And that was the end, as far as her parents were concerned. But not for Y. "My parents wouldn't let me go for treatment," she says. "My parents were not there to hear."

Y. jumped at the slightest noise, panicked at the doorbell, lay awake. "Basically I had a need to go over and over it. And a longing to sleep near somebody," to sleep in safety. "It affected my relationships," she says. "No one was there to say, 'Talk to me.' Friends and other people were freaked out—you know, didn't know how to respond."

She finished high school, went a thousand miles away to college. "Then time did its thing. After a while I had an interesting—a story, interesting in its not affecting me," Y. says carefully. She told her interesting story once in a while, but not to the therapist she began seeing, she says. "I didn't hear any license" to speak about rape from this therapist, who never asked her about sexual abuse or rape. "I needed somebody to draw it out, but that didn't happen," she says. Though she had told her story to police, neighbors, family, and friends, "I hadn't really experienced anybody who could hold it," she says. No one she told could hold the story with her, could hear the story without turning away or withdrawing and withholding empathy until Y. could convincingly pretend that she had gotten over it, she says. "I did have relationships in college, with both men and women, but that whole realm was just very confused for me—sex, violence, love, fear." She didn't *feel* angry, but, she says, "My anger came out in a number of ways—rejecting men, insisting on a kind of independence. I never got angry at the man who raped me, because I was so filled with fear." She thought it was odd that she didn't feel angry, even though she had every cause to. "It's weird, I was more terrified, and other people got angry." It should have been easy to get angry. Unlike other rape victims, she didn't encounter blame. Her story was "more of a TV drama" than most and fit the prevailing myth of rape: the man was a stranger; he was black; he broke in; she fought hard. Sometimes when she told her interesting story, people got angry for her, for a while. But reflecting on her own reaction, "I think terror really characterizes it, not anger," she says. The night of terror was the trauma. The decade of terror was the post-traumatic stress.

Y. wasn't in Herman's book, though the young psychiatrist used dozens of examples like hers to describe simple post-traumatic stress disorder, and when she read it, Y. knew she might have been in it. She read that every aspect of the typical response to danger, overwhelmed by force, "tends to persist in an altered and exaggerated state long after the actual danger is over," and after trauma what Miller might call the feeling-thought-acts of a typical response to danger were often psychic smithereens cut off from memory.

Traumatic events may "recondition the human nervous system" so that for a time victims "no longer have a normal 'baseline' level of alert but relaxed attention. Instead," Herman writes, "their bodies are always on the alert for danger." Heart rate and blood pressure increase when they hear sounds that remind them of the trauma they experienced, and they remain in this state of "hyperarousal" even when they are asleep, so their sleep is hard to come by and often troubled. Dreams and memories of the trauma, exactly repeated, may intrude into normal consciousness as involuntary flashbacks. And they "can recur unmodified for years on end," Herman says, noting that psychiatric observers from Janet and Freud to Kardiner and Robert Jay Lifton were amazed at the persistence of traumatic memories and dreams.[53]

Insisting on keeping the politics behind psychological trauma in the diagnostic picture, whether it is a picture of war or of home, Herman writes that the post-traumatic effects of war are directly comparable to the effects of repeated incest or rape because the context of both is an inescapable political trap, "where the victim is in a state of captivity, unable to flee, and under the control of the perpetrator." The result of this kind of "prolonged, repeated trauma," whose victims might characterize it not as one event but as an epoch encompassing many events, is a syndrome Herman has named *complex* post-traumatic stress disorder. "Examples of such conditions include prisons, concentration camps, and slave labor camps," Herman writes. "Such conditions also exist in some religious cults, in brothels and other institutions of sexual exploitation, and in some families."[54] She combines her own and other researchers' observations of Holocaust survivors, incest survivors, returned prisoners of war, prostitutes, battered women, and survivors of child abuse to create a diagnostic category that describes their "more complex, diffuse and tenacious" symptoms, including "deformations of relatedness and identity" and "vulnerability to repeated harm."[55]

Survivors of prolonged, repeated abuse are left with histories of globalized disturbance. They also sleep with difficulty, wake and startle incessantly in a state of chronic anxiety and upset "without any recognizable baseline state of calm or comfort." Headaches, stomachaches, backaches, tremors, choking, and nausea may plague them.[56]

On the other hand, "people in captivity become adept practitioners of the arts of altered consciousness." This ability to reduce overload by disconnecting awareness of the worst things that happen seems to save victims from immediate psychological short-circuiting. But the long-term cost of dissociation turns out to be high. In fact, "people who enter a dissociative state at the time of the traumatic event are among those most likely to develop long-lasting PTSD," Herman writes.[57] Such an experience hurls victims into mental lives in which memory, emotion, and even aspects of character may be severed in quite involuntary ways that protect them from reexperiencing old, remembered trauma at full force. But these protections prolong an equally involuntary preoccupation with trauma. Victims who develop complex PTSD may achieve "virtuosic feats of dissociation."[58] These dissociative prodigies may include not only the efflorescence of separate personalities who remember different parts of a victim's experience but also quite stunning divisions of psychological labor. For example, of two sisters from an abusive or severely negligent family, one may remember the abuse with no associated emotions, and the other may remember nothing but be overwhelmed from time to time with random-seeming feelings of despair or terror detached from any memory, a trauma in itself. "The traumatized person may experience intense emotion but without clear memory of the event, or may remember everything in detail but without emotion. She may find herself in a constant state of vigilance and irritability," Herman writes.[59]

"Protracted depression" and "humiliated rage," incubated in a hostage whose attempts to flee or protest would result in further trauma or death, are the emotional freight of complex PTSD. Herman traces the lineaments of a relationship between abuser and victim, a relationship dedicated to breaking relationships for the sake of stealing power or controlling the victim. Amnesty International's list of the coercive methods used to control political prisoners, hostages, and concentration camp survivors bears "an uncanny resemblance" to the reports of "battered women, abused children, and coerced prostitutes," Herman observes. Perpetrators use a technology of betrayal, threats, and violence laid on a foundation of physical deprivation and isolation from good relationships. Captive victims have to depend on abusive captors; they bond with them because they come to believe, often rightly, that the only person who can help them is this person who has complete control over them and wants only to harm and exploit them. This dependence on someone intent on harm creates "a constriction in initiative and planning" like the famous dog who is zapped so often when he tries to leave his crate that after the power is turned off and the door left open, the dog will no longer try to escape, having "learned helplessness." In just this way, the coercive, obsessive attention of a captor, and the malign, dependent relationship it creates, become and remain part of the "inner life" of a victim long after captivity is ended. Even if they don't suffer from the idealization that is part of Stockholm syndrome, survivors may feel terrified of, lonely for, and worthless without their captors. Even after other forces set them free, forming new relationships will never feel playful or motivated by simple interest or attraction but will always raise "questions of life and death" for survivors, who may ricochet between "intense attachment and terrified withdrawal."[60] In the end, survivors often have a sense not that they are many people, like our popular picture of survivors with "multiple personalities," but that they are nobody—that they have no self. And this experience of no-self is not a Buddhist meditative state or the empathic identity of relational people who cannot segregate a sense of self from their engagement with the rich, growth-fostering relationships that they experience at the heart of their lives. A person with this symptom of complex PTSD might dream she was a piece of dirt-encrusted ice being kicked down a sidewalk in the dark, or describe herself to a therapist "as reduced to a nonhuman life-form." Herman also saw the repetitive phenomena associated with the aftermath of repeated psychological trauma—self-mutilation, involuntary flashbacks, and violence—all in the light of this new diagnosis.

When severe trauma is prolonged, symptoms are even more prolonged. Half of a group of former hostages still had symptoms six to nine years later. Two-thirds of Vietnam veterans had symptoms of PTSD, and more than one-third still had them fifteen years after discharge. Korean POWs showed symptoms forty years later.

But Herman doesn't find Janet's weaknesses and predispositions to complex PTSD. For instance, the survey of studies of wife beating she looked at turned up only one common characteristic among the wives: they were married to men who beat them. Complex PTSD may happen anytime "ordinary, healthy people . . . become trapped in prolonged abusive situations"—whether they are wars or relationships with abusive mates or parents, she writes. But by the time such victims manage to escape their traumatic captivity, "they are no longer ordinary or healthy."[61]

Eventually, researchers in the new field of seeing violence would go looking for traces of trauma in people who had no recollection of trauma but were known to have suffered it because they had been treated for physical injuries that police or hospitals had records of. Sometimes researchers would find a partial memory, or a suspicion of having been abused. But often, even years later, the researchers wouldn't find memories in known victims of abuse. They would find isolation, paranoia, addiction, self-loathing, chronic self-destructiveness, but no memory that any trauma had taken place.

People who did not identify themselves as feminists or human rights activists often reacted to this research not so much with horror that incest and childhood sexual and physical abuse were epidemic as with horror that researchers were working on it. Nonetheless, an awareness that rape, incest, child abuse, and war had profound and long-lasting destructive effects on all of their victims—and on all of their victims' relationships, on all of the people who loved and lived with victims—moved from the women's movement into psychiatry through Herman's work, and that of other early feminist psychologists and sociologists, and allowed her and her colleagues to work in intellectual territory that only novelists and artists had inhabited before.[62]

Popular culture of the 1980s and '90s blew hot and cold on the new science, called traumatic stress studies, that grew up around seeing violence. The culture itself experienced various states of tolerance and intolerance, sometimes knowing and sometimes not knowing that violence was at the bottom of many psychological disorders, as though civilization itself were experiencing intermittent dissociation about the causes of individual dissociation and other reactions to trauma. At times, journalists and commentators allowed that perhaps more violence was committed against young people than by them, and that common public ills such as addiction, falling victim to further crime and abuse, self-destructiveness, and panic attacks were often signs of and responses to early violence. At other times, the public seemed to revert to blaming young people for the weakness of seeing themselves as victims, forgetting about the huge sink of unreported violence and sexual crime that was going to submerge or at least touch a fourth or more of all American children. During the 1980s, careful new research estimated that one in three American women and one in seven American men had been criminally abused as children. And yet at the time this endemic abuse was becoming known, the mass media focused much of their response to this news on the tiny proportion of cases in which a victim claimed to have "recovered memories" of alleged abuse and accused a parent or other relative who denied the abuse and loudly proclaimed the accuser was making it up. In the mid-1990s, a lobbying group estimated that seven thousand of these disputes had arisen in the United States over several years. During each of these years, about 130,000 children were confirmed victims of sexual abuse, and about 200,000 children were substantiated victims of physical abuse in the United States. During a twelve-month period in the 1990s, only one story on the enormous prevalence and widespread effects of child abuse ran in any of the three major U.S. newsmagazines, and yet five articles appeared about disputed "recovered memories"—mostly about women who believed they remembered crimes, usually incest, long after they took place. Two of the three magazines viewed skeptically or negatively the possibility of remembering abuse years after the fact. Only one was more balanced, mentioning studies that showed more than 75 percent of people who said they remembered forgotten abuse later found corroborating evidence, such as eyewitness or hospital reports. "False complaints do occur for sexual abuse, just as they do for all other crimes. Studies of thoroughly investigated child sexual abuse cases document the frequency of false complaints at between 2 and 7 percent," Herman wrote.[63] "The problem is not that memory recovery is being debated. Rather, it is that today's media devote far more coverage to side issues such as recovered memories than to the indisputable reality that millions of American children grow up in nightmarish conditions of rape, sexual violation and physical brutality inflicted by adults entrusted with their care," Mike Males, a social ecologist, wrote.[64] "False memory syndrome" is not a psychiatric diagnosis; the name simply reflects the successful public-relations campaign of the False Memory Syndrome Foundation, an advocacy group founded by parents who claimed their children had wrongly accused them of sexual abuse.[65]

The allegedly false accusations of a small group of people became a hot topic, widely and prominently covered and debated. And at the same time almost all known and convicted perpetrators of physical or sexual abuse against children denied and continue to deny what they have done, and their routine denials go almost without comment. Once again, relational psychologists notice that gender marks this divide. Individual members of the dominant group, men, have the power to lie without besmirching their entire group as liars, but the subordinate group, women, lacks that power, so false complaints from a tiny number make all women who recall abuse suspect. Relational psychologists mark this difference as a cultural fault line, a politically enforced division between men and women.

"Concerned that the public confusion and dismay over this issue" of remembering sexual trauma years, perhaps decades, after experiencing it, and concerned that "the possibility of false accusations not discredit the reports of patients who have indeed been traumatized by actual previous abuse," in 1993 the board of trustees of the American Psychiatric Association issued a statement about sexual abuse and dissociative amnesia. "Sexual abuse of children and adolescents leads to severe negative consequences. Child sexual abuse is a risk factor for many classes of psychiatric disorders, including anxiety disorders, affective disorders, dissociative disorders and personality disorders," the APA board announced, thereby acknowledging a common injury's potential for causing global damage that even a decade earlier many of its members would have denied or ignored. The APA statement acknowledged that "a lack of conscious awareness of the abuse for varying periods of time" is one "coping mechanism" that victims of abuse use; but it also acknowledged that precision still eludes the scientist who wants to know precisely which memories of traumatic events are historical and potential evidence in a criminal trial, and which memories are what Freud used to call fantasy, and a defense lawyer might call bogus.

By 1996, a federal judge could rule that the possibility of recovering memories of abuse lost for half a century is backed by good science and that juries should be able to hear testimony about them. Van der Kolk offered expert testimony in this case, including evidence about positron-emission tomography (PET-scan) images that showed memories of trauma are actually stored in a different place in the brain from non-traumatic memories that are recalled easily.[66] "We believe this reflects the tendency in PTSD to experience emotions as physical states rather than as verbally encoded experiences. Our findings suggest that PTSD patients' difficulties with putting feelings into words are mirrored in actual changes in brain activity," van der Kolk writes.[67] "This may be why people often describe their memories returning first as isolated visual images or bodily sensations. They say, 'I see his hand coming toward me,' or in the case of a Vietnam veteran who saw his buddies blown up, 'I can smell the smoke,' " van der Kolk told a reporter.[68]

The research that has grown from Herman's first investigations of the politics of psychological trauma is still split along political lines. One group of clinicians supports an expensive, long-term developmental study of victims who are chosen because they are known from police and hospital records to have suffered sexual abuse, though a number of them have no recollection of it.[69] Another study by this group compares documented sexual-abuse survivors who did and did not experience a period of traumatic amnesia with a control group who experienced no abuse. The authors find many common symptoms and complaints, but they report the amnesiac group "differed in several ways. They were more likely to experience fear for their lives, and abuse by persons well-known to them. They were more likely to dissociate and to report psychological symptomatology. They were not likely to have recovered memories through therapy or hypnosis; rather, environmental triggers were the most likely cause of memory return."[70]

Some psychologists, mostly non-clinicians, are highly skeptical of the idea of recovering from traumatic amnesia caused by childhood sexual abuse. Perhaps the best known of these is the experimental psychologist Elizabeth Loftus, whose research is linked to the Web site of the False Memory Syndrome Foundation. Loftus's experiments are about influencing memory, and she generally appears as an expert court witness for the defense. In a typical Loftus experiment, family members convince a person that he or she remembers something that never happened or didn't happen that way—for instance, that he once got lost in a mall, or that the car crash he saw was different in some major way. She extrapolates this result to a belief that therapists or friends, or even strongly worded books about remembering sexual abuse, can influence a person to imagine himself the victim of abuse or torture.[71]

Van der Kolk seethes in his review of Loftus's popular book about her trials and research, *The Myth of Repressed Memory*. Loftus produces "an overall impression of unadulterated madness among psychologists and psychiatrists who deal with adults who claim to have been abused as children by indiscriminately presenting outrageous claims from the self-help literature, excerpts from TV shows such as 'Oprah' and 'Donahue,' scientific publications such as *Playboy* and, when convenient, the work of serious investigators," he writes.[72] And if Loftus's experiments on influencing memory actually prove that social environment influences memory, then they support the premise that an abuser could persuade a child that the abuse had never happened and that child might quite plausibly forget about it, until she was in a social environment that would support her remembering it. Such developments as the widely publicized pedophile priest scandal of the Catholic Church appear to have weakened the appeal of Loftus's position.[73]

One study ferrets out the politics in this controversy, concluding that "people's beliefs about the [in]validity of recovered memories are strongly tied to autocratic misogyny, social denial, and narcissistic self-interest." This study found that "participants' authoritarian opposition to women's equality was as strong a predictor of their beliefs about recovered memories and incest as it was of their beliefs about battered women and PMS," while people who believe that traumatic amnesia can both occur and subside tend to "acknowledge the injustice of child abuse or support women's equality."[74] These researchers emphasize that the controversy about recovered memories is political: it has a chilling effect on women who have been isolated and now believe that someone in authority might listen to them, and it demeans women and men victims, since the people who believe that the epidemic of sexual abuse is really an epidemic of "false memories" of abuse—what Freud called fantasies—assume that women and men who suspect they have been victimized are so malleable and gullible that they cannot be trusted to know or remember what happened to them.

A larger cultural drama about the power of memory—the power to send someone to jail for rape thirty years late, for instance, or the power to rewrite history by recalling events that were politically unspeakable at the time they happened—held center stage when Herman wrote *Trauma and Recovery*. It was a drama being played out around the world. Salman Rushdie, for instance, under threat of death from Iranian Islamic orthodoxy for writing a novel about his native India, quoted the Czech writer Milan Kundera: "The struggle of man against power is the struggle of memory against forgetting." And, in an essay about racism in Britain, where he was hiding out, Rushdie quoted Michael Dummett on "the will not to know—a chosen ignorance, not the ignorance of innocence."[75]

Relational psychologists find the "recovered memory" controversy fits very neatly into their ideas about "patriarchy," that ideologically strident but nonetheless indispensable word for the politics of dominance and subordination. It's like global warming: now that there is a mile-wide strip of open sea across the North Pole, the same fossil-fuel interests that denied the climate was changing, and then denied the climate change was linked to combustion, are celebrating the chance to exploit a new "Northwest Passage" created by global warming while still denying that global warming is taking place. This is the seeing and not seeing of patriarchy. Scorning "recovered memories" and permitting the exploitation of sexually abused women as prostitutes make a very similar political pattern. The difference is that some of the scientists in this debate are, as it were, coal and oil—they are women, they were children, and so it is harder to persuade them that their interests are the same as the interests of the dominant group, or that they will feel more powerful if they speak and act and think as though their interests are the same.

Z. is a former colleague of mine. One afternoon after I had begun working on this book, Z. called me at home. She told me a much older neighbor whom she trusted and liked had jumped her and tried to rape her the night before. She had been able to fight him off, but she knew she was not all right. She needed some kind of treatment, and she needed to find another place to live, she said. She knew I had begun this project and thought I would know where she could turn.

When I answered the phone, I was in the middle of reading *The Rape Victim*, the book Mary Harvey wrote with Mary P. Koss, one of the first of the generation of psychologists of rape who began to track and quantify violence against women at the peak of the women's movement. For instance, Koss and Harvey had discovered that most rapes or sexual attacks have less of a TV look and more of a neighborhood kind of feel—that is, "they are less likely to be committed by strangers, more likely to be committed by someone known, often well-known, to the victim," Harvey says. Seventy-three percent of the women who reported that they had been raped or sexually attacked in Russell's pioneering study knew their attacker, and 84 percent of the girls who said they'd been raped or attacked in a later study of adolescents knew their attackers.[76] Koss and Harvey plotted the reactions of rape victims over time the way other specialists graph recovery from heart attacks, or earthquakes. Because Z. had "won" and had only been attacked and not successfully raped, she said she felt guilty and wrong for feeling raw, endangered, and terrified after her ordeal. But because I was reading a book that described rape as a relational trauma, I knew that even if she had won her fight, she had lost several relationships—to a neighbor, to a home, to a neighborhood, and, depending on how friends and institutions responded to her now, to a whole civilization. I told her some of the facts that were being compiled from surveys of crime victims whom sociologists had never questioned before. Koss and Harvey summarized surveys about rape and recovery from sexual attacks, and they suggested this wouldn't be a quick fix. Rape victims often continued to feel more distress until about three weeks after an attack, and then remained very distressed for another month, Koss and Harvey wrote. I also referred Z. to Harvey, who was able to see her the next day.

Simply hearing that even the quickest recovery from sexual attacks may take months was a relief, Z. said, because it helped her feel normal—there was a normal reaction to attack, and she was having it. She said she was also relieved to hear from Harvey that she could take her time and recover somewhat before deciding whether and how to prosecute the offending neighbor, knowing that a court proceeding might bring a second trauma, supplying all the "conditions of successful degradation ceremonies."[77] But Z. didn't look relieved. When we met a few days later, she stood four or five feet away, an alienating foot or two beyond the normal comfort zone for conversation. She couldn't look me in the eye for more than a fraction of a second at a time. By now, I had read enough to know these acts of distancing were signs of relational disturbances brought on by simple PTSD, signals that a personal balance of empathy and creative relational curiosity had been spun haywire, into terror, by a major breach of trust. I had learned from Herman, Koss, and Harvey, and from other victims and survivors of attacks I had interviewed, that when someone you trust attacks you, an involuntary, typical response is to back away from everyone you once trusted—suddenly to find yourself fearing trust itself as an untrustworthy guide, at a moment when you desperately need people to reassure you and help you rebuild trust. Koss and Harvey cited studies that found ninety days often seemed to mark a phase of recovery, and in fact when we met again three months later, Z. stood in the normal North American comfort zone for conversation and made more eye contact.[78] Z. felt better but she was not "over it," she said. She still had hair-trigger startle reactions, a pervasive uneasiness, and bouts of insomnia and terror.

Z.'s trauma attack also produced a secondary trauma for her boyfriend and her family, since she was unable to relate to them in a normally loving and trusting way. Rape and sexual assault are not just things men do to women, although the culture marks them that way. Even when, as is typically the case, men do them to women, they are also things men do to other men. Because women are marked as the ones who carry relationships for the whole culture—because women are often the mediators, the healers, the ones who reach out, take care,

and make sure that relationships in any family or community are working well—when women are wounded, the men they relate to are
wounded, or suffer loss, too, and Harvey pays attention to that.

I don't think I have ever heard Harvey speak in public without describing her ecological model of trauma. Once, in fact, I saw her walk
onstage and speak about it with confidence, humor, passion, lively clinical vignettes, and clear order for an hour in front of about nine hundred clinicians at a Harvard Medical School teaching conference.
Afterward, over lunch, she told us that she had realized when she got to
the stage and was being introduced that she had left her copy of her
speech in her car and so had had to "wing it." Harvey is a missionary for
the field of community psychology, which was not yet born when she
began graduate school, so she earned a Ph.D. in experimental and developmental psychology at the University of Oregon in 1970 and began
working with advisers who, she says, invented the field that year.

Community psychology is public mental health. Its birth coincided
with deinstitutionalization and the planned creation of a nationwide
network of community psychologists who were to take over from the
centralized, bureaucratic, imprisoning mental hospitals that were
closed in the 1970s. But community psychology is more linked to community organizing, in which schools of social work began to offer degrees in the 1970s, though many have now stopped, since neurobiology
and neurochemistry—pills—have become the name of the game in
psychology and psychiatry. Harvey does what she can to keep her
young and somewhat overshadowed specialty visible, maintaining its
emphasis on studying community dynamics and neighborhood structures with an aim to improve them as psychological environments.
"The ecological framework of community psychology looks at the environment and organizations as being interdependent," Harvey says.
"What does it take for a human community to be life-sustaining, self-
supporting? Tradition, diversity, pluralism" all play a role, she says. The
Victims of Violence program is an example of a complex community
psychology intervention. "In the last twenty years we've built an organization that has dramatically changed the environment for survivors of
trauma in our community," she says.

Harvey notes that Herman, director of training at the Victims of Violence program, where Harvey is overall director, is "fundamentally a

scholar and a feminist activist in spite of a very intellectual and reflective temperament," whereas Harvey has "this temperament that is out there," the spirit and fire of an activist. She's proud to be the namesake of a Scottish grandmother who had two nicknames: she was called "'Wee Mary' because she was tiny and because of the brogue," and she was called "the Iron Hand" because of her fierce will. "She had to have justice in her genes," her granddaughter says. "I really started out as a research psychologist, but I'm so much of a damned activist that I never sit down to do the writing," she said once. But in 1996, she finally published "An Ecological View of Psychological Trauma and Trauma Recovery."[79]

"Each individual's reaction to violent and traumatic events will be influenced by the combined attributes of those communities to which s/he belongs and from which s/he draws identity," she writes. Violence is a kind of "acid rain" in social environments—"an ecological threat to a community's ability to offer its members safe haven," she writes. Seeding this rain of destruction, "racism, sexism and poverty can be thought of as environmental pollutants—i.e. ecological anomalies that foster violence and threaten to overwhelm the health-promoting resources of human communities." On the other hand, "economic well-being and community-wide regard for pluralism and diversity can be understood as ecological contributors to violence prevention"—as it were, clean air and clean water for social environments.[80]

Interpersonal violence is traumatic because it assaults a whole web or ecosystem of social, personal, and emotional connections, Harvey writes. If those connections are strong enough to withstand that assault, or vital enough to regrow quickly after trauma breaks them, victims weather trauma much better than if their connections are weak or tentative. Z. recovered from her single trauma much more quickly than Y. at least partly because Z. had and made connections that supported her recovery right away, while Y. had and found parents, friends, and professionals who left her to cope by herself. For decades, Harvey has paid attention to the way traumatized people respond, recover, or retreat into isolation differently depending on the resources and reactions they meet in their communities of home, neighborhood, work, faith, friends. Today clinicians often look at age, stage, intelligence, prior history of trauma, and the relationship between the victim and the perpetrator when they try to diagnose and devise treatment for traumatized people. But they don't always look at the traditional way of understanding or dealing with trauma in the victim's culture, or the traditional view of asking for and accepting care, or "the modeling of hope, tenacity and resilience that may or may not have been provided by family, friends and other significant figures." In the same way, clinicians may measure trauma by the degree of physical injury or isolation, or the amount of time a perpetrator had a victim trapped, but violations of other community values may be what makes trauma especially painful or shameful to a particular victim. "A combat veteran with a strong religious background may be haunted for years by the crucifix worn by a dead enemy soldier, for example, and a rape victim who found herself too terrified to resist may feel lasting shame for uttering the words of consent and pleasure that her assailant demanded of her." The environment of any trauma and of the care available following the trauma all have cultural meanings and qualities that affect recovery. In a U.S. community that hates and fears immigrants, a tornado victim who doesn't speak English will have a different trauma from one who does, even if all the mainstream—and English-speaking—services are excellent. "A victim of homophobic gay bashing" may try to maximize recovery by seeking help from agencies known to be part of or friendly to the gay community.[81]

Harvey looks at trauma and healing along seven dimensions. Two of them have to do with memory: trauma victims often have too much or too little memory, which really means, Harvey notes, that they have not so much lost memory as lost control over the process of remembering. Sometimes they can't remember their trauma no matter how hard they try; at other times, or in other victims, memory floods them with flashbacks, "traumatic intrusions which disable and terrify even as they elude meaningful appraisal."[82] The traumatic split of memory from feeling means that sometimes trauma victims "will feel waves of terror, anxiety or rage" in response to various triggers—seeing a child the age they were when traumatized, or a place that resembles a place where they were abused—without having any memory that gives them a clue about the source of these runaway feelings. These dissociated feelings are often so unendurable that they drive victims to try to overwhelm the overwhelming with addictions or self-mutilation, or to screen out unpredictable triggers by isolating themselves. Trauma also leads to disorders of meaning; people who have been repeatedly assaulted in war or by violent crimes may live in communities that teach them to believe that violence is cool, inevitable, or not violence.

One of Harvey's favorite clinical tales is about a composite woman she calls Katherine, who comes for treatment saying she feels that sexual abuse by a neighbor during preadolescence has made her feel so bad about herself that her boyfriend has been driven by her low self-esteem and poor appearance to have an affair with another woman. "Thus, she blamed herself for Todd's affair and wanted to develop a self-improvement plan to prevent him from having another," Harvey says.[83] Perking herself up for Todd is Katherine's goal for treatment. Only as her therapy deepens does Katherine confess that Todd has a temper when he drinks, and that he often drinks and beats and rapes her. Katherine does not know that the source of her pain and bad feelings is in the trauma she has suffered and in its perpetrators, not in herself. When Harvey asks clinicians who are listening to her talk about Katherine how many of them have had a Katherine in therapy, hands go up all over the immense hotel ballroom. People whose memories and internal warning systems have been dissociated and disordered by trauma often don't know what reminds them of the trauma; if they do remember it, often they don't know that such trauma is criminal, destructive, and bad, or that there is any alternative, or any good hiding place. As a result, they leave themselves in extreme danger—living with perpetrators, cutting or otherwise hurting themselves, and abusing drugs, Harvey says.

Most perpetrators who commit crimes that traumatize their victims have no *feeling* that what they have done is wrong. Whatever moral sense they have has become completely cognitive, linked to ideas or opinions about what is just, or good for boys and girls, never linked to that integrated, empathic, relational sense of not wanting to do harm. Herman notes the widespread observation that perpetrators lack empathy and quotes a study in which "only 14 percent of offenders expressed remorse or regret for their actions."[84]

"This absence of feelings is described consistently by murderers throughout the world and throughout history," James Gilligan writes. "Moreover, the more violent the criminal, the more notable the lack of feelings. The most violent men already feel numb and dead by the time they begin killing."[85] Gilligan, Carol's husband, is a forensic psychiatrist who led a successful program to reduce violence in Massachusetts prisons. His book *Violence: Our Deadly Epidemic and Its Causes* traces the motivation for committing traumatic crime to shame, or fear of shame. Violence becomes something to be proud of for a man who has been raised in a culture in which it is shameful to be tender or loving and to have less power than someone else. "The most direct way to prevent someone from laughing at you is to make them cry instead," James Gilligan writes.[86] And prison, the place of punishment for violent acts, is a culture of enormous power differences that socializes men "to become as violent as possible" by limiting the ways to avoid shaming almost completely to one way: violence.[87] On the other hand, the high level of violence, shaming, power imbalance, and danger in prison puts a macho mask on the fact that prisons do in some sense nurture and certainly feed, house, clothe, and keep track of the people who live inside them.

James Gilligan also focuses on the political culture of violence, which he calls the "structural violence" that power-laden divisions of race, gender, class, and sexuality do to people who never commit physical, criminal violence. Shame is built into a system that makes everyone shamefully invisible at some point; even tall, straight, white, male plutocrats get old or sick sometime. Societies that have the fewest or shallowest caste-like divisions—and therefore fewer reasons to be shamed—also show the lowest rates of violence, and lower mortality rates from other causes, he writes. This link is true geographically: the United States, which has the greatest inequalities between rich and poor of any developed country, also has a rate of violence that is "five to ten times larger than the other first world nations"; and Sweden and Japan, which have the lowest rates of inequality, have the lowest rates of violence. It is also true over time, so that, for instance, as inequalities in England and Wales increased, rates of violence increased.[88]

"Shame is the experience of feeling unworthy of the compassionate response of another," Jordan says, speaking at the Learning from Women Harvard Medical School conference in April 2000. "When we are in shame, either arising spontaneously within or from the shaming and humiliating that is done to us, we long for connection but feel we are not worthy of connection," she says. Shame is a political emotion rather than a moral one like guilt, and shame is enforced, as humiliation, much more often than it simply arises out of an inner sense of falling short.

"Shame is one's own vicarious experience of the other's scorn. The self-in-the-eyes-of-the-other is the focus of awareness," Herman quotes in a reading from her mother, Helen Block Lewis.[89] Lewis studied and coded transcripts of hundreds of psychotherapy sessions. She found that shame was by far the most common emotion patients expressed, and she began to pay attention to the dynamics of the real power relationship between therapist and patient as well as to the imaginary one Freudians called transference. In healthy relationships, Herman paraphrases, a flicker of shame is "a signal of disrupted relationship" that calls for reconnection. "I once asked her how anyone could ever get over the feeling of shame, and, by way of demonstration, she laughed. It just goes away, she said, when two people can look each other in the eye and laugh together. Mutual acceptance and regard dispel the pain," Herman recalled. "Shame is resolved simply by the affirmation of a restored relational connection."

But in the world of dissing that leads to chronic disconnection and dissociation, "one of the most potent sources of control is shame. It really works. It's hideously effective," Jordan says. And it's a tool psychotherapy teachers use all the way through to postdoctoral internships. "I feel like I've lived with shame since adolescence—not before, interestingly enough," Jordan says. And she thinks that, like her, most "girls are shamed in adolescence into going underground," she says. "It feels very real to me, what I write about shame. It is something I know. It is something I live with and struggle with, and also I see how it does block me from really being with someone." Around the time she was fighting to get girls on the safety patrol and into shop courses, in early adolescence, Jordan says she started feeling ashamed of being tall and smart. Later, as a young psychologist, she felt ashamed when "I'd be doing things that were making people feel better and change their lives," because the mutual, empathic methods that came naturally to her were scorned and spurned by her supervisors as indulgent, enmeshed, not neutral enough, she says. "I felt a tremendous amount of shame about that. I know it. I know that feeling of 'somebody else could be doing this so much better.' Or sometimes, 'gee, this doesn't seem to be working; it must be because I'm so bad at it.' I can remember my whole internship being one string of battles with the training director about penis envy. And I was shamed for this—it was, 'We know what her issue is.' I would read these volumes of psychoanalytic literature, and they were so dense and they made me feel stupid, but I would keep trying." And meanwhile, just as she had come to feel stupid when she went from Pembroke to Harvard to McLean's prestigious internship program, she was not noticing that she was winning awards or that her patients were getting better. Even after she had found the support and inspiration of the group at the Stone Center, she felt ashamed when she got into the huge auditorium at Wellesley and talked about the relational pleasures of sex. "It's very pervasive," she says. "There is an active force that is shaming, that is silencing, that is forcing people into dissociation. Traumatizing someone is actually about silencing them," she says. "In a shaming situation, you're told that it's not happening to you. Then you're told it's your fault. Then you're told you can't tell anyone."

When the meeting at Jean's house got going, the women in the group realized that each of them felt she was the stupidest person in the room, even though each of them also felt an excited sense that what they were doing was right. One night they went around the room and every woman described the shame she felt about not being as good as the others. Judy remembers feeling sad and angry—not for herself but for the other women in the room for whom she already had such respect. "I thought, look at what has been done. Look at the way their brilliance has been dimmed or curbed or questioned—how could this happen?" The answer that came to them was simply that "so much of socialization is about shaming," especially socialization into the dominant mind-set of "independence" and "socialization toward gender compliance." Both boys and girls are shamed into going along with norms about how boys should not appear to depend on others and girls should. The shame that both groups feel prevents them from seeing that they are being pushed by the same prod in completely different directions. It is hard to see anything through shame; one of the few things a shamed person may be willing to do is to prevent others from seeing, without noticing what they are seeing. James Gilligan writes about a murderer who mutilated the eyes and cut out the tongue of a former high-school classmate after he murdered her in her car. She had offered him a ride because his car had broken down. "All the justification he needed for his crime was 'I didn't like the way she was looking at me,' " he writes, and translates the murder itself as a message about shame: " 'If I destroy eyes, I cannot be shamed,' and 'if I destroy tongues, then I cannot be talked about, ridiculed, or laughed at; my shamefulness cannot be revealed to others.' "[90] But shame is not only for white men whose cars break down, or who otherwise don't manage to be as dominant as parents, teachers, and peers often shame them into thinking they should be. "Shame is directed at marginalized groups and serves to put and keep them in a place of disempowerment and silence; they are made to feel that their reality is deficient," Jordan writes. "Dominant groups characteristically use shame against subordinate groups to keep them from expressing their reality in a way that would threaten the dominant view."[91]

Shame can take us into disconnection from almost any direction, but the four cardinal directions of shaming are race, class, gender, and sexual orientation. These and other caste categories such as age and health become aspects of the social environment that can make trauma more isolating and disabling, because they make it shameful. Exits or distractions that work as "quick fixes" for caste shaming—dropping out of school, "food addictions, irresponsible sexual behavior and premature pregnancy or any one of the many ways African-American adolescent women choose to endure the consequences of their devaluation"—are "social and psychological traps" that lead to further disconnection and isolation, Tracy Robinson and Janie Ward write.[92]

"Whether by reason of race, sexual orientation, gender or some temporarily disabling condition such as grad-student-hood, the threat that one's collective identity might be besmirched heightens the potential for trauma," the psychologist Maureen Walker writes. She remembers how her African-American race, feminine gender, and status as a trainee set her early-warning system on red alert about the danger of being shamed when she walked into a counseling session she was supposed to run at a drug treatment program. For his own reasons—addiction, physical deformity caused by a drunk-driving accident—a client she calls Rick was on red alert for shame, too, and managed to paralyze her with a shaming insult about her "Kmart psychology," to which she responded with a shaming retort that she can't remember but that drove him from the room. "From our own private spaces we brought relational images that defined safety as maintaining dominance and control over the other, thus postponing for at least one more day the threat of nobody-ness. He bolted from the room. I dissociated. The lesson of my dissociation is that in my attempt to save face, I lost touch."[93] The relational losses of shaming show up evenly on the sides of the shamer and the shamed, and create a kind of double disconnection and insulation when someone who is dominant in a shaming caste like race realizes what the system of dominance has led her or him to do, and so one begins to feel ashamed of shaming. "I feel very ashamed of the unconsciousness about the privilege of being white that I've lived in in my life," Jordan admits. "I'm just walking around dripping with all this privilege that I don't even notice."

"Shame gets in the way of relational movement, and leaves the person feeling helpless or dependent on the other for release from this painful state, and can lead to withdrawal or avoidance. Women of color have rightfully been angered and frustrated" when white women appear standoffish or cold because they are ashamed of their racist conditioning and worried that they will do something racist. Women of color "need to be able to trust that we are doing our own working through of these feelings, so that we can remain open and connected while discussing racism," Jan Surrey writes.[94]

"Acadian" white middle-class girls in Lyn Brown's Maine study won't express anger, desire, or even self-satisfaction and confidence to any but the most trusted friends and mentors. Other peers and adults are too likely to shame them for expressing these feelings as a kind of caste enforcement, because they don't fit "white middle-class constructions of the feminine woman as pure, nurturing, self-effacing, and always nice and compliant, and the Acadia girls—smart, complex and truly driven—know this," Brown writes. They tell their friends; they tell their favorite counselor; they tell Lyn about "desire or strong feelings like anger" and can make an "astute political commentary on class and the critique of hurtful behavior and unfair school practices." Their teachers, however, get only "stellar public performances of sweet, bland, uncritical acceptance" of gender, class, and race norms. "When the girls take their voices out of public discourse, their questions, emerging perspectives, concerns, and fears are 'left relatively unanalyzed, unchallenged, and in critical ways buried,'" Brown writes, quoting the literary theorist Mikhail Bakhtin. "They lose the power of their collective critique and, in time, they risk losing touch with what they know to be true from experience; that is, they risk dissociating from their thoughts and feelings," she warns.[95] So dissociation is a risk of the prolonged, repeated criminal traumas of rape, incest, assault, and molestation that befall a third of women and a seventh of men in childhood—and also, in a less disabling way, of the prolonged, repeated insults and disconnections from race, gender, and the other cardinal directions of shame that befall every single one of us all our lives. Terrence Real, a family therapist whom Gilligan contacted and began to work with after she read about his study of male depression, writes about the pervasive "psychological patriarchy" in which women dissociate because there is no safe place to experience what they know, and suggests that one of the reasons Gilligan found girls losing their voices at adolescence is that they could no longer tell the truth about men.[96]

For lesbians, merely being shamed is one of the best results they can hope for from being identified as homosexual. The worst results they might expect are to be fired, evicted, assaulted, or killed, or to lose their children. Unlike straight women and most men of color, gay women and men have the option of keeping this difference secret—or rather, they have the option of allowing the cultural assumption that everyone is heterosexual to cover them. No matter how "out" they may be among family, friends, or colleagues, from time to time, for safety's sake, gay people have to make this decision not to correct a misidentification based on bias. Suzanne Slater, a member of the Stone Center's Lesbian Theory Group, tells a story about Terry, who lived openly as a lesbian in Northampton but didn't feel safe acting lesbian when she and her partner went to a play in nearby but much more traditional Springfield. "Throughout the evening, they avoided touching and watched the crowd more vigilantly than felt comfortable. Part way through intermission, Terry spotted her therapist sitting in a nearby section of the theater." She realized that the therapist had spotted her, too, when the therapist "nodded to Terry in an acknowledging but understated way. Privately, Terry felt vaguely amused that two of the most important women in her life were here, and no observer would ever be able to tell," Slater writes. But the joke gets old fast: life in an environment where no one can ever tell what is important to you, an environment where security depends on living in heterosexual disguise, creates daily disconnections that are prolonged and repeated for gay people even when they are not severe.[97] It is hard to imagine the environmental obstacles to recovery for a closeted lesbian who is raped, for instance.

And what about the environment for eating disorders, anorexia and bulimia, which have been disabling and killing young women for decades? As it became possible for women to express sexual desire, or, perhaps more realistically, as it became possible for men to see women as desirous as well as desirable, and it became possible for women to be sexually active without the ultimate female dishonor of losing community, the classic hysterical seizures of the nineteenth century—the raving woman with the arched back screaming for her mother in a dissociated trance in front of the triumphant diagnostician Jean Charcot and his students at the Salpêtrière—simply disappeared. The secret of the symptoms that Freud regarded as the source of the Nile became in a sense unsought after, because the Nile, as it were, dried up. But if we think of hysterical seizures as the body talking about sex when the voice was forbidden to, because "nice" girls couldn't, we can see a similar kind of silencing at work in the incredible growth of eating disorders—so rare in Freud's time that he never even mentioned them, and today so common that talking about them, flirting with them, and treating them are a political culture for American girls.

"Thinness today has replaced virginity" as the common measure of a girl's success, Catherine Steiner-Adair told a gallery full of listeners at the Museum of Fine Arts in Boston in 1996. Steiner-Adair, a clinical psychologist specializing in eating disorders, is one of three clinicians who trained with Gilligan, Brown, Ward, Tolman, Taylor, and others as part of the Harvard Project on Women's Psychology and Girls' Development. Now an associate in psychology at the Klarman Eating Disorders Center at McLean Hospital and a clinical instructor in psychology at Harvard Medical School, Steiner-Adair reads eating disorders as "the body politic" making a stand about "how impossible it is to grow up as a girl in a girl's body in a culture that at adolescence suddenly devalues connection, relationships, all the knowledge you have about life," she says in 2004. Girls are free to express their expertise, but in adolescence this knowledge "must be rewritten as a 'nice and kind' script," she says. At adolescence, "girls lose the safety to speak out about unfairness and meanness; so they often silence themselves. For girls with eating disorders, the body becomes the self that speaks, that says something is terribly wrong. And they use their body to speak because they feel that they are powerless to be heard if they tell their story through the spoken word." In 2004, Steiner-Adair had just completed an eating-disorders prevention program and written a book about it. "It's an eating-disorders prevention program that doesn't mention eating disorders, and it's very successful," she says. She compares anorexia to Gandhi's political fasts and prison hunger strikes, and she sees the purge-and-binge cycles of bulimia as an unconscious attempt to meet an impossible cultural demand on post-1960s Superwomen to be a slender, power-suited "man" with a briefcase at the office, a professional who "doesn't need anybody," and a shapely mother and sex object at home, a private person with healthy connections.[98]

Surrey adds that, like our culture's contemptuous fear of poverty,

> our whole cultural "fat phobia" reflects the interpretation of fatness as a voluntary state, chosen by the individual, either due to "not caring sufficiently," or as indicative of a psychological profile of a weak-willed, docile, passive dependent individual, unable to control "oral" impulses. Could it be that these traits are highly correlated with many of the same traits generally considered to be more "feminine"?[99]

Both Steiner-Adair and Surrey, who did her first Stone Center research on eating disorders in Wellesley College undergraduates, have been struck by the bizarre norms of shape and weight for girls. For four decades, more than 10 percent of women and girls have been estimated to have an eating disorder; and dieting is a major industry, with billions spent and made on spas, books, videos, diet programs, and, of course, special diet food. As early as 1978, more than half of U.S.

women said they were dieting, and most women considered themselves overweight. By 2004, 35 to 50 percent of American men and women were considered obese, while the rate of eating disorders remained unchanged. In the United States, if you are female, you have a 30 to 50 percent chance of being obese, and better than a 90 percent chance of thinking you are. It is normal for women in the United States to believe they weigh too much. For a time, this belief could be attributed to the social environment of popular culture, doctors' visits, and even insurance tables that all told women and post-pubertal girls they weighed too much. But even during the period in the 1980s and early '90s when medical and actuarial weight charts were revised upward, so that ideal weights actually became higher, the ideals for beauty as shown in models and advertisements were revised downward. The recent increase in American obesity—now affecting up to 10 percent of children, as play has become more sedentary and electronic—has done nothing to enlarge the feminine ideal. As the millennium dawned, models' lips and breasts got fatter but everything else got thinner. Models who used to come from the small, abnormal group of women who are naturally both tall and slender now had to diet stringently to get even thinner than the norm for them, Steiner-Adair notes. Some had ribs removed to look thinner; some added lip and breast implants; and some did both. Now designers and art directors use computers to distort those unreal body shapes to make them even thinner in the films and photographs that tell women that they are too big. Some girls are pulled toward eating disorders because these diseases are one way to look like what the culture says they should look like. When they develop anorexia because that's what they have been told by every magazine cover and film will gain them popularity and high-powered jobs, some psychologists may see this social conformity as an individual disturbance.[100]

"The idea that dependency is bad is really problematic for girls, primarily because they really value dependence" in the form of connection, Steiner-Adair says. Girls are taught to pay attention to relationships; at the same time, they encounter a dominant culture that teaches them that relationships are less important than independence and autonomy, Steiner-Adair writes. They are supposed to be good at relationships, and they're supposed to think their own expertise isn't very valuable. And girls are socialized to rely on others' opinions for self-esteem. One form this double bind takes is that "girls are socialized to be unable to accept their bodies," just as they are taught to embody relational values in a world that simultaneously devalues them.[101]

Surrey's early study of women undergraduates at Wellesley showed that most (64 percent) thought they were overweight, and even more than that (72 percent) had "moderate to extreme concern about reaching their ideal body weight."[102] She identifies "the current preoccupation with body image and body weight as a major cultural disturbance, or cultural 'disease.' "[103] This disease in the culture so devalues women's relational strengths that it forces them to keep all their cards off the table, often to look and act like men—or boys, actually—in the public world of work. For women in this environment, "effectiveness comes to represent the ability to *control* oneself rather than to *express* oneself," Surrey writes.[104] In some families, acting out of an uncritical desire to help their daughters make a necessary deal about an impossible body, for the sake of success and power, parents may become the agents of this diseased culture by nagging and taunting their daughters about weight. Girls with anorexia see their families "as a miniature reflection of an equally disturbed culture."[105] Because family and culture mirror each other, many girls can't find a perspective that would lead to what becomes such an abnormal situation—a healthy girl not obsessed with food.

Needless to say, this "diseased" and traumatizing cultural environment isn't good for men, either. Although men escape intense and global pressures to be thin, there is enough cultural pressure for men to be strong that some men lose themselves to drug-and-exercise addiction that is every bit as destructive and potentially lethal as anorexia. Terrence Real cites recent studies that show men's self-esteem is directly linked to their sense of muscular fitness. "In America, it seems, a woman cannot be too thin and a man cannot be too hard," he writes.[106] Being on the other side of the table or the bed from a woman in a power suit may make it easier for a man to "win": no matter how well dressed she is, a woman who is starving is hardly likely to make better decisions than a man who has just had steak and baked potato for lunch. But the cost to the man's sense of what is normal is enormous. Some of Mary Koss's first work on the prevalence of rape found that the closer men approached the stereotype of the masculine, the more likely they were to find rape acceptable. In other words, the culture that puts all relational qualities in women's basket, and puts being tender, being empathic, caring about not hurting, finding out and respecting what the other wants off limits for "real" (stereotypically masculine) men, makes rape normal for "real" men. And this split makes relationships dreadful for men. The 1998 National Violence Against Women Survey found that women were most at risk of violence from men they were close to and men were most at risk from men they didn't know; this difference follows directly from the cultural "disease" that makes relational qualities both feminine and trivial or weak. But it is a disease and a difference that the culture manages to keep remarkably unseen. When these prevalences were first reported in the 1970s, people found them completely counterintuitive. A news story describing the same pattern, known for three decades, called it a surprise in the year 2000. Warnings about the dangers of strangers are still the most common warnings children hear, even though more than three-quarters of child victims of rape—who now make up more than half of all rape victims in Massachusetts—are attacked by fathers, stepfathers, mother's boyfriends, male relatives, or other family friends.[107] Statistically, U.S. women are safer with strangers than with close male relatives or friends. If children were warned about the real risks they face, parents and teachers would teach girls to dread relationships, and they would teach boys to trust them. But despite the risks, our culture invites girls to value close relationships with men above all.

"Aggressive fathers make aggressive sons who turn into aggressive fathers. Nurturant mothers make affectionate daughters who turn into nurturant mothers," Herman and Lewis wrote in their fierce and poignant early paper about mother-daughter anger. "This difference has traditionally been valued ambivalently in our culture. On the one hand, women's nurturance has been culturally fostered as a means of ensuring that women will function as a refuge or haven for men, a relief from their exploitive behavior. On the other hand, these same qualities are denigrated as inferior in a culture that valorizes aggression (Miller, 1976)."

Mothers have to teach their daughters not to show the sort of "autonomy, adventurousness and initiative" that works for boys, because of the risk that girls who show off or take risks will trigger trusted and familiar boys and men to rape or molest them. "Mothers teach daughters that the social price they will have to pay for these qualities is very high and very real. Daughters in families where mothers don't protect them feel more betrayed than girls in families where the mothers are vigilant and restrictive," Herman and her mother wrote. This collaboration in writing about mother-daughter anger was the only time the two ever discussed it, Judy says. And one common source of daughters' anger at their mothers is that mothers often protect their daughters from "predatory male sexuality" without explanation. Mothers often set restrictive boundaries and curfews without explaining the real dangers not only of strange men but of men they may know well, so that girls experience what feels like pointless overprotectiveness from mothers, and children's culture mythologizes this kind of overprotection without explanation, or with a false explanation. Fairy tales—Cinderella, Sleeping Beauty, and Snow White—teach that *women* exploit women; men rescue women, and men can exempt their own princesses from the degraded lot of most women. Many mothers mirror this kind of legendary disinformation by protecting their daughters while misleading them into thinking that it is the mothers who are too restrictive rather than male relatives and friends who may be dangerous.[108]

Boys, on the other hand, learn to dread close relationships, even though, as men, they are actually safer with people they know well than with strangers. And this is the logic of a culture of dominance: men are most in danger of harm at the hands of strangers, and yet most men, women, boys, and girls are taught to beware strangers only.

Bergman first talked about what he calls "male relational dread" at a Stone Center colloquium in 1990. "Men," he explained, "are fashioned by an event that is profoundly different from that fashioning women: the disconnection from the *relationship* with mother, in the name of becoming a man."[109]

And "the issue is not Mother but relationship," he and Surrey stress in *We Have to Talk*.[110] Boys start to lose the relational mode—tears, empathy, tenderness, creativity, and curiosity in relationships—at a very young age. "Everything in the culture forces it to come about, in the name of 'growth,' " Bergman writes of little boys' losses.

> Prompted by father and the male image in the culture, the boy is heavily pressured to disconnect, to achieve maleness. Not only

is he expected to turn away from mother to do this, and not only is mother told she has to support this, but it is bigger than merely mother: It is a turning away from the process of connection. A boy is taught to become an agent of disconnection. The break is not only from connection, from mutual authenticity, but also a break from being in the process with a person, who happens to be a woman, and mother at that.

Boys are not valued for—and learn not to value—relational skills.

This theft of love from little boys is a profoundly political rite of passage, during which boys learn that their mothers are powerless to stop the cultural police who shame, tease, hit, beat, and lock them away from being relational and that the relational way itself leads away from power and success. "Ask any man about his boyhood, and you will hear hair-raising stories filled with incredible cruelty, violence, and daily terror. Boyhood is not a 'latency' in any sense of that word," Bergman writes.[111] Although our culture allows girls to go on practicing the art and science of relating with their mothers and others, girls, too, begin to learn they are spared because they simply aren't considered important enough to be forced to be non-relational, and that in fact their relational skills may make them targets of abuse by powerful men and boys who are close to them.

"Freud, as everyone knows, believed that the little girl as early as three years of age was profoundly shocked when she became aware that she did not have a penis," Stiver wrote in 1986, "and, furthermore, was devastated to learn that her mother did not have one either. I would suggest that both little girls and little boys experience shock and devastation when they confront indications that their beloved and highly valued mothers are often treated with contempt, harshness, and sometimes cruelty."[112] So here in the relational world we have boys losing love—not access to sex—around the time of the "Oedipal crisis" that Freud imagined tore boys from their imagined dream of sex with Mom, under the threat that Dad would castrate them if they tried anything. And here we have girls not crushed to learn they don't have penises but crushed to learn that they and their mothers do not have as much power as boys and men.

"Boys," my daughter tells me as a wise fourteen-year-old, sardonically in tune with her culture, "are supposed to destroy each other. Girls are supposed to destroy themselves."[113]

Bergman puts it more clinically:

> A primary violation in women's lives is the early realization that men are strong and can hurt them, physically and sexually. Little girls pick up the violence in a lack of connection—as subtle as a look in a man's eyes, a sexual objectification. Little boys often notice this fear in little girls. Boys learn about their physical power, to enjoy it, and to fear it.
>
> The last thing men can talk about with each other is their feelings about their potential for sexual violence. Often, it is not part of their awareness. For example, one day at my swim club, I was walking toward the whirlpool, wearing only my bathing suit; a woman in the whirlpool turned, saw me, and I saw in her eyes a sudden fear of me, a man; it made me realize how deeply women carry this, all the time.[114]

Men, harboring "relational dread," may feel afraid of what being at a loss with actively relating women may do to them; so men may fail to notice that women fear their greater power. Similarly, a white woman, crossing the street to avoid a black man she stereotypically fears may rob or rape her, may fail to register the shame that man feels because she is shunning him, and may fail to imagine the fear he feels of the trouble her greater power as a white person might call down on him, almost without her noticing. The system of dominance very neatly and personally protects dominant people from sensing the effects of their power in all but the most observant and open members of the dominant group. "The subordinate groups often can see more clearly some of the things the dominant group is not seeing, not only what is invisible about the subordinate groups but about the dominant group itself," Bergman and Surrey write.[115] But Bergman has tried to become one of the observant, open ones, and he ventures some of his reflections about being a white man:

> While men are taught that they have power and are supposed to act powerfully, men may sense women's fear of it. Men too are

afraid of it, in themselves, and from other men. In a patriarchy, men may also be victims. Hierarchy means that there's always someone more successful and more powerful, and men are haunted by failure. The biggest winners are potentially the biggest losers. In a power-over model, it isn't safe to take an authentic vulnerable, relational stance.[116]

A client Bergman and Surrey call Bill was six when he felt his first frisson of "male relational dread"; that was the day when comfort, understanding, and home first seemed more dangerous than the assaults that drove him to hunt for comfort:

> I had been beaten up at school, and I was walking home along the railroad tracks. I hadn't been hurt physically, much, but had been humiliated by the other boys in my class. Waves of feeling rose up, came out in sobs which I tried to choke off. I knew that my mother would be home, and I couldn't wait to tell her what happened . . . She heard me come in and turned around. I saw her seeing on my face my dried tears. I sensed her sensing my pain. She asked, "What happened? What's wrong, dear?"
>
> In that instant something shifted in me. I had been yearning to tell my mother what had happened, but as I saw her concern in her face, as I sensed her moving toward me with concern, I stiffened up inside.
>
> "Nothing," I said, and turned away, and went back out the door.

But Bill's mother didn't want to let the meanies win and leave him with no way to express what was so obviously real distress:

> I remember my mother facing me, asking me something, and my not knowing what to say. And then she got angry, or maybe she started crying. But she kept asking me, and the feeling I had, it was like she was ripping at my heart, my guts. Not only could I not say anything, but I had to steel myself against showing her any reaction. I made my face freeze, showing her no reaction, and tried my hardest not to respond, saying to myself: "Stay like this and it will be over." I felt like something horrible might happen. I wanted

desperately to respond to her, but could not, because if I said anything it would only get worse. I was in the searing spotlight of my
mother's love. I froze.

"Just as important as Bill's not showing his feelings is his *not being
moved* by the feelings of someone else, in this case the person most
dear to him in the world," Bergman and Surrey comment. And they
note that this dread is not something that belongs to Bill:

> Dread arises in the connecting.
> Dread is not carried inside him like a sickness. Dread arises not
> in the "I" or the "you" but in the "we." This is a radically different
> view from that of traditional theory, which views pathology, or neu-
> rosis, as residing within the person. In fact, male dread is not even
> pathological but something that often arises in the field of "normal"
> relationship, when men and women attempt to open up to each
> other, often in the most intimate situations.[117]

This distinction is a truly radical break with academic psychology and
psychiatry, a corollary of the idea that "self" is not the most accurate
way to describe human experience. Bergman, like the other relational-
cultural theorists, is saying psychological dysfunction originates and resides *between* people rather than *in* them, more like wars and enmity
than illness or disability.

Stiver tells a story about the way this dread can affect not just personal relationships but the practice of psychotherapy and the administration of mental hospitals. Speaking of the time when she was chief of
psychology at McLean Hospital, she says, "I was talking to a male colleague about something I considered to be extremely important. I
needed his support, and I was talking with a good deal of feeling. He
minimized what I said and downplayed its importance," Stiver says.
The more strongly she disagreed, the more dismissive her colleague
became.

"I was getting more and more exasperated. He kept saying, 'Well,
it's really not that important,' or 'Let's wait and see.' Finally, in a kind of
apathetic way, I said quietly, 'Well, there's this, this, and that.' "

Magic. As soon as Stiver drained her words of feeling, she recalls, "he said, 'Oh, why didn't you say that before—instead of coming on like a witch on a broom!' At first I was hurt; then I thought further—I tried to tell him something and let him know it was important, but he couldn't hear me. My intense expression of feeling made him too anxious to hear the message, yet I felt that my feelings were just as important to the communication as the words!" Even this male colleague of a female senior psychologist took the opportunity to enforce the cultural rule that women "need to curtail such feelings, as though one cannot harmonize cognitive effectiveness with affect. But one can be strong about convictions and emotionally expressive; can be involved in tasks, master them, and be concerned about people; can be analytic in problem solving and be intuitive. None of these qualities has to be polarized."[118]

A relational education, the kind Gilligan observed girls getting from mothers and from girl and women friends, builds "a basic sense of 'learning to listen,' to orient and attune to the other person through feelings," Bergman and Surrey write. By contrast, some of the men they have worked with have described their childhoods as what one man called "learning *not* to listen, to shut out my mother's voice so that I would not be distracted from pursuing my own interests" and could ignore his mother's requests for help or attempts to interest him in things she cared about or thought were important.[119] Bergman lists many ways that men are taught to twist relational skills into aids to disconnection. One of the most disabling is "compare, don't identify."[120] Instead of feeling connected by a sense of likeness or common ground, find the ways that you, or the other person, don't measure up to some ideal—and then compete, don't join. A question Bergman took from a man in the audience at the end of his first talk about male relational dread showed this disconnecting disease of comparison at work. "Are you saying that men are an inadequate version of women in the ability to be in relationship?" the man asked. "The issue is not to compare genders," Bergman answered. If you walk a mile in someone else's moccasins and spend the whole time wondering whether these moccasins are better or worse than yours, or paralyzed by fear that someone will see you wearing girl moccasins and will conclude that you're gay or a wimp and therefore not a real man, you'll never learn what the exercise is intended to teach. Bergman spent a long time qualifying his thesis with this questioner: many men are quite relational, and many women aren't; there are always individual exceptions to any cultural norm. But, in the aggregate, he said, "I think we men must face the facts: If the focus is mutual relationship, we have a lot to learn."[121]

In the late 1990s, Gilligan began to follow boys' early development to see how their development compared with girls'. "It's so parallel it's eerie," she was saying by 1999, "except it's happening at four or five." First of all, in the very youngest boys she and her students were studying in all kinds of school settings—public, private, urban, suburban—she often found the same kind of relational listening she found in preadolescent girls. These boys were listening, and they were completely unafraid to talk about what they heard. "Mommy, you have a happy voice, but I also hear a little worried voice," one boy said. In a lecture on gender she gave at Cambridge University in May 2003, she quoted a father's account: "Alex recalls that when he expressed his remorse for having 'lost it' and hit Nick the previous day, five-year-old Nick observed, 'You are afraid that if you hit me, when I grow up, I'll hit my children.' Alex, who had been hit by his father, had vowed to break the cycle; Nick registered his father's fear that the pattern will now continue into the next generation." But these clear, honest voices began to fade by kindergarten. "You hear the voice take on the voice-over voice," Gilligan says. Boys start to speak with the "objective" voice from nowhere that pretends it has no social location—no class, gender, or race and little empathy or imagination. "I feel like I've seen the initiation into patriarchy."

Judy Chu was one of the first of Gilligan's graduate students to join her in her study of boys. Chu had already studied adolescent boys in a number of school settings when she began to interview and observe preschool and kindergarten boys in a private school in the Boston area. She had seen older boys who had "learned from experience that when you put yourself out there, not only have you made yourself vulnerable, nine out of ten people will take advantage of that vulnerability," Chu says. The older boys she had studied had learned that peers and adults were likely to use, say, an admission of depression or weakness as a way to mock or hurt them. She had seen a boys' version of the conflict she calls "compromise versus overcompromise." For instance, she says, girls are famous for paying attention to others' feelings but "overcompromising" by losing connection to their own feelings. Now she began to see young boys excluding parts of themselves because they weren't boyish enough. For instance, a little boy who loved art and loved sports heard from his boy peers that he couldn't have both those interests. The first year Chu observed him, it was not hard for him to see himself differently from the way many of the other boys saw him. But a year later, he shows self-doubt. "This year he's saying, 'Maybe they're right.' Maybe he can't be artistic and love sports. He's starting to lose the connection with himself." The pressure behind his veering toward "overcompromise" comes mostly from other boys. They let him talk all he wants about art. But because he enjoys and talks about art sometimes, other boys exclude him at all times from the sports talk that is such a lingua franca among young males. "When he talks about sports, the other boys won't let him. The popular boys don't like it, and they all give him a hard time."

In the coed class Chu was observing, there was a girls' "team" and a boys' "team." The boys and girls called the boys' team "the mean team." These groups or gangs got together on the playground and also more or less ran the underground life of the classroom. In the second year of Chu's study, the boy who was "the boss of the mean team" became especially tough on resisters, boys he felt were on the fence about boy stuff or, worse, had friends on the girls' team and liked to play with them. One boy told Chu he had to pretend he didn't like the girls who were his friends. When Chu asked why, he said, "If the boss of the mean team finds out, he'll fire me from the team, and then I won't have a team, and that would be a bummer." In other words, he chose to isolate himself from girls so the other boys wouldn't isolate him. "He doesn't want to be on it, but if he quit the mean team, then they would all be against him," Chu says.

"Can a boy be on the girls' team?" Chu asked another boy.

"Not the boy-boys," he told her.

"Who are the boy-boys?" she asked him.

"Well, me definitely," the five-year-old said.

"That happens so young," Chu says. And boys think boy-boys are not good. "They are really attuned to what people think about boys—they know that people think they're sexual predators," she says. "They know that everyone thinks boys are bad—boys are violent." And because they get such heavy pressure not to think of themselves as broader or more complex than the boy-boy image—to the extent that, for instance, other boys won't allow them to talk about sports if they admit they like art—their options, as Chu puts it, are very limited. "Boys will be boys" means *to boys* "boys will be bad." At least that's what it means to the very young boys Chu has studied. But their attitudes are also remarkably adaptable. Chu tells a story to illustrate: the boys' teacher had a talk with the boss of the mean team and another boy, both of whom told the teacher they thought boys were bad. She insisted that boys were good. They gave an example: they would pick up another boy's pencil if they found it, and that would be bad. But their teacher insisted that they would tell the boy they had the pencil, and then he would know it wasn't lost but that they had found it for him, and that would be good. "She pushed the point with them," Chu says, "and then they acted totally different. Once they felt they were being perceived as good," they started to act more that way. "They responded so quickly," Chu says.

At the Harvard Medical School teaching conference Learning from Women, in April 2000, Gilligan gives an update on the work with preschool boys and their fathers that she, Chu, and other graduate students are doing. She talks about the way the fathers of the boys she observes in a small private-preschool class notice openness and integration of thought and feeling in their sons and prize it, as they recall having had and lost similar qualities as young boys. She describes a man she calls Jim, the father of a boy she calls Jake, "on all fours with Jake on his back, Jake's arms wrapped around his father's neck, his face reaching around like a turtle's, kissing his father tenderly on the cheek," and she talks about the empathy Jim's "open affection" calls up in her: "I am moved by this father's ease in receiving the love of his small son, his steadiness, his unhurried presence."

"Getting close and getting quiet and hearing and talking on sort of a personal, very personal level. Those are the things we do together," Jim says of his best times with Jake. He and his son love to "have these great conversations and be really physical and have this very sweet time, so unself-consciously," Jim says.

"Sweet" is also the word that John uses to talk about his four-year-old son Ben's "sensitivity" and "real joy" in his drawings, which show real talent, and in his friends. "They just make me feel so good," John says.

But when Carol meets these same fathers the next year, outside the kindergarten classroom, they respond very differently, she says. Jim is now worried that Jake is too concerned about the relational life of his classroom; he fears that Jake has been referred for testing for a learning disability or attention disorder because of the very "qualities he treasured and nurtured in Jake" during their "great conversations" of the year before, Carol says. "Jake is tracking the relationships, Jim says, rather than paying attention to what he needs to do in school. It is separating him from the other boys, and he is losing his position in the group.

"I see Jim's concern, his fear really that maybe he was leading Jake down a wrong path," Gilligan says, using her own empathic responses the way another scientist might use other sense data. "I try to make emotional contact, but I have the impression that Jim is not open for the conversation I want to have, or at least not at that moment. He is focused on helping Jake make the adjustment to school. I feel I am in the presence of a different man" from the one who had found his son's openness so sweet—and so poignantly reminiscent of a lost openness of his own childhood.

"John also seems different to me the following year," Gilligan says. "He tells me proudly that Ben, now five and in kindergarten, is into soccer and coin collecting. 'What about his drawing?' I ask. I could be speaking a foreign language. John brushes off the question and repeats that Ben is now playing soccer and collecting coins."[122]

Boys at four were "direct, attentive, articulate and authentic," Chu concluded in the dissertation she wrote under Carol's supervision about their work with boys. But Chu found that over the year they turned five, the boys changed, Gilligan says. "She captured the change through a series of 'in-' words, negating or muting the qualities in the boys that she found so astonishing the previous year: 'inattentive, inarticulate, indirect, inauthentic,' " Gilligan comments.

Chu also worked as an assistant to William Pollack, a clinical professor of psychology at Harvard Medical School who has treated hundreds of boys at McLean Hospital as an appreciative colleague of Judy

Jordan's. Like Bergman, Gilligan, and Chu, Pollack sees in boys the same culturally enforced, premature separation from mothers and families and also from situations boys can count on to be safe. In his surprising bestseller *Real Boys*, Pollack writes:

> We expect them to step outside the family too abruptly, with too little preparation for what lies in store, too little emotional support, not enough opportunity to express their feelings, and often with no option of going back or changing course. We don't tolerate any stalling or listen to any whining. That's because we believe that disconnection is important, even essential, for a boy to "make the break" and become a man. We do not expect the same of our girls. In fact, if we forced our daughters to disconnect in the same manner as we do boys—with so little help and guidance—we would expect the outcome to be traumatic.[123]

During his decades of work as a therapist and teacher at the Family Institute of Cambridge, Terrence Real followed the link in memory, back from male depression to this traumatic, socially enforced disconnection that makes a boy a man. He titled his book on the subject *I Don't Want to Talk About It: Overcoming the Secret Legacy of Male Depression*. Children, Real writes, citing Herman, try to preserve their connections to their parents even when those connections have to become pathological because the parents abuse or neglect them. In fact, because they are being injured, they paradoxically need those attachments more than if they were not being abused. But if they are boys, they can't talk about these needs, because "in our culture expressiveness—even talking in an animated way with great emotional range—is reserved for women," he writes. "Recent research indicates that in this society most males have difficulty not just in expressing but even in identifying their feelings. The psychiatric term for this impairment is *alexithymia* and psychologist Ron Levant estimates that close to *eighty percent* of men in our society have a mild to severe form of it."[124] So for boys, Real thinks, first there is the traumatic loss of connection, then the loss of expressiveness, then the dissociative loss of knowing what they feel, and this is called becoming a man. In his second book, he calls it "the toxic legacy of masculinity."[125] Real has memories of his own about this kind of splitting, which he calls "doubling," citing the psychiatric pioneer investigator of the effects of brainwashing and political terror, Robert Jay Lifton.

"I remember, from the earliest age, teaching myself how to dissociate, consciously schooling myself in the art of leaving my own body to hover somewhere close to the ceiling. Looking back, I can recall it all clearly from an aerial view, my father's face suffused with blood, purple with exertion, his eyebrows drawn in concentration. The boy, bent over, his pants at his ankles, like an embarrassed spectator, turning away. The whiteness of the boy's skin," Real writes, remembering his father beating him. "When my father was carried away by his rage, both he and I dropped into different variations of trance. My father moved into the intoxication of dominance while I split off from my own body, hovering above the scene."[126]

Of course, as Herman especially likes to stress, most men who are traumatized by violent abuse do not become violent themselves. Many learn from the pain and shame never to do such a terrible thing to another person. Real cites the research of the psychologist David Lisak, who studied 250 men who had been abused as children. Half were supermacho, much more rigidly and stereotypically masculine or "hypermasculine" than a control group. An equal number were thoughtful nonconformists, "radically untraditional in both the ways that they envisioned themselves and in their concepts about the male role" and "far more unconventional" than the control group of men who hadn't been abused, Real reports. "Having found themselves unmanned"—not by violence itself but by violent defeat—"these men rewrite the criteria for manhood," Real concludes.[127] The violence they suffered made them examine and reject the masculine role associated with violence and love of violence. In Lisak's study, the game of violence didn't seem worth the candle of masculinity to half of these men who had been abused.

Lonnie H. Athens, a criminological sociologist who began his lifelong exploration of violence with his own personal history of abuse by his father, describes four stages of what he calls "violentization" a person must go through to become violent and dangerous. "Brutalization"—

the stage of childhood victimization, of repeated trauma to bodies and relationships—is only the first stage of this process. Victims who become abusers also have to win a fight and become notorious for it in a way they feel makes their lives better. And they have to be coached, by people they believe have been violent or are violent themselves, to believe that using enough violence to defeat or disable an adversary "is a *personal* responsibility which they cannot evade" because the world is such a nasty place that "grave harm should be done to certain people," Athens writes. In other words, apprenticeship in violence doesn't require just the absence of good relationships, and thus the absence of those five good things Jean Miller writes about (zest, empowerment, knowledge, sense of worth, and desire for more and better connection). People can only learn violence in actively bad relationships that bring trauma and betrayal. Richard Rhodes, a journalist whose personal history of childhood abuse has inspired him to explore violence from its source in individual experience to its apocalyptic apogee in nuclear weapons, has rescued Athens, who teaches at Seton Hall University, from the obscurity of academic journals and texts. In *Why They Kill*, his book about Athens's work, Rhodes notes that people who are qualified to be violence coaches don't coach just anybody. Like everything else in the world of human relationships, violent coaching has its politics: "Women are evidently discriminated against as candidates for violent coaching, if you will, just as they are discriminated against in other athletic, social and employment processes dominated by men, simply because they are female."[128]

Most abusers abuse in secret, and sacrifice the notoriety their violence or sexual abuse would bring them, because they don't want to get caught. These people do not become the violent and dangerous criminals Athens has studied. They become violent and dangerous parents, adult relatives, teachers, coaches, and religious leaders. As Herman notes again and again, perhaps 90 percent of abusers are never studied, because they don't get caught. And most victims of trauma—if only the near-universal trauma of disconnection our culture makes part of growing up for boys and girls—are also silent about both the way parents and other important adults disconnect from them at four or fourteen and the way they themselves later disconnect from children and adults. Gilligan and Real interviewed couples together and "were struck by the extent to which both women and men know in some sense where they have sealed off love, the deals they have made and the compromises struck, always for good reason but often at enormous cost," Gilligan writes in a draft of her book about relationship and trauma, *The Birth of Pleasure*. The draft she shows me in 2000 is a kind of fugue that returns again and again to a few key themes—preschool boys, adolescent girls and Anne Frank's diary, Abraham and Isaac, the Oedipus story, couples in crisis, and the story of Cupid and Psyche that Gilligan sees as the Western myth that teaches how to resist, reconnect, and even create pleasure after trauma. "The trauma inherent in patriarchy and which fuels its continuation is a break in relationship with women and boys on the part of both women and men," Gilligan writes.[129]

> Trauma is the shock to the psyche that leads to dissociation: our ability to separate ourselves from parts of ourselves, to create a split within ourselves so that we can know and also not know what we know, feel, and yet not feel our feelings. It is our ability, as Freud put it in Studies on Hysteria, to hold our experiences not as a secret from others but as a "foreign body" within ourselves. So that we can be angry without feeling our anger, feel sad without knowing we are sad. We can separate our sense of ourselves, from our knowing of pleasure, feel and yet not feel our joy. This sense of inner division, like the split between ourselves and our relationships, has become so much a part of our history that for the most part we take it for granted. Yet we have come collectively in the late twentieth century to a crisis of relationships, when old forms of relationships that were based on not knowing and inauthenticity or outward forms of threat and oppression no longer seemed desirable or even tenable, and when we are experimenting with new forms, uncertain of the outcome, unsure of the way.

And again, a few pages later, from a slightly different direction: "Trauma is inherent in patriarchy; to be patriarchal is to disrupt connection—in splitting fathers from sons, in dividing men from women. When we stop and think about what we are reading, in the Bible and in Greek tragedy, we see how consistently we are reading stories about a traumatic disruption of love and desire that leads to some kind of crushing of the soul."[130]

The symptoms of relational dread and PTSD that disconnection and trauma cause look startlingly like traditional, stereotypical machismo. "Our findings suggest that PTSD patients' difficulties with putting feelings into words are mirrored in actual changes in brain activity" that record traumatic events in catastrophic feelings rather than words, van der Kolk writes. People who suffer PTSD can't rely on empathic responses—say, the way Gilligan does in her studies of boys and girls—because their responses are distorted by constant hyperalert attention that paradoxically gives them no help in figuring out what is more or less important, menacing, or safe in any situation. So "they respond with fight-or-flight reactions. This causes them to freeze, or, alternatively, to overreact and intimidate others in response to minor provocations," van der Kolk writes.

> Having been chronically aroused, without being able to do much to change this level of arousal, persons with PTSD may (correctly) experience just having feelings as being dangerous. Because of their difficulties using emotions to help them think through situations and come up with adaptive solutions, emotions merely become reminders of their inability to affect the outcome of their life. In PTSD, extreme feelings of anger and helplessness can be understood as the reliving of memories of the trauma; like other memories of the trauma, they become reminders that are to be avoided.[131]

In other words, people who commit violence that causes trauma are often living out an extreme masculine stereotype of toughness or are using intimidation to enforce political dominance. And some of the aftereffects of trauma look a lot like that very masculine stereotype, but they only take that form in the people who develop post-traumatic disorders and are in a political position to dominate. The post-traumatic disorders of people who have little or no political power don't resemble machismo; PTSD in subordinate people makes them look like sissies, wimps, or borderlines.

Herman unfailingly points out a fallacy in the concept of a so-called cycle of violence. Most people who are abused do not become abusers, and in fact abuse survivors often motivate themselves to protect children or other dependents even when they have lost or never developed a sense of worth that would motivate them to protect themselves. A history of abuse does not necessarily make someone an abuser. However, the chances of becoming an abuser are greater when an abuse history is combined with a position of power—sometimes simply by virtue of being young, adult, and male—in which "kicking butt," for instance, may be regarded as an achievement or perhaps even a prerequisite for respect, and "kill" may be a man's transitive verb for having sex with a woman. In this analysis, the general contractor for the social construction of masculinity and femininity is psychological trauma, but the architect is the system of dominance.[132] In fact, given the political way "violent coaching" or another form of cultural valorization of violent men is used to turn abused boys but not girls into abusers, trauma becomes indispensable as the culture's dominance factory, turning out subordinate and dominant with cruel efficiency. The study Herman, Perry, and he made of so-called borderline patients led them to portray typical borderline behavior relationally, van der Kolk writes: "Most traumatized patients were clinging and dependent on the one hand, but socially isolated without mutually rewarding relationships on the other. Many had retreated into social isolation after years of frantic searches for rescuers." His profile of this group sounds a great deal like the people on both sides of Jean Miller's paradigm of dominant and subordinate behavior and shows in psychiatric and even neurological terms the cause-and-effect relationship that feminists and civil rights activists had long suspected of the culture at large—that dominance is created and enforced by violence. Because these patients had learned about power and relationship by being beaten or raped by people they loved or depended on, scanning any situation to discern who had power over whom became a survival tool. "Having a history of helplessness with people in power, they tended to cast most subsequent relationships in terms of dominance and submission. When they were in a position of power, they often inspired fear and loathing" in their subordinates; "when they were in a subordinate position, they often felt helpless, behaved submissively, did not stand up for themselves, and tended to engage in idealization (and/or devaluation) at the expense of being able to experience their own competence."[133]

" 'If I were to say what I was feeling and thinking, no one would want to be with me, my voice would be too loud,' seventeen-year-old Iris says, half to me and half to herself," Carol writes in her draft of *The Birth of Pleasure*. "Looking straight at me, Iris adds with an edge of defiance, 'But you have to have relationships.' 'Yes,' I agree. 'But if you are not saying what you are feeling and thinking, then where are you in these relationships?' It is my question for girls and women; it is my question for myself. Iris sees the paradox in what she is saying: she has given up relationship so that she can have relationships, muting her voice and hiding herself so that 'she' can be with other people."[134]

Miller first wrote about what she called "one major paradox" in a paper she read at a Harvard Medical School Learning from Women conference in April 1987, using her composite middle-class mother Ann as an example: Ann's husband and other friends continually stop or dismiss her when she is saying what she really thinks and feels, mostly because they don't or won't listen, but Ann still tries to stay in these relationships in some form by "keeping more and more of herself out of her relationships"—saying less and less about how she really is.[135] Miller described how growth-stopping relationships could lead to "the most terrifying and destructive feeling that a person can experience"—a kind of isolation that leads to "feeling locked out of human connection. This feeling of desperate loneliness is usually accompanied by the feeling that you, yourself, are the reason for the exclusion. It is because of *who* you are." And yet, because the isolation is really caused by someone's refusal to listen to you, or to stop pressuring you to pretend you think or feel something you don't, "you feel helpless, powerless, unable to act to change the situation," Miller wrote. "People will do almost anything to escape this combination of condemned isolation and powerlessness."[136]

Miller lists the ills—"depression itself, phobias, eating problems and others"—that "have all grown out of attempts to find a possibility of acting within connections when the only connections available present *impossibilities*—when the people in available relational contexts have threatened or actually carried out disconnections and violations."[137] Depressed and anxious people have repeatedly tried to form good, mutual, empathic relationships with the people around them, and those people have been impossible—unresponsive at best and abusive at worst.

Dana Crowley Jack, a second psychology clinician who got her doctorate working with Gilligan and the Harvard Project researchers, has found that

> self-silencing, or keeping anger and other vital feelings out of the relationship, appears particularly linked to depression, because anger demands positive, interpersonal expression; its function is to regulate relationships, restore connection, and have an interpersonal effect. Silencing anger doesn't change what aroused anger in the first place. And self-silencing can make a woman feel separated from others and from herself and can present a "false self" to others. Her anger over this disconnection can contribute to depression, as can hopelessness about changing the conditions that instigate anger.

The price of expressing anger—perhaps shaming, isolation, or violence—may seem impossibly high, Jack and Lyn Brown write in *The Complete Guide to Mental Health for Women*, a practical handbook of relational psychology published in 2003.[138]

Miller notes that physical and sexual violations combined with relational violations make "a most extreme impossibility" for human psychological growth.[139] Then she describes the five bad things that come from disconnections in bad relationships and can drive a person into the relational paradox: trying to keep out of a relationship so you can stay in it.

First, you feel "the opposite of zest," Miller says. Call it blah. Miller's colleague Nikki Fidele calls it "feeling disconnected about being disconnected." Miller says it's hard to pick out because it's the general background feeling most people find in their jobs and many women feel in their lives.

Second, the motivation to act shrivels, because people have the experience that "if I act in what seems to me a moment to act in, it leads to this disconnection." Miller describes this tentativeness as an attitude born of repeatedly feeling unheard or put down, a feeling that "your desires are going to lead to this big trouble—this terrible feeling that you don't like."

Third, the more someone pushes you away or rejects you for expressing your real thoughts and feelings, the less you feel you know about the person, the relationship, yourself, or any relationship. "There can be great confusion because you don't understand what's going on," Miller says. One of the injuries a battered woman suffers is bewilderment about why her batterer is assaulting her. She scans the relationship to learn what she does to cause mistreatment, but she can learn nothing, because the mistreatment is not about anything she does but about her batterer's need to show dominance through violence. When people complain that they "feel crazy," Miller and Stiver write, "this 'feeling crazy' often refers to their confusion about what they are feeling when there is no adequate response to them from other people."[140]

The fourth bad thing that comes with bad connection or chronic disconnection is "a diminished sense of worth," Miller says. Being disregarded or being asked to obey rather than listen and respond, or having to manipulate other people and make them obey, assaults and erodes anyone's sense of worth. This particular bad thing is much more obvious in the subordinate person—the victim of racism or gay bashing, the abused child, the demeaned adolescent, the ignored wife. But dominant people can't develop or maintain a sense of worth based on good connection, because money and power can't buy good connection. So, Miller says, dominant people may actually develop differently. They may develop "according to other theories," the self-at-the-apex kind, like Freud's, where "if they've been lucky and had these wonderful mothers, then they've developed this great sense of their own egos." So on the subordinate, bossed end of disconnections we find people who feel worthless and oppressed, and on the dominant, bossing end we find people who have big egos but little dignity. These disconnected, often disconnecting dominant people use "ego inflation as a kind of intoxication" that pumps them up so they don't notice, or at least don't often notice, how unworthy they feel.

Then there are hybrid relationships, in which "big shots who get to the top of the heap," for instance, "have women around them, but also some men, who play that role" of the empathic listener and connector, Miller says. These are the dominant people who allow some underlings to speak truth to power. But instead of relating creatively as equals, "they're really using other people's ability to try to engage" in a mutual relationship; these dominant people dabble in good connection as a way of getting close to the five good things, and they do get some benefit. But they can't let go of their dominance enough to make it truly mutual. And for the subordinate people who are trying to engage them but get very little mutuality back, it is still "a kind of relational activity, so it feels better" than not being allowed even to try to engage as equals, empathically, at least for a time. But eventually, if the dominant person continues only to toy with connecting and continually retreats out of relationship into shaming, rejecting, neglecting, unlistening coercion, based on a sense of superior power, the person who is trying to relate comes to feel "mixed up, angry, hurt, disappointed" and exhibits "a great tendency to feel 'it must be me.'"

This impulsion out of relationship into a sense that there is something wrong with oneself leads to the fifth bad thing that comes from disconnection, the sense of isolation that feels as though it will never change. Because the other person won't honestly connect or won't connect for long enough for a coherent relationship to form, "you can't find a way to move, to do something." And this sense of stasis, "stuckness," is as profound as the sense of being wrong.

Disconnections can be brief and minor—a husband or father changes the subject immediately after a wife or child has revealed something very important to her—or they can be prolonged, repeated, and severe, like incest, racism, or war. But any disconnection leaves the people on each end of a relationship at best feeling blah, stuck, confused, worthless, and alone in a caroming and intensifying isolation for which they feel they must somehow personally be to blame. For the more powerful person, who uses power and a sense of entitled privilege to disconnect, these bad things are often masked by an intoxicating rush of narcissism. Rapists and murderers described these kinds of feelings to James Gilligan. Doing bad and feeling good, even great, these dominant disconnectors are on the converse side of the women or subordinate men Miller described as doing good and feeling bad.

This relational paradox—keeping your true feelings out of relationship to maintain some semblance or remnant of relationship—makes it possible to reframe the ideas of conscious and unconscious, Miller says. Consciousness and unconsciousness become simply the experiences or memories that a person can and cannot represent—perhaps even to herself or himself—in a given relationship. Based on their past experiences of disconnection, "people develop strategies of trying to stay connected by keeping important parts out of connection," Miller says, and that idea comes "very close to Carol. In fact, that's where, without really speaking about it, she and I wrote almost the same sentence."

"Jean and I wrote versions of the same thing," Carol agrees. Carol's version appeared in her essay "Joining the Resistance," which she first read as the Tanner Lecture on Human Values at the University of Michigan in the spring of 1990. In adolescence, she wrote, "Paradoxically, girls are taking themselves out of relationship for the sake of relationship and self-consciously letting go of themselves." Gilligan found girls deliberately, skillfully noticing what aspects of their experience the people they love and need rejected in their interactions. So when peers, women, boys, and men ignore or mock certain ideas or feelings, they simply leave that stuff out of those relationships—in order to preserve any sense of relationship at all. A teacher at the conference she and her colleagues had with Laurel School teachers about the results of their years of interviewing Laurel girls put it to Carol this way: " 'I think,' Sharon Miller says, 'they have let go of themselves. I think it is the unusual middle school girl who can say . . . if you don't like me the way I am, fine. Most girls can't say that because there is no one there.' " No inner or outer authority backs them up enough to give them this kind of confidence. "Why not, I ask her," Carol continues. "I am thinking of the girls who are so resolute, so present at eleven. 'Well,' " Sharon Miller continues, " 'that's the question, you know: what happens to girls when they get to that age? Well, because that is the age when girls start identifying with adult women.' And then, suddenly, seeing the circle"—of her own logic—"closing, she says, hand rising, covering her mouth, 'My God,' as tears begin flowing, 'And there is nothing there.' "[141] This teacher is saying that at times when girls look to older women for models of holding on to their unique voices, those women often respond by silencing themselves and turning away from the girls.

The women literally or figuratively abandon the girls rather than stay with them in relationship. "You're on your own" is a common message from women to girls at moments when adolescent girls look to women for support for their passions and their honesty.

The idealized image of the perfect girl that Catherine Steiner-Adair and Lyn Brown find girls starving and stifling behind is often an image that is handed to girls for emulation by teachers, parents, and adults they admire. And at the same time, adults often trivialize or demonize the sprawling, sloppy, angry and "fresh," brutally honest, ceaselessly, shamelessly questioning kid who longs only for world peace or ten dollars to see the latest sex comedy or horror flick. When adolescents turn to the nearest adults with their tough questions and rising feelings about just what is going on in the system of dominance, here, today, in this classroom or kitchen, they often encounter parents and teachers or mentors who act as though they have become devils or ditzes by asking these questions. At these moments of need, when one might say adolescents are asking adults how to stay in "To Be" as they move from childhood to adolescence, the adults, as Sharon Miller saw, often disappear into "Not to Be." Often women do not listen to girls or empathize with them or show them how to live with these dilemmas. Instead, the adults to whom girls turn with the messy passions and agonies of their age often withdraw from good, honest, mutual relationships. Often without really understanding what they are doing, women may retreat into expectations that girls should quiet down and act like selfless "good little girls," or the women simply give the girls the silent treatment.[142]

Jean Miller talks about Ann, who becomes convinced that her husband doesn't listen to her because there is something wrong with her, even as she says less and less to him to try to keep that wrong thing under wraps. Carol writes about Anna, the working-class girl who taught Lyn Brown so much.

At twelve, Anna says she is starting to think about things she accepted on faith earlier, because "you just kind of trusted the teacher." Most of the time, she says, "I'm in a pretty good mood, and sometimes I'm not. Sometimes I am mad at the world." In her interview at thirteen, Anna gives the response "I don't know" sixty-seven times, more than three times as often as she said it at twelve in an interview of the same length. Now she talks about how much she loves reading and singing because "I can just kind of get lost in them and not have to think about things." "She watches others to see which way to go and does not, she says, 'massively disagree on anything.' With friends, if she disagreed, she would be 'kind of mad at myself, have kind of a messed up feeling.' With adults, 'they would overpower me most of the time,' " Anna says. "Paradoxically, for the sake of relationship and also for protection, she is disconnecting self from others," Carol writes.

A year later, at fourteen, Anna says she is "really loud" again. She peppers her interview with more than twice as many "I don't know"s as last time, but now they alternate with "you know"—"punctuating a tale of resistance which is clearly political," Carol writes. Anna is still feeling pressure to fake being too nice to notice pain and hypocrisy—pressure to not know what she knows, as Carol puts it—but she is deciding to resist that pressure and look for allies wherever she can find them, "you know," even among Harvard Project interviewers. "I see things from lots of points of view" is the way Anna now frames her ability to see beyond the Pollyanna blinders of the "perfect girl," and the adjective she chooses for this breadth of perspective has changed in a year from "crazy" to "creative."

Anna has found the courage to hold on to her own perceptions, and she asserts it in English class when her teacher assigns a theme about a hero. Anna knows what she's supposed to write: "There was a ladeedah hero who went and saved all humankind." But Anna sees heroism differently: she sees it as part of the problem of the system of dominance, a system in which some people are seen as heroic giants, nearly immortal, and others are seen as peons and wimps. This kind of valorizing serves evil as often as it serves good, Anna sees, and so she decides to write her theme from the point of view of a young German boy in the Hitler Youth, admiring his hero, *der Führer*. Anna is part German; her father has been out of work, and her father and brothers "easily resort to what she calls 'brute force' in the face of frustration." They hit her, and each other, demonstrating to Anna "how the need to appear strong or heroic can cover over vulnerability and lead to violence," Carol writes. Anna's teacher, however, disses Anna's need to explore the causes and the perils of making heroes. "She really did not go for that at all," Anna says. "I started to write, and she got really mad, and she was like, 'I am afraid you are going to come out sounding like a little Nazi.'" To Anna, her teacher's insistence on calling Hitler an "antihero" and saving the word "hero" for good guys "was just narrow-minded," a refusal to see the danger in heroism. But this was a question close to Anna's heart, and she just couldn't let go of it. Here is the Anna of fourteen, trying again to insist on being honest in relationships after backing off a year earlier. Perhaps because she is giving honest self-expression a second chance, she cares passionately about convincing her teacher to hear what she is saying about the dangers of idealization. "I had to write that paper because I was so mad," Anna says. "I had to write it to explain it to her, you know," she says (looking for some resonance from her interviewer, a nod or a noise of agreement, with that "you know"). "I just had to make her understand."

"This urgent need to 'make her understand,' the overwhelming desire for human connection—to bring one's own inner world of thoughts and feelings into relationship with the thoughts and feelings of others—feels very pressing to girls who fight for authentic relationships and who resist being shut up, put down, turned away, ignored," Gilligan writes. Anna's friend went to her teacher as an ambassador from Anna; Anna's mother told her to write the paper but to be careful not to turn her teacher against her. Anna wrote two papers, "a ladeedah one and the one I wanted to write," she explains. Her teacher gave her an A on "the normal one." Anna showed she could do what the teacher wanted, retail the myth of glorious heroism. And then Anna asked her teacher to do what Anna wanted—to listen to her ideas about the corrupting dangers of heroic myths. In the end, Anna says she learned "not to antagonize people," by listening to her mother and writing two papers. She believes her teacher didn't learn much and "probably saw it as more annoying than anything." She doesn't think her teacher ever got it, but at least she read both papers, and Anna at least tried to represent her experience, to connect.

Interviewed at fifteen, Anna is now asking "questions about religion and violence" in class, Carol writes. Anna learns these questions are as unwelcome to her classmates as her essay about Hitler and hero worship was to her English teacher. Talking to her Harvard Project interviewer, she recalls taking part passionately in what Carol calls "an intensely controversial classroom conversation" and noticing "a bunch of people who just sat there like stones."[143] Anna is realizing that even if she finds a way to remain honest about her beliefs in school, she will often have to feel like a member of a resistance movement, speaking out among the silenced and against the silencers, finding support in literature and a few very close relationships.

The last time Gilligan taught her big adolescence course at Harvard, in 1991, a student came up to her and asked a question during the break. "I work with adolescents. I work with kids who kill themselves and kill other people," the woman student said. "If I come into relationship with them—there's no counseling available to these kids in the place where I work—if I come into relationship with these kids, what happens to me when they kill themselves or kill other people? Are boundaries always a bad thing?"

When the class reconvened, Carol tried not to answer the question but to rephrase it relationally: "Can I be in relationship with this other person? Is that relationship making it impossible for me to be in relationship with myself? Because if I can't, then I have to make one of two moves, if you will remember *In a Different Voice*: I will either become in the terms of that book 'selfish' and say 'I have no time for your world,' or 'selfless,' meaning I will give up my entire world to be with you in your world—anything. You can come in, I'll give up everything I care about and believe in so I can be with you." Both of these moves force you out of relationship, Carol says. But they have different values. "One is called good for women, and one is called bad for women. Selflessness is 'good.' It's how you get to be known as a good woman. And then you ask yourself—the chapter title in Jean Baker Miller's book captures this: 'Why am I doing good and feeling bad?' " Women's laughter rippled up. "No, seriously, because you're doing good all the time, but you're feeling more and more isolated, because of course you're being selfless in relationship, meaning you're not in relationship. It's the paradox," Carol said: in order to keep up some kind of conversation, some appearance of relationship, women often have to keep their true needs and likes and thoughts and feelings out of a relationship for the sake of pleasing the other person, who they fear or know would reject their true feelings or ignore their needs, if they tried to express them and thereby make the relationship real.

But this is the paradox adolescents are up against, too, and later Carol draws another picture of Anna. "Her question is, 'How do you know if what someone is saying is true?' And she resists silencing her voice when she disagrees with her mother, her teacher, her friend." Anna is frank about her background, Carol says: " 'The centerpiece on our dining room table is a pile of unpaid bills.' That's a quote from her interview. She's a child growing up in the midst of domestic violence who has a confiding relationship with her mother. And all the studies on resilience, psychological resilience, the ability of a child to flourish in a difficult situation, stress—this is the work of E. James Anthony on what he called 'the invulnerable child' and the work of Michael Rutter." Gilligan is careful to cite her sources. And of course these sources are saying just what Freud told Elisabeth von R.'s mother when he appealed to her, because they show that "the presence of a confiding relationship, meaning a relationship in which one can speak one's psychic life, is the best protection against psychic illness. So Anna's relationship with her mother becomes key.

"She's not a popular girl in her school," Carol finishes her portrait, "but she is the editor of her school newspaper, which means that she is someone who is determined to be outspoken."

Her portraits of adolescent girls are different from those of other psychologists, Gilligan says. "Adolescence may be a 'second individuation' for boys—that's Peter Blos's term—or a time of 'identity crisis'— that's Erikson's term—or as Harry Stack Sullivan sees it, it's a time of relational opportunity, where the desire for a chum and then what he calls 'lust dynamism' bring people out of loneliness, are powerful propellants back into relationship, or as Freud says a time for 'object refinding.' Object finding is object refinding, Freud said.[144] The implication is there has been an early loss, and here's a chance to mend it or repair it.

"For girls in the work of our research taking women's development back into girlhood, the suggestion that comes so strongly out of that work is this is the time, so to speak, of first individuation, in the sense of coming up against a chasm which forces or tries to force a separation of self from relationships—that that separation has not been made until adolescence." So girls are only asked to endure the mind/body, thought/feeling, self/relationship split at adolescence, whereas boys are pushed to start splitting off their feelings much earlier. And "if you want to see the cultural mandating of those separations, you can see how they're written into the course catalog of this university: courses on cognition, courses on emotion, the notion of the self, the notion of relationships, and so forth," Gilligan adds.

A decade before, Gilligan had explained to her class that the culture of adolescence reflects the selfish/selfless split in groups—so there are the "good" groups of adolescents who have given in to the cultural pressure and have split thought from feeling and try to match the traditional ideals of perfect girls and heroic boys. And then there are "the dissidents: imperfect girls, and the boys who are not heroic," Carol said. It's important for students of adolescence "to appreciate, to see what's at stake then: the power over adolescents of these judgments, the power of the cultural voices, one senses the power to overwhelm, to destroy relationships. Experience seems so small compared to the hugeness, the power of the social construction of reality and its institutions, in churches and schools, in the media and so forth."

Just talking about adolescents brings them into the room, she said, since even when you speak *about* people, and not just to them, you are in some kind of relationship with them and your attitude to them and to their integrity will affect that relationship and your voice as you speak, Gilligan said. "How easy it is to lose the voice or the voices of adolescence, and how easy it is particularly as professionals in the fields of psychology and education to speak in a voice-over voice of authority which does not first take the time and trouble to hear and sort of draw out the complexity of adolescent voices, children's voices"—and their differences.

A few years later, talking with Normi Noel and me on that splendid fall day in Cambridge, Carol says it was in 1991, working with middle-school girls in the Theater, Writing, and Outing Club, that she and her colleagues and students really learned what girls are protecting when they resist adult co-optation. It was here that the Harvard Project joined the resistance and began to make a language for what they themselves were resisting and what they were protecting out of their own deepest experience (of great art, of love and hope, of their own questions). "To Be" and "Not to Be" were the names Normi and Carol gave to the worlds of love and hierarchy, connection and disconnection. And "the Accident" became their term for the way "Not to Be deals its blow," as Normi put it.

"The Accident," she explains, is "when you hit the patriarchy, when the culture hits you."

By the final year of their study, "nail polish and boys and dates started to replace the conversation" for all but two of the girls, Normi says. "I remember Carol saying, 'I can't bear watching this.' The two girls both hung on to 'To Be,' to who they are, and what I watched with Kate was—I didn't know what to say about their voices. Their voices were huge and big and full, that's what I saw," Normi says. "They weren't puzzled. They seemed to know that women were in shards, generally. But a generosity of spirit that I cannot forget.

"They didn't reject me, and they didn't make me feel like a fool for being an adult and being crippled in a way that they were whole. And I felt a lot of humiliation. It was never spoken about, but that's my take, that's how I felt." But the shame she felt for being less whole than the girls she was supposed to guide and observe did not stop Normi from making precise observations about the changing quality of their voices. As a trained voice teacher, she noticed that as time went on, their voices generally had less volume and were "more on one note," even though they were still showing the honesty and ease that characterize "To Be." It was almost as though they could sense that the end of their freedom was imminent, the voice teacher says. "Just before the Accident, coming into the Accident, their voices get smaller and smaller," Normi says. And then one day she saw the Accident happen.

"I remember Kate standing up for one little girl who was being really maligned by the rest of the group," Normi says. "And Kate said, 'It's not fair, you guys. She just—she's moved four times this year, and she's having a hard time.' And they all jumped on her and said [huge and brash], 'Oh, what do you know, blahlahlahlah, she's a jerk.' And she *was* hard to deal with, but Kate stood up for her, and then I watched her go. This is what happened to her voice: She said [loud and full], 'You guys, it's—' Then she got hit—Accident. Then, just from the side of her mouth to Carol and Annie: 'It's just not fair, she had to—' And it goes into this," Normi says, and she falls into a dead quiet. "We didn't say anything. We didn't know what to say." But Kate had one more drop of the courage to stay connected to the girl who was being maligned, Normi says. "She went [whispered and slurred], 'I just—' And then she lifted her eyes up and looked at them. And I'll remember that moment as long as I live." What Normi believes she was seeing was a human being learning that she could not speak honestly to her friends and choosing to take her directness and honesty out of her voice and put it in her heart, as it were—deciding to feel rather than speak her truth. "I thought, that's where her voice is going, deep, deep inside her body, and it's resonating just as surely as the voice resonates on sound, but it's resonating on feeling. And then I started to watch. If the thought and the feeling is alive but it's not voiced, it's inside them, then they go through all the things that Carol and Annie were showing me, you know, they go underground, they go crazy, they revolt, they turn into broken-off, split-off personalities" and grow up to become adults "in shards."

Normi says she had the sense that Kate might someday recover her voice, an actual spoken, honest, direct voice rather than a stream of feeling that she could hide and protect from further Accidents, further occasions when the people she was relating to refused to listen to her. But she had no idea how. Then she began to think that this bewilderment itself might be the key. Maybe her inability to imagine how Kate could reverse the process of protecting her voice might be a threshold that she and other women could recross back into the girlhood world of an open voice that carries the soul, the psyche, direct personal experience strongly.[145]

"The word 'Accident'—it's not 'accident' as in 'accidentally,' " Carol says. "You're walking on the road and a truck comes with its headlights full on you and it just runs over you and goes on down the road." The Accident is no accident, she says. The victim sees it coming but doesn't believe it's going to hit or hurt her.

"And nobody picks you up," Normi says.

The Accident came to Carol in a dream.

"My dream was this turnpike dream: that Tina was having this ladies' lunch in the middle of the road—you know, with pink tablecloths and flowers on the tables—and it was a lunch that I liked, and I was invited to the lunch, and meanwhile, down the turnpike further toward Boston, out of the woods, I saw these police lights, and you know the swirling red and blue lights of police cars and ambulances, and a child was being carried on a stretcher out of the woods." Somehow in the dream she knew that the only way to save the child was to name what had happened to the child. And so she said the words "radical isolation." In the dream they sounded like "a medical term, like anorexia nervosa." The child's diagnosis was "radical isolation," she says. "In the dream I heard it as Latin words. And I screamed in the dream that this is what the child is suffering from, and it would die if people didn't understand what the disease was."

Carol was working with children who she could see and hear were coming into a time when they were becoming disconnected from one another and the child in her dream by coercive cultural forces. So she dreamed of a child "in a near-fatal accident, and I think that is the perfect image" for what happens to adolescents, she says. The driver in the dream "is just going from here to there," in a very common way that also happens to hold the risk of killing anyone he runs into.

Jean Miller's insight is relevant here: the dominant group of people know much less about what they're doing than the people they dominate. Because they have the power to ignore their own motives, they don't have to admit or even notice that they are attacking subordinates. Subordinates, however, certainly know they've been attacked, and when they respond by defending themselves, the dominant people can call that defense an attack.

Normi talks about "the subtlety of the Accident. It can happen in a room five times a minute—I've seen my most beloved get hit over and over, and I'm at the point where I feel like I'll die if I watch it for one more second, but no one else around seems to be having that feeling. It's very subtle."

Yet "how quickly it isolates you," Carol says. "And how psychology isolates you: 'This seems to be your problem. What is your problem?' " The discipline tends to blame the victim, instead of asking, "Who hit you? What is their problem?"

"It's as though it never happened," Normi says.

"What I realize, too, is it's the As-If," Carol says. "It wipes out the relationships, as if the relationships hadn't existed, as if what happened in the relationships wasn't real, as if the other person really didn't hear what I spoke, as if all that didn't happen." Nearing adolescence, girls' big voices start to shrink, along with their pleasures, Carol says. Entering adolescence, the girls whom Carol, Normi, and Annie studied would begin to put down "their group and their relationships and the things that had given them pleasure—like that little game they played at the beginning, that circle thing?" Carol reminds Normi. Then Carol mimics the girls moving into the phase when they renounce their old group fun: "Oh, that was really stupid and we didn't really like that." Even within one life or the lives of a group of friends, there can be an Accident, a cultural revisionism that simply erases loves, pleasures, and interests that the friends felt would last forever while their bonds lasted. It might be a game or a song or a favorite place to go with someone, and then one day the person tells you it never meant anything. "And you realize that if you loved that or cared about that, it was unprotected. It was going to be as if that had never happened, or as if it had never happened to the other person. It's like in a love affair, when the other person says, 'Actually, I have no feelings for you,' and that's devastating in itself, but what's even more devastating is the fact that you have to lose this."

Irene Stiver remembers certain meetings of department heads at McLean where she tried to bring up the relational theory she and the women who met at Jean's house were talking into being. She sounds a bit like Anna at fifteen, or Normi's Kate: "If I spoke up at a meeting, I would feel two things. I would feel invigorated and much better for having spoken, and I would feel absolutely alone." Surrounded by men who she felt fawned over a shaming, bullying administrator, Irene just couldn't fawn along with them or say what she felt were the completely fabricated compliments her colleagues paid the emperor about his new clothes. "I'm not a courageous person particularly," she says, but "if my life depended on it, I couldn't say some of those things." She could lie if she had to, she says, but she couldn't kiss up. "I can't say, '[Boss's name], you're wonderful.'" So instead, when meetings got to be about one administrator loudly praising another who she and many others felt was eviscerating care at the hospital in the name of the bottom line,

Irene learned "to dissociate. You say, 'I'm not here,' and I would do my budget. I would just leave. I wasn't there. That was when it became just unbearable, watching this charade" in which it was impossible to disagree with the boss and therefore impossible to speak.

Writing about a patient she calls Ruth, "a very accomplished young woman in her thirties," Jean Baker Miller describes the other side of this silence: "Ruth had a very clever, articulate, and witty way of talking, often using ridicule and contempt in speaking of the many people she criticized. I often felt put off and ineffectual and also critical of her contemptuous approach. This was particularly so when I felt this fire directly turned on me. Because I didn't believe it would be helpful to express criticism, I probably used a strategy for staying out of connection—which was to be more silent." Eventually, though, Ruth is able to talk to Jean, without contempt, "about what it would have been like to raise questions in her family about her father's drinking and realized that it felt, even now, like an absolute impossibility. She said no one would tolerate hearing it and in fact would turn on her and attack her. She began to get the sense that she may have been caught up in the family's denial and secrecy about this whole topic." Ruth remembered a time when she had been sick and had reached out for her mother, but her depressed mother hadn't been able to respond. Ruth "spoke of being able to feel that longing and of feeling terribly alone, frightened, and humiliated to even think about feeling this desire and having it be rejected," Miller writes. Reflecting about these memories with Jean, Ruth stopped her protectively playful but distancing Mercutio act. "She talked haltingly, without any of her cleverness and wit. As she told of her longing, she spoke with much more fear. I was very moved and felt that we were making progress." Jean realized that Ruth was now asking her to respond to her story with the sort of care Ruth usually made sure no one would believe she needed or would want to provide. But Ruth was unable to sustain this frank appeal:

> At the next session, Ruth seemed totally back to her old clever style. She conveyed none of the emotion of the prior session. I felt pushed away and much less connected. But she did bring a dream. In the dream there was a terrible explosion in a house. Ruth knew that a child was in the house and she was struggling through it to

reach the child. She had a sense that other people were there, too. She managed to reach the child, who was lying unconscious. Now, however, no one else was there.[146]

Ruth's dream is a version of Carol's dream about "radical isolation." It belongs to a genus of dreams of people who've been in cultural Accidents, hurled into "Not to Be" by overpowering negligence or abuse. For instance, a woman I'll call W., a civil servant whose mother severely beat and burned her as an infant and child, tells me she dreamed when she was in her forties that she was in a terrible car crash. In the dream, she crawled lame and bleeding from the car, but an ambulance at the scene took off without her. So she limped along the street, terrified and nearly getting hit again and yet again by other cars racing past, until she came to a familiar town house. She dragged herself up the steps and found the door open. Inside she saw dozens of her friends having a party. "Oh, W., how are you?" the first friend she saw called out. "You look terrific!"

"I've just been in a terrible accident. I'm bleeding. I'm sure I've broken bones. I feel horrible," W. answered weakly. "Please call an ambulance."

"Look at W.!" her friend raved to the others. "Doesn't she look great?"

"Oh, W., you look great!" "You look terrific!" "It's just great to see you," her friends in the dream chorused giddily. So W. turned away and limped off, dripping blood, to find a phone and call an ambulance for herself.

Like Carol's and W.'s dreams, Ruth's dream is a picture of what Miller and Stiver came to call the "central relational paradox." Miller writes:

It helped me to really "get with" Ruth's strategies for staying out of connection. It told about the reasons for retreating from connection, for continuing the strategies of disconnection, and at the same time, the dream itself was a way of moving toward connection. The images of the explosion and the hurt child helped me feel more deeply how terrifying it was to see and speak the truth of Ruth's experience in her family, and how painful is the feeling of being so hurt with no one there to respond. In a way, this is one of those dreams that is everywoman's—and everyman's—dream.[147]

Stiver describes Joan, another client, who began to bring up associations and memories that were really what Stiver and Miller call "relational images," inner flash cards about what life teaches us to expect from relationships, and again, Joan found that explosive isolating silence: "In one memory she saw herself at age seven, sitting in the back seat of her parents' car en route to the hospital where she was to have surgery. She recalled saying, 'I'm not afraid to die.' And no one said a word. She had no memory of being frightened. Just the awfulness of the silence that followed," Stiver writes.[148]

Plotting out the way the five bad things about disconnection lead to the central relational paradox, Stiver writes:

> When a child's expression of her thoughts and feelings is neither heard nor responded to, when she feels that who she is or what she expresses has no impact on the important people in her life, when she experiences a profound sense of powerlessness in her relational interactions, and when her painful feelings cannot be shared with another person, there are profound consequences, in a marked erosion of trust, in the impaired capacity for empathy, and a lack of empowerment. Growing up in dysfunctional families, children learn how to *stay out of relationships*, while behaving *as if* they are *in* relationships.[149]

In some families, trauma is at home in the form of alcoholism, incest, or the post-trauma of surviving political atrocities such as the Holocaust, torture, and disappearance squads in Central and South America, or hostage taking and other acts of terrorism. Here, secrecy, inaccessibility, and "parentifying" children by expecting them to take more and better care of parents and each other than parents take of them are the mechanisms of chronic disconnection, Stiver writes. And in a world where patriarchy, dominance, and subordination touch all families, all families are "to varying degrees" dysfunctional, Miller adds. "What I mean is that our families are not grounded in mutuality. Once you have a power imbalance, where one person can determine what is allowed to occur in the relationship to a very large extent and also has material power, value, and prestige in the world, then you have a set-up for non-mutuality," Miller comments.[150] Anna might call it the built-in hero worship of the modern American family.

The simplest example Miller and Stiver use is of a child who puts a blanket over an alcoholic parent who has passed out and who later wakes with no memory of what happened and no thanks for the child. Parents who are being parented by their children simply take, absorb the parenting, and dose themselves with whichever of the five good things they can get, often for the sake of the good feelings and not for the sake of the relationship, which can only be said to exist because their children keep trying to find a way to have one. In such families, "the burden of responsibility that children assume for the well-being of others overrides their own entitlement to receive care and devotion, yet taking on this burden may be the only way they can make some connection with family members"—the central relational paradox in a particularly virulent form: forcing a child to act like a parent in order to get child care. "Despite their yearnings for connection, these children grow into adulthood regarding relationships in general as burdensome, nongratifying, and often incomprehensible. In their interactions they often continue to 'take care' of others but with little access to their own feelings for other people." And should they ever get to their own feelings, they find they feel "unworthy, confused, depleted, and with a sense of hopelessness that anything can change." These bad feelings naturally come from having had to "take care of parents whose complex psychological problems the child cannot begin to understand, let alone solve."

When children who have parented their parents grow up, they fit very smoothly into the hybrid kind of work relationships in which the boss may act relational in order to get some of the zest, will to action, knowledge, self-esteem, and solidarity that come from good relationships or to benefit from an underling's relational skills, but without any real or lasting mutuality. These are vampirish relationships, where the more powerful person bleeds the relationship of energy and vitality, intent on using relationship as a feel-good experience rather than as a means of fostering growth, and then walks away feeling full for the moment, leaving the weaker person feeling robbed or used.

Carmen, for example, entered therapy complaining about her bosses and saying she felt used and unappreciated at work but would never dream of looking for a better job; she didn't think she deserved her bosses' respect. Gradually she revealed that she had essentially been in this situation all her life. Her father died when she was nine. Right away, she had to go to work after school to help support her family; but she found it next to impossible to please her exhausted mother, who was usually crabby and critical of her, leaving young Carmen continually anxious about having to help her family and yet, according to her mother, failing. "Carmen was amazed to realize" that she still felt this same general anxiety and that any work assignment would ratchet up her anxiety to "the same acute panic reaction she remembered as a child," Miller and Stiver write.[151]

Throughout the 1990s, Stiver and Miller set themselves the task of describing what they called the "strategies of disconnection." By this they meant the approaches that people who have been pushed into inauthenticity in their own relationships use to try to stay safe from shaming and neglect by keeping out of relationships. Yet Miller and Stiver found the same people use these same approaches to express at least their longing for connection, based on the "relational images" their experience has etched in their memories.

When people have grown up with chronic disconnection, in bad formative relationships, the images that guide them in forming or conducting new relationships develop in the confusion and isolation of the five bad things. "The experience of disconnection often leads people to form relational images of others as people who cannot understand, cannot feel with them, will not be there for them, will leave them in isolation, will turn against them, will scorn, humiliate or abuse them." They will always expect others to act this way, and their relational images will keep them from being able to notice how well or badly others really behave. "Within these expectations they develop a variety of responses: for example, they believe they must be compliant or silent, serving and responding to others' needs, not asking anything or outwitting, controlling, or triumphing over others. They may have to respond to other people in all kinds of complicated ways," Miller and Stiver write, "but what they cannot do is respond with their own thoughts and feelings."[152] Corporate success, or getting to the top of the ladder in any hierarchy, can be thought of as a strategy of disconnection; so can the formation of an individualistic, Western notion of a "self."

These responses are really strategies for getting as much good as people with histories of disconnections can get out of relationships while avoiding explosions, accidents, and radical or condemned isolation. Often these images are in two layers or levels that reflect attitudes people were supposed to have as children about their parents and teachers. The upper level is that others are kind, all-powerful, and unconditionally loving—an ideal that people may think of first when they think about forming or deepening relationships. This common sense of approaching an ideal when forming a new relationship covers a deeper strategy based on experience, "that longings for connection will be met with various degrees of disappointment and rejection," Miller and Stiver write.[153] People who find themselves bound by "a compelling and unrelenting need to repeat, over and over, old traumatic interactions" are so deeply convinced that they are the cause of their problems that they may not even know they feel this way.[154] But this behavior—which Charcot and Janet noticed, and Freud first described as a repetition compulsion, and Gilligan, too, rediscovered as a kind of psychic law—is another face of the relational paradox. Repeating a betrayal by someone you love is a way of staying close to that person if you believe there is no other way to be together except by betrayal. Miller and Stiver write:

> In this way, replications represent a most poignant attempt to be with the important people in one's life when it has been impossible to truly be with them. The child, in search of all of the "five good things" that follow from authentic engagement in mutual relationships, chases an illusion of relationship. She remains disempowered, often without valid knowledge of herself and others, feeling totally unworthy and out of connection, often taking on her parents' terrors, depression, or isolation, all the while believing it is all her fault.[155]

Victims of chronic trauma may also repeat their traumas because they never learned any other way of relating and simply don't know how else to go about it. Russell found that two-thirds of the victims of child incest in her study reported that they were later raped, and the longer incest lasted, the more likely they were to be raped later.[156] Some incest victims simply do not find support or any strategy in their environment for living in an unexploited way, as was true of the women who first made Herman think that the incest they described was likely to be real; for others, an incestuous past leads them to form relational images that bring only sexual predators into focus as appropriate partners. Even discounting a possible "wish to relive the dangerous situation and make it come out right," a trauma survivor's "desperate longing for nurturance and care makes it difficult to establish safe and appropriate boundaries with others," Herman writes. "Her tendency to denigrate herself and to idealize those to whom she becomes attached further clouds her judgment. Her empathic attunement to the wishes of others and her automatic, often unconscious habits of obedience also make her vulnerable to anyone in a position of power or authority. Her dissociative defensive style makes it difficult for her to form conscious and accurate assessments of danger." If a trauma survivor does relive her trauma, "whether in the form of intrusive memories, dreams or actions," she finds herself "continually buffeted by terror and rage" that are "outside the range of ordinary emotional experience and they overwhelm the ordinary capacity to bear feelings." But trying to hide from repetition may only make complex PTSD worse, since "the attempt to avoid reliving the trauma often results in a narrowing of consciousness, a withdrawal from engagement with others, and an impoverished life."[157]

And because many systems for interacting are forms of the system of dominance, repeated disconnection is often built into environments like schools and workplaces, even neighborhoods, regardless of the personal histories of students, employees, and residents. Joyce Fletcher, now the co-director of the Working Connections Project at the Jean Baker Miller Training Institute, sat at her dining room table with Miller, Stiver, Jordan, and half a dozen other interested women union organizers, high-tech executives, a doctor, and a lawyer one night a month for nearly a decade to think about the way that relational practices succeed or fail in businesses and other large organizations. Much of the talk was about how these practices become distorted, disconnected, and "disappeared" by systemic organizational assumptions—and about how those assumptions can be changed. Gilligan also uses this idiom of "being disappeared" to describe the fate of girls and other subordinate groups who are simply not seen or heard by dominants, and of course the idiom was invented in Buenos Aires by the Madres de Plaza de Mayo, protesting the loss of their dissident or simply unlucky children and grandchildren, who had been kidnapped and often murdered—"disappeared"—and pointedly refusing to disappear themselves during the Argentine military junta's "dirty war" of the late 1970s. Fletcher's book, *Disappearing Acts*, follows a group of women software engineers as they respond to pressure both to use relationships to make a project or an organization better *and* to pretend that their relational work has no value. Her book features a table of disappearances that really tabulates the appearance in one workplace of the more general social phenomenon Miller identified in 1976: recasting women's relational strengths as trivial, private idiosyncrasies or weaknesses.

The first category in Fletcher's table is "misinterpreting the intention": many corporations and other organizations run on the assumption that the relational work women and some men engineers do to create and maintain teams, to empower other workers to contribute, and to contribute themselves to the good of a whole project is just being nice, or naive, or just something they do because they want to be liked or even because they feel insecure. This widespread, systemic misreading disconnects what Fletcher would call good relational outcomes from their causes, and makes it look as though a workplace in which a few women are being nice just happens to have a strong esprit de corps and is full of workers who are willing to go beyond the minimum to make sure not only their part but a whole project is successful. This trivializing misinterpretation means that "the *strategic intention* of the behavior—the attempt to put into practice a different model of effectiveness—is lost," Fletcher writes.[158] The women engineers she followed wrote thank-yous, spent hours listening, tried to teach in a way that didn't leave the other person feeling one down, and did menial jobs if they saw something important about to slip through the cracks of job responsibilities—but they didn't adopt these relational practices because they were nice. They worked relationally because they believed that was the best way to do the job, Fletcher says, and this "belief system is the real casualty in the disappearing dynamic."

In another study, Fletcher found some men who also believed in and practiced relational ways of working. Predictably, they "tended to be men of color who came from another culture, not the USA," she told a Stone Center audience. "How *Western* male this focus on individualism and autonomy is," Sung Lim Shin, a Korean-American psychologist, responded. "It is not just gender." But though these relational men "weren't rewarded for their behavior and they often were seen as just being helpful or nice people," Fletcher told a Stone Center audience in 1996, "they didn't have the gender dynamic operating on them. They didn't get labeled as mothers and they didn't get punished or called names for helping or listening or whatever."[159] An insidious side of the pressure on girls to be nice and kind is the pressure to read one's own often difficult choice to live and work in a relationally honest, mutually respectful way as a cute personal attribute that every good girl or woman must always show no matter what, and that no manly man should let himself exhibit.

By "clustering support positions at the bottom of the hierarchy," organizations also disappear what professional athletes get credit for: "assists" that relational people give to corporate big shots, Fletcher writes. Because of this hierarchy, if an ambitious, rugged individualist makes it to the top, he can ignore the help he received on the way up, from people on the bottom, because they become subordinates too distant to be seen, thus "perpetuating the myth of individual achievement," like Freud forgetting his patients, including the wealthy, influential patient who got him his university professorship, when he talked about working alone.[160] An ambitious man who has confided his problems to a secretary need never worry that she will use this information against him, because the organization is built to keep her from ever competing with him for a job he wants. In this way, relational work is put into a female or foreign ghetto in organizations, and habitual, built-in disconnection is par for the course of the man or woman on the rise.

The second category on Fletcher's table of disappearances is the "limits of language": Fletcher noticed that all the work buzzwords like "competence, skill, knowledge," even "teamwork," were defined in a way that left out relational competence, skill, and knowing what you are doing with people and not just with numbers and products. In a sense, without being culturally marked as such, they were words for things at which only males were supposed to excel. Conversely, the relational words—"nurturing, empathy, caring"—were "girl" words, associated with mothering and femininity, leaving a strong connotative perfume on these practices that reserved them for women or for sissies, female-identified men. Listening to Fletcher talk about the way our words for relational acts restrict them to girls or people who are being nice (that is, not getting paid for being relationally competent), a woman expresses her frustration about being asked to use the necessary relational skills to initiate and guide productive and long-lasting organizational change. "What I have noticed in years of working in organizations is that many men espouse the values of organizational change and talk as if they understand the intricacies of the process but they don't *actually* value these things. I am a consultant and I have actually been forced to reduce my billable hours because the organization didn't believe that what I was doing was 'real' work," she says. A woman "team leader" Fletcher talked to "had given a presentation to top management, intentionally using the pronoun 'we' to represent what had in fact been a team effort. She was taken aside afterwards by her mentor and told that she would never get ahead if she didn't 'stop with this "we" stuff.' She was told the presentation would have been a lot stronger if she had used the pronoun 'I' because 'we' sounds weak and overly general."[161] Fletcher's point is that it takes a whole system of disconnection to make "we" dangerously, career-threateningly weaker than "I."

Her third category is "social construction of gender," and it works like a syllogism: (1) Girls and women in organizations are supposed to just "be nice"; they are not seen as deliberately choosing, training for, and mastering relational practices based on beliefs about the best way to create organizations. (2) "Behavior coded as feminine is devalued in workplace settings"; you will never get ahead by "being nice." (3) "Female engineers are simultaneously *expected to* [act] and *devalued for* acting relationally."[162]

This pervasive, disconnecting double bind in their corporate culture may not stop organizations from priding themselves on trying to hire and promote women, or minorities, or team players. But for women engineers in the workplace she studied, Fletcher saw it bring on the five bad things like clockwork. "In fact, in my analysis I had a separate category labeled 'Am I Crazy?' to reflect the ambiguity and self-doubt they often expressed," she writes. "The problem is, the loop constructs all these issues in terms of personal aberration. What gets lost is the fact that women's experience is being *systematically distorted* in order to protect the status quo from challenge. So it is natural that women start to think of these issues as their problem." Women believe that the bad fit between their relational skills and the system that requires and ignores them is their problem; in fact, each woman believes it is her problem, one she has to solve alone. But since it is a problem in a system she has no power to alter, she can never make her bad feelings about doing good go away. So, Fletcher concludes:

> It is no wonder that lots of women—even those who have made it to the top—are leaving organizations to start their own small companies or are refusing promotions or refusing to compete for top positions. Again, conventional wisdom holds that these women are leaving because they can't hack it. Either career and work aren't important enough to them or they can't take the pressure. But interestingly, follow-up interviews with women who have left high-level jobs indicate that they can do these jobs, they've just decided they don't want to."[163]

Neither white middle-class women nor women of color who have left top jobs cite work-family conflicts, Fletcher writes. Instead, "when interviewed they talk about their inability to work the way they want to work in the current structure and about the inefficiency and ineffectiveness of many work norms."[164]

These deficiencies become more devastating when the organization that is disappearing relational practices is in charge of meting out psychotherapy for traumatic injuries. The health maintenance organizations that offer the only psychotherapy many traumatized people have access to are often for-profit businesses with dominant, nonrelational norms. Health maintenance organizations have more than decimated the average stay in a mental hospital from ninety days in the mid-1970s to thirty in the 1980s to four or five at the turn of the twenty-first century. The outpatient services these organizations offer, referred to as McTherapy by many of the therapists who have no realistic financial choice but to work for them, are defined in training manuals that HMO therapists are supposed to follow. And the guidelines for short-term managed-care therapy often specifically forbid relationships. Surrey describes one managed-care training manual that another therapist showed her: "It literally said the words, 'Do not make a relationship with the client. This will keep people in treatment longer than they need.' " Here the central relational paradox—stay out of relationship for the sake of relationships—is enshrined as a commandment for psychotherapists as an organizational system builds disconnection into what it calls "care."

7.
Healing

Two years after she finished college, six years after her rape, Y. moved to Boston and decided to try therapy again. She chose to see a male therapist. "It's not as though he had a wealth of experience in working with women survivors," she remembers, but he was "very warm, sincere, and generous" in a way that broke through the cynicism and distrust that her earlier, ineffective attempts to tell her story to family, therapists, and friends had taught her. "It's not as though I presented with great affect," she says, using the distancing, diagnostic phrase for showing a lot of feeling at the start of therapy. Instead, her new therapist presented with great affect.

"He welled up with tears as I told him the story, and I thought, Well, somebody's moved. Somebody's doing something," Y. says.

He was being "very present," she says, "and that demonstrated an ability to hold it."

We have heard about this "ability to hold it" as the mutual empathy that the Stone Center theorists make so much of. Jordan theorizes that mutual empathy is the engine of relational healing, or reconnection. A client who long ago dissociated the pain of a horrible story so she could stop feeling horrible tells the story, sees that it moves the therapist, and is finally moved, by the response of the therapist, to experience the horror of her own story again or perhaps for the first time—but now with a witness, with an ally, in an empathic relationship. At this moment, the empathizing therapist is the catalyst that transforms dissociation into reconnection and healing. "I think what Judy [Jordan] says describes it best, when she talks about being moved—to be moved when the person is, *and* the person knows that you're moved by it, which moves the relationship further," Stiver reiterates. As a therapist, or just as a friend who listens to relationships as well as to the people in them, "you bring a whole way of experiencing relationship that changes everything. And I think that's our task," Stiver says. To change everything.

About a year after Y. entered this last psychotherapy, and everything began to change, her therapist suggested that she think about supplementing their work with a time-limited, fourteen-week group for survivors of rape at the Victims of Violence program of the Cambridge Health Alliance. Y. listened. Then she thought about it, thought and felt about the possibilities of healing in relationships with a whole group of survivors, for a long time. She went on working with the therapist, and about a year after he made his suggestion, she decided to try the group.

The rape survivors' group Y. joined had two leaders and five members, one of whom dropped out before the fourteen weeks were up. It met at the hospital, and there Y. finally found anger. "I was the person for whom the rape had occurred the longest ago. So for myself it was hard to hear people who were getting help sooner. It brought up anger for me," she says. "I felt their wounds were open, and mine was somewhat scarred." The others had experienced date rape and stranger rape—"I want to say worse than mine," Y. says, carefully marking the common tendency of victims to downplay the severity of their own pain, in a kind of etiquette that too often invites neglect from the people who are supposed to help them recover. She felt it was easier for her to talk than for the other survivors of rape but, more than seven years after her rape, harder to feel. Time, she felt, had not so much healed her trauma as ingrained her dissociation. "I improved over time and had hardened," she says. "I was more vocal, because it wasn't as close, so on some level it was easier for me to talk about it. But I could see I was more cut off, whereas it seemed to me they were a little closer to their feelings." And the feelings of the other survivors in this group woke up hers. "I was very moved," she says. "That was where I felt like the essence of much of the healing was for me—hearing those stories and hearing other people's pain." Her work with her individual therapist, present as he was and precious as it was, simply didn't have the efficiency of the group work. "In mutual sharing, there isn't that power differential," she says. The other survivors of rape in her group had the same amount of power she did, and the same kind of experience. "You're seeing someone else's pain that you can identify with" in a way that helps you, she says. "You're sort of able to provide an empathy" and take empathy in "from other people who you know for a fact know what you're talking about—where there's no projection." The survivors who heard her story weren't so thrown that they started to see her as some kind of cripple, Madonna, or whore. Though they were moved, they weren't thrown at all; her story was their story, and they were all telling it. This candid sisterhood was a first for Y. Despite statistics that told her as many as one in three or four women have been raped or sexually abused, Y. had only met one other person, in college, who admitted that she'd been raped.

The group leaders made things easier. Once when Y. was casually sitting on a couch with her legs crossed, talking about what had happened to her, one of the leaders suggested that she plant her feet on the floor while she talked. "She was saying, 'I can see that you're not really very connected,' " Y. remembers. The leader was encouraging her to retract the careless, offhand, and to that extent dissociated style she had had to assume in the past when she was talking about being raped; the leader was inviting Y. to take herself and her pain more seriously. "It meant a lot to me, because I had spent so much time protecting people from having to endure what I had endured," Y. says. And then she states Miller and Gilligan's relational paradox as she had had to live it: "In order to maintain connection with people, I didn't want to overwhelm them with my story." At last she was in a group of four or five people who were connecting in order to share the most difficult kinds of stories to hear, with two experts at keeping connection alive. "One of them in particular was really good at sort of stating what she'd learned and making you feel really understood," Y. says of a group leader.

The survivors' group wasn't perfect. For instance, the leaders asked members to choose goals for themselves in the group. When Y. said her goal was "to get in touch with my feelings about it," the leaders pushed her to "come up with something more concrete. So I sort of fabricated a goal of telling my parents I was in this group," and that felt kind of fake, or at least not right, since she didn't feel it would help to try to talk to her parents, whose response to her rape had always been more or less a plea or demand to downplay it or dissociate. Worse, in Y.'s mind, was a bias in the group leaders somewhat in favor of dissociation—a leaning toward the patriarchal premise that not to feel is to be in control and that to be in control is good. She felt this bias emerged when a woman in the group began to describe a dream she had had that seemed to point not just to rape but to a history of incest that had preceded the rape. The woman was screaming and crying about the dream when one of the leaders stopped her and told her that in this group they were only to talk about dreams or other psychic events that concerned the rape they were there to talk about. Y., on the other hand, talked about a couple of times she had been molested as a child, and yet she wasn't stopped, because, she thinks, she didn't show that those memories still upset her. "That's like saying, 'You referred to it without affect, so we'll let it go.' "

Overall, though, in this group, "I felt like I was doing what I wanted to do," Y. says. "I trusted the clinical intelligence of the leaders and their sensitivity. And I really had the sense from the members that we really had helped each other." She no longer felt a strain in relationships with her closest friends or with her family, especially her parents, from whom "the message was silence." She no longer needed to ask them to listen to her with empathy they had long refused; she had found other, willing listeners. She says she learned that when you need to talk about something as "traumatic and tense" as rape, "you need a special clinical place for that, and I felt like I finally got it." The group became "a place to go where I was, like, allowed—encouraged—to talk about it. It was a place to talk about the rape, and I was so barred from doing this" everywhere else except in the therapist's office. When she talked to the group about being raped, the responses she got were healing. "Nobody said, 'It was your own fault,' " although "the women in that group all struggled with that." For the second time since Y. started therapy, talking about rape began to feel better than not talking about it. And by the end, "It was very validating."

"It did relieve me," she says. After fourteen weeks, Y. says she felt, "I've done justice to the part of me that's been hanging around and holding me back." She felt she'd both found and begun "to assuage my anger a bit, because my pain had been heard and tolerated." Three years after this group had ended, Y. was completing graduate training so she could run similar groups. "It did for me what I needed," she says.

Mary Harvey always illustrates her work about the ecology of healing from psychological trauma with a stark chart of possibilities. Y. belongs in the first of Harvey's four categories: *"Trauma victims who have received clinical care and have psychologically recovered from their experience."*

When we last heard of Bertha Pappenheim, the brilliant patient whom Dr. Breuer dumped in terror when he realized she imagined she was pregnant by him, she had relapsed to Harvey's second category: *"Trauma victims who have received clinical care but have not benefited and have not recovered."* Pappenheim more or less drops out of sight from 1882, when Breuer abandoned her, to 1888, when she reappears in Frankfurt, volunteering in an orphanage during the day and staying up at night to translate Mary Wollstonecraft's revolutionary eighteenth-century tract, *A Vindication of the Rights of Woman*, into German for the first time (this from the sequestered young Anna O., whose separate English-speaking and German-speaking personae never talked to each other during the worst of her psychotic agonies). Pappenheim's translation was published in 1899, the year Freud's *Interpretation of Dreams* came out in Vienna, and in 1900 her play *Women's Rights* appeared. In 1902, Pappenheim started Care by Women, an association of volunteer social workers in Frankfurt. In 1905, as a social worker focused on abused and abandoned orphan girls in Frankfurt, she began a lifelong campaign against white Jewish slavery throughout Europe. Neither Ernest Jones, Freud's disciple and biographer, who first identified her publicly in the 1950s, nor the journalist Lucy Freeman, who wrote a popular biography of her in the 1970s, speculated about what trauma in her own life led to the psychosis Breuer treated her for in the 1880s. In 1930, she was still refusing to let any of her charges near a psychoanalyst; she never married or so much as allowed a man to serve on her board. "Her dedication, education, and commitment were legendary," Herman declared about her at the biennial Harvard conference in 1991, quoting Martin Buber: "A volcano lived in this woman.

Her fight against the abuse of women and children was almost a physically felt pain for her."

In a life dedicated to bringing healing to poor women and girls *"who have not received clinical care and have not recovered"* (Harvey's fourth category), Pappenheim managed to shift herself into Harvey's third category: *"trauma survivors who have recovered without benefit of clinical intervention."*[1] It might even be fair to call her a trauma survivor who recovered despite clinical intervention. In her decision to complete her own healing by serving trauma victims, Pappenheim was like Y., and like many of the women who were moved to become psychological healers by the second wave of the women's liberation movement. This movement's long first wave swept Pappenheim from translating Wollstonecraft to a sense of vocation and competence in the 1890s, and Pappenheim's healing was capped by becoming a healer herself, helping to repair the cultural and social imbalance that led, as she wrote in 1929, to a "nature of things" in which "the girls are the ones who get hurt, the boys are the ones who derive the pleasure."[2] Her legendary case did so much for psychoanalysis, and yet psychoanalysis did so little for her. To her death she despised the kind of psychotherapy that had hung her out to dry.

Pappenheim's recovery is obvious from the outside: she created a career, righted wrongs, loved and worked with passion and intelligence, and was loved and worked for in return by legions of admirers. But Harvey says recovery is ultimately experienced inside, not simply as the end of symptoms—which in fact may intensify for a period during treatment—but as the beginning of a new equilibrium she measures by seven criteria.

She calls the first criterion for healing "authority over the remembering process." Treatment teaches survivors to remember at will, by choice, "events that previously intruded unbidden into consciousness," as well as events that may have been shrouded in traumatic amnesia. Memory no longer controls the survivor; instead, the survivor controls memory, so that he or she "is able to call upon and review a relatively complete and continuous life narrative."

In the same way, recovered trauma survivors achieve "integration of memory and affect," so that they never call to mind inner pictures of atrocities that arrive without any feeling, and they never find themselves awash in "waves of terror, anxiety or rage" without a clue as to what has triggered them or what memories the feelings belong to. "In recovery, memory and affect are joined. The past is remembered with feeling," Harvey writes. Dissociation reassociates. Survivors remember what they felt when they were traumatized, and they also feel new feelings about what happened—like the new anger and sadness that Y. felt for the first time in the survivors' group, years after rape had left her feeling simply terrified and the responses of the people she cared about left her feeling isolated.

Not all symptoms of trauma go away when survivors recover. But trauma survivors do learn what Harvey calls "symptom mastery." They learn what things—violent films, for example—trigger flashbacks or panic attacks for them and they learn to avoid them. To calm and comfort themselves when symptoms come up, they learn to "practice specific stress management techniques or make appropriate use of prescribed medications."

Citing the work of Lenore Terr on kidnapped children and Herman on adult trauma, Harvey explains that "early, prolonged and repeated victimization is associated with severe identity disturbances and with a discontinuous and fragmented self-experience." Survivors recover "self-esteem and self-cohesion." They learn to soothe themselves with "healthful, self-caring routines," instead of distracting themselves with substance abuse, self-mutilation, or other injuries. They learn to feel like themselves all the time. They learn to feel worthy of care instead of guilty about whatever it was that caused a parent or mate to abuse them.

Trauma victims may swing from terrified isolation—Miller's "condemned isolation"—to reckless partnering with new abusers. If the person who loved them abused them or exposed them to abuse, then they may have learned that love only comes with abuse—that bad relationships are the only kind—and may choose either to seek love from abusers or to avoid abuse by isolating themselves. Recovered survivors learn "safe attachment," Harvey says. Treatment teaches trust; not only does the therapist act in a trustworthy way, but she or he guides the survivor toward other trustworthy, healing relationships, as Y.'s last therapist did. Eventually, Harvey writes, perhaps after much grief for

intense, injurious relationships, "the recovered survivor is able to negotiate and maintain physical and emotional safety in relationships and
views the possibility of intimate connectedness with some degree of
optimism."

At last, the recovered survivor can make sense, make meaning, of it
all. This "meaning-making" is the creative part, the art of recovery,
Harvey writes. She characterizes it as "a deeply personal and highly
idiosyncratic process, particularly when the trauma has entailed interpersonal violence and direct encounter with the human capacity to
commit atrocity." Insights about what happened, about whom they
have become, and about "the world in which traumatic events occur
and recur" move survivors to make art, to take social action, or to find,
as Y. and Bertha Pappenheim did, lifework that opposes and undoes
abuse that is part of the system while doing and supporting the work of
love and growth. "Whatever the process, the recovered survivor will
have named and mourned the traumatic past and imbued it somehow
with meaning that is both life-affirming and self-affirming," Harvey
writes.[3]

Harvey has come to understand that for some people, making
meaning of their life "entails giving up their focus on the trauma," she
says in 2004. A survivor who was part of an ongoing Victims of Violence
study of trauma recovery has brought home to her that for some people, the path to a meaningful existence leads past what remains a
meaningless atrocity. The researcher who interviewed this woman
about her healing asked, "So tell me, how do you make meaning of this
trauma?" The woman replied, "I don't." She expanded her answer to
explain that all of the meanings she had imputed to the incest she had
suffered as a child proved to be false: she had thought that if she bore
it, at least her sister wouldn't suffer, but then she learned that her father moved on to her sister when she left. She had thought that maybe
the incest helped keep her parents' marriage intact, but then her parents got divorced. "I spent the first half of my life trying to make sense
of my life," she told the interviewer. "I'm not giving another minute of
my life to try to understand an incomprehensible event." "You confront
it, you metabolize it in some way, and then you . . . move on," Harvey
summarizes. "The best revenge is to love your life."

During recovery, survivors use the personal qualities and skills that escaped traumatic injury—their resilient capacities—to help heal the capacities that are injured. And of course the communities and environments in which they heal have their own resiliencies and limitations: sometimes they are riddled with shaming prejudices or lack support groups and clinics; sometimes they have enlightened and well-funded resources and residents, and these differences factor hugely. Harvey fashions two composite examples, based on hundreds of cases, to illustrate.

Sarah, twenty-one, white, raised by parents who shared child-rearing tasks, is now in college. She is a campus activist involved in several feminist groups. In a campus pub with friends one night, she starts a conversation with a man she'd noticed there before and liked the look of. He asks to walk her home. She says yes willingly, but then is turned off when he comes on to her sexually very aggressively during their walk. She pushes him away. He responds with "angry, violent and life-threatening sexual assault."

JoAnn is also twenty-one and white, raised in a close-knit, religious family in a working-class suburb. Her parents tear their hair at this "unladylike" tomboy who turned into a good athlete before she married right out of high school. Now divorced, JoAnn lives with her two toddlers in a small apartment near her old neighborhood and works in a nearby restaurant. One night after a softball game, she and a friend hit a lively local bar; JoAnn stayed when her friend left and later accepted the offer of a man she'd "seen around" to walk her home. He forced her into his car, drove her to "a remote area, raped her and left her to fend for herself."

Sarah and JoAnn are the same race and age. And the events that traumatized these women are very similar. Both involved an illusion of safety, familiarity, alcohol, and "physical brutality and humiliation." Both women are left with "intrusive recollections" that force each of them to "revisit her fear and her pain," Harvey writes. "Sarah will recall with particular shame the fact that she was initially attracted to the man who assaulted her. JoAnn will revisit the humiliation she experienced when her physical strength failed her and she felt too frightened to fight."

But because of their environments, their prospects for recovery vary greatly, Harvey writes. Think of the differences between the people, perspectives, and values of Sarah's ecosystem and of JoAnn's, Harvey says. Their communities differ "in their understandings of rape, their views of women, their attitudes toward alcohol, and their comfort and familiarity with professional assistance and psychiatric intervention." Think of the difference between the professional resources of a Boston college campus and those of a country town where there is "no rape crisis center, no specially trained medical emergency room personnel, and no sexual assault unit of the local police department." JoAnn has no obvious person to go to about her rape. "She, herself, is not sure what she thinks of her experience. Was she raped? Many in her home community, including perhaps her own father and mother, believe that a 'nice girl' can't really be raped."

Sarah's "resource-rich urban community," her family, friends, and colleagues, and her own college-educated attitudes almost funnel her into a strong recovery. Her recovery may still be painful, slow, and erratic. But even if she struggles with doubters and with self-doubts of her own, many of the people and institutions she trusts most will support her.

If she can decide on her own to try to prosecute, JoAnn will be lucky to find someone in the court system who will encourage her to fight. ("Only one percent of rapes are ultimately resolved by arrest and conviction of the offender," Herman notes.[4]) And it is hard to imagine how JoAnn could find her way to clinical care, since her family distrusts headshrinkers and believes family business shouldn't be shared with outsiders. Her brothers—who respect her physicality—her teammates, and perhaps a victim advocate in the court system are her best chances for beginning an education about gender, rape, and support that Sarah already had when she was raped, Harvey speculates.

Sarah knows she was raped; JoAnn isn't sure. Both have had little exposure to violence. Add childhood abuse and adult battering to their histories, or change their ethnicities or race—make them poor or locate them in high-crime neighborhoods—and the "ecological challenges to their recovery would clearly multiply," Harvey writes. Treatment has to begin with assessments that include how victims' environments are likely to support or thwart recovery. What have the victims been taught to believe about rape or other violent crimes? Who and where are those teachers? What treatments can they afford? What are the politics of their situation? What kind of power and how much power did this abuser and past abusers have over the victim? What kind of power does the victim have? What kind of power is ranged against her?[5]

In the worldwide effort to reduce the incidence of psychological trauma and to heal it once it happens, it is as important to organize communities to pay for services and institutions that support healing and to discourage attacks as it is to offer psychotherapy, and therapists have to be part of this community organizing, Harvey insists. "The therapist is a social activist," committed to combating hate crimes, since "the level of violence that is directed toward women and children is best understood as an expression of hate, or at least of contempt," Harvey says, speaking in 2000 at the Harvard Medical School's Learning from Women conference. "Any therapist working with trauma survivors has to be prepared to be a social activist, because you can't be neutral about atrocity," Harvey says again in 2004. And one element of the Victims of Violence program that Harvey is proudest of is the Community Crisis Response Team, which draws on volunteers from across the metropolitan area to respond to schools, town governments, and fire or police departments when they ask for help in the wake of crimes and catastrophes such as murders and fires. She calls it "community psychology at work."

"It changes everything if you demand to listen, to hear, to think about women's experience as well as men's, and start looking at the context," Harvey says.

Trauma itself can be an environment. Studies both of men tortured and traumatized by "brainwashing" techniques in war and of women victims of prolonged domestic battering demonstrated that most victims "show no evidence of serious psychopathology before entering into the exploitive relationship," Herman writes. "Chronic abuse causes serious psychological harm."[6] Atrocious relationships, relationships that feature prolonged and repeated abuse accompanied by threats of more abuse if the victim doesn't lie about it, tie people into the agonizing knots Herman calls complex post-traumatic stress disorder.

Along with other relational therapists, Herman discovered that these knots can begin to come untied in healthy relationships, including a therapy relationship, in which the healthier, more powerful person uses her knowledge and skills to benefit the victim and encourage truth telling. Just as relationships have the power to destroy people, they also have the power to heal them. But, very important, "therapy is a bridge to community, not a substitute for it," Herman says.

> The core experiences of psychological trauma are disempowerment and disconnection from others. Recovery, therefore, is based upon the empowerment of the survivor and the creation of new connections. Recovery can take place only within the context of relationships; it cannot occur in isolation. In her renewed connections with other people, the survivor re-creates the psychological faculties that were damaged or deformed by the traumatic experience. These faculties include the basic capacities for trust, autonomy, initiative, competence, identity, and intimacy. Just as these capacities are originally formed in relationships with other people, they must be reformed in such relationships.[7]

The relationships that Herman says are indispensable for healing are growth-fostering relationships, to use the relational-cultural language; they restore power or teach victims to assume power if they have been in abusive relationships all their lives and have never been empowered. "Empower" and its opposite, "disempower," are nineteenth-century coinages. The words have been burnished by use in the twentieth-century feminist and civil rights movements and evoked no resistance until they encountered the late-twentieth-century conservative strategy that spurns efforts to achieve social justice as "politically correct." The power "empowerment" conveys is not, however, some feminist or minority delusion of grandeur but simply the unit of political power that citizenship grants to every person in a democracy—the power to live, earn a living, learn, form associations, express opinions, worship or refrain from worshipping, reproduce or refrain from reproducing, seek and receive protection from crime, and travel or remain at home by personal choice. Herman says that "the first principal of recovery is the empowerment of the survivor."[8] The neutrality of the psychotherapist, conceived as a lack of personal involvement and responsiveness in the neo-Freudian model, becomes political neutrality for Herman. The therapist is politically neutral; therefore, she or he will not abuse the patient or tell the patient what to do. The therapist is a supportive witness, an ally, someone whose respect for the survivor is so profound that the survivor learns self-respect from it; the therapist is someone whose belief in the patient's ability to tell the truth and live is so secure, so trusting, that the patient learns to trust this process and heal. The therapist teaches and empathizes. The old Freudian notion that a patient in psychoanalysis should not read or learn about his treatment or his ailment is seen as yet another effort to disempower and maintain dependence. Abuse, especially child abuse, not only actively injures children; it also neglects them. Victims of abuse may have chosen unlikely soothing activities—self-mutilation, substance abuse, even the endorphin rush of further danger—simply because they were the only available possibilities for something like relief in a life where "relational possibilities for self-soothing were not possible," Herman says, and a warm bath, a cup of cocoa, a good read, a relaxed moment of spacing out, or a nature walk never happened or was never safe.

So the therapist and survivors' groups that focus on self-care and on information about trauma teach basics that healthy children learn from loving parents and healthy communities. Safety first, for instance. Safety is the first lesson, the first stage, of recovery in Herman's three-stage paradigm.

"What would the world be like if closeness to another human being meant death?" Amy Banks asked at the Harvard Medical School teaching conference Learning from Women in April 2002. "That's what our clients walk in with."

Banks is a former staff psychiatrist at the Victims of Violence program who is now in private practice while she raises twins. She tells the hundreds of therapists who attend the conferences and workshops where she teaches how to express willingness to enter a healing relationship with a trauma victim in a way that doesn't trigger symptoms that were caused by abusive family members in the past and how to reconnect when symptoms are triggered. "A major trigger in therapy is too much closeness," Banks says. Because of a flooding of neurochemical mechanisms that normally help people pick out particularly threatening stimuli, complex PTSD victims are "less able to discern what stimuli are *likely* to represent danger." When a patient enters the "panic room" of a full-blown attack of PTSD, she may lose all capacity to judge or speak, and no explanation will calm her until the neurochemistry "dies down," as it eventually does, Banks says. But in victims it dies down to a state that is chronically amplified, a state in which the brain has been chronically overstimulated so that it careens from neurotransmitter depletion to overstimulation. Medications can help slow and lessen these reactions until the patient begins to form new neurochemical patterns in response to healthy relationships, but "we do not have a drug that treats PTSD" with 100 percent effectiveness, Banks says. The best—serotonin reuptake inhibitors like Prozac and Zoloft, or alpha- and beta-blockers of adrenaline that may help with sleep and hyperarousal—are only 30 to 50 percent effective, she says. And even these potential benefits may be blocked if traumatized patients are afraid to take drugs a therapist prescribes, since powerful abusers may have given them harmful substances, and the offer of drugs may feel like a power play rather than an offer of help. Even meditation, acupuncture, and other non-pharmacological ways of calming down may be frightening, at least initially, and leave patients feeling tortured or abandoned to memories of abuse. For therapists trying to teach patients how to be safe, "abuse is devastating," Banks says. "All of the ways that we want to try to help are toxic" or at least potentially toxic, especially before memory has become a reliable guide, while therapist and patient are first cataloging the kinds of things that may trigger traumatic reactions of panic and terror. "The ordinary response to atrocities is to banish them from consciousness," Banks says in 2000, quoting Herman. "This is the meaning of 'unspeakable.'" Banks quotes an incest survivor from a 1998 interview: "We became a family of amnesiacs." In many cases these amnesiacs experience memory as one of Gilligan's "Accidents"—a hit-and-run of neural stimulation that leaves them feeling like victims once again. One way for therapists to cope with the downward plunges of the roller-coaster ride of therapy is to create and agree upon a signal with each patient that the therapist can give to remind her that she is not in actual danger when something triggers terror, Banks suggests. This phase of healing can take years, but it can be done, Banks says. And it is essential to build in elements of self-care before the phase of exploration of memory, so that episodes of panic or neurochemical flooding do not lead to new injuries or leave the patient feeling helpless or incompetent.

During treatment, the patient may not be able to feel any difference between trauma and post-traumatic healing. Both can be equally painful. In the beginning, healing pain often feels all too familiar, and safety simply means escape: getting out of danger, not living with or depending financially on an abuser, not being stalked or threatened or raising children who are being threatened, not depending on narcotics or alcohol, not cutting or hurting oneself for comfort as a signal from the present moment that gets through the panic with the information that now is not then. Eventually, a patient realizes that the pain of trauma brings injury, and the pain of healing is like teething: you get something for it. Safety comes to mean replacing dangers with safe resources—learning to use a public library instead of a bar as a safe haven, learning to live in a place that is safe enough to relax in, learning to use soothing teas or incense or carefully prescribed drugs instead of intoxicants to cope with disabling emotional crises, learning yogic breathing or meditation. Sometimes, especially in cases of a single or relatively short period of trauma, self-soothing techniques such as eye movements, bilateral patting, or counting combined with specific recall protocols may be effective. But the most important step toward safety is making the kinds of friends who will protect you from abuse and stick with you while you are healing. The "condemned isolation" Miller writes about becomes a terrifying physical and mental imprisonment at moments of post-traumatic neurochemical flooding, Banks says. And everything—even the beautifully clear and schematized booklet Banks and trauma sufferers have written to explain the neurochemistry of trauma—can be a trigger to a person who has been attacked so often that she no longer has a sense that attacks have a source outside herself.[9] "Survivors feel unsafe in their bodies," Herman writes—in danger from other people and at risk of emotional flooding.[10] But for "condemned isolation," as for the abuse that causes it, "the antidote is to be listened back into voice and ultimately back into connection," Miller says, responding to Banks's talk at the 2000 conference.

Safety starts with the most immediate environment, the victim's own body and mind, but any system of protection or security has to be social, has to involve dependable protectors and comforters in some form, however remote, and victims smell it—smell the interdependence that any comfort represents—and at first that scent of connection terrifies them. If there are injuries, doctors need to treat them rather than repeat them. Herman quotes an emergency-room physician: "The most important thing in medically examining someone who's been sexually assaulted is not to re-rape the victim."[11] If there are mind-altering sleep and eating disorders, the victim needs information about what will make it possible for her to sleep and eat more normally. These helps might include drugs, but both Herman and Banks stress that the psychopharmacological job of therapists is to educate victims about drugs and their potential benefits and side effects until the patient is able to make and then continually revisit a truly informed decision. Just to achieve real consent in a matter this intimate and important requires profound healing, since in many ways all the traumatic disorders can be seen as disorders of the ability to give or withhold consent. That is why empowerment and all the political dimensions of the victim's circumstances must be seen as paramount throughout treatment.

After the weeks or months it may take the victim of a single, brief traumatic event, and after the years it may take for the victim of prolonged, repeated psychological trauma, to feel safe inside her body come weeks or months or even years of learning to feel safe inside her life—safe in the house, safe on the job, safe with strangers, safe with friends. Sometimes this step involves fleeing an abuser to a carefully organized, secret safe house. Sometimes it means psychologically detoxifying homes, bedrooms, cars that abuse may have caused to feel anything but safe—a mature look into closets and under the bed to reassure the traumatized mind that the monsters are gone. Whatever trust has not been broken or has been built or restored becomes the flashlight that burns through a monstrously shadowy, doubt-filled environment. The need to plan how and whether to prosecute perpetrators of crimes may create painful, frightening conflicts with the need to plan how to get and stay safe, since the justice system almost always moves faster than victims' recovery, which in the best conditions is only helped by confronting the perpetrator during the later stages. For a typical victim of rape or sexual assault, "just as her life is stabilizing, a court date is likely to revive intrusive symptoms."[12] Once again, Herman underlines the necessity for the victim to make her own decision, and to be empowered to make it by therapists, by survivors of similar crimes, and by victim advocates who can teach her about the risks of being re-traumatized and of her assailant being acquitted, as well as about the powerful satisfaction of getting a sexual predator off the streets.

Within ninety days, with good support and empowering treatment, survivors of "a single acute trauma" that may have lasted for no more than minutes, diagnosed with simple PTSD, can usually restore the sense of safety and the knowledge of how to care for themselves in the still-fragile state that Herman sees as the first stage of recovery. The Victims of Violence program offers crisis intervention, usually between one and six sessions of individual counseling, for people who want to focus on an acute reaction to a single traumatic incident. A survivor of "prolonged, repeated trauma," by contrast, diagnosed with complex PTSD, may need months of patient teaching and listening simply to develop the "psychological capacity to protect herself."[13] Physical safety may be elusive because a victim of incest or repeated rape in long-lasting abusive relationships may have "come to view her body as belonging to others," Herman writes.[14] She may still be hanging out with her longtime attacker, whom she may regard as her best friend or most torrid lover. Couples therapy is a mistake as long as the perpetrator's covert or overt goal is to regain control of the victim. It probably won't work even if the attacker promises to give up violence, since commonly "in return for his pledge of nonviolence, he expects his victim to give up her autonomy," Herman writes.[15]

Herman tells the story of Vera, who took out a restraining order against her boyfriend "after he had beaten her in front of the children":

> Since his departure she could not eat or sleep and found it difficult to get out of bed during the day. Nightmares and intrusive memories of violence alternated with fond memories of the good times during their relationship. She had frequent crying spells and thoughts of suicide. She sought therapy in order to "get rid of him once and for all." On careful questioning, however, she acknowledged that she could not imagine life without him. In fact, she had already begun to see him again. She felt like a "love addict."

Though the therapist privately would have liked nothing better than to see Vera separate from her boyfriend, she did not agree to this as a therapeutic goal. She advised Vera not to set goals that seemed unattainable, since she had already had quite enough experiences of failure. Instead, she suggested that Vera postpone her final decision about the relationship until she felt strong enough to make a free choice and that in the meantime she focus on increasing her sense of safety and control of her life. It was agreed that during the initial phase of treatment, Vera would continue to see her boyfriend on occasion but would not allow him to move back into her home and would not leave the children alone with him. These were promises she felt she could keep.

At first Vera was erratic about keeping appointments. The therapist was not critical but pointed out the importance for her own self-respect of following through on plans she had made. Therapy settled into a fairly regular routine after it was agreed that Vera would only schedule appointments that she was sure she could keep. Each session focused on identifying some positive action, however small, that Vera felt sure she could take on her own behalf. Initially she would rummage through her purse to find scraps of paper on which to write down this weekly "homework." An important milestone was reached when she bought herself a notebook in which to record her weekly tasks and began to check off each accomplishment with a bright red felt tip marker.

One of Vera's chief complaints was depression. The only times she felt good were during brief romantic interludes with her boyfriend. Occasionally he also supplied her with cocaine, which gave her a transient sense of power and well-being, followed by a "crash" that made her depression even worse. The therapist raised the possibility of a trial medication for both depression and intrusive post-traumatic symptoms, but explained that she could not prescribe it unless Vera was willing to give up her recreational drug use. Vera chose to accept the medication and felt increased pride and self-confidence after refusing her boyfriend's offer of cocaine. She responded well to anti-depressant medication.

As Vera's symptoms abated, the focus of treatment shifted to her children. Since the boyfriend's departure, the children, who used to be quiet and submissive, had gone completely out of control. She complained that they were clinging, demanding, and insolent. Overwhelmed and frustrated, she longed for her boyfriend to return so that he could "knock some sense into them." The therapist offered information about the effects of violence on children and encouraged Vera to seek treatment for her children as well as for herself. She also reviewed practical options for help with child care. The situation improved when Vera, who had been estranged from her family, invited a sister to visit for a few weeks. With her sister's help, she was able to reinstate predictable routines of child care and nonviolent discipline.

The work of the therapy continued to focus on concrete goal-setting. For example, one week Vera agreed to a goal of reading her children a bedtime story. This activity gradually developed into a soothing routine that both she and her children enjoyed, and she found that she no longer had to struggle to get her children to go to bed. Another milestone was reached when Vera's boyfriend called during one of these peaceful times and demanded to see her immediately. Vera refused to be interrupted. She told her boyfriend that she was tired of being available whenever he was in the mood to see her. In the future he would have to make a date with her in advance. In her next therapy session, she reported with astonishment and some sadness that she no longer needed him so desperately; in fact, she really felt capable of getting along without him.[16]

Finally, sober, safe, and able to care for herself and her children, Vera was ready to go, if she chose, for the goal she had wanted to set on the first day of therapy. And she was ready for the second phase of recovery. Before they started to talk about the history of abuse that had caused Vera's depression, substance abuse, desire to kill herself, and enslavement—that is, her profound conviction that she was not the owner of herself—Vera's sense of safety and her trust in her therapist were well enough established to stand the stress of remembering. So now she and her therapist were ready. They would avoid what Herman calls the most common therapeutic errors: not talking about a traumatic history at all, or talking about it too soon. It was time to talk about it.

The second stage of recovery from psychological trauma is telling the story—"completely, in depth, and in detail."[17] Herman calls this stage "remembrance and mourning." The therapist's job is to restrain the patient from starting this process until safety and trust have been established and tested, and to wait to begin listening to the story until the patient chooses to start telling it.

The smallest things can make it hard to make this choice. Y. couldn't start until she found a therapist who cried when he heard what had happened to her, even though she herself felt unmoved. V., on the other hand, had to wait until she found a therapist who wouldn't cry. "I was so afraid of being violated," V. says about her initial search for a therapist. "I didn't care if my therapist cared about me. I didn't care if she loved me, if she wanted to take me home with her," V. says. "I just cared about clarity." Once she decided that psychotherapy might help her, she found a therapist through a local women's organization. She met with the therapist a number of times and found that whenever she began to tell her therapist about her history of abuse, her therapist would cry. "Tears would come to her eyes," V. says. "In the beginning that was scary." To V., at that early stage when she still didn't feel safe in her own body, tears in the eyes of a therapist might mean "that my needs aren't going to get met—that she's not going to be detached enough from what's happening to meet my needs," or perhaps a therapist's tears would mean that the therapist would be so upset and involved in her own reaction that V. would feel she needed to take care of the therapist in a way that might feel like or might even become fresh abuse. Maybe she would have to watch what she said to protect the therapist from feeling pain, or to keep the therapist from creating a diversion from the hard things that V. had to talk about by hurting V. in some way that would be easier for the therapist to talk about. So V. went through the Victims of Violence intake process and chose to work with a therapist they recommended, "because she was so clear," V. says. "I would say, 'I'm an abuse survivor,' and she wouldn't go like this," V. says, frowning deeply. "She would just look at me. She wouldn't bring her emotional reaction into the therapy."

After this therapist helped V. learn to anticipate and soothe her own reactions to her trauma and to make herself feel safe, her sense of what she wanted from therapy shifted. She began to want to see tears in therapeutic eyes. When I speak to her, she is grateful that her therapist has never aroused any fears or worries that the therapist might abuse her in any way. But now she is thinking about going back to the first therapist, the one who cried. "I want someone who it's going to bother. I want someone who's going to be sad for me—that they're going to feel genuinely about that. I want some kind of emotions. I want a feeling that they brighten when they see me." Now she wants to see the therapist moved when she is moved—empathy, a kindred show of emotion in the give-and-take of good relationship.

Telling the story must include telling what happened to the victim—and what happened always includes emotions as well as traumatic events. The victim experienced rape, assault, betrayal, terror, crushing disappointment, and distrust, including distrust of herself. All these elements of trauma must be recalled and recounted in detail, so that the victim can integrate and survive them. The therapist is a witness and an anchor in this process, keeping the victim at the task of reconstructing the trauma by the quality of her respect and the pull of her listening, but also constantly keeping the victim in the rhythm of remembrance and recollection, conjuring and collecting memories into a story, and reassembling and restoring faculties and even moral qualities—composure, courage, compassion—that have been injured and dissociated. The victim may experience this integration as a coming to believe and take seriously events she has remembered without belief or moral concern. The therapist's powerful, unmistakable example of listening and believing helps the survivor learn to listen to herself and believe what she hears herself say. While she begins to experience the horror of her story and the restoration of her ability to represent her own experience, and to give or withhold consent, the survivor also has to reroot her sense of right and wrong very deeply, below the depth of the crime against her, below the level of harm to her sense of trust in civilization. Herman is eloquent on this moral aspect of the therapeutic task:

> The traumatic event challenges an ordinary person to become a theologian, a philosopher, and a jurist. The survivor is called upon to articulate the values and beliefs that she once held and that the trauma destroyed. She stands mute before the emptiness of evil, feeling the insufficiency of any known system of explanation . . .

The arbitrary, random quality of her fate defies the basic human faith in a just or even predictable world order. In order to develop a full understanding of the trauma story, the survivor must examine the moral questions of guilt and responsibility and reconstruct a system of belief that makes sense of her undeserved suffering. Finally, the survivor cannot reconstruct a sense of meaning by the exercise of thought alone. The remedy for injustice also requires action. The survivor must decide what is to be done.[18]

Complex PTSD is a reaction to trauma. Listening to victims tell their stories, therapists do much of their work simply by informing their clients that their reactions are understandable, that the obvious names for their experiences and symptoms—incest, rape, trauma—are accurate, that their feelings evoke compassion and empathy, that their predicament is as moral and political as it is physical and psychological. The therapist can't lead the witness—mustn't assume that one part of a story is worse or more harmful than another, or that the story is complete, or that it isn't true, or, in a more recent error, that "merely on the basis of a suggestive history," it will turn out to be a story of abuse the patient hasn't yet remembered, Herman writes.[19] Just following the signs that are in plain sight—describing memories and feelings that do survive, studying flashbacks, the triggers of panic attacks—usually uncovers all the lost or missing memories necessary to flesh out a full enough story, though some of the same specialty techniques military psychiatrists used in World War II to get traumatized soldiers back into service—such as skilled hypnosis and even Amytal—are still available if other paths lead to an inner stone wall. Simply telling the story to a respectful witness—whether victims of rape, combat stress, or political torture do the telling—"can actually produce a change in the abnormal processing of the traumatic memory," a change that relieves many physical symptoms of PTSD.[20] But the therapist must also help the survivor deal with the relational aftermath of the story, rebuilding trust and also, eventually, deciding what to do about the people who hurt her or who were hurt with her. The Victims of Violence program runs groups of about six survivors, for women, for men, and for mixed groups of men and women. Most of these groups run for three or four months, though a few ongoing groups have met for more than a decade. Jayme Shorin, a social worker who is the administrator of the program, has seen "huge changes in the community and what kind of groups are being offered" outside of Victims of Violence. Several developments discouraged some therapists from running private groups for survivors for a time: a campaign of intimidation by a group of parents who were accused of abuse by their adult children was one factor. "And also, it's really hard work, and it's hard to keep up and take care of yourself," Shorin says; secondary traumatization from working with high-risk, severely injured patients has reduced the number of therapists who run survivors' groups.

For therapists who continue to work with trauma victims, there's no getting out of mourning, once the story of any trauma is told, though "resistance to mourning is probably the most common cause of stagnation" in this phase of healing, Herman writes.[21] The victim who has learned not to cry and dreads making anyone else cry with her story may come to pour out tears every day in this stage of therapy. Herman quotes a survivor, remembering her mother: "Even when that woman beat me, no way was she going to make me cry. I never cried when my husband beat me. He'd knock me down and I'd get up for more. It's a wonder I didn't get killed. I've cried more in therapy than in my whole life. I never trusted anyone enough to let them see me cry. Not even you, till the last couple of months."[22]

"Fantasies of both revenge and forgiveness can constitute obstacles to processing" trauma therapeutically, Herman says. "Trauma survivors who become obsessed with revenge eventually come to the realization that this obsession" is part of the harm that their abusers did to them, she says. And "fantasies of unilateral forgiveness" also impede healing, since forgiveness is a relational process. "I forgive you" is "the response to a heartfelt apology and request for forgiveness," Herman says. If the apology is never made, the process of forgiveness cannot take place. And "genuine contrition in a perpetrator is a rare miracle," Herman writes, after decades of experience.[23] For a victim to attempt to forgive a perpetrator who never asked for forgiveness, or who is unrepentant and still lying and refusing to admit any wrongdoing, would be an empty exercise, like kissing oneself in the mirror. A trauma survivor needs to tell her story to "an open-minded, compassionate witness," her therapist, her closest friends—and to other survivors in therapy or support groups—until she realizes that she needs to mourn the fact that she will probably never be asked for forgiveness. "Forgiveness is based on the principle of mutuality, and that really requires explanation and apology and acknowledgment of the crime and the willingness to make amends," Herman says in May 2002, just finishing a year of research for a new book about restorative justice as a fellow at the Radcliffe Institute. The common failure of perpetrators to seek forgiveness or make amends often rules forgiveness out, she finds. The healing response when forgiveness is impossible is often simply giving up, ending the relationship—or at least the expectation that it will ever be a good relationship—and looking for love from more likely candidates. "Paradoxically," for instance, "the patient may liberate herself from the perpetrator when she renounces the hope of getting compensation from him," Herman writes, though it is important to many victims to know that victim services in courts and at many clinics are subsidized by fines paid by convicted rapists and sexual assailants.[24] A victim who knows she has no chance of achieving a mutual relationship with a perpetrator, because she knows he believes he has a right to betray and assault her, has to mourn her broken trust.

At times, the phase of telling the story may seem frighteningly endless, especially since it focuses on a kind of frozen memory, paradoxically timeless, that is being unfrozen by truth, tears, and empathic listening into a living, supple, integrated memory—and especially since certain phases, such as the phase of realizing that no one protected her as a small child and mourning that absence of care, expose the victim to a potentially suicidal vacuum of remembered neglect. The therapist tries to help the victim remember, mourn, and resuscitate her trust at the same time, relying on good current relationships. "Her healing depends on the discovery of restorative love in her own life," Herman writes. "Once the survivor has mourned the traumatic event, she may be surprised to discover how uninteresting the perpetrator has become to her and how little concern she feels for his fate."[25] She may even find that her trauma itself no longer interests her so profoundly, mostly because it no longer cries out for healing. Healing doesn't make it not have happened; however long or short her trauma history, she will think of it every day and grieve, but not at the heart of her day, not in the center of her life. Her attention will now be available for other things—love, trust, commitment, and justice.

As traumatized patients tell their stories and mourn the losses their stories are about, they arrive at the third stage of healing: they begin to feel it is time to reconnect. They may take a self-defense course, especially one like IMPACT Model Mugging that acknowledges the special styles and circumstances of attacks on women and can become an effective survivors' group itself. They may speak out in their families about what may be long traditions of abuse cloaked in silence. Schatzow and Herman quote an incest survivor at the stage of reconnection, when this woman had finally told her family about the years of secret incest with her father. She recalls relief, bereavement, and finally freedom:

> Initially I felt a sense of success, completion, incredible relief! Then, I began to feel very sad, deep grief. It was extremely painful and I had no words for what I was feeling. I found myself crying and crying and not knowing exactly why. This hardly ever happens to me. I am usually able to have some kind of verbal description to explain my feelings. This was just raw feeling. Loss, grief, mourning, as if they had died. I felt no hope, no expectations from them . . . I knew there was nothing unspoken on my part. I didn't feel, "Oh, if only I had said this or that." I had said everything I wanted to say in the way I wanted to say it. I felt very complete about it and was very grateful for the lengthy planning rehearsals, strategizing . . .
>
> Since then I have felt free . . . I feel HOPE! I feel like I have a future! I feel grounded, not like I'm manicky or high. When I'm sad, I'm sad; when I'm angry, I'm angry. I feel realistic about the bad times and the difficulties I will face, but I know I have myself. It's very different. And it's nothing I could ever imagine, not at all. I always wanted this freedom and was always fighting to get it. Now it's no longer a battle—there's no one to fight—it's simply mine.[26]

Just as the loss of relationships through the betrayals of psychological trauma leads to the loss of a sense of self, so with reconnection comes self-possession, or maybe self-repossession. In this third stage of heal-

ing, the creation or restoration of a network of good, mutually respectful, and responsive relationships brings a sense of initiative. Desire is
no longer feared as a key to Pandora's box but welcomed as one point
of departure for trying and accomplishing satisfying, pleasant, and socially valuable acts. One patient may find she can have orgasms while
replacing her old sadomasochistic fantasies with images of waterfalls.[27]
Another finds she can walk down the street feeling confidence instead
of panic, or fear that she may panic. For some, this phase is a kind of
treatment for the addiction to endorphin highs that was the silk purse
victims made out of the sow's ear of post-traumatic symptoms. At the
same time, once patients are able to experience normal comfort, relax-
ation, alertness, and something like contentment, many also recognize
the immense courage it took for them to be able to achieve, say, a quiet
Sunday at home, or a peaceful walk by the river with friends. Every
survivor may now find a real use for forgiveness—forgiving the afflicted
person she used to be for self-mutilation, suicide attempts, substance
abuse, and other risky behavior, and often asking forgiveness of the
friends, spouses, relatives, partners, children, and therapists she may
have neglected or demanded too much of through months or years of
dissociation and healing.

Like Bertha Pappenheim's, the final healing for many survivors is a
commitment to the kind of social and political action that led to the
creation of rape crisis centers, treatment centers like the Victims of Violence program, and court-related victim advocacy programs. Y.'s ambition to become the kind of therapist who helped her is one common
way survivors live this out. Others volunteer for rape crisis centers,
abuse hotlines, safe houses, or battered women's shelters, or lobby on
behalf of abuse victims, or write, act, or make art about them. "While
there is no way to compensate for an atrocity, there is a way to transcend it, by making it a gift to others. The trauma is redeemed only
when it becomes the source of a survivor mission," Herman writes.[28]
On the other hand, "resolution of the trauma is never final; recovery is
never complete."[29] Major life events or milestones—marriage, a death,
the birth of children, or children reaching the age when abuse began
for their mother—can trigger symptoms a survivor hasn't known for
years. But of course, the survivor who returns to therapeutic work
trusts the process and knows healing is possible. She knows the five

good things and knows that survivors' groups—effective at any stage of healing—may help her again now.

At the turn of the twenty-first century, the Victims of Violence program was providing eight thousand purely clinical hours a year, including intake and assessment, individual psychotherapy and crisis intervention, and a wide array of information and support groups, for people at all stages of healing. About four thousand clinical hours were individual psychotherapy sessions. Much of the program's funding comes from the federal Victims of Crime Act of 1984 and its revolutionary provision of compensation for treatment of traumatic injuries, based on complaints made to an administrative authority (rather than criminal proceedings) and funded by fines on convicted offenders. The VOV staff has more than quadrupled in the past two decades from six to twenty-nine. "We serve men and women and have both men and women on our multicultural staff," says Herman, who continues as director of training. In addition to its clinical program, VOV runs the Victim Advocacy and Support Team, the Community Crisis Response Team, and a new Center for Homicide Bereavement and has a federal grant for aid to first responders to provide services to people and service providers bereaved and traumatized by the attacks in New York and Washington on September 11, 2001. Victims of Violence staff members have taught on five continents and taught foreign visitors to Cambridge and Somerville (their current home) about the repercussions of abuse, war crimes, and political torture.

Jayme Shorin, who started at the program in 1988, right out of social work school, has worked in Canada with First Nations people about integrating the Victims of Violence model into native healing rituals. Now associate director of the program, Shorin says that at the start of the twenty-first century she saw "more polarization" in the field: political opponents seemed better organized, but the general public was also much better educated, she says. Some private therapists were shunning work with survivors of sexual abuse, both fearing and participating in a backlash against trauma survivors and their therapists; some had gone overboard and doled out "some questionable treatment," Shorin says. "There were people who were told they had trauma histories that they didn't. There were people who landed up living with their therapists who were going to nurse them back to health; there were people who did all sorts of unbounded things." But by 2004, she says, thanks to such professional organizations as the International Society for the Study of Dissociation and the International Society for Traumatic Stress Studies, "there are really good new ethical guidelines out there" for treating PTSD, and "people are really working much more responsibly. A lot more empirically based treatments are being studied, and there's a lot more interest in physiological correlates of trauma. There's a new emphasis on body-oriented psychotherapy." For the most part, she says, private therapists have gotten better at treating trauma victims; most trauma treatment programs have learned from successes like the Victims of Violence program and routinely screen for abuse during evaluations. "When we started, we were the only show in town, teaching everybody how to do this. Now clinicians in general are pretty educated in how to do the simpler cases," Shorin says. "Our team over the years has gotten the more complicated cases—multiple diagnoses, dual diagnoses, substance abuse, intergenerational family problems, and lately a lot of major mental illness interfaced with a really chronic trauma history." Unfortunately, if predictably, the "managed-care-ization of health care" has had a destructive impact on trauma services, Shorin says. "There is a huge emphasis for productivity. It's really hard to take care of yourself, because they keep pressing for numbers." Poor clients, too, are harder pressed to pay, since the state raised their sliding fee scale.

Herman herself is looking beyond the immediate need for treatment to the political part of the healing. In the late 1990s, she began a new phase of research on justice for rape, battering, and incest victims. What would justice be from the victims' perspective? Certainly not a system like the current one, in which, Herman says, "95 percent of perpetrators do not suffer any consequences," a system that produces what the United Nations' Joint Declaration of the Special Rapporteurs on Women's Rights calls a worldwide "climate of impunity" for perpetrators of rape. It interests her that legally, the injured party in rape— most of whose victims in the United States are minors—is the state. Historically, this construction was a way of avoiding endless vendettas. But Herman believes it has produced a kind of justice that often hands victims the opposite of what they need.

Herman enumerated the difficulties in a paper she read in Washington, D.C., to a government-sponsored symposium on the mental health needs of crime victims in 2000:

> Victims need to establish a sense of power and control over their lives; the court requires them to submit to a complex set of rules and procedures which they may not understand, and over which they have no control. Victims need an opportunity to tell their stories in their own way, in a setting of their choice; the court requires them to respond to a set of yes-or-no questions that break down any personal attempt to construct a coherent and meaningful narrative. Victims often need to control or limit their exposure to specific reminders of the trauma; the court requires them to relive the experience by directly confronting the perpetrator.

Some elements of a less re-traumatizing system already operate in some parts of the United States. Victim advocates in courts are paid by states, funded by fines paid by offenders, to support and inform victims who decide to prosecute through the court process, and these court officers are agents of a victim-centered justice. Thirty-two states have adopted victims' rights amendments to their constitutions: these amendments entitle victims to be treated respectfully, to confer with prosecutors, to speak at sentencing, to be assured of safety, and to be informed of these rights. Police and judges in many jurisdictions are enforcing restraining orders, and "women are using them in droves," Herman says; women seek and obtain between thirty-five thousand and forty thousand civil restraining orders a year in Massachusetts alone.

Herman's research on alternatives to the criminal justice system in its current, adversarial state has led her to the movement for restorative justice, in which "the violation of relationships, between offender and victim, and between offender and the wider community, is considered the fundamental problem, rather than the abstract violation of the law," she explained in Washington. A system of justice focused on repairing broken relationships is a noble concept, but she cautioned her audience about its suitability for criminal cases: "Restorative justice programs can be effective only when the safety of the victim and other potential victims has already been secured." How can an offender nurtured in the culture of denial at all costs be brought to see that his crime is an injury to a community and to a member of it, and to want to heal that injury, and to actually do the work of healing it, and how could a community and a victim ever be sure that he was sincere and no longer a threat? "Though many anecdotal reports have been published, no systematic, data-based studies have yet been conducted to document the mental health effects (healing or otherwise) of victims' participation in restorative justice programs," Herman said.[30]

Herman is still asking questions about how to use science to heal injustice. For example, she writes of domestic abuse, "We do not yet understand how individual perpetrators, in privacy, manage to reinvent the same coercive methods that are practiced in totalitarian political or religious systems." And she is still hypothesizing startling answers, always suggested by known data, that explain a lot if they are true. For instance, she wonders if "the sex trade might also be considered an endemic reservoir in which methods of coercive control are maintained and refined, to be called upon in times of war."[31]

Herman is uncomfortable talking about social dissing—dissociating from someone and isolating that person as punishment for seeing and saying things that are not supposed to be seen or spoken—in the same breath as the psychological state of dissociation that is the result of being traumatized and lied to about it. An outspoken political partisan for human rights, she is an equally passionate psychiatric empiricist; she wants to save the word "dissociation" for the specific psychological state she studies and treats in trauma victims. But she does describe a kind of mass social dissociation; she first encountered it when she realized that incest was a common crime in a society that insisted it was rare, and she now encounters it as she and others begin to examine the means by which we live so easily with knowing and not knowing about prostitution—"a worldwide enterprise that condemns millions of women and children to social death and often to literal death, for the sexual pleasure and profit of men," and that thrives everywhere. "The choice to avoid knowing operates at the edges of our consciousness; this is how dissociation is practiced as a social norm," she writes.

Thirty years ago, rape, domestic violence, and incest were similarly invisible, despite their high prevalence. A mass movement was required to bring these abuses into public awareness. In the social analysis developed by feminists, these crimes were understood as intrinsic features of a system of male dominance. It was recognized that the purpose of these crimes is to impose power, and that the methods used in furtherance of this goal are essentially the same as the methods of torture practiced in political prisons worldwide.

In 2003, she published these observations in a paper in which she told a story about social dissociation operating in her own field. The paper serves as the introduction to a special double issue of the *Journal of Trauma Practice*. The issue, called *Prostitution, Trafficking, and Traumatic Stress*, is packed with research and protocols by a dozen investigators about the way complex PTSD shows itself in the lives of women who have been used in prostitution and about how to treat them; so it represents a sizable breach in the wall of willed ignorance that surrounds prostitution. In her paper, Herman describes one healing moment when her appeal for professionals to show what they knew began to move this social dissociation about prostitution into reconnection and association:

> Recently, when preparing a lecture for a conference on trauma, I proposed to address the subject of prostitution. The conference organizer was not pleased with my suggestion. Most of the program was devoted to the response to terrorist attacks and the formation of a national center for traumatic stress in children. Here was plenty of "clean" trauma, with many innocent victims whose plight aroused general sympathy. Prostitution, by contrast, was embarrassing, shameful, in a word, dirty. Did it even make sense to speak of victims? Wasn't prostitution, after all, a "victimless crime"?
>
> I noted that our staff at the Victims of Violence Program . . . were seeing a remarkable number of patients who had been used in prostitution, and that these were among the most cruelly abused people we had ever treated. My colleague acknowledged that he, too, had seen such cases, but surely they were unusual. I suggested as an empirical test that we poll the audience at the conference. If few of the participants had seen such cases, I promised not to pursue the subject any further.
>
> At the start of my lecture, with about 600 people in attendance,

I asked how many had treated or were currently treating patients who had been used in prostitution. By my rough visual estimate, 450 people (75%) raised their hands. It was a moment of surprise, not only for my colleague, the conference organizer, but for those in the audience as well. Here was a common experience that by common, unspoken consent was simply not discussed in public, not even by a group of mental health professionals who had already amply proved their willingness to bear witness to terrible stories. It was also a moment of illumination and relief, as members of the audience looked around and realized they had lots of company.[32]

As she had done a quarter of a century before with her questions about father-daughter incest, Herman, by asking questions about prostitution, had once again brought a common crime and its traumatic aftermath out of the psychiatric shadows and into the light of clinical observation, empirical study, treatment, and healing. This kind of effort brings healing not merely to victims of these crimes but also to the culture that turns a blind eye to them.

At the end of the day, the Girl Scouts at Lyn Brown's demonstration of girl power meet a special guide to the perils of perfection and the art of seeing through cultural scams. Josette Huntress, Miss Maine in 1994 and a Colby College student in Lyn's class on girls' development when she wasn't being Miss Maine, regards Lyn Brown as her mentor in trying to "tell people not to be trapped in a role," especially when the role is "Penelope Perfect" and the people are girls. "What if MTV were run by and for girls?" a student asks the Girl Scouts who have been assigned to her group to design a set for it and talk about the music such a channel might carry. One scout draws a space alien; another draws a girl in baggy pants; somebody else says it would be cool to play the songs of humpback whales. The girls talk about the things people are picked on for in the guise of pressure to look and dress a certain way: race, class ("You must have gotten that shirt from Goodwill"), obesity, size ("I don't like being called shrimp"), age ("I get so sick of being called Baby Face").

Then Josette leads an exercise in which the girls are asked to pick

Penelope Perfect out of magazines, and their notion of perfection in young women is so stereotyped and limited that even in airbrushed teen fashion magazines, they find far more to pick on than to praise. "She's not Penelope—she's not that pretty," one says, and turns the page. "She's not Penelope—her eyes are brown, not blue," a brown-eyed girl says. "That's not Penelope—Penelope's not Chinese," another girl says, and then wonders, "So what happens if you're Chinese and you want to be perfect?" In general, the Girl Scouts comment that the perfect girl is "prissy" and "pretty" and "can't keep a best friend but has lots of friends."

"What do these girls have to do to be in magazines? Do you think they have to wear a lot of makeup? Do you think they have to have someone else do their hair?" Huntress asks. "Do you think you want your friends to be like that—to spend forty-eight hours doing their hair?"

Huntress is dressed in casual clothes; her hair is glossy and short but not "done." With a cast on her hand, she looks like an active, lively undergraduate who knows what she wants, and being a beauty queen is not it. No one has told the girls in this group that she is Miss Maine, but the girls' underground is operating, and somehow the word is getting out. Huntress is here to help them expand their ideals to include real girls, girls with imperfections like their own. She offers them poster boards and markers. "Let's write on these posters what we really want to be like," she says. What would the magazine photos show if they were about girls like them? Then she holds up her hand and says, "They should show someone with a cast." The girls get into it right away: "They should show someone with a zit," one says.

Huntress takes a couple of the photos that the girls chose from teen magazines for the Penelope file and asks, "What if this person was really mean to you? I mean, you can't tell" from just looking. "Can you tell if these girls are smart or not? No. Can you tell if these girls are sweet or not? No." And what would they eat if they wanted to look like that, to look perfect, she wonders. Huntress likes pizza and ice cream, plays basketball, and broke her arm playing "tackle Frisbee," she says. "Your hair isn't perfect," a girl tells her. "That's because she's wearing a cast," another girl deduces. "My definition of perfect is to be and act like yourself," Huntress says.

"Perfect is anything you want to be," a girl says.

Other girls chime in: "People are perfect in their own way." "Perfect is everyone." "It's better to be a true friend than a perfect friend."

"What should we do with all these perfect Penelopes?" Huntress asks about the pictures they've cut out of magazines. "Throw them away?" Huntress suggests. "First, let's have a screaming contest," she says with a grin.

The message is clear, and now it gets loud: girls should be themselves, and girls should be heard. It comes with the rumor that's been whispered around the room all through this exercise: Huntress is Miss Maine. At the very end of this exercise, Huntress admits it in a whisper to a little girl who asks her point-blank. "I never wanted to bring up the fact that I was Miss Maine at all," Huntress says later. But she felt she had to answer the girl's question, because the girl looked so confused, Huntress says. "Then when I left, she put her arms around me and said, 'I love you, Josie.' And I was very glad she didn't say, 'I love you, Miss Maine.' "

Huntress, who had to diet to a size four to win the competition, regained weight during her reign and was back up to "a healthy size ten," she said, when she led this exercise for Girl Scouts. She talked later about living on egg whites and anger in a world that praised her for anorexia. "No one in that environment said, 'You haven't had your period in three months and we're worried about you.' Everyone was like, 'Oh, you look good.' " Her dad was the only dissenter. "Josette, you're too thin, and I don't like it," he said. "He saw it as a loss of strength when other people saw it as empowerment," Huntress said. Long after the egg whites were gone, Josie's anger kept her at work as a mole in the pageant business—a remarkable example of what Gilligan and Brown mean by resistance—appearing as Miss Maine without a crown so she could say, "Your crown is on the inside, not the outside," when people asked where it was. "I need to be in pageants not because I need the acceptance but because I have this message," Huntress said. "You don't have to be someone you're not."

"I want to explore whether love in and of itself sets in motion a resistance to patriarchy," Gilligan writes in *The Birth of Pleasure*.[33] A decade before she wrote the book, which she calls "a new map of love," she identified the myth of Cupid and Psyche as an overlooked "map of resistance that takes you out of a tragic landscape, to get to good relationships—comedy rather than tragedy"—whereas the story of Oedipus that Freud picked as paradigmatic of human development is a map of betrayal that leads to tragedy. She told the story of Cupid and Psyche, in the last lecture course on adolescence she taught at Harvard, as the ultimate reconnection, the legitimate happy ending Western culture has for stories that start with illusion, loss, and even trauma. Telling this story became Carol's way of offering her students and then her readers a paradigm and guide for successful, loving, and pleasurable relational living.

The version she used in her course and uses in her book is the version of Lucius Apuleius, a man born in northern Africa to a well-to-do Roman family in about 130 C.E. Like other colonials in Africa—Augustine of Hippo, Albert Camus, Doris Lessing, Nadine Gordimer—Apuleius forged his own connection to place and culture by writing and by activism. In his case, as in Augustine's, it was religious activism. His career foreshadowed Augustine's almost completely, until the climax. Like Augustine after him, Apuleius attended the university at Carthage and later became an orator and advocate in Rome. In between he studied in Athens and traveled all over the imperial Roman world as a searcher after religious rites and mysteries. For a time he may have been as down on his luck and impoverished as the hero of his famous novel, a hero who bears his own first name. Gilligan notes that "in Rome, he was accused of witchcraft and returned to North Africa." The religion that captured Augustine had no allure for the elitist Apuleius. Apuleius had nothing but scorn for the young Christian cult, whose ethos of spiritual equality between slaves and freemen repelled him. He married a rich widow, the mother of a friend who had saved his life, and became a priest of Isis and Osiris, the Egyptian goddess and god of life and resurrection, and a priest of Asclepius, the Greek god of healing. So he was able to connect with the cultures of Africa and Greece, cultures he was born and bred in but not of, and at the same time he was able to maintain his sense of himself as a Roman aristocrat, rich enough to pay the high fees and noble enough to show the patrician bloodlines that priesthood required. He became a famous defender of pagan traditions against the new sect of Christianity. His defense of the Greek tradition, *The God of Socrates*, survived the many later Christian purges of pagan literature. And one edition of *The Golden Ass*, his celebration of the polytheistic way and of the great goddess Isis, managed to slip by the Inquisition.[34]

The Golden Ass is a kind of book that a Christian apologist couldn't write. It's the product of a classic attitude toward good and evil, tacky and sublime, that recognized these opposites as bedfellows and soul mates, seeds and soil for each other—two sides of a coin, not two sides of a war. It's *Tom Jones* and *Pilgrim's Progress*, a picaresque pilgrimage that includes bawdy satire and solemn epiphany. Unlike the pilgrims of Geoffrey Chaucer's *Canterbury Tales*, which also mixes folly and holiness, the Lucius of Apuleius's novel doesn't even know he's on a pilgrimage until the very end, when Isis literally transforms him from an ass to a priest. And tucked within this double metamorphosis, in which a man first becomes an ass and then a priest, is a tale within the tale, the story of Cupid and Psyche. Apuleius puts this story of the god of love and the most beautiful woman alive (who is also Psyche, the soul) into the mouth of a thieves' drudge, "a trifling and drunken old woman," who tells it to comfort a virgin the thieves carry off to their den from a rich house they rob. The old woman reminds the captive girl of the paradoxical method of dream interpretation common at the time, in which a dream of riches and joy presages loss, and a dream of loss presages bounty.

This story she tells is a myth that has been found throughout the world, from India to Scotland. Some later, European versions transformed this myth into Beauty and the Beast, in which the maiden has to fall in love with the beast before he can be transformed back into a man. But Apuleius's early version is more subtle.

Psyche's curse is not that she is sent to wed a beast, like Beauty, but simply that she is very, very beautiful in the first place. She is so beautiful that people call her the New Venus and swarm around her like groupies and paparazzi. People stop worshipping the old Venus, the real Venus, and start worshipping Psyche instead. But she is only idealized—like the beautiful woman in Herman's consciousness-raising group. She has no friends, and no man wants to marry her. "She's totally isolated, because if you're an object of beauty, you're not in relationship," Carol tells her class in 1991. To find out what to do with her, Psyche's parents consult the oracle of Apollo—"that is, the old version of a therapist," Carol tells her class. "The oracle is a woman with the wisdom of Apollo. What does she advise to solve your relational problems? What does she say is the solution, echoing the wisdom of Apollo? Separation," Carol says. The oracle tells Psyche's parents to have a funeral for her and abandon her on a hill outside of town, "since she is destined to marry a monster," Carol says. "Psyche's parents are devastated."

But Psyche tells them, in Carol's translation, "When you should have grieved was when everybody honored me and called me the New Venus as if I had been then dead."

"That's the voice of Elisa," Carol says. "That's the voice of the eleven-year-old girl," looking for real relationship rather than idealization, and saying so.

Psyche feels she'd rather die than go on living as the New Venus, but after the whole town has walked in her living funeral procession and left her with tears and speeches, she meets pleasure, not death. First a wind awakens her sense of pleasure, and then a husband visits her in darkness every night and brings her "great pleasure," Carol translates, though Psyche never sees him. She does not know that he is Cupid—Eros, in Greek—the son of the very same Venus whose worshippers Psyche had won without wanting to.

Psyche gets pregnant, and her sisters visit and tell her this unseen husband is really a monster who will kill her and her child. And here Gilligan contrasts the Oedipal myth that Freud held up as the tragedy of all families: Jocasta, Oedipus's mother, decides to give away her baby in order to save her marriage. By contrast, Psyche, in Apuleius's version of a myth as old as Oedipus or older, decides to kill what her sisters tell her is a monster husband so she can save her child. "But she looks at Eros under the light she'd brought to kill him by and sees that this is not a god" or a monster, Carol says. "This is a man, because he's vulnerable. She sees his vulnerability 'and thereby of her own accord, she fell in love with Love,'" Carol translates. "Seeing his humanness, she fell in love with him—not when he was a god. What she also discovers in this moment is that all the stories she was told about love and relationships aren't true. It's like all the stories that cannot be sustained as true if you

take as text these voices of girls, because girls obviously know a different reality that is contradicted by these stories about idealization."

This opposite of epiphany, Psyche's vision of the human as love's inspiration, is not the end of the story. "No—huge turmoil and conflict,"
Carol says, "because the women are seeking and speaking." So now the
story moves away from a choice between the ideal and the relational
into relationship. The adventure continues as "Eros has to see what the
differences between Psyche and his mother are, and Psyche has to
learn that others will help her."

Jungians make much of this story, seeing it as a very early description of the progress of the soul, the path of individuation, as they call it,
whereby a person—Apuleius himself, or Everyman, or Everywoman—
accomplishes an annealing of internal aspects that cohere into selfhood.[35] But Gilligan sees it as a story about relationships "and a map
showing how a path headed for tragedy can turn into a road to freedom."

And the end of the myth, at the end of this path, is "what's called a
just and lawful and everlasting marriage, and the birth of a daughter
named Pleasure," Carol concludes triumphantly.

It's so different from Freud's Oedipus, which Gilligan says is a myth
about what we would call a dysfunctional family: the father blinded, the
mother strangled, silenced. "The sons set out to war with one another
and kill one another off, and the daughters are summoned to accompany the father in his blindness." The Oedipus story hides, in a tangle
of hatred and blood feud, what Freud could no longer risk hearing about sexual abuse from young women—although, as we know,
mother-son incest is quite rare, while father-daughter incest is common. But the Oedipus story does tell the common story of boys' early
loss of relationship, in tones of inexorability and doom.

The Psyche story is about the pressures on adolescent girls to sacrifice relationships, but it is more about the way girls can resist these
pressures or see through them successfully, if with great difficulty. "The
Psyche story says that there are two crucial points of resistance," Carol
says. First, the adolescent girl "holds on to her relational knowledge"
despite pressure to succumb to seeing and talking about herself and
others as objects that can be idealized or put down. "The second point
is the young mother, who faces this choice of whether to risk sacrificing

her child to save her marriage or sacrificing her marriage to save herself and her child; if she chooses not to risk her child's life and her own, she will basically transform the story about love," Carol says.

And so Gilligan's last big lecture class on adolescence concluded with the happy ending of Apuleius's Cupid and Psyche. It was a big class in more than numbers, for Carol transformed the course she was told to teach because nobody else wanted to; ultimately she taught not only a new psychology but a new reading of Western culture and its Greek foundations.

In *The Birth of Pleasure*, Gilligan uses the story of Cupid and Psyche as a kind of lifeline for love, for the possibility of living with happiness, respect, and pleasure rather than dominance, hubris, and suffering. And she describes the way she and Terrence Real, the psychologist of men's post-traumatic depression, listened for notes of comedy and tragedy in the accounts of couples seeking help with relationships that were stuck at best and doomed, they feared, at worst. "As Terry picked up the signs of trauma and I tracked the voice of pleasure, we charted a terrain of loss" in the lives of the couples they listened to. But like a hidden window in a computer game or an alternative ending on a DVD, "the voice of pleasure . . . created an opening in the tragic story" of couples losing love to the relational paradox, she writes.[36]

Gilligan and Real track couples back to moments of intense relational pleasure, in marriage or in childhood. For instance, a man who closes down after experiences of pleasure with his wife remembers being "pals" with his mother at the age of four or five. Another man remembers how much he respects his wife's courage, and how passionately he loves being with her, only when she summons the courage to say she will leave him if he doesn't put more of himself into their married life.[37]

Carol writes:

I will never lie to you. I will never leave you. I will never try to possess you. These became the vows of relationship that Terrence Real and I came to in the course of our work with couples in crisis. They hold a promise not necessarily to stay married but to stay in relationship by creating the grounds for trust—making it possible to open oneself freely to another and to find the other again after the inevitable breaks in connection. It is the condition for living with change.[38]

I met Carol in March 2003 for lunch and a long talk in Cambridge. She talked about New York as a place that felt like home, and New York University as a place where she felt "ordinary" instead of alternately idealized, valorized, vilified, trivialized, or ignored. Now that she had become a University Professor there, she was "freed to move across disciplinary boundaries and go where my work was taking me—back into history, into literature and theater." She spoke about "Jane Fonda's extraordinary gift of $12.5 million to take my map of development as the basis for strengthening healthy resilience and courage in boys and girls—in primary and middle schools." It had seemed like a happy ending for Carol's work at Harvard, she said. "Fonda's personal gratitude to my insights about voice led her to endow a chair in my name at Harvard, knowing that I was preparing to move to New York. Having raised funds for three professorships in gender studies, I felt I could move on to the next phase of my work without jeopardizing the gender studies program at Harvard."

Despite this endowment, Carol had refused to reconsider her decision to leave Harvard; instead, she agreed to advise the center and lend her name to the chair as a way of honoring and preserving her work. Harvard, however, delayed the appointments to the three open professorships in gender studies until the steep decline in the value of the AOL Time Warner stock Fonda had given made them impossible. By now, Fonda had withdrawn most of this gift to the Harvard Graduate School of Education.

Carol had stayed at Harvard long enough to finish her research and see the last of her students graduate. "I went to NYU because I was looking for a free space," she says. At Harvard, she had tried to create such a space in her research, but no matter how successful she was, there was always a power difference: she was the professor; her fellow researchers were her doctoral students, officially studying "under" her. She was their supervisor. To achieve a truly free space, "I had to do with colleagues what I had done with graduate students," she says. "At NYU in the late 1990s, I found a free space and the relationships with colleagues that became essential to taking the next step in my work." At

NYU's Steinhardt School of Education, Carol's colleagues included Niobe Way, a former student, and Pedro Noguera and Carola Suárez-Orozco, former Harvard colleagues who had helped her set up the Fonda program. Carol still had her questions: What is love? What is truth? It had taken her two and a half decades to come to the edge of an answer, she says. "What I didn't know in 1982 is that it would take me twenty years"—first to follow the path where girls led, and then to follow boys, and then to look at couples in crisis and to read up on the infant research that showed inborn relational skill. Now "I had my maps," she says. And they led to a different set of questions:

> If we are born with a voice and into relationship, if we register our experience in our bodies and our emotions, if we are inherently re-lational, responsive beings, delighted by pleasure and capable of knowing our experience, then a basic question about development changes, marking a paradigm shift. The question is no longer how do we become capable of love and knowledge, but rather what keeps us from loving and knowing? How do we come not to know our experience, our feelings, and the feelings of others? How do we become divided from others and from ourselves? What leads us to forgo pleasure for the sake of gaining competitive advantage? And how do we find our way back to delight, to our natural voice that is a guide to love?[39]

Now, in New York, she wrote *The Birth of Pleasure*. With support from colleagues like David Richards, a constitutional lawyer and philosopher with whom she teaches, and Peggy Cooper Davis, a historian of Recon-struction, she created a portrait of her knowledge rather than a more typical scientific magnum opus, because part of what she had to say about what she knows was the way she said it.

As we talked, Gilligan said she believed that now, in 2003, the movement against war and for human and civil rights that had in a sense carried her into her work was "at the boiling point." A president who had gained a minority of votes cast, including the largest gender gap in history, now occupied the White House, she noted. The federal government was backing a suit to dismantle university affirmative action programs; the disenfranchisement of thousands of African-

Americans in Florida wrongly barred from voting because they shared names and zip codes with former felons had led to this odd minority presidency of the "compassionate conservative" George W. Bush, who was retreating from arms treaties and waging "preemptive" war on Iraq. Carol pinned onto her sweater a button with a dove and an Iraqi child's name on it that I offered her and said she had taken her strengthening-healthy-resistance-and-courage project to NYU law students and was writing fiction. Rather than running a center to study gender in education at the Harvard Graduate School of Education, she was "choosing again to live on the edge—to pursue my life as an artist"—and working on a novel and a collection of short stories. She talked about the shock of meeting psychology students who had never heard a teacher tell them that research was about asking a question you really wanted, maybe even needed, to know the answer to. She talked about the shock of recently learning that Jane Addams, whom she'd studied in middle school, had won the Nobel Peace Prize in 1931 for teaching heads of state to listen and talk to each other in respectful relationship instead of as competitors and gamesmen. "I learned all about her work at Hull House and the settlements. Why didn't they say anything about her peace work?" I replied that Emily Balch, who taught at Wellesley, home of the Stone Center and the Center for Research on Women, where Gilligan had held a fellowship in 1977, had won the Nobel Peace Prize in 1946 for founding after World War I the Women's International League for Peace and Freedom, an organization that still exists—and whose name I couldn't remember at the time. I mentioned the Kellogg-Briand Pact of 1928, outlawing all war between nations and ratified by sixty-two countries, including Japan, Italy, Germany, France, Great Britain, and the United States (to list them in the order in which they broke the pact). She said she was beginning to feel the first waves of the waters of oblivion that have covered women's relational work from one era to another. And it seems to her now, she said, that the way to stay on her own cutting edge, the way to stay in "To Be," to keep learning right on the border between what she knows and what baffles her, is to make art about it. To stay in psychology as a typical psychologist would force her to teach the basics of her work, discovered a generation ago, over and over, to students who are no longer convinced that love and politics have a place in psychology, or it would force her to defend those old discoveries to critics who use the tactics of saboteurs to get attention for their polemics.

Nonetheless, she stunned me with her optimism. At one point in our conversation about the state of the world, I repeated the current half-full speculation that the reluctance of Europe and Asia to jump onto Bush's military bandwagon in Iraq, and the fact that acquiring territory by conquest has been against international law for a couple of decades, might say more about the future of peace than the future of war. War, that epitome of bad, nonrelational conflict, might even be behind us in a thousand years, I ventured. Carol agreed that people are growing out of war. But she thought my guess about how long it would take was way off. "Ten years," she said.

Any relationship with a community or a segment of society that lies to, violates, abandons, or tries to possess members of another segment—say, whites to blacks, or middle-aged to young, or high-income to low-income—requires teachers to lead the lied-to to resist, to free themselves by joining with people who don't lie to, violate, abandon, or possess them. This is the classic story of the end of slavery, the story of the civil rights and women's liberation movements. Janie Victoria Ward, working at the Ed School in what survives of its gender studies program—now expanded to include race and class—finds that black parents teach their adolescent children four steps to freedom from racism in the United States: "Read it. Name it. Oppose it. Replace it."

"Racism can be psychologically overwhelming to kids," Ward says at a talk about her book, *The Skin We're In*, at the Wellesley Center for Research on Women. "When kids get mad or feel shamed, they don't always think that clearly." In interviews with black parents and adolescents (not in the same families) about whether and how black parents talk to black adolescents about race, Ward discovered that parents often teach their kids first just to discern when difficulties are caused by prejudice.

"We are constantly telling black children that racism doesn't exist," Ward says. For instance, one new teacher at Ward's talk said school administrators had forbidden her to say anything about race to her elementary-school students. And in the face of institutions where racism is officially, literally unspeakable, black parents often feel very isolated breaking white communities' loud and embarrassed silence about race. "Both parents and kids shared with me the pain that's associated with acknowledging that some problem has to do with racism," Ward says. And yet children who learn to see everything or nothing as racist are at grave risk of a kind of institutional trauma that can wreck lives; knowing this all too vividly, many black parents take it as a very serious duty to teach their children definite criteria for determining if something is racist. "I am not giving a particular definition for what racism is. Within families, the families themselves are determining what they want to call racism. What's important is to talk about it," Ward says.

Opposing racism the right way can make a self-respecting life possible for a black teenager. Opposing it the wrong way can have very damaging consequences. "Kids need to feel safe and in control of their lives and feelings," Ward says. And that means being able to express their feelings about injustice or prejudice. "Parents want their children to understand the difference between an opposition that is constructive and an opposition that is destructive," she says. They try to teach their children to oppose racism in ways that build their own communities and that they can live with for a long time; "it's not just getting your teacher out of your face," she says.

And that's what makes replacing racism so important. "Parents put a lot of energy into talking about opposition, but resisting takes creativity; it takes energy; it takes insight. And that energy gets depleted," Ward says. Parents teach their children that they need to take shelter from the harm of racism and recharge their resistance, often in fervently energizing churches; these are the "extended home places" that teach "our sense of purpose as a community" and provide "the holding-on tools that we have developed" in a world that too often wants to knock black people off balance. "When parents talk about what they want their children to experience" as healing alternatives to racism, Ward says, they talk about "learning the power of prayers and faith, and knowing about its ability to energize us and bring us peace. 'You can't always be fighting. You get tired, and sometimes you lose your way,'" the parents she talked with say they tell their kids. "It's very important for kids to know how to take a rest" from a white-dominated world that can feel like a battlefield or an occupied zone to them sometimes. "Music is very important, especially gospel music—the message, the inspiration, the back-and-forth expressiveness, instilling faith that, though things may be tough, they are going to get better; the struggle is worth it," Ward says.

"What was so beautiful for me," she says of her study, was to find the link between individual and group advancement and growth constantly reiterated and redeveloped. "Embedded in a sense of racial identity is the sense of the moral terrain: the idea of the extended self, the idea of kinship networks. As a people we are very diverse; there is no one way to be black, and yet all black people have a connection." And of course, the connection for African-American children touches European-American children, too. "African-American children are, after all, American children. They're children who are growing up in the same toxic environment" as white American children. "What do you do in the consumer culture that puts money ahead of everything?" That is a question for all parents of teenagers, Ward says.

In her current work as project director of the Alliance on Gender, Culture, and School Practice at the Harvard Graduate School of Education, she is trying "to create a curriculum for women and men who are going to work with girls and boys around gender, race, and class issues." Such a curriculum has to support women supporting girls beyond surface compliance with the idea of a racially and sexually just world. Ward and her colleagues are trying to write out of their curriculum the dead end where women can get quiet and just abandon girls to their anger at injustice. They want to develop a curriculum for women to work with girls that does not, as Sojourner Truth said of the United States Constitution, have a weasel in it.

Unfortunately, even as Ward is trying to describe this goal, a white woman at her talk has perhaps unthinkingly weaseled out of understanding the model of antiracist teaching that Ward found in black parents. The woman says she thinks the step Ward calls "replacing it" should mean replacing or changing racist behavior in white people. But Ward, and the black parents, mean replacing the degrading experience of racism with another, uplifting experience, like being swept away by music that "ignites passion around freedom, justice, and love," the kind that brings you out of your seat a dozen times or that "sounds like it's being sung just for you," Ward says. Somehow this well-meaning white woman still carries the defeating notion that the victims of racism are supposed to end racism. Even after Ward spends some time trying to explain, the woman doesn't seem to understand that black parents and teenagers simply want to get away from racism and racists; only white people have the power to change racism; only white people can open themselves up and listen to what black people say and feel.

In the hands of relational psychologists, therapy is one proven way of healing violence and broken relationships, one relationship at a time. And yet "therapy is a weird relationship," Catherine Steiner-Adair once told a roomful of women therapists at McLean Hospital. "To not say 'this is really strange' is to say 'this is normal.' " And too often, the implicitly "normal" style of therapy with anorexic girls simply reprises the bad relationships that have injured them. Steiner-Adair, the clinician who trained with Gilligan in the Harvard Project in the early 1980s, was the first to describe the basics of a relational psychotherapy, one "that integrates connection."[40] We've already seen how her study of girls with and without eating disorders had shown her that girls who tried to live out current cultural ideals of physical and mental health— "the super-thin, high-earning, independent woman who has a husband and children not because she needs them but because she can fit them in," she says—were more at risk of becoming anorexic or bulimic. Girls who saw through these ideals and deliberately rejected them in favor of valuing actual relationships with real people—girls who valued dependence and interdependence and saw autonomy as an isolating danger—stayed healthy. In other words, the girls who thought the ideal of needing no one was sick didn't get sick. The girls who believed that ideal was healthy "showed more symptomatic behavior indicating eating disorders," and girls like them in Steiner-Adair's private practice often did get sick. Steiner-Adair called the girls who were able to see through these impossible ideals "Wise Women." Unlike the "Superwomen" in Steiner-Adair's study, the Wise Women saw that this ideally super-thin superwoman was literally incredible, and when they talked about their own ideals, they said what was important to their own ideal woman was "relationships with other people, you know, partly what decisions she makes—how is that going to affect other people, and not society, but people you are close to? The inner person is important to her, not what people look like."[41] Ironically, the girls who didn't believe in this glamorous image of feminine autonomy showed more autonomy by being able to hold a value against the social tide. But the believers in Superwomen who came to Steiner-Adair for treatment seemed to get sick because their relationships were often as false as their ideals. Steiner-Adair found anorexic girls arrived for therapy as "experts in false relationships"; though they often weren't aware that they had this expertise, "they have vast experiences of what it is like to be in a relationship that has the outward form of connection but is lifeless or dead at the center, in which the other is emotionally absent and therefore cannot be directly engaged."

If you practice "therapy as a way to teach girls to manage not to need people anymore, you've just become a professional who is enabling the cultural norm which is so disabling to girls' development," Irene Stiver told the same audience, most of whom were women therapists dying to hear someone give them permission to support girls' relational expertise. Steiner-Adair learned to help girls with eating disorders realize what experts they were in bad relationships; at the same time she tried to maintain good relationships with them herself— that is, honest, mutually responsive relationships "where one is able to move and be moved by another, to influence and be influenced." The girls got better.[42] "It became very clear to me that the traditional forms of therapy were completely iatrogenic to girls getting better. So you have this voiceless, silent, neutral nonperson sitting across the room to which you're supposed to tell your deepest stories," she said later. "It's horrendous instruction in one-sided, hierarchical, false relationships." Working with Carol Gilligan—like her, she says, an amateur dancer who knew how to talk with her body—and with a couple of other sympathetic supervisors, one Jungian, one trained in "experiential" therapy, Steiner-Adair learned to say "I" and "we," instead of using the impersonal constructions that prevailed in the neutral, self-centered, psychoanalytic therapy of the time. "I'll say something simple like 'I'm sorry you felt that way for so long,' or 'Hearing you say this makes me feel so good,' or 'I see how important this is to you.' The communication is 'What you are telling me moves me.' "[43] Decades later she would say, "The way I practice is to form a very safe and palpable visible connection to the people I work with. And this is very challenging, of course, because the people with eating disorders that I work with are very terrified of relationship. They're both terrified and longing for it." In this process, "it's essentially the relationship that is healing, and then you revisit and reexamine and reflect on what are the complexities, the enormous complexities of the relationship, and that is the work that the therapist has to do on him- or herself in the relationship. Now, this requires far more of the therapist than the old way."

In psychotherapy, healing starts—again and again and again, Miller and Stiver write—with their "central relational paradox": people disconnect in order to salvage elements or wisps or sometimes no more than hopes of connection. Both therapist and patient will disconnect in this way, for the sake of connection, throughout any therapy. The therapist's job is to pay attention to "how connected or disconnected she and the patient are at all times," with the goal of letting the patient see and feel that the therapist is following, is "with" her. By sharing her thoughts and feelings about the patient's experience with the patient, the therapist guides the relationship through the spectrum of the five good things; the end of the therapy marks a happy relational beginning, or, more realistically, middle, for the patient. The patient who has learned to reconnect after disconnection knows the old "strategies of disconnection" and "relational images" she invented or learned long ago, in order to keep as much relationship as possible and at the same time to keep herself safe; she also knows new protective strategies and images of relationships, based on healthier ways of relating to the therapist, and eventually to others, that lead to increased zest, trust, knowledge of herself and others, action, and relationships. The strategies she brings to therapy are best seen not as shields against relationship but as filters that have allowed the patient as much relationship as she has felt was safe, given the risks that relationships presented after the painful disconnections of childhood and later traumatic or hurtful and relatively powerless times.

Judy Jordan performs this therapeutic duty to track her own connectedness by noticing a reemergence of "ego," a defensive sense of self: "The evocation of empathy in another person has to be almost without ego. When I actually start to feel that ego piece come back in, that *me*, that defensiveness—the ego comes back in and that moves me away and out of" connection with her patients. "I don't think that's necessarily wrong. I think it's actually a place of tremendous learning for me and my patients," she says. "When is that moment when I start climbing back into my ego, or when I start getting defensive, or when I start disconnecting? That's a place where hopefully I'm going to learn something about me and I'm also going to learn something about the person I'm with. You know—what makes it necessary to move into that space of separation? Because it is a space of separation. That's what ego is, in my understanding. I probably use it more in the way Eastern thinkers use it than the way traditional psychologists or psychotherapists use it. That's where I go out of that movement, where I go out of the flow." Jean and Irene's idea is that "when the therapist goes into disconnection," he or she uses the experience "to learn about the patient and the relationship," Judy says. Maybe the disconnection starts in the therapist's own "strategies of disconnection." Maybe the therapist disconnects because the patient's yearning for and terror of connection are pushing the therapist away. And maybe it's some of both. Whatever its genesis, the therapist has to use her reaction to any disconnection as a starting point for reconnection, and she has to talk with the patient about how they are both experiencing any particular episode of connection, disconnection, and reconnection. "I really struggle a lot with having to see the very real ways that my shortcomings and my limitations and my struggles around connection and disconnection are impacting the people I work with or are triggering something in them," Jordan says.

Working with patients who are self-destructive, who cut themselves or hurt themselves in other ways, brings "a kind of terror and a kind of urgency and a kind of paralysis—like I've got to say something, I've got to do something right now. I feel it in my body," Jordan says. The feeling is a professional requirement. "There has to be a certain amount of that terror in the therapist," a certain amount of doubt in the face of assured danger, or the therapist is not adequately connected to a self-destructive patient, she says. She traces the shift from courage and hope for healing to actual healing in the therapeutic relationship. As a therapist, "I feel like I actually resonate with the terror and . . . also can sort of stay steady with somebody, but I don't *know* yet inside sometimes, even when I'm looking steady with them; I don't know yet for sure that we're going to make it through. And actually as I build a relationship with them and as I go through these what some people call enactments with them"—the connections and disconnections—"I really get to know it, I get to know the strength and I get to know the endurance, and I get to know we're going to get through it."

Reconnection starts when a listener's empathy, something that is not part of a patient's image of how a relationship is going to go, comes across in a way the patient notices, Miller and Stiver write. Some patients can be so out of touch with their own experience that they only notice that they have moved by noticing that someone else is moved by them. "When the therapist can truly *be with* a patient's experience, something happens *in the therapist*. She is changed. If the patient can feel this happening, feel the therapist move in this sense, something very important occurs: she knows she has had an impact on the therapist simply by expressing her feelings and thoughts. This may be very new, and even hard to believe, but if a patient can begin to believe it, she will be moved in turn," they write.[44]

This movement takes the patient beyond simple reaction into a basic shift in her experience of being human. "She moves toward seeing the possibility that a relationship can include all of one's complicated mixture of feeling-thoughts, positive and negative, rational and irrational. She can feel and think about the feelings and sort them out in the process of experiencing them *with another person*. Experiencing them with another person is what she did not have the chance to do before."[45] And there comes that repeated finding about how much better teenagers, traumatized children, students at risk of dropping out, and so many other studied groups do when there is at least one confidant, one other person to listen to their experience. Miller and Stiver write:

> At these moments of interchange, a person moves into more connection based on her more real representation of her experience. Simultaneously, she comes to feel in greater connection with her own inner experience, and to feel a right to that experience. She develops a more accurate awareness of herself as she becomes more accurately aware of the other person's responsiveness to her. She begins to create relational images, in which the other person can be seen as more empathic and responsive. She, in turn, can be more truly and fully herself and simultaneously more truly with the other person.[46]

Reconnection is of course never stepping back into the same river. Instead, "when this process occurs, each person and the relationship itself inevitably move on to a new level, to being *more* than they were before. This growth to a new level may be a small step, and it does not go on at every minute of life or at the same rate for all people involved, but it happens at times for all of us," especially when we are dealing with children, they write.[47]

The examples Miller and Stiver give are composites or carefully disguised retellings of the kinds of breakthroughs into mutual empathy that teach therapists and patients more about how to be empathic. There is Pat, whose recitation in therapy of all the things she does for a husband and children who never appreciate her leaves Irene feeling bored and distanced. But as soon as Pat begins to talk about how sad this situation makes her, Irene feels jarred from her boredom into a sharp, aching sadness, suddenly feeling very sad "with" Pat. As the session ends, Irene tells Pat how distanced she felt during the recitation, and that she reckons Pat may have been trying to convey how walled off she feels from her own experience. "Then suddenly I felt your sadness and heartbreak," Irene tells her. Pat replies, now with feeling, "It feels hopeless to me." But Irene finds hope in the courage it takes to communicate that very hopelessness: "As we moved to the door, I said, 'The fact that you were able to feel that here, and I could feel it with you, tells me we're moving and I am really hopeful about that.' "[48]

Ruth's dream of the explosion in the house and of herself running in to find everyone gone but an unconscious child, whom she rescues, was a way of sharing her experience of growing up in a family she sensed would explode if she told the truth about the alcoholism it sheltered. Her telling Jean about the dream was a breakthrough that led Jean to realize how very threatened Ruth felt by the prospect of letting go of the family silence that had come to mean family. Ruth and Jean moved dozens of times after that from expressions of real sadness about her family back to Ruth's habitual, strategically off-putting sarcasm. "But both Ruth and I were able to keep finding the ways to a new connection," Jean writes. "My empathy with Ruth's fear of giving up her strategies also helped me stay connected whenever Ruth withdrew from me again."[49]

Eve admits that she feels expressing grief at her mother's death would make her look "like some kind of slimy bug found crawling in the mud." Her relational image, based on the way her family responded to her as a child, is that she will drive people away unless she always appears "cheerful, competent, and pretty." Hearing about this slimy bug, Jean can tell Eve, "Now I can feel much more how awful it feels even to think of expressing sadness." Because Jean resonates with Eve's horror of expressing sadness, and takes this horror as an important feeling in itself, one that needs sharing, Eve begins to move toward expressing the sadness it holds off. This kind of movement toward a new relational image only happens when a therapist understands the patient's familiar images and strategies of disconnection and can also "really be able to 'get with' the feeling of them. This combination of thought and feeling makes the difference; it allows the patient to 'feel the therapist feeling with her,' so that the therapy *moves*."[50]

Businesses and other large organizations can learn to reconnect with employees and clients or customers using this model of "transformational mutuality," in which both sides of any difference make the institution more responsive and productive when relationships are good. In the best-case scenario, where there are power differences and differences of race, ethnicity, gender, and class, "both the insider, dominant group and the 'outsider,' nondominant group are seen as participating in *mutual* learning and change," the Jean Baker Miller Training Institute's manual for groups, called *Relational Practice in Action*, states. Administrators should be asking themselves how to listen to dissent, not how to shut it up or ignore it. "It's not, 'What's wrong with these women?' but 'How come these organizations don't learn from these women and begin to do business differently?'"[51]

The institute's manual, written by Jordan and Cate Dooley, teaches relational-cultural theory by suggesting ways for study groups to do what it says and feel it work. It offers handouts in big print that spell out relational approaches in acrostics. To reconnect, for instance, Jordan and Dooley suggest:

C onnection must be affirmed as a priority

O ffer positive memories from the relationship's past and new hopes for the future of the relationship

N ame the disconnection

N   eed to apologize if you have hurt the other person
E   mbrace the differences
C   all for a relational "time out" when needed
T   alk to a third person together to get help[52]

And then, in small print, they offer key concepts and exercises for the groups reading the manuals to try. One of the key concepts comes from a Gilligan-like review of classic studies of animals and stress: asking the question "Where are the females?" women researchers uncovered the fact that the fight-or-flight response imagined by early stress researchers was arrived at by studies with only male subjects. Even the rats in the studies were male. When Shelley Taylor and her colleagues at the University of California at Los Angeles looked at reactions to stress among females, human and otherwise, they saw a reaction they called, in an instantly classic article, "tend-and-befriend, not fight-or-flight."[53] Later research only reinforced Taylor's findings. "When you listen to men and women talk about the different ways they cope with stress, as I have done for over two decades, it doesn't take long to realize that women's responses are profoundly more social," Taylor writes in the book that grew from her research. About thirty scientific studies have looked at what men and women do in response to stress. Do they turn to others for help or go it alone? All thirty studies show that women draw on their friends, neighbors, and relatives more than men do, whether the stress results from unemployment, cancer, fear or crime, a death in the family, or simple sadness. "From a scientific standpoint, this is an amazing consistency," Taylor writes. "In the social sciences, you rarely see thirty studies all showing the same thing. The difference between women's and men's inclination to turn to the social group in times of stress ranks with 'giving birth' as among the most reliable sex differences there are."[54]

But males are not barred from learning the typical female response to stress "by engaging in growth-fostering, nurturing behavior" and staying to help rather than fighting or fleeing, Jordan and Dooley write. "Evidence suggests we are all—men and women—capable of developing more complicated and socially proactive responses to stress and conflict."[55]

For instance, staying on the vulnerable end of the spectrum of emotions that signal disconnection ("hurt . . . misunderstood . . . disappointed . . . left out") rather than flying to the aggressive, dominant end ("accusing . . . attacking . . . furious . . . rageful") makes it possible to keep empathy going during a conflict. The manual teaches users how to tell who is a safe risk for "good conflict": who is likely to keep on trying to reconnect and avoid declaring war. "Can this relationship hold and work through the conflict? Are both individuals willing to deal with the issue openly?" Jordan and Dooley ask. Can you be honest with the people you're in conflict with even if you're feeling hurt? Can you trust them to hold the goal of reconnecting, rather than winning, as the purpose of the conflict? Can you respect them even while staying clear about the difference that is creating conflict? Can you trust the other person to respect you while you are in conflict?[56] One of their big-print handouts is an eleven-step program for "navigating and engaging in good conflict": Stay with the feeling of pain that led you to feel in conflict. Name what you think hurt you "without accusing or attacking" the other. No shaming—"avoid indirect sarcasm or ridicule." Above all, "listen actively and responsively"; don't pretend that making up your response while the other person is talking is listening. Listen even when you're being criticized; if you're in conflict with a person you respect, you're going to learn something valuable from the conflict: you're in conflict because your relationship is telling you that you have reached a point together where you both have an opportunity to learn something important. Stay empathic and feel for the empathy coming to you from the other person. Be mutual: "try on" the other person's position and help him or her to "try on" yours, so the relationship itself and not one or the other of you can "hold" the conflict. Give yourself permission to change: if the relationship is healthy, both sides will change as the conflict plays out; if you stifle that change, the relationship will die a little, or a lot. Experience the way listening to each other pulls you back into connection. Be personal; put your heart into this: "avoid impersonal, disconnected negotiations and strategies done by a third person at the bargaining table," because those kinds of negotiations are for winning and losing, or at best creating a tie, not for growing in relationship. In fact, call in a relational expert to help keep you both honest, authentic, and respectful if you need to.[57] If your conflict is in an organization, with a whole staff, level, or team of people, make sure you have "relational allies" who are feeling the same conflict and feel in it with you. That way the people you're in conflict with can't tell you the problem is that you alone see a problem.

The manual ends with Joyce Fletcher's four Ns for community and organizational change. The fourth N is "networking," another name for making alliances at work that make work smoother, more mutual, and more egalitarian. The first of the three Ns is "naming": "calling attention to relational practices" at work that are otherwise trivialized as "being nice" or not seen at all. Then "norming": naming the practices that are seen as important at work, so that they can be questioned. Why is "being tough," say, more important for productivity than "being nice"? Aren't both important? But then why should the toughies get more credit than the people who have chosen collaborative good cheer as their modus operandi? The third N is "negotiating": once relational practices are named and seen as possible norms, and previous norms are also named and seen as not the only possible norms, networks of people who favor working relationally can negotiate to try to build relational practices into workplaces and other organizations as new, additional norms.[58] What if every conflict at work or between individuals or groups of different ranks, races, classes, ages, sexual orientations, degrees of health, ethnicities, political or any other kinds of beliefs were truly seen as an opportunity, a relational call for growth on all sides? "Oh, I feel that you just really hurt me. This is really tough for me to say, but I think our relationship can hold the tension of this conflict. I'm going to try to be honest here, and I hope you will be, too, so we can be more authentic together and come to trust each other more."

This view of conflict shows very starkly how the relational approach "changes everything I understand about everything in the world," Miller says. What if "winning" always meant a win for the relationship? What would conflict be if we lived it as challenging turns in the road to better relationships? "If you make a shift like that *as a man*, it's a very radical shift. Everything changes. Everything," Steve Bergman says. The difference from the way conflict is usually handled—as a polite, or at least less rude, form of war—is enormous. Some communities, some families, some groups of friends or colleagues are mutual enough that their members really do see the most desired outcome of any conflict as more closeness and better relationships.

But institutions that maintain and therefore protect power differences—and that means every institution where somebody has more power than somebody else—are often Teflon for the relational view. A number of parts of institutions that the Stone Center group started as relational organizations went down with the institutions that housed them: The women's program at the Charles River Hospital that Jean headed in the 1980s was scrapped a few years before the hospital itself, as hospitals became privatized and for-profit. The women's unit at McLean Hospital—along with some of the trees that Judy Jordan found so healing—got cut. The Stone Center itself, once run as a research and counseling unit based on relational theory and practice, has reorganized so that the relational emphasis is limited to the Jean Baker Miller Training Institute.

On the other hand, an ongoing Toronto study Jean cites is showing that even when used short-term, the relational model of psychotherapy is effective. Short-term therapy is relational when it "stresses connection not separation, support not confrontation, relational awareness in addition to symptom reduction, and the building of relational strengths and networks," Jordan writes.[59]

Groups of women all over the world are using the new relational-cultural manual. These theorists' books are still in print, in bookstores, in libraries, and on mountaintops: in 2004, the institute's research and action report drew a picture of a microeconomic support group of women weavers high in the Sierra Madre of Mexico discovering the Spanish edition of *Toward a New Psychology of Women* with "wide eyes and delight." The Jean Baker Miller Training Institute has held training institutes for more than twelve hundred clinicians since 1996, and its Working Connections Project has held workshops for scores of executives, administrators, and entrepreneurs. Linda Hartling, the associate director of the Jean Baker Miller Training Institute, and Jenny Ly compiled a bibliography of academic writing about relational-cultural psychology in 2001; it contains nearly 350 items, and it doesn't include the Victims of Violence work or much of the Harvard Project psychologists' work.[60] Hartling's latest count tops 500 items. Lyn Brown, Judy Chu, Elizabeth Debold, Dana Jack, Jill Taylor, Deborah Tolman, and Janie Victoria Ward are among Gilligan's students who have gone on to publish and teach all over the United States. The Women Teaching Girls/Girls Teaching Women retreats that the Harvard Project led in Cleveland and Boston, guided by Judith Dorney's protocols; their Strengthening Healthy Resistance and Courage in Girls projects; and their Company of Women/Company of Girls theater troupes and workshops inspired creative programs around the country, including the Ms. Foundation's Take Our Daughters to Work days, which at their peak involved thirty-five million participants. The Victims of Violence program is twice the size it was when I started research for this book. These women pioneers of relational psychology teach, consult, speak, and write all over the world. Their biennial Learning from Women conferences sponsored by Harvard Medical School draw hundreds of conferees. And beyond the propagation of their theories and methods, these innovators can take some credit for the presence of victim advocates in courtrooms and for the persistence of rape crisis centers. The same movement toward mutual help supports now burgeoning and widely effective twelve-step programs. For every small professional program that got shut down by the "managed-care-ization" of all health services in the last two decades, relational theory can claim to have influenced major national policy shifts: an emphasis on girls' development and boys' relational development in education, an emphasis on victims' rights in the treatment of crimes, an emphasis on relational strengths and histories in hospital assessments and medical education. When the Salvation Army went to Ground Zero on September 11, 2001, they brought water and grief counseling. Kaethe Weingarten writes in her grim and yet deeply heartening book about our ever-more violent environment, *Common Shock: Witnessing Violence Every Day*, that these days, "FBI culture makes counselling a standard operating procedure," recognizing that law enforcement can be as traumatic as the crimes it seeks to prevent and that agents need to find trained relational witnesses to what they have endured when they return from the field.[61] On September 1, 2004, a teenage boy spoke in a National Public Radio report about gangs shooting at ghetto graffiti-removal crews in East Los Angeles; he talked about how hard it was to go back to work after his crewmate, like him a former gang member trying to go straight, was murdered on the job. "I was really traumatized," he said. He spoke fluently and accurately, with vulnerability in his voice, open to empathy, assuming that his listeners would understand his trauma and his need to heal from having a friend shot down beside him. The words he found for his experience came to him easily and readily, and yet they had traveled from the earliest observations of the first relational psychologists and psychiatrists, years before he was born, into the wider culture, and from there to his East LA neighborhood and to his lips.

The women and men who moved the focus on relationships from the civil rights movement and the women's movement into psychology lost some battles and won a lot of wars, because they weren't fighting for power. They were moving with a democratic movement, a movement for equality—for the right to base education, psychiatry, psychotherapy, labor, and law enforcement on the kinds of equal, honest, authentic, creative, and searching relationships that generated the twentieth-century movements for peace, women's liberation, and civil rights. They were simply "putting it out there" that relationships are real, are the source of human growth, can wound, can heal, and they were confident enough "to trust that the world will change if you put this out," Miller says. They were right.

"Learn empathy" for fellow physicians, Steve Bergman writes under his pen name, Samuel Shem, in the *Annals of Internal Medicine*.

How do we learn to see, in our patients, ourselves? How do we learn, in doctor-patient interactions, to transform our role from "power-over" to "power-with"? How do we play our part in those moments that heal, those moments of what I would call mutual empathy when not only do I see the patient clearly, and the patient sees me clearly, but *each of us senses the other feeling seen?* Those moments in which you can almost hear the *"Click"* of healthy connection? These are healing moments, and not just in my specialty, psychiatry. Think, for a moment, of a surgeon discussing with a patient whether or not to have an operation. In the old days, a paternalistic surgeon might say, "I'm telling you you need this operation." Lately this has changed to, "I've given you all the information, and now you have to decide." A few surgeons have gone further, toward a more mutual approach, saying, "What are we going to decide to do?" Note that in this last example, using "we" does not take the decision away from the patient; rather it lets the patient know that the surgeon is with him or her in the decision-making process. Such a statement empowers not only doctor and patient, but also empowers the relationship between doctor and patient.[62]

These kinds of doctors, if they are male, join the ranks of "men-in-relation," Bergman writes in his earlier classic on "male relational dread." Women in the gender workshops he and Surrey teach all over the world, for children and adults, see the relational moments and qualities of men and name them: "caretakers; deep loyalties; relationship through action, through projects, through doing; lifting heavy objects; rational thinking; focusing on one thing at a time; honesty; directness; can let things go and move on to other things; breadwinners; protectors; know how to deal with fear; alliance builders; not so overwhelmed by feelings; strategic; product-makers; purposeful; killing spiders; frisky about sex."[63]

Despite temporary setbacks, "I see lots of room for change in this society if both men and women get on the side of the young," Bergman says. The United States is more fluid and interested in change than any of the dozens of countries where he and Surrey have worked, he says. "We are in the forefront of trying to make things better. We break roles. We break roles more than any other country. We break roles with awareness."

Janet Surrey tells and writes about a white man—culturally cast in the most dominant role and therefore the most obstructed from learning mutual empathy—who "got it" in therapy with her. He was dying. But that came later. "He came into therapy basically calling himself a recovering white man who had terrible relationship problems. He was going through a second divorce, very estranged from his kids, and yet very highly successful," Jan says. In fact, he was very successful as an editorial-page editor who was in a sense the public voice for social justice in Boston. But, as Jan says, his deep values about service to people in need were "disconnected from relationship." He could not live according to his own values in his close personal relationships.

"Hey, I'm a man, what can you expect?" he would tell Jan when he had exposed yet another area of relational insensitivity or bleakness in his life. "He desperately wanted me to help him learn to be a father,"

Jan said when she told this story at a conference in 2000. "We talked in the greatest detail about his children, in the process building interest, curiosity, understanding, and connection. Through this conversation, he began to touch on his own sadness and loneliness as a young boy, growing up in an isolated rural area as an only child" with a severely diabetic, bedridden mother who died when he was twenty-two and depended on him to entertain her every day after school without ever touching on how sad they all were about her illness. His father took care of him reliably but also avoided expressing any feelings, and Kirk, Jan's patient, loyally avoided expressing his own feelings as he told this story. Working with Kirk was tough "and not something I looked forward to," Jan admitted. Kirk's "relational dread" and his "strategies of disconnection—humor, anger, sarcasm, and especially self-denigration—were well-developed and very controlling," Jan writes. "I found myself empathizing with the women in his life; the gender issues were always with us." Kirk began to sense the relational need in his fear of his feelings: "that he was not simply 'empty' and not simply afraid of feeling his sadness and loneliness—but was more afraid of feeling alone with them. He had no experience of or images of relationships where feelings moved between and connected people," Jan writes in what became a Stone Center paper.

> One year into therapy, Kirk was at a routine medical appointment to investigate a chronic cough and was diagnosed with fast-growing metastatic lung cancer. He lived for 13 months after this diagnosis. I remember that he called me between sessions to tell me this news. I remember that when he came in the next time, I changed my seat and moved from a chair further away to sit right next to him. I was startled to observe how much more open and willing to be with him I was in the face of illness and possible death. What a lesson about my own personal and professional strategies of disconnection![64]

Therapy continued; with a literal deadline looming, Kirk's need to complete his growth propelled him into bodywork, a cancer support group for men, a meditation group, all on Jan's recommendations. "We began to start our sessions in silence. He began to talk about his life as a mosaic of moments with each moment having its own completeness and beauty," Jan writes. But still there was always the question of whether Jan was a kind of psychological travel agent—arranging silences or guided, meditative fantasies for Kirk to be alone in—or a therapeutic partner. Was the work for him or with him?

During one session about halfway through this last year of therapy, Kirk asked Jan to help him create an inner refuge. "He had been trying to imagine a place of peace and comfort in himself as a 'meditation' " to help him calm down when things got sad and scary, Jan says as she tells me the story in an interview. "He had an image from childhood of an old abandoned house looking out on a meadow in the Berkshires with a brook running by, and of an old rocking chair, abandoned, and of course I had a very strong connection to the geography," Jan says, since she grew up nearby and has revisited the area all her life.

"As he was describing it to me, I had this sense of not knowing if he wanted me to sit on this porch with him—or if he wanted to be alone. And I had this incredible experience of—the history of all my experience with men, a collective experience of knowing they want you but not quite knowing where and whether they're going to let you be there, and you have to do all the work to figure that out.

"I just said to him, 'I don't know about whether you want me there.' And he really started to cry. And he heard how it felt to me—you know, what it felt to not know." For once, for the first time, Kirk felt, empathically with Jan, the loneliness of waiting to be with someone who is not sure whether or not he wants you. Before this, Kirk had only been in himself, not sure how close he wanted to be, or self-critical about relational failure in a way that made self the cynosure and kept relationship out of focus. "Up to this point in time, everything had been all about him, in terms of 'I can't do it; I'm a failure; I'm not enough in relationships,' " Jan says. His kind of self-criticism walled him off from empathy; his way of operating meant "being so self-centered that you can't simply connect to the other person's pain, without having to refer it back to yourself," Jan says.

But in that moment when Jan told him she didn't know whether or not he wanted to imagine her with him on the porch of his inner refuge, "he just made that connection. It was unbelievable, for both of us, a real experience. Very hard to capture in words, but it really was an experience of connection and breaking out of self that was a very, very important part of making reparations. The real piece of healing was not about him." At last, he experienced relationship rather than himself failing at relationship. For once, he didn't apologize for chronic failure to relate. His epiphany "was about breaking out of that and making a real connection." He felt Jan's pain. There is so much resistance in the dominant culture to empathy that "I feel your pain" is a laugh line, a cliché used for mockery and shaming. But Kirk had traveled so far from what Jean and Irene would call that cultural strategy of disconnection that he was crying as he felt Jan's pain about not knowing whether he wanted her to be with him. And that feeling enabled him to "get with" her, to notice that they had a relationship and to assume its point of view, for the first time. "He got it," Jan says.

> He began to talk about feeling something grow between us. He noticed that he could just stay with my pain without taking it back to how it reflected on him, on how he had failed again. He described a feeling of love and compassion for me—for women, feeling women's struggle to relate to him, to men.
>
> He then described feeling a sense of expansiveness and buoyancy and feeling a new energy surging through his body, particularly through his hands.
>
> Our eyes met and he held the gaze with me for some time, both of us tearful but smiling.

"This 'seeing together,' this understanding reverberated between us." So there were mutual empathy and the five good things:

> Healing connection, zest, spirit, interbeing, relational being, I and Thou, We.
>
> After that, Kirk described in his life a growing capacity to be with others, which brought him great joy. He let friends be with him in new ways as he died, although some important relationships remained very difficult and unmoving.
>
> Our relationship remained immensely important to both of us and I saw him up to the day before his death. I promised him I would share his experience.[65]

At a panel discussion at the Learning from Women conference, on April 28, 2000, a question for therapists came up about love. If you know that love is what heals your patients, and you know that you and they love each other—not erotically, not as friends or as siblings, but with the particular love that grows in that kind of healing relationship—can you ever say it out loud? Should you even admit it to yourself? Or has the idea of love been used so often to cover sexual exploitation, eroticism, dominance, or guilt-tripping that a therapist shouldn't get near it in any single case?

Stiver's response was positive, though she was circumspect enough to express herself with a negative. Almost the very last thing she ever said in public was her reply to this question. "It's not possible to hear a person's true story without love," she said: love is the normal result of listening to honesty.

Three days later, Stiver learned she had advanced bone cancer. The disease became debilitating very quickly, and she didn't have time to say goodbye in person to many of her patients, whom she carefully referred to former students and colleagues. So she asked Judy Jordan and another therapist who was a former student to draft a letter to her patients. In Jordan's typically self-effacing way, she remembers the draft they came up with—written in the honest but reserved, slightly warmer than noncommittal, professional tone the Stone Center group had spent years trying to leave behind. Jordan knew better; she knew what Irene meant. Several years earlier, Judy had been eloquent about her own experience of love in psychotherapy. "When I feel love for a patient," she had told me in a long interview about her style as a therapist, "we are in the experience of love together. There is some envelope that embraces both of us," and that envelope is the relationship. "It isn't about 'I love you' or 'you love me'; it's almost more about love is here with us." But Judy hadn't been bold enough to attribute that sentiment to Irene in a letter to Irene's patients when Irene was dying.

"This needs work," Irene said when she read the letter; then she drafted another farewell that managed to hit every note with warmth, candor, and professionalism. Almost immediately, Irene's letter started to become famous in the psychotherapy world, because she found a way to say she loved her patients and knew they loved her. Her words were clear and yet in no way exploitive; on the contrary, they were exactly what Irene had tried to be as a therapist for forty years: growth-fostering.

It made sense that Irene would act this way as her life ended. Her career, as she had told me about it, was really a story of withstanding one kind of oppression or silencing after another while constantly looking for ways to move to places where she could use her insight and fierce commitment to the power of relationships in order to help people grow better. She began by sneaking out of Wellesley, where she was Miss Pierce, the experimental psychologist who wasn't careful enough about taking attendance and making sure that only debutantes absent for parties could be excused. She moonlighted as Dr. Pierce, a psychological tester at McLean, where she recognized Alfred Stanton's milieu therapy as an early form of relational therapy and Stanton himself as an administrator almost miraculously uncorrupted by power. When McLean inevitably became compromised by managed care and the short-term McTherapy model, she was already part of the Stone Center group that became the relational-cultural theorists of the Jean Baker Miller Training Institute, another escape hatch that turned into a gateway, a Monday night meeting that became a lifework and a movement.

Irene could argue, but she didn't fight. "She was a master of the psychological martial arts," the psychiatrist Alan Stone, for years her colleague at McLean, said at her memorial service. "If you came at her on a power move, you met no resistance, and you crashed into your own defenses and ended up chuckling with her," Stone said. She had a candy dish in her office. For all her sophisticated brilliance, she offered everybody a little sweetness, perhaps as a way to suggest that therapy, which is so hard, would ultimately be like the candy, hard and sweet, and here was a little of the sweetness right now, and she was not above sampling it herself. She had an unforgettable speaking voice, low, beautifully modulated, fierce and soft at the same time. And she could write in that voice. The letter Irene took in hand and rewrote to her satisfaction was quoted on the cover of the program at her memorial service at Wellesley in November. It became a kind of motto to promote and explain the scholarship fund the Jean Baker Miller Training Institute started in her memory.

"It has become even clearer to me that love is what it's all about,"

Irene wrote to her patients, a few weeks before her death. "Not only at this time, but throughout our relationship, I have felt your love and deep caring for me. In turn, I hope that you feel my love for you. My hope is that you will hold onto this love and build on it in your life. Thank you for the privilege of being part of your life."

Laura Benkov is a lesbian therapist and mother who for most of the 1990s was in a Stone Center theory group that focused on mothering. In 1998, this group published *Mothering Against the Odds*, an ingeniously edited collection of essays and conversations that explore diverse "social locations" of mothering—lesbian, adoptive, minority, immigrant, single, low-income, ill, or incarcerated. Benkov's daughter Elizabeth was four and "at the stage of endless questions" when Benkov wrote about her for this collection. "One night she came padding out of her room with the 14th question of the evening: 'Mommy, someday will you be a language instead of a mommy?' Anxious to get her back to bed, I answered hastily, 'No, Elizabeth, I'll always be your mommy,' " Benkov writes. But the child's question stuck in her mind, and on reflection Laura realized that there would ultimately come the day when her mothering lived more in Elizabeth's memory than as a current experience. "With that image in mind I realized that, of course, I hope someday to be a language for her, or more aptly, that we together will be a language—one she knows deeply in her soul. One she takes pride in, one she can add to or change, one she can teach others. I hope it is a language of vision, joy, love and strength," Benkov writes.[66]

Irene Stiver became a language on September 24, 2000. Her transformation might be called a model of relational death. In a world where human growth counts as the center point of civilization, death is precisely the time when relationships begin to live in traditions and memories. Language is the medium of tradition and memory as well as of invention and connection. Language is humankind's voice; its existence requires ears—requires listening and empathy that result in love and more growth.

"I don't believe relationships end with death. I don't believe relationships end when people say goodbye," Jordan said one afternoon when she and Irene were both still working at McLean Hospital, in the mid-1990s. Jordan was talking about how, after therapy with a patient ends, her relationship to the client doesn't. "The meetings end; the work ends—that particular piece of work ends. But these people are in my life for the rest of my life. I continue to learn in relationship to them in their absence. You know—things that I thought I understood, or things that happened that I thought had had their full impact on me, come back to me and come in a completely new way. And that to me is relationship."

Notes

Introduction

1. Rosalind Barnett and Caryl Rivers, *Same Difference: How Gender Myths Are Hurting Our Relationships, Our Children, and Our Jobs* (New York: Basic Books, 2004), p. 29.
2. Christina Hoff Sommers, *Who Stole Feminism?* (New York: Simon & Schuster, 1994) and *The War Against Boys* (New York: Simon & Schuster, 2000).
3. *Time*, Jan. 17, 2005, pp. A1–A65.

1. Difference I

1. Carol Gilligan, "In a Different Voice: Women's Conceptions of Self and of Morality," *Harvard Educational Review* 47, no. 4 (Nov. 1977), p. 482.
2. Richard J. Herrnstein, *I.Q. in the Meritocracy* (Boston: Atlantic Monthly Press/Little, Brown, 1973), p. 14. The passage continues onto p. 15:

   > Cultural factors, general surroundings, and racial discrimination complicate the analysis in unknown ways. Given the interest and the data, one might succeed in teasing apart the genetic and nongenetic factors for various groups, but such was neither my goal nor my subject. Instead, I hoped to call attention, first, to the genetic spine running through the social class continuum, giving it a rigidity that few social theorists, let alone ordinary laymen, recognize; and, second, to the likely stiffening of the genetic spine if society manages to wipe out the complicating factors like racial discrimination and varying social inheritance and give everyone an equal chance.

3. Ibid., pp. 136–37.
4. Flora Davis, *Moving the Mountain: The Women's Movement in America Since 1960* (New York: Simon & Schuster, 1991), p. 333.
5. He meant by this odd phrase that educated women would not be able to bear children and would not want to. Quoted from *Adolescence*, vol. 2 (New York: Appleton, 1904), p. 634, in Scarborough and Furumoto, *Untold Lives*, p. 4.
6. After merging with Radcliffe in 1977, Harvard College was accepting 123 men for every 100 women undergraduates in 1996.

7. Gilligan, "In a Different Voice," p. 484.

8. Ibid., p. 485.

9. Ibid., p. 514. Gilligan quotes Erik H. Erikson's quotation from Gandhi's autobiography in *Gandhi's Truth* (New York: Norton, 1969), p. 233.

10. Ibid., p. 490.

11. Ibid., p. 487.

12. Susan Faludi is the best known. See her attack on relational thinkers in general and Gilligan in particular in *Backlash: The Undeclared War Against American Women* (New York: Crown, 1991), pp. 325–32.

13. "Kohlberg's research on moral development has confounded the variables of age, sex, type of decision, and type of dilemma by presenting a single configuration (the responses of adolescent males to hypothetical dilemmas of conflicting rights) as the basis for a universal stage sequence." Gilligan, "In a Different Voice," p. 515.

2. Difference II

1. Betty Friedan, *The Feminine Mystique* (New York: Norton, 1963), p. 336.

2. Sigmund Freud, *General Psychological Theory* (New York: Macmillan, 1963), pp. 69–70.

3. Friedan, *Feminine Mystique*, p. 308.

4. Jean Baker Miller and Ira Mothner, "Psychological Consequences of Sexual Inequality," in *The Women's Movement: Social and Psychological Perspectives*, ed. Helen Wortis and Clara Rabinowitz (New York: American Orthopsychiatric Association/AMS Press, 1972), p. 80.

5. Ibid., p. 81.

6. Ibid., p. 87.

7. Jean Baker Miller, ed., *Psychoanalysis and Women* (Baltimore: Penguin, 1973), p. 3.

8. Ibid., p. 39.

9. Clara Thompson, "Penis Envy in Women," ibid., p. 53.

10. Clara Thompson, "Some Effects of the Derogatory Attitude Toward Female Sexuality," in *Psychoanalysis and Women*, ed. Miller, p. 75.

11. Clara Thompson, "Cultural Pressures in the Psychology of Women," in *Psychoanalysis and Women*, ed. Miller, p. 375.

12. Alfred C. Kinsey, W. B. Pomeroy, C. E. Martin, and P. H. Gebhard, *Sexual Behavior in the Human Female* (Philadelphia: Saunders, 1953), p. 582, cited in James H. Jones, *Alfred C. Kinsey: A Public/Private Life* (New York: Norton, 1997), p. 695. See also William H. Masters and Virginia E. Johnson, *Human Sexual Response* (Boston: Little, Brown, 1966).

13. Miller, *Psychoanalysis and Women*, p. 399.

14. Ibid., p. 397.

15. Friedan, *Feminine Mystique*, p. 77.

16. Miller, *Psychoanalysis and Women*, p. 383.

17. Ibid., pp. 395–96.

18. Ibid., p. 384.

19. Ibid., p. 386.
20. Miller, *Toward a New Psychology of Women*, p. 96.
21. Ibid., p. 13.
22. Ibid., p. 80.
23. Ibid., p. 8.
24. Ibid., p. 58.
25. Ibid., p. 11.
26. Ibid., p. 24.
27. Ibid., p. 83.
28. Ibid., p. 86.
29. Ibid., p. 29.
30. Ibid., p. 59.
31. Ibid., pp. 47–48.
32. Ibid., p. 126.
33. Ibid., p. 131.
34. Ibid., p. 10.

3. Difference III

1. D. James Henderson, "Incest," in *Comprehensive Textbook of Psychiatry*, 2nd ed., ed. A. M. Freedman, H. J. Kaplan, and B. J. Sadock (Baltimore: Williams and Wilkins, 1975), p. 1532, cited in Herman with Hirschman, *Father-Daughter Incest*, p. 11.
2. Linda Gordon, *Heroes of Their Own Lives: The Politics and History of Family Violence* (New York: Viking, 1988), p. 207.
3. Kathie Sarachild, "Consciousness-Raising: A Radical Weapon," in Redstockings, *Feminist Revolution* (New York: Random House, 1978), p. 144.
4. Ibid., p. 145.
5. From Francis Quarles, "Wherefore hidest thou thy face, and holdest me for thy enemie? (Job xiii.24)," in *The Metaphysical Poets*, sel. and ed. Helen Gardner (London: Oxford University Press, 1967), p. 88.
6. Judith Lewis Herman and Lisa Hirschman, "Father-Daughter Incest," *Signs: Journal of Women in Culture and Society* 2, no. 4 (Summer 1977), p. 742.
7. Russell began looking at rape in 1971, and her rape study *The Politics of Rape: The Victim's Perspective* (New York: Stein & Day) appeared in 1975.
8. Flora Davis, *Moving the Mountain: The Women's Movement in America Since 1960* (New York: Simon & Schuster, 1991), p. 308.
9. Herman and Hirschman, "Father-Daughter Incest," p. 739.
10. John Boswell, *Same-Sex Unions in Premodern Europe* (New York: Villard Books, 1994), p. 40.
11. Juliet Mitchell, "Women: The Longest Revolution," repr. from the Nov.–Dec. 1966 *New Left Review* by the New England Free Press, Boston, 1966, p. 1.
12. Sigmund Freud, *The Origins of Psychoanalysis: Letters to Wilhelm Fliess, Drafts and Notes: 1887–1902* (New York: Basic Books, 1954), quoted in Herman and Hirschman, "Father-Daughter Incest," p. 737.

13. Peter Gay, *Freud: A Life for Our Time* (New York: Doubleday/Anchor, 1989), p. 751.

14. Herman and Hirschman, "Father-Daughter Incest," p. 737.

15. L. Bender and A. Blau, "The Reaction of Children to Sexual Relationships with Adults," *American Journal of Orthopsychiatry* 7 (1937), p. 518, quoted in Herman and Hirschman, "Father-Daughter Incest," p. 738.

16. Alfred C. Kinsey, W. B. Pomeroy, C. E. Martin, and P. H. Gebhard, *Sexual Behavior in the Human Female* (Philadelphia: Saunders, 1953), p. 121, quoted in Freyd, *Betrayal Trauma*, p. 37.

17. Kinsey, Pomeroy, Martin, and Gebhard, *Sexual Behavior in the Human Female*, p. 121, cited in James H. Jones, *Alfred C. Kinsey: A Public/Private Life* (New York: Norton, 1997), p. 689. In Jones's opinion, "His focus was not at all on little girls, but on the misunderstood and much maligned adult males who abused them" (p. 688).

18. Nancy Lukianowicz, "Incest," *British Journal of Psychiatry* 120 (1972), pp. 301–13; Herbert Maisch, *Incest* (London: Andre Deutsch, 1973); Atalay Yorukoglu and John P. Kemph, "Children Not Severely Damaged by Incest with a Parent," *Journal of the American Academy of Child Psychiatry* 5 (1966), pp. 111–24, cited in Herman and Hirschman, "Father-Daughter Incest," p. 738.

19. Herman and Hirschman, "Father-Daughter Incest," p. 737.

20. Ibid., p. 740.

21. Phyllis Chesler, "Rape and Psychotherapy," in *Rape: The First Sourcebook for Women*, ed. Noreen Connell and Cassandra Wilson (New York: New American Library, 1974), p. 76, quoted in Herman and Hirschman, "Father-Daughter Incest," p. 740.

22. Ibid., p. 741.

23. Herman and Hirschman, "Father-Daughter Incest," p. 744.

24. Ibid., p. 745.

25. Ibid., p. 747.

26. Ibid., p. 748.

27. Susan Brownmiller, *Against Our Will: Men, Women, and Rape* (New York: Simon & Schuster, 1975), p. 281.

28. Herman and Hirschman, "Father-Daughter Incest," p. 748.

29. Ibid., p. 751.

30. Ibid., pp. 750, 752.

31. Ibid., p. 753.

32. Ibid., p. 754.

33. Ibid., p. 756.

4. Free Space

1. Noel explains her metaphor this way: "I saw that if a silent person was like a silent instrument, you'd first have to have the desire to be 'plucked' by an idea, but to sound it, grow voluble, you'd need the wood, the resonance around you, to re-sound."

2. John Locke, *Locke's Essay Concerning Human Understanding, Books II and IV*, ed. Mary Whiton Calkins (La Salle, Ill.: Open Court, 1962), "The Epistle to the Reader," p. 9.

3. R. B. Freeman, *Charles Darwin: A Companion* (Folkstone, Kent, U.K.: Dawson, 1978), p. 133.

4. Stephen Jay Gould, *Full House: The Spread of Excellence from Plato to Darwin* (New York: Crown, 1996), p. 63. Speaking of survival of the fittest: in 1998 bacteria were discovered thriving in water used to cool the radioactive rods that run nuclear reactors, and scientists expressed fears that the tiny creatures might eat through metal storage tanks for nuclear waste.

5. Ibid., p. 137.

6. Thomas S. Kuhn, *The Structure of Scientific Revolutions* (1962), International Encyclopedia of Unified Science, vol. 2, no. 2 (Chicago: University of Chicago Press, 1970), p. 94; Kuhn quotes the physicist Max Planck on the need to wait for old scientists to die before a new theory takes root (p. 151).

7. *The Autobiography of Charles Darwin*, ed. Nora Barlow (New York: Harcourt, Brace, 1958), p. 237; Freeman, *Charles Darwin*, p. 143.

8. Quoted in Janet Browne, *Charles Darwin—Voyaging: Volume One of a Biography* (New York: Knopf, 1995), p. 240.

9. "At some future period, not very distant as measured by centuries, the civilized races of man will almost certainly exterminate, and replace, the savage races throughout the world." Charles Darwin, *Descent of Man and Selection in Relation to Sex* (1871; New York: Heritage Press, 1972), p. 241.

10. Adrienne Rich, "North American Time," in *Your Native Land, Your Life: Poems* (New York: Norton, 1986), p. 33. Rich writes of poetry, but we can read "biology," "psychology," "feminism," or any science.

11. Tatum, *Why Are All the Black Kids Sitting Together in the Cafeteria?*, p. 118.

12. Pamela Allen, *Free Space: A Perspective on the Small Group in Women's Liberation* (New York: Times Change Press, 1970), p. 6.

13. Ibid., p. 40.

14. Ibid., p. 8.

15. Ibid., p. 14.

16. Ibid.

17. Ibid., p. 29.

18. Ibid., p. 40.

19. Ibid., p. 30.

20. Ibid.

21. Ibid., p. 42.

22. Ibid., p. 51.

23. Ibid.

24. Ibid., p. 60.

25. Flora Davis, *Moving the Mountain: The Women's Movement in America Since 1960* (New York: Simon & Schuster, 1991), p. 9.

26. Belenky, Clinchy, Goldberger, and Tarule, *Women's Ways of Knowing*, p. xii.

27. Mary Field Belenky, Lynne A. Bond, and Jacqueline S. Weinstock, *A Tradition That Has No Name* (New York: Basic Books, 1997), pp. 53, 13.

28. "Feminist research," the sociologist Joyce McCarl Nielsen observes, "began as a result of consciousness-raising that would not have occurred without the women's movement that began in the 1960s." *Feminist Research Methods*, ed. Joyce McCarl Nielsen (Boulder, Colo.: Westview Press, 1990), p. 22.

29. Joseph Adelson, ed., *Handbook of Adolescent Psychology* (New York: Wiley, 1980), pp. 114–15, cited in Carol Gilligan, "Exit-Voice Dilemmas in Adolescent Development," in *Mapping the Moral Domain*, ed. Gilligan, Ward, and Taylor, with Bardige, p. 147.

30. Audre Lorde, "The Master's Tools Will Never Dismantle the Master's House," in *Sister Outsider*, pp. 110–13.

31. Later, Lyn Brown notes, wanting to leave room for "many psychologies and ways to define development," they excised the definite articles and renamed it the Harvard Project on Women's Psychology and Girls' Development.

32. In the last year of the Understanding Adolescence Study, five of the Harvard Project researchers, joined by Kristin Linklater, a dramatic voice teacher and actor, went on half a dozen Women and Race retreats to explore the developmental impacts of race and gender with a number of women of color—Janie Ward, then a Harvard Project researcher; the theologian Katie Cannon; Wendy Puriefoy, an administrator in an agency that was funding their work; the Latina psychiatrist Teresa Bernardez; Christine Robinson, a public health policy analyst; and Joyce Grant, a public-school administrator.

33. Brown and Gilligan, *Meeting at the Crossroads*, p. 53.

34. Brown, *Girlfighting*, p. 2.

35. Brown and Gilligan, *Meeting at the Crossroads*, p. 43.

36. Ibid., p. 50.

37. Lyn Mikel Brown, "A Problem of Vision: The Development of Voice and Relational Knowledge in Girls Ages 7 to 16," in *A Selection of Working Papers Through 1991*, by the Harvard Project on the Psychology of Women and the Development of Girls, Human Development and Psychology, Harvard University Graduate School of Education, 1991, pp. 8–9.

38. Brattle Theatre, Cambridge, Mass., Sept. 23, 1993.

39. Mark B. Tappan and Lyn Mikel Brown, "Hermeneutics and Developmental Psychology: Toward an Ethic of Interpretation," in *The Role of Values in Psychology and Human Development*, ed. William M. Kurtines, Margarita Azmitia, and Jacob L. Gewirtz (New York: Wiley, 1992), p. 120. Fish believes that the agreement of interpretive communities is truth, more or less, and his phrase really harks back to Kuhn's "agreement of the relevant community." Tappan and Brown argue that unless the interpretive community's agreement involves a caring relationship with its subjects as well as with other interpreters, its interpretations can be as bogus as Nazi science or Soviet history.

40. Darwin, *Autobiography*, p. 70.

41. Carol Gilligan, "Remembering Larry," *Journal of Moral Education* 27, no. 2 (1998), p. 237.

42. Brown and Gilligan, *Meeting at the Crossroads*, p. 166.

43. Ibid., pp. 219–20.

44. Ibid., p. 221.

45. Ibid., p. 222.

46. Lyn Mikel Brown and Carol Gilligan, "Listening for Self and Relational Voices: A Responsive/Resisting Reader's Guide," in *Selection of Working Papers Through 1991*, p. 2. See also Carol Gilligan, Renee Spencer, Katherine M. Weinberg, and Tatiana Bertsch, "On the Listening Guide: A Voice-Centered Relational Method," in *Qualitative Research in Psychology: Expanding Perspectives in Methodology and Design*, ed. P. M. Camic, J. E. Rhodes, and L. Yardley (Washington, D.C.: American Psychological Association Press, 2002.)

5. Relationship

1. Judith V. Jordan in Janet L. Surrey, Alexandra Kaplan, and Judith V. Jordan, "Empathy Revisited," Work in Progress, no. 40 (Wellesley, Mass.: Stone Center, Wellesley College, 1990), p. 14.

2. Miller and Stiver, *Healing Connection*, p. 48.

3. Jean Baker Miller, "What Do We Mean by Relationships?" Work in Progress, no. 22 (Wellesley, Mass.: Stone Center, Wellesley College, 1986), p. 3.

4. Ibid., p. 7.

5. Ibid., p. 9.

6. Ibid., p. 20.

7. Janet L. Surrey, "Relationship and Empowerment," in *Women's Growth in Connection*, ed. Jordan and others, pp. 163, 168.

8. Judith V. Jordan, "Clarity in Connection," in *Women's Growth in Diversity*, ed. Jordan, p. 53.

9. Miller and Stiver, *Healing Connection*, p. 32.

10. Miller, "What Do We Mean by Relationships?" p. 10.

11. Ibid., p. 11.

12. Shem and Surrey, *We Have to Talk*, p. 61.

13. Miller, "What Do We Mean by Relationships?" pp. 5, 21.

14. *A Portable Medieval Reader* (New York: Viking, 1949), p. 366, cited in Ashley Montagu, *Touching* (New York: Harper & Row, 1978), p. 81.

15. "Learning itself is motivated and affect-laden. Similarly, in an intense affective moment, perception and cognition go on." Daniel N. Stern, *The Interpersonal World of the Infant: A View from Psychoanalysis and Developmental Psychology* (New York: Basic Books, 1985), p. 42.

16. Ibid., p. 118.

17. Ibid., p. 147.

18. Sarah Blaffer Hrdy, *Mother Nature: A History of Mothers, Infants, and Natural Selection* (New York: Pantheon, 1999), p. 392.

19. Renee Spencer, "A Comparison of Relational Psychologies," Project Report, no. 5 (Wellesley, Mass.: Stone Center, Wellesley College, 2000), p. 5.

20. Allan N. Schore, quoted from an article by Benedict Carey in the *Los Ange-*

les Times, March 31, 2003, in "Hardwired to Connect," a report by the Commission on Children at Risk convened and published by the Institute for American Values, New York, 2003, p. 24. Schore reports on his research in three technical medical and psychiatric texts: *Affect Dysregulation and Disorders of the Self* (New York: Norton, 2003), *Affect Regulation and the Repair of the Self* (New York: Norton, 2003), and *Affect Regulation and the Origin of the Self: The Neurobiology of Emotional Development* (Mahwah, N.J.: Lawrence Erlbaum, 1994).

21. Judith V. Jordan, "The Meaning of Mutuality," in *Women's Growth in Connection*, ed. Jordan and others, pp. 87–88.

22. Miller in Shem and Surrey, *We Have to Talk*, p. 50.

23. Jean Baker Miller, ed., *Psychoanalysis and Women* (Baltimore: Penguin, 1973), p. 375.

24. Miller and Stiver, *Healing Connection*, p. 22.

25. Janet L. Surrey, "The Self-in-Relation: A Theory of Women's Development," in *Women's Growth in Connection*, ed. Jordan and others, p. 53.

26. Miller, "What Do We Mean by Relationships?" p. 3.

27. Judith V. Jordan, "The Meaning of Mutuality," Work in Progress, no. 2 (Wellesley, Mass.: Stone Center, Wellesley College, 1986), p. 15.

28. Janet L. Surrey, "Women and Empathy: Implications for Psychological Development and Psychotherapy," in *Women's Growth in Connection*, ed. Jordan and others, p. 38.

29. *Letters of John Keats*, sel. Frederic Page (London: Oxford University Press, 1968), p. 53.

30. Judith V. Jordan, "Courage in Connection: Conflict, Compassion, Creativity," Work in Progress, no. 45 (Wellesley, Mass.: Stone Center, Wellesley College, 1990), p. 6.

31. Stolorow first called his approach "psychoanalytic phenomenology" and said its "units of analysis are the distinctive configurations of self- and object-representations which pervade subjective experiences. These configurations are distinguished not only by their ideational content, but also by their predominant affective coloring." Robert D. Stolorow and George E. Atwood, *Faces in a Cloud: Subjectivity in Personality Theory* (New York: Jason Aronson, 1979), p. 183.

32. Weingarten also describes this session in Kathy Weingarten, "Side-Lined No More: Promoting Mothers of Adolescents as a Resource for Their Growth and Development," in *Mothering Against the Odds*, ed. García Coll, Surrey, and Weingarten, pp. 27–31.

33. Judith V. Jordan, "Empathy and Self Boundaries," in *Women's Growth in Connection*, ed. Jordan and others, p. 69.

34. Surrey, "Self-in-Relation," p. 62.

35. Judith V. Jordan, "Relational Learning in Psychotherapy Consultation and Supervision," in *How Connections Heal*, ed. Walker and Rosen, p. 24.

36. Surrey, "Relationship and Empowerment," p. 173.

37. Joyce K. Fletcher, "Relational Theory in the Workplace," Work in Progress, no. 77 (Wellesley, Mass.: Stone Center, Wellesley College, 1996), pp. 2–7.

38. Jordan in "Empathy Revisited," p. 11.

39. "Psyche Embedded: A Place for Body, Relationships, and Culture in Personality Theory," in *Studying Persons and Lives*, ed. A. Rabin and others (New York: Springer, 1990), p. 2.

40. Surrey, "Self-in-Relation," pp. 51–66. In her groundbreaking study *The Reproduction of Mothering: Psychoanalysis and the Sociology of Gender* (Berkeley: University of California Press, 1978), Nancy Chodorow used this phrase to describe an infant's development of "self in relation" to her mother (p. 78), but in the psychoanalytic scheme Chodorow envisioned in 1978, this stage is normally and properly followed by a stage of self in separation from mother and father (p. 151n.). Chodorow believed that a child's lingering longing for "primal unity" with a mother who is the primary parent creates a "threat to selfhood" absent in the father-child relationship (p. 194). Her influential insight was that the cultural tradition of primary-parent mothers and more or less absent fathers created an unbalanced sense of self in girls and boys, an imbalance that would improve if parenting practices were more equal. But her scheme is a paradigm shift away from the empathic continuum of "selves-in-relation" that Surrey described in 1983.

41. Jean Baker Miller, "Connections, Disconnections, and Violations," Work in Progress, no. 33 (Wellesley, Mass.: Stone Center, Wellesley College, 1988), p. 7.

42. See, for example, Shem and Surrey, *We Have to Talk*, p. 10: "I hold the faith that if the quality of Tom's connections is healthy," Bergman (Shem) writes about a client, "we won't have to worry about his 'self.' "

43. Miller and Stiver, *Healing Connection*, p. 52.

44. Jean Baker Miller, Judith V. Jordan, Alexandra Kaplan, Irene P. Stiver, and Janet L. Surrey, "Some Misconceptions and Reconceptions of a Relational Approach," Work in Progress, no. 49 (Wellesley, Mass.: Stone Center, Wellesley College, 1991), p. 5.

45. Miller in Jean Baker Miller and Janet L. Surrey, "Rethinking Women's Anger," in *Women's Growth in Diversity*, ed. Jordan, p. 200.

46. Brown and Gilligan, *Meeting at the Crossroads*, p. 187.

47. Margaret Bullitt-Jonas, *Holy Hunger: A Memoir of Desire* (New York: Knopf, 1999), pp. 130–31.

48. Miller and Stiver, *Healing Connection*, p. 30.

49. Surrey in "Empathy Revisited," p. 3.

50. Surrey in Cynthia García Coll, Robin Cook-Nobles, and Janet L. Surrey, "Diversity at the Core: Implications for Relational Theory," Work in Progress, no. 75 (Wellesley, Mass.: Stone Center, Wellesley College, 1995), pp. 9–10.

51. Judith V. Jordan, "Clarity in Connection: Empathic Knowing, Desire, and Sexuality," Work in Progress, no. 29 (Wellesley, Mass.: Stone Center, Wellesley College, 1987), p. 7.

52. Miller and Stiver, *Healing Connection*, pp. 34–35.
53. Ibid., p. 38.
54. Jordan, "Clarity in Connection," Work in Progress, p. 13.
55. Jordan, "Clarity in Connection," in *Women's Growth in Diversity*, ed. Jordan, p. 56.
56. Jordan, "Clarity in Connection," Work in Progress, pp. 11–12.
57. Deborah L. Tolman, "Female Adolescent Sexuality in Relational Context: Beyond Sexual Decision-Making," Center for Research on Women, Wellesley College, pp. 12–13, repr. in *Beyond Appearances: A New Look at Adolescent Girls*, ed. N. Johnson, M. Roberts, and J. Worrell (Washington, D.C.: American Psychological Association, 1998). Tolman cites Sharon Thompson's essay "Putting a Big Thing into a Little Hole: Teenage Girls' Accounts of Sexual Initiation," *Journal of Sex Research* 27 (1990), pp. 341–61.
58. Tolman, *Dilemmas of Desire*, p. 163.
59. Shem and Surrey, *We Have to Talk*, pp. 191–92.
60. Annie G. Rogers, "Voice, Play, and a Practice of Ordinary Courage in Girls' and Women's Lives," draft, Jan. 1993, p. 10; published in *Harvard Educational Review* 63 (1993), pp. 265–95.
61. Ibid., p. 14.
62. Ibid., p. 47.
63. Jordan, "Courage in Connection," p. 3.
64. Brown and Gilligan, *Meeting at the Crossroads*, p. 45.
65. Shem and Surrey, *We Have to Talk*, p. 33.
66. Jordan, "Courage in Connection," p. 4.
67. Irene P. Stiver and Jean Baker Miller, "From Depression to Sadness in Women's Psychotherapy," Work in Progress, no. 36 (Wellesley, Mass.: Stone Center, Wellesley College, 1988), pp. 2, 4.
68. Miller in Jean Baker Miller and Janet L. Surrey, "Revisioning Women's Anger: The Personal and the Global," Work in Progress, no. 43 (Wellesley, Mass.: Stone Center, Wellesley College, 1990), p. 2.
69. Jean Baker Miller, "The Construction of Anger in Women and Men," Work in Progress, no. 83-01 (Wellesley, Mass.: Stone Center, Wellesley College, 1983), p. 7.
70. Ibid., p. 11.
71. Brown and Gilligan, *Meeting at the Crossroads*, p. 117.
72. Ibid., p. 114; brackets and ellipses are in their text.
73. Ibid., p. 115.
74. Ibid., p. 116.
75. Brown, *Raising Their Voices*, p. 11.
76. Ibid., p. 177.
77. Taylor, Gilligan, and Sullivan, *Between Voice and Silence*, pp. 37, 33.
78. Ibid., p. 193.
79. Beverly Harrison's words about anger are in *Making the Connections: Essays in Feminist Social Ethics*, ed. Carol S. Robb (Boston: Beacon Press, 1985),

p. 14, cited in Katie G. Cannon and Carter Heyward, "Alienation and Anger: A Black and a White Woman's Struggle for Mutuality in an Unjust World," Work in Progress, no. 54 (Wellesley, Mass.: Stone Center, Wellesley College, 1992), p. 7.

80. Surrey in Miller and Surrey, "Revisioning Women's Anger," p. 5.

81. Miller and Surrey, "Rethinking Women's Anger," p. 215.

82. Miller in Miller and Surrey, "Revisioning Women's Anger," p. 9.

83. Sharry Langdale interviewed Tessie in 1981 as part of an early Harvard Project study; Gilligan quotes Tessie in "Joining the Resistance: Psychology, Politics, Girls, and Women," p. 19, in the Harvard Project's self-published anthology Working Papers (1991); also published in Michigan Quarterly Review 29, no. 4 (1990). (The ellipsis is in Gilligan's essay.)

84. Gilligan, In a Different Voice, p. 2.

85. From "Ode on a Grecian Urn," in The Poems of John Keats, ed. H. W. Garrod (London: Oxford University Press, 1961), p. 210.

86. When one listens to women, "the concept of identity expands to include the experience of interconnection. The moral domain is similarly enlarged by the inclusion of responsibility and care in relationships. And the underlying epistemology correspondingly shifts from the Greek ideal of knowledge as a correspondence between mind and form to the Biblical conception of knowing as a process of human relationship," she wrote. Gilligan, In a Different Voice, p. 173.

87. Belenky, Clinchy, Goldberger, and Tarule, Women's Ways of Knowing, pp. 112–13.

88. Ibid., p. 18.

89. Miller, Jordan, Kaplan, Stiver, and Surrey, "Some Misconceptions and Reconceptions of a Relational Approach," pp. 12–13.

90. "To be someone is to be somehow connected with someone else," an African-American woman called Sandra says in another three-way conversation about culture and spirit, recorded by Margo V. Perkins, an African-American literary scholar, in "Exploring New Spaces: A Dialogue with Black Women on Religion, Culture, and Spirituality," in My Soul Is a Witness: African-American Women's Spirituality, ed. Gloria Wade-Gayles (Boston: Beacon Press, 1995), p. 165. Sandra's words are a concise explanation of Normi and Carol's concept.

91. Kristin Linklater, Freeing the Natural Voice (New York: Drama Book Specialists, 1976).

92. Gilligan in Carol Gilligan, Annie Rogers, and Normi Noel, "Cartography of a Lost Time: Women, Girls, and Relationships" (paper presented at the Harvard Medical School–Stone Center conference Learning from Women, May 1992), p. 8.

93. Noel, ibid., pp. 13–14.

94. Gilligan, Rogers, and Noel, ibid., pp. 17–18.

95. Job 2:13.

96. Shem and Surrey, *We Have to Talk*, pp. 51–52.
97. Ibid., p. 110.
98. Ibid., p. 153.
99. Cannon in Cannon and Heyward, "Alienation and Anger," pp. 7–8.
100. Cook-Nobles in Cynthia García Coll, Robin Cook-Nobles, and Janet L. Surrey, "Building Connection Through Diversity," in *Women's Growth in Diversity*, ed. Jordan, pp. 184–85.
101. Heyward in Cannon and Heyward, "Alienation and Anger," p. 8.
102. Cook-Nobles in García Coll, Cook-Nobles, and Surrey, "Diversity at the Core," pp. 4, 5, 6.
103. García Coll in García Coll, Cook-Nobles, and Surrey, "Building Connection Through Diversity," pp. 176–77.
104. Cook-Nobles, ibid., pp. 182–83.
105. Surrey, ibid., pp. 188–89.
106. Surrey, ibid., p. 193.
107. Carol Gilligan, "Exit-Voice Dilemmas in Adolescent Development," in *Development, Democracy, and the Art of Trespassing: Essays in Honor of Albert O. Hirschman*, ed. Alejandro Foxley, Michael S. McPherson, and Guillermo O'Donnell (Notre Dame, Ind.: University of Notre Dame Press, 1986), pp. 283–99.
108. Surrey, "Relationship and Empowerment," p. 170.
109. Janet L. Surrey and Rosalie G. Surrey, "Mother-Daughter Relationships over the Life Span" (unpublished), p. 11.
110. Ibid., p. 14.
111. Alexandra G. Kaplan, Nancy Gleason, and Rona Klein, "Women's Self-Development in Late Adolescence," in *Women's Growth in Connection*, ed. Jordan and others, p. 127.
112. Irene P. Stiver, "Beyond the Oedipus Complex: Mothers and Daughters," in *Women's Growth in Connection*, ed. Jordan and others, p. 107.
113. Cynthia García Coll, Janet L. Surrey, Phyllis Buccio-Notaro, and Barbara Molla, "Incarcerated Mothers: Crimes and Punishments," in *Mothering Against the Odds*, ed. García Coll, Surrey, and Weingarten, pp. 262, 265.
114. Surrey in Surrey, Kaplan, and Jordan, "Empathy Revisited," p. 4.
115. Linda Harris, Robert W. Blum, and Michael Resnick, "Teen Females in Minnesota: A Portrait of Quiet Disturbance," in *Women, Girls, and Psychotherapy*, ed. Gilligan, Rogers, and Tolman, p. 131.
116. Carol Gilligan, "Women's Psychological Development: Implications for Psychotherapy," in *Women, Girls, and Psychotherapy*, ed. Gilligan, Rogers, and Tolman, p. 12.
117. Carol Gilligan and Annie Rogers, "Reframing Daughtering and Mothering: A Paradigm Shift in Psychology," in *Daughtering and Mothering: Female Subjectivity Reanalysed*, ed. Janneke van Mens-Verhulst, Karlein Schreurs, and Liesbeth Woertman (New York: Routledge, 1993), p. 128.
118. Jane Attanucci, "In Whose Terms: A New Perspective on Self, Role, and Re-

lationship," in *Mapping the Moral Domain*, ed. Gilligan, Ward, and Taylor, with Bardige, p. 216.

119. Brown and Gilligan, *Meeting at the Crossroads*, p. 225.
120. Taylor, Gilligan, and Sullivan, *Between Voice and Silence*, pp. 70, 76.
121. Ibid., p. 81.
122. Surrey, "Relationship and Empowerment," p. 167.
123. Joyce McCarl Nielsen, ed., *Feminist Research Methods: Exemplary Readings in the Social Sciences* (Boulder, Colo.: Westview Press, 1990), p. 9.
124. Marcia Westkott, "Feminist Criticism of the Social Sciences," repr. in Nielsen, ed., *Feminist Research Methods*, p. 62.
125. Miller, "Women and Power" in *Women's Growth in Diversity*, pp. 198–99, 205.
126. Gilligan, "Joining the Resistance," p. 15.

6. Disconnection

1. Shem and Surrey, *We Have to Talk*, p. 216.
2. William Shakespeare, *Hamlet*, act 4, scene 7, line 177, *The New Shakespeare*, ed. John Dover Wilson (Cambridge, U.K.: Cambridge University Press, 1964), p. 112.
3. Emily Dickinson, *The Complete Poems of Emily Dickinson*, ed. Thomas H. Johnson (Boston: Back Bay/Little, Brown, 1960), no. 599, p. 294.
4. Brown, "A Problem of Vision," p. 8.
5. Quoted in *The Origins of Psychoanalysis: Letters to Wilhelm Fliess, Drafts and Notes by Sigmund Freud*, ed. Marie Bonaparte, Anna Freud, and Ernst Kris (New York: Basic Books, 1954), p. 134, cited in Herman, *Trauma and Recovery*, p. 18.
6. First published in Max Shur, *Freud Living and Dying* (New York: International Universities Press, 1972), p. 104, cited in Jeffrey Moussaieff Masson, *The Assault on Truth: Freud's Suppression of the Seduction Theory* (New York: HarperPerennial/HarperCollins, 1992), p. 9.
7. Letter of May 4, 1896, in *The Complete Letters of Sigmund Freud to Wilhelm Fliess, 1887–1904*, trans. and ed. Jeffrey Moussaieff Masson (Cambridge, Mass.: Harvard University Press, 1985), p. 105.
8. Sigmund Freud, *Autobiographical Study* (1925), trans. James Strachey (New York: Norton, 1963), p. 82.
9. Ibid., p. 97.
10. Pierre Janet, *Psychological Healing*, trans. Eden Paul and Cedar Paul (1925; New York: Arno Press, 1976), p. 595.
11. Ibid., pp. 595, 597.
12. Ibid., p. 674.
13. Josef Breuer and Sigmund Freud, *Studies on Hysteria* (1893–95; New York: Basic Books, n.d.), repr. of *The Standard Edition of the Complete Psychological Works of Sigmund Freud*, vol. 2, trans. and ed. James Strachey, with Anna Freud, Alix Strachey, and Alan Tyson (London: Hogarth Press, 1955), p. 26.
14. Ibid., p. 12.

15. Ibid., p. 35.

16. Lucy Freeman, *The Story of Anna O.: The Woman Who Led Freud to Psychoanalysis* (1972; New York: Paragon House, 1990), p. 201.

17. Hammerschlag is quoted in Freeman, *The Story of Anna O.*, p. 220.

18. "The patient, whose life became known to me to an extent to which one person's life is seldom known to another, had never been in love; and in all the enormous number of hallucinations which occurred during her illness that element of mental life never emerged." Breuer and Freud, *Studies on Hysteria*, pp. 21–22.

19. Breuer in a letter of 1907 to the psychiatrist Auguste Forel, cited in Freeman, *Story of Anna O.*, p. 192.

20. Breuer and Freud, *Studies on Hysteria*, p. 286.

21. "In all cases, the father, not excluding my own, had to be accused of being perverse." In Masson, *Complete Letters*, p. 264; and Freud, *Autobiographical Study*, p. 57.

22. Breuer and Freud, *Studies on Hysteria*, p. 138.

23. Ibid., p. xii.

24. Ibid., p. 161.

25. Ibid., p. 148.

26. Peter Gay, *Freud: A Life for Our Time* (New York: Doubleday/Anchor, 1989), p. 72.

27. Breuer and Freud, *Studies on Hysteria*, p. 160.

28. Gilligan retells this story in *Birth of Pleasure*, pp. 418–27.

29. James called dissociation the psychiatric find of his lifetime, really agreeing with Freud's early assessment of his own achievement:

> I cannot but think that the most important step forward that has occurred in psychology since I have been a student of that science is the discovery, first made in 1886, that, in certain subjects at least, there is not only the consciousness of the ordinary field, with its usual centre and margin, but an addition thereto in the shape of a set of memories, thoughts, and feelings which are extra-marginal and outside of the primary consciousness altogether, but yet must be classed as conscious facts of some sort, able to reveal their presence by unmistakable signs . . . In the wonderful explorations by Binet, Janet, Breuer, Freud, Mason, Prince, and others, of the subliminal consciousness of patients with hysteria, we have revealed to us whole systems of underground life, in the shape of memories of a painful sort which lead a parasitic existence, buried outside of the primary fields of consciousness, and making irruptions thereinto with hallucinations, pains, convulsions, paralyses of feeling and of motion, and the whole procession of symptoms of hysteric disease of body and of mind. (William James, *The Varieties of Religious Experience* [1902; New York: Collier, 1961], pp. 191, 193)

30. Masson, *Assault on Truth*, pp. ix–x.

31. Herman, *Trauma and Recovery*, p. 18. Freud never mentioned anywhere in his

writings, including his letters, two cases of child abuse and murder that got huge play in the Viennese press in the late 1890s while he was retreating from his ideas about childhood sexual abuse and hysteria. But in both cases, the mothers were blamed and the fathers acquitted. And when fathers testified that the children, whom they had tortured, "tormented" them past endurance, this testimony was admitted with respect. Police testified they failed to respond to neighbors' reports of extreme abuse because they found them "unbelievable." Freud's blindness to child abuse was the blindness of his age. In Freud's Vienna, the "sentimental myth of the loving parent" coexisted with the reality that "children were regarded as the virtual property of their parents." This combination of attitudes made it almost impossible to believe that parents would abuse their children—or that, if they did, it was anybody's business but their own. By 1895, when Freud's book about hysteria was published, his own family of six children was complete; the following year, his father, whom Freud suspected of having abused his siblings, died. "The secret of child abuse was safe from Freud, for it could not open to his particular picklocks," the European historian Larry Wolff writes in *Child Abuse in Freud's Vienna: Postcards from the End of the World* (New York: New York University Press, 1995), pp. 61, 139, 150, 211.

32. C. Henry Kempe and others, "The Battered-Child Syndrome," *JAMA* (July 7, 1962), pp. 18–19, cited in Wolff, *Child Abuse*, p. 241.
33. Cited in Mary R. Harvey, "Making a Difference in the Lives of Women and Children: A Call for Clinical and Community Action," and Judith Lewis Herman, "Shame and Violence in Women's Lives" (speeches delivered at the Harvard Medical School–sponsored conference Learning from Women, Boston Park Plaza Hotel, April 29, 2000).
34. Herman, *Trauma and Recovery*, p. 20.
35. W.H.R. Rivers, "Mind and Medicine" (lecture delivered at John Rylands Library, Manchester University, September 4, 1919) (Manchester, U.K.: Manchester University Press, 1920), pp. 11–12.
36. W.H.R. Rivers, *Conflict and Dream* (London: Kegan Paul, Trench, Trubner and Co., 1923), p. 66. Rivers could not begin to imagine that the traumatic nightmares of thousands of men who had been sent back from the trenches of World War I were sexual wish fulfillments, or that, as Freud claimed for dreams in general, their deepest content was a memory of early childhood. He continues: "It is difficult to see how such awful and terrifying experiences as those of dreams of this kind can be the result of wishes of the dreamer. Even if there were no other facts to lead us to regard Freud's view that the dream is a wish-fulfillment as unduly simple, and in my opinion there are many such facts, the nightmare and the battle-dream would themselves be sufficient to lead us to revise the Freudian view" (pp. 67–68).
37. Rivers, "Mind and Medicine," p. 12.
38. Herman, *Trauma and Recovery*, p. 25.
39. Ibid., p. 26.
40. Elaine Showalter, *The Female Malady: Women, Madness, and English Culture, 1830–1980* (New York: Pantheon, 1985), p. 250.

41. Jeffrey Moussaieff Masson, *A Dark Science: Women, Sexuality, and Psychiatry in the Nineteenth Century* (New York: Farrar, Straus and Giroux, 1986), p. 8.

42. Jonathan Shay, *Achilles in Vietnam: Combat Trauma and the Undoing of Character* (New York: Atheneum, 1994), p. 5, cited in Richard Rhodes, *Why They Kill* (New York: Knopf, 1999), p. 299.

43. Herman, *Trauma and Recovery*, p. 32.

44. Herman with Hirschman, *Father-Daughter Incest*, p. 4.

45. Russell, *Secret Trauma*, p. 123.

46. Quoted by Richard Kluft in "On the Apparent Invisibility of Incest," in *Incest-Related Syndromes of Adult Psychopathology*, ed. Richard Kluft (Washington, D.C.: American Psychiatric Press, 1990), p. 25.

47. Herman with Hirschman, *Father-Daughter Incest*, pp. 108, 125.

48. Jeffrey B. Bryer, Bernadette A. Nelson, Jean Baker Miller, and Pamela A. Krol, "Childhood Sexual and Physical Abuse as Factors in Adult Psychiatric Illness," *American Journal of Psychiatry* 144, no. 11 (Nov. 1987), pp. 1426–30.

49. Herman cites Nancy Lukianowicz, "Incest," *British Journal of Psychiatry* 120 (1972), pp. 301–13, and Alvin Rosenfeld, "Incidence of a History of Incest Among 18 Female Psychiatric Patients," *American Journal of Psychiatry* 136 (1979), pp. 791–96, in *Father-Daughter Incest*, pp. 177–78.

Sappho Durrell, for instance, wasn't asked about incest. She was in therapy in London with the psychoanalyst Patrick Casement but found herself unable to tell him that her father, Lawrence, the great author of *The Alexandria Quartet*, was an incest perpetrator. "How much do you know about depressions arising from incest as vs. *mental* trauma?" she quizzed Casement, after she had learned about some of the work on incest that Herman and others were just beginning. "Existential depression, yes but I suspect more than just that. Wouldn't have been able to know enough about my problems to ask you this question when I last saw you." Two days later, she wrote Casement again, and in this note she strains against the political limits of the Freudian psychoanalytic I-know-best-but-I-won't-tell-you mode:

> I feel that you are blocking me from saying things because you can't bear to hear them.
>
> You don't want to hear certain things about my father or to consider them deeply because they strike a chord in you of something that you should have resolved and come to terms with and so you are trying to shield him. Defector. And you are trying to get me to protect both him and you against the truth in yourselves.
>
> Up to now I've been saying things obliquely and slowing myself down in places to protect you. This is insane—I shouldn't be feeling I have to protect you—the reverse should be true. You're anxious to protect yours and my father's guilt (actually his is very different from yours) from my ex-

posure. Face yourself and then you can face my father and you needn't block me.

Less than three months later, Sappho Durrell wrote another letter, this time using a pseudonym:

Dear Ms Herman,

I read with great interest yours and Ms Hirschman's article in The Sciences on the subject of Father/Daughter Incest and its attendant consequences.

I gather from asking psychologists and psychiatrists over here that relatively little work has been done on this particular problem and this impression is strongly borne out by the tenor of your article. Then again, the US seems to be well ahead of Europe and the UK in researching or indeed correlating incidences of this form of abuse.

I am at present preparing an article to submit to the feminist magazine Spare Rib on the long and short-term psychological effects of this and I would be extremely grateful to know of any recent books, research papers, or of people working in this field either here or in the States.

I look forward to hearing from you in the near future,

Yours sincerely

Ms Vivien Gantry

Herman didn't remember this correspondence until she saw it reprinted in *Granta* twelve years later, but she says she received hundreds of inquiries like it—just as hundreds of therapists were beginning to receive clear, courageous, direct, and challenging complaints like Durrell's to Casement. Durrell never found the support she was looking for except perhaps in death. At the same time she was writing Herman, she was joining the British Society for the Right to Die with Dignity. Durrell married and separated, took up and separated from lovers, had five abortions, wrote letters to her analyst, and killed herself in January 1984. Sappho Durrell, "Journals and Letters," in *Granta* 37, *The Family* (Autumn 1991), pp. 55–92 (notes to Casement, July 24 and 26, 1979; letter to Herman, Oct. 9, 1979).

50. Judith Lewis Herman, "Sexual Violence," Work in Progress, no. 83-05 (Wellesley, Mass.: Stone Center, Wellesley College, 1984), pp. 3, 8.
51. Judith Lewis Herman, J. Christopher Perry, and Bessel van der Kolk, "Childhood Trauma in Borderline Personality Disorder," *American Journal of Psychiatry*, 146, no. 4 (April 1989), p. 491.
52. Herman, *Trauma and Recovery*, p. 33.
53. Ibid., p. 37.
54. Judith Lewis Herman, "Complex PTSD: A Syndrome in Survivors of Prolonged and Repeated Trauma," *Journal of Traumatic Stress* 5, no. 3 (1992), pp. 377–78.

55. Ibid., p. 379.
56. Ibid., p. 380.
57. Judith Lewis Herman, *Trauma and Recovery*, 2nd ed. (New York: Basic Books, 1997), p. 239.
58. Herman, "Complex PTSD," p. 381.
59. Herman, *Trauma and Recovery*, p. 34.
60. Herman, "Complex PTSD," pp. 382–85.
61. Herman, *Trauma and Recovery*, p. 116.
62. Doris Lessing, for instance, had joined the tradition of Virginia Woolf and Rebecca West that Pat Barker has joined more recently; Lessing made the effect of the omnipresence of men traumatized by war a theme of her novels, as she writes that it was of her life. Lessing, too, observes the way she knows and then doesn't know how much war hurt her father, who lost his leg and his faith in World War I, and then hurt her brother, who fought in World War II, which shadowed her own coming of age in what was then southern Rhodesia. She describes noticing for the first time, as an adult whose children are grown, that war-born post-traumatic stress was the most striking quality her father and her brother had in common:

> Suddenly I understood something: again, I could have seen it before: nothing is more exasperating than this, that you can flounder about in a mist, and then, all at once, everything is clear. What my brother and my father had in common was not genes: at least, genes were not why both were slow, hesitant, cautious, dream-logged men who seemed always to be listening to some fateful voice only they could hear: they were both men hurt by war. This thought was such a shock to me, illuminating all kinds of old puzzles, old questions, that I had to set it aside for the moment. (Doris Lessing, *African Laughter: Four Visits to Zimbabwe* [New York: Harper-Collins, 1992], p. 61)

"We are all made by war, twisted and warped by war, but we seem to forget it," Lessing writes in her autobiography:

> I used to joke that it was the war that had given birth to me, as a defense when weary with the talk about the war that went on—and on—and on. But it was no joke. I used to feel there was something like a dark grey cloud, like poison gas, over my early childhood. Later I found people who had the same experience. Perhaps it was from that war that I first felt the struggling panicky need to escape, with a nervous aversion to where I have just stood, as if something there might blow up or drag me down by the heel." (Doris Lessing, *Under My Skin: Volume One of My Autobiography, to 1949* [New York: HarperCollins, 1994], p. 10)

63. Herman with Hirschman, *Father-Daughter Incest*, p. 237. Herman cites D. Jones and J. M. McGraw, "Reliable and Fictitious Accounts of Sexual

Abuse to Children," *Journal of Interpersonal Violence* 3 (1987), pp. 27–45. The theologian Carter Heyward's memoir *When Boundaries Betray Us: Beyond Illusions of What Is Ethical in Therapy and Life* (San Francisco: HarperSanFrancisco, 1993) presents an example of false memories of abuse occurring during psychotherapy.

64. Males surveyed the newsmagazines for Fairness & Accuracy in Reporting (FAIR), a media watch group: Mike Males, " 'Recovered Memory,' Child Abuse Media Escapism," *Extra!* Sept./Oct. 1994, pp. 10–11.

65. Herman interviewed Stephen Fried, a reporter for *The Philadelphia Inquirer* who was one of the first to begin questioning the FMSF's side of the story in this period. Fried spoke about why the group's PR worked so well—on top-rated, mainstream news organizations like his own and *The New York Times*:

> In public, political disputes, he explained, journalists count on both parties to argue their side of the story aggressively, assuming that balance will emerge from a vigorous adversarial process. In family disputes, however, he could see that this process did not work fairly: it rewarded those who wanted to fight, and punished those who wanted to avoid conflict. He noted that most of the FMSF parents had not been publicly accused by their children, and very few faced formal legal charges; most often the children simply wanted to be left alone. When FMSF parents spoke to the press, they knew that their children would be unlikely to contest their statements, no matter how outrageous. (Herman, speech to the Nieman Fellows at Harvard University, repr. in *Nieman Reports*, April 1994.)

66. Judge Edward F. Harrington ruled for the First Circuit on May 9, 1996, in a case involving a sixty-eight-year-old woman who said she remembered that an older cousin had sexually abused her more than fifty years before; the ruling was reported in *The Boston Globe*, May 10, 1996, p. 28.

67. Bessel van der Kolk, "The Body Keeps the Score: Approaches to the Psychobiology of Posttraumatic Stress Disorder," in *Traumatic Stress*, ed. Bessel van der Kolk, Alexander McFarlane, and Lars Weisaeth (New York: Guilford Press, 1996), p. 232.

68. Alison Bass, "Hidden Memories," *Boston Globe*, March 18, 1996, Health/Science section, p. 25.

69. This study, led by the psychiatrist Frank W. Putnam, is documented in three articles that Herman cites in her afterword to the 1997 edition of *Trauma and Recovery*: M. D. De Bellis, G. P. Chrousos, L. D. Dorn, L. Burke, K. Helmers, M. A. Kling, P. K. Trickett, and F. W. Putnam, "Hypothalamic-Pituitary-Adrenal Axis Deregulation in Sexually Abused Girls," *Journal of Clinical Endocrinology and Metabolism* 78 (1994), pp. 249–55; P. K. Trickett, C. McBride-Chang, and F. W. Putnam, "The Classroom Performance and Behavior of Sexually Abused Girls," *Development and Psychology* 6 (1994), pp. 183–94; F. W. Putnam, K. Hermers, L. A. Horowitz, and P. K. Trickett,

"Hypnotizability and Dissociativity in Sexually Abused Girls," *Child Abuse and Neglect* 19 (1995), pp. 645–55.

70. Judith A. Sheiman, "Sexual Abuse History With and Without Self-Report of Memory Loss: Differences in Psychopathology, Personality, and Dissociation," in *Trauma and Memory*, ed. Linda M. Williams and Victoria L. Banyard (Thousand Oaks, Calif.: Sage Publications, 1999), p. 147.

71. Loftus has written that she believes her own lifelong, never-dissociated memories of being abused by a babysitter, but doubts her brother's belief that he is recovering memories of some family abuse. Elizabeth Loftus and Katherine Ketcham, *The Myth of Repressed Memory* (New York: St. Martin's Griffin, 1994), p. 225.

72. Bessel van der Kolk, "The Minefields of Memory," *Boston Sunday Globe*, November 6, 1994, p. B19. Van der Kolk goes on to say:

> Loftus is an equal opportunity witness for the defense: She ignores both her own and other people's research that contradicts the point of her book. For example, she fails to report her own published research on a group of 57 sexually abused women, which showed that 19 percent had total memory loss for their abuse during some period of their lives, while another 12 percent had large memory gaps. She even-handedly ignored the well-known study of 100 girls who had hospital records of having been sexually abused, of whom 38 percent did not remember having been molested when interviewed 17 years later.

73. In January 2005, Loftus appeared as the only witness for the defense in the Massachusetts trial of Paul R. Shanley, a defrocked priest accused of decades-old sexual abuse of boys. The only victim whom prosecutors could persuade to testify against Shanley was a man who claimed to have recently remembered that Shanley abused him sexually decades before. Despite Loftus's expert testimony casting doubt on recovered memories of abuse, Shanley was found guilty. (Shanley had been accused by more than a score of men who said they had never forgotten the sexual abuse they alleged they suffered at his hands, but they only came forward after a Massachusetts judge ordered secret administrative church files about pedophile priests released and the media began revealing their contents, decades after the alleged abuse took place. By that time, the Massachusetts statute of limitations on sexual abuse of children had run out, so their complaints had no legal standing.)

74. Connie M. Kristiansen, Carolyn Gareau, Jennifer Mittleholt, Nancy H. DeCourville, and Wendy E. Hovdestad, "The Sociopolitical Context of the Delayed Memory Debate," in *Trauma and Memory*, ed. Williams and Banyard, pp. 343–44.

75. Salman Rushdie, *Imaginary Homelands* (London: Granta/Viking, 1991), pp. 14, 134.

76. Mary P. Koss and Mary R. Harvey, *The Rape Victim: Clinical and Community*

Interventions, Sage Library of Social Research 185 (Newbury Park, Calif.: Sage Publications, 1991), p. 12.

77. Koss and Harvey cite T. W. McCahill, L. C. Meyer, and A. M. Fischman, *The Aftermath of Rape* (Lexington, Mass.: D. C. Heath, 1979), ibid., p. 55.

78. Koss and Harvey, *Rape Victim*, pp. 57, 61.

79. In *Journal of Traumatic Stress* 9, no. 1 (1996), pp. 3–23.

80. Ibid., p. 5.

81. Ibid., p. 8.

82. Ibid., p. 11.

83. Mary R. Harvey and Patricia A. Harney, "Addressing the Aftermath of Interpersonal Violence: The Case for Long-Term Care," *Psychoanalytic Inquiry*, 1997 supp., p. 32.

84. Herman with Hirschman, *Father-Daughter Incest*, p. 232.

85. James Gilligan, *Violence*, p. 36.

86. Ibid., p. 184.

87. Ibid., p. 155.

88. James Gilligan, *Preventing Violence*, pp. 39ff. Gilligan also cites studies that show higher mortality rates in areas where gaps in power between classes are greatest, including an American study that used Sweden as a baseline and found that the "structural violence" in other countries with greater gaps in wealth and earnings than Sweden accounted for fourteen to eighteen million deaths a year worldwide (*Violence*, p. 195). Similar studies in the United States have shown that the states with the largest earning gaps between rich and poor also have the highest mortality rates across class lines ("Income Inequality, Mortality Linked," *Boston Globe*, April 19, 1996, p. 14).

89. Herman cited Helen Block Lewis, ed., *The Role of Shame in Symptom Formation* (Hillsdale, N.J.: Lawrence Erlbaum, 1987).

90. James Gilligan, *Violence*, pp. 60, 65.

91. Jordan in Linda M. Hartling, Wendy Rosen, Maureen Walker, and Judith V. Jordan, "Shame and Humiliation: From Isolation to Relational Transformation," Work in Progress, no. 88 (Wellesley, Mass.: Stone Center, Wellesley College, 2000), p. 10.

92. Tracy Robinson and Janie Ward, " 'A Belief in Self Far Greater Than Anyone's Disbelief': Cultivating Resistance Among African American Female Adolescents," in *Women, Girls, and Psychotherapy*, ed. Gilligan, Rogers, and Tolman, p. 96.

93. Walker in Hartling, Rosen, Walker, and Jordan, "Shame and Humiliation," pp. 9–10.

94. Cynthia García Coll, Robin Cook-Nobles, and Janet L. Surrey, "Building Connection Through Diversity," in *Women's Growth in Diversity*, ed. Jordan, p. 193.

95. Brown, *Raising Their Voices*, pp. 98–99.

96. Real, *How Can I Get Through to You?* pp. 20, 90, 102.

97. "Homophobia imposes a continual need for lesbians to present their most in-

timate and private relationships either as nonexistent or as superficial to the surrounding mainstream community," Slater writes. "Lesbian couples face pressures to hide the true nature of their relationships due to the very real dangers associated with coming out. Similarly, therapists deliberately keep the treatment relationship secret, resulting in the powerful duality of great intimacy behind closed doors and little or no acknowledgment that any such attachment exists in front of others." Suzanne Slater in Natalie Eldridge, Julie Mencher, and Suzanne Slater, "The Conundrum of Mutuality: A Lesbian Dialogue," in *Women's Growth in Diversity*, ed. Jordan, p. 123.

98. "If we look at the collective phenomenon of starving young middle- and upper-class girls in this culture as a body politic instead of a body pathology, the emaciated females become a symbol of a culture that does not support female development or the value of relationships, which is central to the adolescent girl's identity," Steiner-Adair writes. "It seems possible that anorexia nervosa is a natural outgrowth of a culture that outcasts that which is most important to its female population and does so in a symbolic idealization of thinness in women. And it is a form of protest adopted by the adolescent who finds, for whatever reasons, that her voice is silenced." Catherine Steiner-Adair, "The Body Politic: Normal Female Adolescent Development and the Development of Eating Disorders," in *Making Connections*, ed. Gilligan, Lyons, and Hanmer, p. 175.

99. Janet L. Surrey, "Eating Patterns as a Reflection of Women's Development," in *Women's Growth in Connection*, ed. Jordan and others, p. 241.

100. "Becky," a college-aged woman with bulimia, told Steiner-Adair:

> If I haven't exercised I haven't purified myself today of the fat, flab, passivity, helplessness, powerlessness that is everything my mother is. When I see women with thunder thighs, I think, "those poor slobs"; all they do is sit at home and wonder when their husband is going to take them out this month, which will be the highlight of their life. I pity them, because they have nothing in their lives, nothing takes up their lives except housework, gossiping with neighbors, taking care of the kids, cooking a nutritious balanced meal; they are totally dependent on their husbands financially and emotionally. Even if their husbands don't treat them well, they have to stay because they have no ability to support themselves. If I see a woman with no bulge, straight thighs, I think "what an attractive woman"; she's sexually in control, successful personality, you know a well-balanced life, successful at what she does at work and a well-balanced personal life. It's funny, when I see a lawyer at the office I'm interning at who's thin, I'm so impressed, and if I read a brief of hers, it's like I want to take it home and memorize it. But if I were to read the same brief written by a fat woman lawyer, my opinion would go right down. I think to myself, "She's fat, she's a lost soul, an unhappy woman." Part of it is that I feel so sad for her, like a handicapped person. I feel so much pain for them because I know they're isolated from society. Then I scorn the fact that they don't fight the

weight, they must feel like such rejects, such mutants. (Catherine Steiner-Adair, "Developing the Voice of the Wise Woman: College Students and Bulimia," in *The Bulimic College Student: Evaluation, Treatment, and Prevention*, ed. L. Whitaker and W. Davis [New York: Haworth Press, 1989], pp. 159–60.)

101. Steiner-Adair, "Body Politic," p. 167.
102. Surrey, "Eating Patterns as a Reflection of Women's Development," p. 240.
103. Ibid., p. 242.
104. Ibid., p. 245.
105. Steiner-Adair, "Body Politic," p. 176.
106. Real, *I Don't Want to Talk About It*, p. 37.
107. Jordanna Hart, "Statistics Say Abuse Hits Close to Home: Most Young Victims Know Their Molester," *Boston Globe*, May 20, 2000, p. B1.
108. Herman and Lewis also write:

> Feminist thinkers, too, have often viewed women's nurturance with ambivalence, and for good reasons. First there is always the danger that any observation of widespread sex differences can be cited in support of biological determinist theories which rationalize women's oppression as part of the natural order. Second, feminist thinkers cannot help but share in the attitudes of an extremely aggressive culture, in which female nurturance is alternately sentimentalized and despised (Chodorow, 1979). And finally, even if the nurturant qualities of women are positively and unambivalently valued, the danger that these very qualities sometimes render women more vulnerable to exploitation must be recognized. The attachments which are a great potential source of female strength can also be a potential trap. (Judith Lewis Herman and Helen Block Lewis, "Anger in the Mother-Daughter Relationship," in *The Psychology of Today's Woman: New Psychoanalytic Visions*, ed. Toni Bernay and Dorothy W. Cantor [Hillsdale, N.J.: Analytic Press, 1986], pp. 148, 151–52; the references are to Miller, *Toward a New Psychology of Women*, and to the paperback edition of Nancy Chodorow's 1978 classic, *The Reproduction of Mothering*.)

109. Stephen J. Bergman, "Men's Psychological Development: A Relational Perspective," Work in Progress, no. 48 (Wellesley, Mass.: Stone Center, Wellesley College, 1991).
110. Shem and Surrey, *We Have to Talk*, p. 47.
111. Bergman, "Men's Psychological Development," p. 5.
112. Irene P. Stiver, "Beyond the Oedipus Complex: Mothers and Daughters," in *Women's Growth in Connection*, ed. Jordan and others, p. 110.
113. Terrence Real cites a study of psychiatric inpatients who were incest and abuse victims: "33 percent of the males had histories of becoming physically aggressive compared with 16 percent of the females. 66 percent of the fe-

males turned hostility inward and had histories of self-destructive behavior, compared with only 20 percent of the males." He cites E. H. Harmen, P. P. Reiker, and T. Mills, "Victims of Violence and Psychiatric Illness," *American Journal of Psychiatry* 141, no. 3 (1984), pp. 378–79, noted in *I Don't Want to Talk About It*, p. 362.

114. Bergman, "Men's Psychological Development," p. 7.
115. Shem and Surrey, *We Have to Talk*, p. 81.
116. Bergman, "Men's Psychological Development," p. 7.
117. Shem and Surrey, *We Have to Talk*, pp. 44, 48–49.
118. Irene P. Stiver, "Work Inhibitions in Women," Work in Progress, no. 82-03 (Wellesley, Mass.: Stone Center, Wellesley College, 1983), pp. 4–5.
119. Shem and Surrey, *We Have to Talk*, p. 56.
120. Bergman, "Men's Psychological Development," p. 5.
121. Ibid., p. 13.
122. Gilligan addresses some of this material in *Birth of Pleasure*, pp. 57–74.
123. William Pollack, *Real Boys: Rescuing Our Sons from the Myths of Boyhood* (New York: Henry Holt, 1998), p. xxiv.
124. Real, *I Don't Want to Talk About It*, p. 146.
125. Real, *How Can I Get Through to You?* p. 113.
126. Real, *I Don't Want to Talk About It*, pp. 126, 176.
127. Ibid., pp. 234–35.
128. Rhodes, *Why They Kill*, pp. 120, 136.
129. In the introduction to the paperback edition of 2003, Gilligan describes its music this way:

> The structure of this book is orchestral. A voice that is introduced in one key returns in another; themes and variations develop. I hope in this way to capture a process of discovery I went through and that moves through association, through the experience of reading and listening and coming to hear and see relationships. I sought to re-create the harmonies and resonances that led me to cross space and time, to follow a stream of human consciousness that moves, as love can move, across the boundaries of class and caste, nationality and culture, age and gender, past and present. (Gilligan, *The Birth of Pleasure* [New York: Vintage/Random House, 2003], p. 8.)

130. Cf. ibid., pp. 6–8.
131. Van der Kolk, "Body Keeps the Score," p. 233.
132. Ibid., p. 219.
133. Bessel van der Kolk, "The Complexity of Adaptation to Trauma: Self-Regulation, Stimulus Discrimination, and Characterological Development," in *Traumatic Stress*, ed. van der Kolk, McFarlane, and Weisaeth, p. 197.
134. Cf. Gilligan, *Birth of Pleasure*, p. 10.
135. "She is maintaining relationships at the price of not representing her own ex-

perience in them. To this extent, she cannot be relating fully in the ways which lead to growth. Moreover, the parts of herself which she has excluded are unable to change from experience. Her continuous construction of a sense of self and others cannot benefit from the interchange within connections." Jean Baker Miller, "Connections, Disconnections, and Violations," Work in Progress, no. 33 (Wellesley, Mass.: Stone Center, Wellesley College, 1988), pp. 9–10.

136. Ibid., p. 7.
137. Ibid., p. 10.
138. Lyn Mikel Brown and Dana Crowley Jack, "Anger," in *Complete Guide to Mental Health for Women*, ed. Slater, Daniel, and Banks, p. 130. See also Jack, *Silencing the Self* and *Behind the Mask*.
139. Miller, "Connections, Disconnections, and Violations," p. 10.
140. Miller and Stiver, *Healing Connection*, p. 106.
141. Carol Gilligan, "Joining the Resistance," in *A Selection of Working Papers Through 1991*, by the Harvard Project on the Psychology of Women and the Development of Girls, Human Development and Psychology, Harvard University Graduate School of Education, 1991, pp. 42–43.
142. "Is there no pity sitting in the clouds, / That sees into the bottom of my grief?" Juliet cries out to her mother, because her father has threatened to disown her and throw her out—a fate worse than death for a Renaissance girl—if she doesn't marry the man of his choosing in two days, at the age of fourteen, less than a week after her favorite cousin, Tybalt, is killed by the young man she has just secretly married.

> O, my sweet mother, cast me not away!
> Delay this marriage for a month, a week;
> Or, if you do not, make the bridal bed
> In that dim monument where Tybalt lies.

But Juliet's mother, Lady Capulet, is deaf to her daughter's cries. Lady Capulet in this scene is a picture of Sharon Miller's words: "There is nothing there." She has only this to say to Juliet before she exits: "Talk not to me, for I'll not speak a word: / Do as thou wilt, for I have done with thee." William Shakespeare, *Romeo and Juliet*, act 3, scene 5, lines 196–203 (New York: Dover, 1963).

143. Gilligan, "Joining the Resistance," pp. 19–23.
144. Peter Blos, *On Adolescence* (New York: Free Press, 1962), pp. 10–11. Erik H. Erikson, *Identity, Youth, and Crisis* (New York: Norton, 1968). Harry Stack Sullivan, *The Psychiatric Interview* (New York: Norton, 1970), pp. 142–45. Sigmund Freud, *Three Essays on the Theory of Sexuality* (1905), trans. and ed. James Strachey, (New York: Avon Books, 1965), p. 125: "The finding of an object is in fact a refinding of it."
145. By 2004, Normi had realized that this protective silence "holds the inter-

rupted 'truth,' the 'accidented' truth, and finding the way back onto the voice begins with one note, and if there is outer resonance, will find the full wild range of voice, (inner and outer) perceptions, intuition, feeling," she said.

146. Miller and Stiver, *Healing Connection*, pp. 153–54.
147. Ibid., p. 155.
148. Ibid., p. 166.
149. Irene P. Stiver, "Dysfunctional Families and Wounded Relationships: Part I," Work in Progress, no. 41 (Wellesley, Mass.: Stone Center, Wellesley College, 1990), p. 2.
150. Ibid., p. 12.
151. Miller and Stiver, *Healing Connection*, pp. 98–100.
152. Ibid., p. 150.
153. Ibid., p. 126.
154. Ibid., p. 113.
155. Ibid., p. 117.
156. Russell, *Secret Trauma*, pp. 200–203.
157. Herman, *Trauma and Recovery*, pp. 111, 42.
158. Fletcher, *Disappearing Acts*, p. 104.
159. Joyce Fletcher, "Relational Theory in the Workplace," Work in Progress, no. 77 (Wellesley, Mass.: Stone Center, Wellesley College, 1996), pp. 13–14.
160. Fletcher, *Disappearing Acts*, p. 131.
161. Ibid., p. 116.
162. Ibid., pp. 98, 113.
163. Fletcher, "Relational Theory," p. 12.
164. Fletcher, *Disappearing Acts*, p. 119.

7. Healing

1. Mary R. Harvey, "An Ecological View of Psychological Trauma and Trauma Recovery," *Journal of Traumatic Stress* 9, no. 1 (1996), pp. 9–10.
2. Lucy Freeman, *The Story of Anna O.: The Woman Who Led Freud to Psychoanalysis* (1972; New York: Paragon House, 1990), p. 237.
3. Harvey, "Ecological View," pp. 11–13.
4. Herman, *Trauma and Recovery*, p. 73.
5. Harvey tells Sarah's and JoAnn's stories in "Ecological View," pp. 14–20.
6. Herman, *Trauma and Recovery*, p. 116.
7. Ibid., p. 133.
8. Ibid.
9. Amy Banks, "Post-traumatic Stress Disorder: Relationships and Brain Chemistry."
10. Herman, *Trauma and Recovery*, p. 160.
11. Ibid., p. 161.
12. Ibid., p. 165.
13. Ibid., p. 171.
14. Ibid., p. 166.

15. Ibid., p. 168.
16. Ibid., pp. 169–70.
17. Ibid., p. 175.
18. Ibid., p. 178.
19. Ibid., p. 180.
20. Ibid., p. 183.
21. Ibid., p. 189.
22. Ibid., p. 188.
23. Ibid., p. 190.
24. Ibid.
25. Ibid.
26. Ibid., pp. 201–202. The survivor is quoted from Emily Schatzow and Judith Herman, "Breaking Secrecy: Adult Survivors Disclose to Their Families," *Psychiatric Clinics of North America* 12 (1989), p. 348.
27. Herman, *Trauma and Recovery*, p. 203.
28. Ibid., p. 207.
29. Ibid., p. 211.
30. Herman's paper, "The Mental Health of Crime Victims: Impact of Legal Intervention," was later published in the *Journal of Traumatic Stress* 16, no. 2 (April 2003), pp. 159–66.
31. Herman asks these and other provocative questions in "Peace on Earth Begins at Home: Reflections from the Women's Liberation Movement," in *Breaking the Cycles of Hatred: Memory, Law, and Repair*, ed. Nancy Rosenblum (Princeton, N.J.: Princeton University Press, 2002), pp. 188–99.
32. Judith Lewis Herman, "Introduction: Hidden in Plain Sight: Clinical Observations on Prostitution," in *Prostitution, Trafficking, and Traumatic Stress*, ed. Melissa Farley, *Journal of Trauma Practice* 2, nos. 3–4 (2003), pp. 1–3.
33. Gilligan, *Birth of Pleasure*, p. 17.
34. William Aldington's Elizabethan translation gives a great sense of Apuleius's flamboyant and archaic Latin. Robert Graves has a better understanding and a better Latin text to work from. See *The Golden Ass of Apuleius*, trans. William Aldington (New York: Modern Library, 1928); and Lucius Apuleius, *The Transformations of Lucius, Otherwise Known as The Golden Ass*, trans. Robert Graves (Harmondsworth, U.K.: Penguin, 1950).
35. Marie-Louise von Franz, *The Golden Ass of Apuleius* (New York: Spring Publications, 1970), and "Psyche and Eros in Apuleius," in *Projection and Recollection in Jungian Psychology* (Peru, Ill.: Open Court, 1985), pp. 122–34.
36. Gilligan, *Birth of Pleasure*, p. 18.
37. Ibid., pp. 41ff.
38. Ibid., p. 232.
39. Gilligan, *The Birth of Pleasure* (New York: Vintage/Random House, 2003), pp. 6–7.
40. Catherine Steiner-Adair, "New Maps of Development, New Models of Therapy: The Psychology of Women and the Treatment of Eating Disorders," *Psy-*

chodynamic Treatment of Anorexia Nervosa and Bulimia, ed. Craig Johnson (New York: Guilford Press, 1990), p. 226.

41. Catherine Steiner-Adair, "Developing the Voice of the Wise Woman: College Students and Bulimia," *The Bulimic College Student: Evaluation, Treatment, and Prevention*, ed. L. Whitaker and W. Davis (New York: Haworth Press, 1989), p. 156.

42. Steiner-Adair, "New Maps," p. 230.

43. Ibid., p. 237.

44. Miller and Stiver, *Healing Connection*, p. 129.

45. Ibid., p. 131.

46. Ibid., p. 133.

47. Ibid., p. 148.

48. Ibid., p. 127.

49. Ibid., pp. 155, 161.

50. Ibid., pp. 151–52.

51. Judith V. Jordan and Cate Dooley, *Relational Practice in Action: A Group Manual*, Jean Baker Miller Training Institute Project Report, no. 6 (Wellesley, Mass.: Stone Center, Wellesley College, 2000), p. 25.

52. Ibid., p. 39.

53. S. E. Taylor, L. C. Klein, B. P. Lewis, T. L. Gruenewald, R. A. Gurung, and J. A. Updegraff, "Biobehavioral Responses to Stress in Females: Tend-and-Befriend, Not Fight-or-Flight," *Psychological Review* 107, no. 3 (2000), pp. 411–29.

54. Taylor, *Tending Instinct*, p. 24.

55. Jordan and Dooley, *Relational Practice*, p. 41.

56. Ibid., pp. 44–45.

57. Ibid., p. 47.

58. Ibid., p. 55, citing Fletcher, *Disappearing Acts*.

59. Judith V. Jordan, Maryellen Handel, Margarita Alvarez, and Robin Cook-Nobles, "Applications of the Relational Model to Time-Limited Therapy," in *Complexity of Connection*, ed. Jordan, Walker, and Hartling, p. 254.

60. Linda M. Hartling and Jenny K. Ly, "Relational References: A Selected Bibliography of Research, Theory, and Applications," Project Report, no. 7 (Wellesley, Mass.: Stone Center, Wellesley College, 2001). Renee Spencer's "A Comparison of Relational Psychologies" includes more Harvard Project material among its 175 references and a summary of relational infant research (Project Report, no. 5 [Wellesley, Mass.: Stone Center, Wellesley College, 2000]).

61. Weingarten, *Common Shock*, p. 108.

62. Samuel Shem, "Fiction as Resistance," *Annals of Internal Medicine* 137 (2002), pp. 934–37.

63. Stephen J. Bergman, "Men's Psychological Development: A Relational Perspective," Work in Progress, no. 48 (Wellesley, Mass.: Stone Center, Wellesley College, 1991), p. 7.

64. Irene P. Stiver, Wendy B. Rosen, Janet Surrey, and Jean Baker Miller, "Cre-

ative Moments in Relational-Cultural Therapy," Work in Progress, no. 92 (Wellesley, Mass.: Stone Center, Wellesley College, 2001), p. 6.

65. Ibid., p. 7.

66. Laura Benkov, "Yes, I Am a Swan: Reflections on Families Headed by Lesbians and Gay Men," in *Mothering Against the Odds*, ed. García Coll, Surrey, and Weingarten, p. 131.

Bibliography

Works by Carol Gilligan, Her Former Students, and Harvard Project Researchers

Belenky, Mary Field, Blythe McVicker Clinchy, Nancy Rule Goldberger, and Jill Mattuck Tarule. *Women's Ways of Knowing*. 1986. New York: Basic Books, 1997.

Brown, Lyn Mikel. *Girlfighting: Betrayal and Rejection Among Girls*. New York: New York University Press, 2003.

———. *Raising Their Voices: The Politics of Girls' Anger*. Cambridge, Mass.: Harvard University Press, 1998.

Brown, Lyn Mikel, and Carol Gilligan. *Meeting at the Crossroads: Women's Psychology and Girls' Development*. Cambridge, Mass.: Harvard University Press, 1992.

Debold, Elizabeth, Marie Wilson, and Idelisse Malavé. *Mother Daughter Revolution*. Reading, Mass.: Addison-Wesley, 1993.

Gilligan, Carol. *The Birth of Pleasure*. New York: Alfred A. Knopf, 2002.

———. *In a Different Voice: Psychological Theory and Women's Development*. Cambridge, Mass.: Harvard University Press, 1982.

Gilligan, Carol, Nona P. Lyons, and Trudy J. Hanmer, eds. *Making Connections: The Relational Worlds of Adolescent Girls at Emma Willard School*. Cambridge, Mass.: Harvard University Press, 1990.

Gilligan, Carol, Annie G. Rogers, and Deborah L. Tolman, eds. *Women, Girls, and Psychotherapy: Reframing Resistance*. Binghamton, N.Y.: Harrington Park/Haworth Press, 1991.

Gilligan, Carol, Janie Victoria Ward, and Jill McLean Taylor, with Betty Bardige, eds. *Mapping the Moral Domain*. Cambridge, Mass.: Center for the Study of Gender, Education, and Human Development, Harvard University Graduate School of Education/Harvard University Press, 1988.

Jack, Dana Crowley. *Behind the Mask: Destruction and Creativity in Women's Aggression*. Cambridge, Mass.: Harvard University Press, 1999.

———. *Silencing the Self: Women and Depression*. Cambridge, Mass.: Harvard University Press, 1991.

Rogers, Annie G. *A Shining Affliction: A Story of Harm and Healing in Psychotherapy*. New York: Viking, 1995.

Taylor, Jill McLean, Carol Gilligan, and Amy M. Sullivan. *Between Voice and Silence: Women and Girls, Race and Relationship.* Cambridge, Mass.: Harvard University Press, 1995.

Tolman, Deborah L. *Dilemmas of Desire: Teenage Girls Talk About Sexuality.* Cambridge, Mass.: Harvard University Press, 2002.

Ward, Janie Victoria. *The Skin We're In: Teaching Our Children to Be Emotionally Strong, Socially Smart, Spiritually Connected.* New York: Free Press, 2000.

Way, Niobe, and Judy Y. Chu, eds. *Adolescent Boys: Exploring Diverse Cultures in Boyhood.* New York: New York University Press, 2004.

Works by Relational-Cultural Theorists (Stone Center and Jean Baker Miller Training Institute)

Banks, Amy. *Post-traumatic Stress Disorder: Relationships and Brain Chemistry.* Wellesley, Mass.: Jane Baker Miller Training Institute, 2001.

Fletcher, Joyce K. *Disappearing Acts: Gender, Power, and Relational Practice at Work.* Cambridge, Mass.: MIT Press, 1999.

García Coll, Cynthia, Janet L. Surrey, and Kathy Weingarten, eds. *Mothering Against the Odds: Diverse Voices of Contemporary Mothers.* New York: Guilford Press, 1998.

Jordan, Judith V., ed. *Women's Growth in Diversity: More Writings from the Stone Center.* New York: Guilford Press, 1997.

Jordan, Judith V., Alexandra G. Kaplan, Jean Baker Miller, Irene P. Stiver, and Janet L. Surrey. *Women's Growth in Connection: Writings from the Stone Center.* New York: Guilford Press, 1991.

Jordan, Judith V., Maureen Walker, and Linda M. Hartling. *The Complexity of Connection: Writings from the Stone Center's Jean Baker Miller Training Institute.* New York: Guilford Press, 2004.

Miller, Jean Baker. *Toward a New Psychology of Women.* 1976. Boston: Beacon Press, 1986.

Miller, Jean Baker, and Irene Pierce Stiver. *The Healing Connection: How Women Form Relationships in Therapy and in Life.* Boston: Beacon Press, 1997.

Shem, Samuel. *Fine.* New York: St. Martin's, 1985.

———. *The House of God.* 1978. New York: Delta Trade Paperbacks, 2003.

———. *Mount Misery.* New York: Fawcett Columbine, 1997.

Shem, Samuel, and Janet Surrey. *Bill W. and Dr. Bob.* New York: Samuel French, 2000.

———. *We Have to Talk: Healing Dialogues Between Women and Men.* New York: Basic Books, 1998.

Slater, Lauren, Jessica Henderson Daniel, and Amy Elizabeth Banks, eds. *The Complete Guide to Mental Health for Women.* Boston: Beacon Press, 2003.

Tatum, Beverly Daniel. *Why Are All the Black Kids Sitting Together in the Cafeteria? and Other Conversations About Race.* New York: Basic Books, 1999.

Walker, Maureen, and Wendy B. Rosen, eds. *How Connections Heal: Stories from Relational-Cultural Therapy.* New York: Guilford Press, 2004.

Weingarten, Kaethe. *Common Shock: Witnessing Violence Every Day*. New York: Dutton, 2003.

Weingarten, Kathy. *The Mother's Voice: Strengthening Intimacy in Families*. New York: Guilford Press, 1997.

Works by Victims of Violence Program Authors

Herman, Judith Lewis. *Trauma and Recovery*. 1992. New York: Basic Books, 1997.

Herman, Judith Lewis, with Lisa Hirschman. *Father-Daughter Incest*. 1981. Cambridge, Mass.: Harvard University Press, 2000.

Koss, Mary P., and Mary R. Harvey. *The Rape Victim: Clinical and Community Interventions*. Newbury Park, Calif.: Sage Publications, 1991.

Other Helpful Works

Breuer, Josef, and Sigmund Freud. *Studies on Hysteria*. Ed. and trans. James Strachey. 1895. New York: Basic Books, 1957.

Frankenberg, Ruth. *White Women, Race Matters: The Social Construction of Whiteness*. Minneapolis: University of Minnesota Press, 1993.

Freyd, Jennifer J. *Betrayal Trauma: The Logic of Forgetting Childhood Abuse*. Cambridge, Mass.: Harvard University Press, 1996.

Gilligan, James. *Preventing Violence*. New York: Thames & Hudson, 2001.

———. *Violence: Our Deadly Epidemic and Its Causes*. New York: Grosset/Putnam, 1996.

Lorde, Audre. *Sister Outsider: Essays and Speeches*. Trumansburg, N.Y.: Crossing Press, 1984.

Okin, Susan Moller. *Women in Western Political Thought*. Princeton, N.J.: Princeton University Press, 1979.

Pinderhughes, Elaine. *Understanding Race, Ethnicity, and Power*. New York: Guilford Press, 1989.

Real, Terrence. *How Can I Get Through to You? Reconnecting Men and Women*. New York: Scribner, 2002.

———. *I Don't Want to Talk About It: Overcoming the Secret Legacy of Male Depression*. New York: Fireside, 1998.

Russell, Diana E. H. *The Secret Trauma: Incest in the Lives of Girls and Women*. New York: Basic Books, 1986.

Scarborough, Elizabeth, and Laurel Furumoto. *Untold Lives: The First Generation of American Women Psychologists*. New York: Columbia University Press, 1987.

Stout, Linda. *Bridging the Class Divide and Other Lessons for Grassroots Organizing*. Boston: Beacon Press, 1996.

Taylor, Shelley E. *The Tending Instinct: Women, Men, and the Biology of Our Relationships*. New York: Henry Holt, 2002.

Wolff, Larry. *Child Abuse in Freud's Vienna: Postcards from the End of the World*. New York: New York University Press, 1995.

Related Web Sites

Center for Research on Gender and Sexuality (Deborah Tolman): crgs.sfsu.edu/.
Jean Baker Miller Training Institute: www.jbmti.org.
Support for Girls' Development (Lyn Mikel Brown):
www.hardygirlshealthywomen.org.
Victims of Violence Program:
www.challiance.org/departments_ii/victimsofviolence.htm.

Acknowledgments

It takes a village to make a book. And my first, best thanks must go to the extraordinary women who are my primary subjects. Carol Gilligan has been a friend and sometime subject for the seventies, the eighties, the nineties, and the first decade of the twenty-first century, both at Harvard and at New York University. She acknowledged me in her first book in 1982, and it is such a pleasure to be able to return the compliment—and for such responsive and collaborative cooperation, over years, across oceans, over tea, across that indispensable kitchen table. Her colleague Lyn Mikel Brown invited me into her home as well as into her Colby College classroom. Over decades, in her always clear and respectful way, Jean Baker Miller included me as an observer, participant, and faculty member in the doings of her developing Jean Baker Miller Training Institute at the Stone Center of Wellesley College, and ultimately as a friend. Judith V. Jordan and Janet L. Surrey began as friends as well as subjects and by now are virtually my sisters. The late Irene P. Stiver was an enthusiastic and insightful interview collaborator over several years. Judith Lewis Herman has been a generous and patient teacher whose lectures at Harvard Medical School conferences and trauma seminars at the Victims of Violence program of the Cambridge Health Alliance I have followed and whom I have interviewed over more than a decade. Mary Harvey, the director of the Victims of Violence program, has shared her creativity and keen insight in many interviews.

Many other women and men were crucially helpful: the late Sandy Kaplan, who was a member of the core Stone Center theory group for more than a decade, until illness made it impossible for her to continue; my friend from graduate school Stephen Bergman; Jessica Henderson Daniel, Linda Hartling, Maureen Walker, Kaethe Weingarten, Nancer Ballard, Lotte Bailyn, the late Susan Eaton, Joyce Fletcher, Maureen Harvey, Laura Woodburn, Cynthia García Coll, Robin Cook-Nobles, Jackie Fields, Heidie Vázquez-García (Hangen), Roberta Kelly, Yvonne Jenkins, Sung Lim Shin, Barbara Watkins, Ray Stiver, Holly Aldrich, Lucy Murray Brown, the late Lisa Hirschman, Peter Gourevitch, Emily Schatzow, Jayme Shorin, Janet Yassen, Bessel van der Kolk, Judy Reiner Platt, Marion Woodman, Kristin Linklater, Normi Noel, Tina Packer, Mary Belenky, Judy Chu, Elizabeth Debold, Sarah Hanson, Josette Huntress, Annie Rogers, Ellen Snee, Catherine Steiner-Adair, Mark Tappan, Jill Taylor, Deborah Tolman, and Janie Ward allowed me to interview them and often to participate in their classes and research groups. Dozens of others answered questions and shared research papers, presentations, and lectures. Relational psychologists are a fascinating and inspiring group, and the many who shared their work with me made writing this book a profoundly educating joy. They have left me grateful to many more informants than I can name here. I must also express my deep thanks to the many consumers of this psychology who shared their stories of healing with me—the former clients, patients, and trauma survivors who discussed their experiences with me in return for anonymity.

I also need to acknowledge and remember the people who made it possible for me to write any book—the sine qua non friends of my own development as a writer and cultural reporter: Lorraine Bishop, Ross Emmet, Emma Ward, Harriet Brockett, the late Faith C. Lee, Arlene Drake Dickinson, Rose Ravida, Arvilla Cline, Jean Rich, Trudy O'Connell, Mary Valentis, Barbara Wheeler, Bob Garvin; Susan Dickman Campbell, Karen Ruoff Kramer, Charlotte Mills Seligman, Linda Wheeler, the late Irene Mangold Lenon, Del Kolve, Ron Rebholtz, Carol Holmes; the late Susan Moller Okin, who asked Gilligan's question—where are the women?—about political philosophy; the late Hugo Dyson, the late Rosemary Woolf; Don McGoldrick, Rich Gillum, Ellery Sedgwick, Robin Sedgwick, Irene Briedis; the late Tom Winship, Matt Storin, Jan Shepherd, the late Margaret Manning, Mike Janeway, Mike Larkin, and Al Larkin, my educators and friends at *The Boston Globe* from 1971 to 1992; David Brownell, Sara Linnie Slocum,

Eileen Nielsen; Julie Breskin and the staff and patients of South Belknap I at McLean Hospital when I volunteered there in 1977–80; Elie Wiesel, Deborah Jacobs, Leslie Winer, Dick Cooper, Susan Berger; Maeve, George, Harry, Tony, Hamish, and Ian Blackman, and the late Rufus and Smoky; Wendy Sanford, Emily Mitchell, Dick Chasin; Pat Brennan, Ruth Ice, and the women of our writers' support group from 1979 to 1983; Kip Tiernan, Fran Froehlich, Jon Goldman; Muriel Cohen and the *Boston Globe* women's group of 1991–92; the late Flora Courtois, the late Ellie Ricker, Kathleen Moore Alpaugh, Tommy Thompson, the Northfield Conference Community, Tommy Zixi, Harry, and Blue.

Dave Scott got me the computer I wrote on. Cathy Connor-Moen lent me her tape-copying machine. Access to Harvard University Libraries, especially the Countway Medical Library and the Gutman Library of the Harvard Graduate School of Education, was essential; but interlibrary networks now turn local public libraries into research centers, and I thank the staffs of the Sharon Library in Sharon, Massachusetts, and of the Boyden Library in Foxborough, Massachusetts, especially its former director Bertha Chandler. The staffs of the Stone Center and later the Jean Baker Miller Training Institute, the Victims of Violence program, the Harvard Project on Women's Psychology and Girls' Development, and the New York University School of Law fulfilled every request promptly and graciously.

I began my research as a fellow of the Mary Ingraham Bunting Institute of Radcliffe College in 1992–93, supported by a legacy from my great-aunt Victoria Berlet, a Nebraska farmer who would have been completely bewildered by this book and extremely proud of it. I am grateful to my sister-fellows at the Bunting—especially Linda McCarriston, Letitia Obeng, Marilene Phipps, Ann Thomas, Mary Vogel, Ann Ferguson, Jane Midgley, Malena de Montis, Linda Stout, Kathleen Weiler, Norma Wikler, Zipporah Wiseman, and Linda Eisenmann, who took part in study groups with me—and to Florence Ladd, the novelist and incomparably connected former director.

Virginia Barber found this book a home with Farrar, Straus and Giroux, where Jonathan Galassi took it in, awaited it with great patience, and worked through it with me chapter by chapter; Denise Oswald "got it," polished it, and made it shine. Suzanne Gluck and Dorian Karchmar advised me through the production process. Ingrid Sterner, Judy Kiviat, and Lyn Rosen, angelic copy editors and proofreaders, insisted on accuracy. I am deeply grateful to all of them.

My mother and my brother died while I was working on this book, and their loss and the way my family came together around their deaths, and around the weddings and births that followed them, helped make all the theory about relationships much more vivid. I am blessed to have Victoria McGoldrick and Deborah Twombly as sisters. My children, Rachel and Susannah, grew up while I researched and wrote this book, and they let me observe as well as engage in the most intense growth-fostering relationships of my life. My husband and computer consultant, Bill Kondrath, stretched his patience and his software expertise beyond anything he had imagined in order to help me with this project. These people are no longer simply my family; they are this book's family, and both book and I are incalculably better for them.

Index